THE GROWTH OF
SOUTHERN CIVILIZATION

The

New American Nation Series

EDITED BY

HENRY STEELE COMMAGER

AND

RICHARD B. MORRIS

THE GROWTH OF SOUTHERN CIVILIZATION

1790 ★ 1860

By CLEMENT EATON

NEW YORK, EVANSTON, AND LONDON

HARPER & ROW, PUBLISHERS

D-U

*To MARY GASTON EATON, my mother,
and to MARY ELIZABETH,
who has sought to abolish the
Mason-Dixon Line*

Contents

Illustrations

Editors' Introduction

TO PRESENT a balanced picture of the Old South, with its extraordinary variety and startling paradoxes, is indeed an ambitious undertaking, and it is the virtue of this volume that it has managed to capture both the elegance and charm of this region as well as its repressions and cruelty, that it reveals alike its wealth and its poverty, its cultural pretensions and its illiteracy. Clement Eaton underscores the Old South's obsessive pride, along with its obsessive concern with the institution of slavery, which it made peculiarly its own. He sees the ante-bellum South not as a monolithic region of popular legend, but as a vast congeries of different geographic, cultural, and economic complexes. We are given glimpses of town and country, of the lowland rice planter, the upland tobacco farmer, the Georgia cracker and the South Carolina sand-hiller, the piney-woods people and the Creole gentleman.

The result is nothing like a stereotype of the Old South of the classic-pillared plantation, the courtly planter, and the deferential servant. True, the stereotype reflects an ideal that can find occasional substantiation, but the people we meet in Mr. Eaton's pages are proud, ambitious, aggressive, dwelling in decaying elegance or living in the crudest cabins in the Appalachian highlands. They might be chivalric and gentle, but they could also be downright unruly as well as unmoral. Mr. Eaton has enlisted an impressive scholarly apparatus to banish the stereotype of the omnipresence in the Old South of an aristocratic society and has convincingly demonstrated how important a role was played by the middle class.

It is a rich tapestry that the author has woven; yet, despite the vastness and complexity of the scene, he has deliberately eschewed vagarious generalizations, and documents his story with authentic accounts of persons, places, and things taken from firsthand and often from fresh sources. This book introduces us to many people of the Old South, some famous, some obscure, but all of whom played their role in the shaping of Southern civilization.

If, then, Mr. Eaton is a latter-day Frederick Law Olmsted, with his concern for the common people of the Old South, he has managed to bring to his study a breadth and objectivity which are the product of ripe scholarship and a perspective that no contemporary observer, regardless of his motive or integrity, could possibly possess.

Although Mr. Eaton writes of the Old South with affection, he is too good an historian to overlook its paradoxes, its repression of free thought, its tightening of the bonds of slavery, its involvements in speculation and the more sordid aspects of an unrestrained profit system, its extraordinary degree of self-preoccupation, and its uncritical self-esteem. In short, the author has managed to capture the flavor of the Old South without capitulating to it. Above all, he has observed the change from the unhurried society of the older South to an aggressive plantation capitalism which became dominant when King Cotton fastened its monocultural grip on so great a part of the region. He has caught, as it were, a restless people always on the move, always searching for the pot of gold beneath the rainbow in the next territory just opened to settlement. This westward movement, he is careful to point out, was more accelerated in flush times than during depressions and hardly conforms to Turner's conception of westward migration as constituting a safety valve. In the period under review, as Mr. Eaton points out, the South in large measure remained an unstable frontier civilization.

It is only proper that slavery should receive a substantial measure of attention in a volume dealing with the civilization of the Old South, because that civilization was in effect organized around the system of human bondage. Even yeoman farmers and tenants who did not own slaves themselves identified their interests with the slaveowners, with whom they were bound by ties of kinship, business and professional relationships, church affiliations and common aspirations. Everybody in the South, except the Negro, it would appear, was operating on the basis of great expectations. But the author feels that Southerners never seriously extended these aspirations onto the arid plains, and that the free territories were never really threatened by the slave system. No apologist for the institution of slavery, Mr. Eaton shows that nonetheless it was not always a repressive system, that certain features like slave hiring had upgrading potentialities, and that there was a shadowland between freedom and bondage wherein many people of the Old South dwelt. He recognizes that before Emancipation it was in the interest of the slaveowner to use Negro slaves in whatever ways proved profitable, in handicrafts and manufactures as well as in planting, and that considerable job upgrading took place under the slave system which was reversed in the South after Emancipation.

While judiciously evaluating recent evidence of the advance of political democracy in the South during the Age of Jackson and the widespread distribution of landownership, Mr. Eaton finds the South deficient in other criteria of progressive growth. He sees its leadership lagging, its political ideas retrograde, and he has little sympathy for the deep conservatism and religious orthodoxy which have fastened themselves upon the Southern mind. When he leaves the Old South he has completed a guided tour through a beleaguered section of extraordinary variation and complexity, a region seeking to hold to a way of life that was destined not to endure.

This volume is one of The New American Nation Series, a comprehensive and co-operative survey of the history of the areas now embraced in the United States from the days of discovery to our own time. It is concerned chiefly with the society of the South rather than its intellectual activity. That subject is considered in other volumes in the series devoted to thought and culture. Similarly, the impact of slavery on the North, the politics of the "peculiar institution," and the trends in national politics from the Age of Jackson to the coming of the Civil War are dealt with by other contributors to The New American Nation Series.

HENRY STEELE COMMAGER
RICHARD BRANDON MORRIS

Preface

THE SOUTH, or the Southern states, in 1860 constituted a geographical and cultural region that is difficult to define with exactness. Certainly the eleven states that formed the Southern Confederacy should be included, and I should include Kentucky as well as the southern part of Missouri within the South of 1860. Both of these states were accorded stars in the Confederate flag and both had "governments in exile" that sent representatives to the Confederate congress. The census authorities of 1860, however, classified Kentucky and Missouri as Western states and Maryland as belonging to the Middle states. Thus they ignored the Mason-Dixon Line, which, after John Randolph of Roanoke had popularized the term during the debates over the admission of Missouri into the Union, became the symbolic boundary between the North and the South. Despite the census classification, I should include Maryland in the South of 1860, primarily because the Eastern Shore was a land of plantations and slavery, and even today has retained somewhat of a Southern character.

Since I regard the South of 1860 as a land of considerable variety, I have sought to present a federalism of cultures—the Creole civilization, the lowland and the upland cultures, the mores of the black belts and of the pinelands of the Southwest, and city life. I have preferred to follow the method of the Northern traveler, Frederick Law Olmsted, of writing concretely, of recording observations instead of excessive generalizing, and of paying attention to significant details that reveal the humanity and the inner thoughts and emotions of the people of the ante-bellum period.

The title of this volume does not imply that I think the Southern states between 1790 and 1860 were continuously progressing toward a higher civilization. In some important fields, I think, the opposite was true. There can be no doubt that the South made notable economic progress during this period. From a declining economy it changed in the 1850's to an expanding economy. Southern planters with their slave gangs and yeoman farmers brought vast areas of arable land into cultivation in the Southwest, developed a more scientific agriculture, and provided three-fourths of the exports of the country. In the last decade of the ante-bellum period the South rivaled the North in the rate of its expansion of railroads, and manufactures increased significantly. Its schools, its academies, and its universities improved. At the opening of the nineteenth century the Southern states had virtually no literature, but by the time of the Civil War they had produced a considerable number of romantic novels, poems, and works of earthy humor. Finally, a significant advance had occurred during the age of Jackson in political democracy, and economic democracy had increased during the decade 1850–60 through a wide distribution of land.

On the other hand, in several respects the South had taken a backward step. Its political leaders and political thought were not comparable in quality with those of the early Republic. Although the Southern people had become far more religious formally, it is questionable whether their religion was more enlightened. A deep conservatism and orthodoxy had seized the Southern mind. In 1860 the South was a beleaguered section, an ever-weakening minority group, that had lost its earlier sense of nationalism. It was fighting to preserve a way of life that, despite many charming and admirable facets, was fundamentally at variance with its own liberal philosophy of an earlier period and was bound to pass.

Believing that history should primarily be concerned with people rather than vague and impersonal forces, I have, accordingly, filled my book with the lives of people: planters, mechanics looking for jobs, unsuccessful as well as successful farmers, pine-woods pedagogues as well as eminent professors, hard-working yeomen, Negroes as human beings and as slaves, "poor whites," a New York girl trying as the bride of a planter to adjust to Southern ways, unspecialized businessmen, men borrowing money to get ahead or merely "to live it up," land speculators, puritan cavaliers, men tormented by sex and conscience, earthy humorists, editors and preachers, romantic writers, actors and politicians—the last only as they represented the Southern sense of values or aspects of social and economic life.

At the suggestion of Professor Richard B. Morris, who has had the principal responsibility of editing this volume, I have omitted two chapters of the manuscript concerned with education, literature, and the fine arts. Not only did the space requirement of the series require a reduction of pages but the subjects will be considered in another volume of the series. Some of the omitted material in this study will be included in a volume of my Fleming Lectures in Southern History to be published by the Louisiana State University Press under the title *The Mind of the Old South*.

CLEMENT EATON

THE GROWTH OF
SOUTHERN CIVILIZATION

CHAPTER 1

The Land of the Country Gentleman

CHARLESTON was a unique Southern city, where an unusual blend of planters and gentleman merchants formed the upper class, as the Reverend Abiel Abbott of Beverly, Massachusetts, found in 1818. Among the cultivated people he met was the son of Ralph Izard, one of the grandees of the rice country, who took him to his estate, the Elms, seventeen miles from the city, and showed him the kind of life led by affluent country gentlemen.[1]

The plantation mansion was a spacious building in the Adam style, erected in 1809. Abbott was pleased with the "perfect servants" who brushed his clothes and polished his shoes, and with the Carolina breakfast of tea, coffee, johnnycake, grits, and eggs. The mildness of the task system of slavery, which allowed the slave one-third to one-half of the day for leisure, surprised him. The daughter of the family entertained him with a concert on the harp and the master conversed at tea "with much knowledge of the world and books." The Izards were representative of the Carolina country gentry, a well-knit ruling class, whose power and prestige had been diminished by the Revolution but who nevertheless retained great vitality even after the rise of Jacksonian democracy in the 1820's.

A potent force in the development of plantation society was the ideal of the English country gentleman. Although there were country

[1] Abiel Abbott, "A Journal of a Voyage to South Carolina," MS. in archives of the South Carolina Historical Society, Charleston, pp. 58–60.

squires in other parts of the United States, notably in the Hudson Valley and around Narragansett Bay, they did not fix the tone of society or dominate the social pattern as those in the Southern tidewater did. The majority of planters did not know at first hand how English squires lived, but the tradition had been handed down from the colonial period and strengthened by the reading of English and Scottish novels. This institution had been modified greatly by the Southern environment, particularly by the discarding of its tenantry basis and the exaggeration of certain aspects of the English model, such as carrying the defense of personal honor to ridiculous extremes. The growth of large plantations and of Negro slavery in the eighteenth century immeasurably strengthened the position of the country gentry in the South. Other forces which tended to perpetuate the old English institution here were the vestry system of the Church of England; the county court, with its justices of the peace; the sway of family in local government; and, to some degree, the illusion of cavalier origins. These influences counteracted the leveling effect of the American frontier.

The ideal of the country gentleman was carried by emigrating Virginians and Carolinians to remote corners of the South. At the close of the ante-bellum period Henry Stanley, the future explorer of Africa, encountered this powerful social force while clerking in a country store in Arkansas. In Cypress Bend he was amazed to see his fellow clerks and the plain farmers who visited the store bowing to a stern code of conduct that was aristocratic in origin—the obligation to uphold personal honor. Even the proprietor of the store, a German Jew, quickly resented any suggestion of insult and used a dueling pistol. And Stanley too, who had spent his childhood in a workhouse in Wales and had been cuffed about as a sailor on a merchant ship, succumbed to the pervasive mores of this Southern community. When he was sent a package containing a chemise and a petticoat because he was tardy in volunteering for the Confederate army, he immediately enrolled in the company of the Dixie Greys.

Pondering the reasons for "the proud sensitive spirit prevailing in Arkansas," Stanley concluded that it was the fruit of a unique type of provincialism nourished on the plantations and lonely homesteads. The touchiness of the people, he thought, was accentuated by the fevers and chills of chronic malaria that affected so many of them. "In New Orleans," he observed, ". . . the social rule was to give and take, to assert an opinion, and hear it contradicted without resort to lethal weapons, but, in Arkansas, to refute a statement was tantamount to giving the lie direct, and was likely to be followed by an instant appeal to the revolver or bowie."[2]

The farther Southern civilization extended from the seacoast, the more diluted were European traditions, but in the tidewater traces of English institutions survived strongly. In the country-gentleman ideal, in the use of British nomenclature in the currency, in government and religion, and in retaining old English pronunciations and even outmoded vestiges of English court practices, such as benefit of clergy, the South of the early republic revealed its affinity for the mother country. Riding through Maryland and the Northern Neck of Virginia in 1796, the Irish traveler Isaac Weld observed that the great plantation residences were "exactly similar to the old manor houses in England." The occupants of these houses lived in "a style, which approaches nearer to that of the English country gentleman than what is to be met [with] any where else on the continent. . . ."[3]

In the same year, the architect Benjamin H. Latrobe, freshly arrived from England, noted a striking likeness between the rural society of Virginia and that of his native Yorkshire. So congenial did he find the company of Virginia planters that he remarked, "In Amelia [County] I could have again fancied myself in a society of English country gentlemen . . . had not the shabbiness of their mansions undeceived me."[4] At Petersburg he attended a horse race which he described as "a duodecimo edition of the Newmarket race in folio." Some years later, in 1819, Adam Hodgson, an English traveler, reported that the best society of Charleston was "much superior to any which I have yet seen in America." The manners of the upper class resembled those of "the more polished of our country gentlemen and are formed on the model of what in England we call 'the old school.' "[5]

Yet the Southern planters did not keep up their estates as the Eng-

[2] Dorothy Stanley (ed.), *The Autobiography of Sir Henry Morton Stanley* (Boston, 1909), p. 157.

[3] Isaac Weld, Jr., *Travels through the States of North America* . . . (London, 1799), I, 83.

[4] Benjamin Henry Latrobe, *The Journal of Latrobe* (New York, 1905), and Talbot Hamlin, *Benjamin Henry Latrobe* (New York, 1955), pp. 70, 71, 78.

[5] Adam Hodgson, *Letters from North America* . . . (London, 1824), I, 48–49.

lish squires did.[6] In contrast to the green and neatly tilled farms of England, the countryside of Maryland and Virginia had an unkempt and worn-out aspect, for much of the arable land had been exhausted by unremitting tobacco culture and ruined by erosion. The dilapidated mansions behind stately groves of trees, the abandoned tobacco fields covered by yellow sedge and old field pines, the deserted log cabins, the decay of the Episcopal churches, whose broken-out windowpanes and sagging doors permitted the invasion of pigs and cattle, indicated a serious lack of prosperity and a profound apathy of spirit. Planters and small farmers alike were forced to be largely self-sufficient, making for themselves such domestic articles as cloth, shoes, soap, candles, and furniture. The decline of the tobacco trade after the Revolution had reduced contacts with the great world of Europe. Indeed, before the coming of steamboats and railroads, the farmers and planters of the early republic were isolated both from Europe and the Northern states and were less cosmopolitan in outlook than their fathers and grandfathers had been.

The planters of the tidewater region were reluctant to recognize the realities of a changing economy. Although their plantations might be run down and their Negroes miserably clad, they maintained an unconquerable pride and refused to alter their ways. Virginians, especially, continued to practice the lavish hospitality of former days. At the close of the eighteenth century, nearly every plantation was overstocked with slaves. Instead of working industriously to improve conditions, many of the planters, according to Weld, "give themselves but little trouble about the management of their plantations."[7] Relying on overseers, they spent many hours hunting and fishing, drinking alcoholic liquors, and simply "doing nothing." Travelers found the inflated manner of speaking of these run-down aristocrats ridiculous, and they were amused by the titles that Southerners profusely conferred on plain citizens. Frequently a stage driver would be addressed as "Captain," an innkeeper as "Colonel," a lawyer or a large planter as "Honorable" or "General."

The economic distress of the old tobacco country was owing partly to the unreliability of the foreign markets upon which it depended. The

[6] William Faux (an English farmer), *Memorable Days in America* . . . (London, 1823), I, 192–193; II, 123–124.

[7] Weld, *Travels,* I, 141.

decline in the tobacco trade to England after the Revolution turned many of the planters of the tidewater area to raising wheat. In the newer lands of the Piedmont, on the other hand, tobacco culture expanded and became the money crop. The Napoleonic wars opened a good, though fluctuating, market for cereals in Europe and the West Indies. When prices of tobacco rose temporarily, the planters abandoned wheat for their old crop. As a consequence, between 1818 and 1822, European markets became glutted with tobacco. When tobacco prices declined, the planters returned to wheat, but the ravages of the Hessian fly and of rust drove them once again to tobacco—"the old hopeless shifting from one crop to another began again."[8] Jefferson gave up tobacco as a money crop at Monticello after 1812, but he continued to cultivate "the royal weed" as the principal crop of Poplar Forest, his plantation in southwestern Virginia.

The towns and ports of the tobacco country reflected the languishing state of agriculture. Particularly noticeable was the decline of Georgetown, Alexandria, Tappahannock, Yorktown, and Norfolk, ports at which great quantities of tobacco had formerly been inspected and exported. By 1800, since little tobacco was now grown in the tidewater, Yorktown had dwindled to a third of its size before the Revolution. Norfolk, the largest commercial town in Virginia, contained only four hundred houses, its unpaved streets were filthy, and it lacked a single bank. Williamsburg, once the center of government and fashion, had so rapidly declined after the removal of the capital to Richmond in 1779 that it was a shadow of its former self. When Benjamin Latrobe walked down its principal street seventeen years later, he noticed that the wooden columns of the capitol were stripped of their moldings and all awry, and many of the houses were ruined and uninhabited. William and Mary College had only thirty students; Jefferson's alma mater had become little more than a grammar school where the boys went barefooted. The fine old Episcopal church of Bruton Parish nearby was neglected and out of repair.

The richest and most flourishing parts of the South at the end of the eighteenth century were the rice and sea-island-cotton districts of the Carolinas and Georgia. Unlike the tobacco lands, the rice fields did not suffer seriously from erosion or the depletion of the soil. The rice

[8] Avery O. Craven, *Soil Exhaustion as a Factor in the Agricultural History of Virginia and Maryland, 1606–1860* (Urbana, 1926), p. 81.

district was a narrow strip of swampy land less than fifty miles wide; its extent was determined by the limits within which the tidal ebb and flow of the fresh-water rivers and streams could be used to flood and drain the fields. On sea islands that fringed the coast long-staple cotton was very profitably grown. The cultivation of indigo, a crop of the higher lands of the interior, had largely been abandoned as a result of Oriental competition and the loss of the British bounty after the Revolution. In its place planters had turned, after the invention of the cotton gin, to growing short-staple cotton. In sharp contrast to Virginia, Maryland, and North Carolina, South Carolina enjoyed a period of prosperity and vigorous growth until the panic year of 1819. The exports of sea-island cotton increased enormously, and the cultivation of short-staple cotton expanded rapidly into the Piedmont.[9] Yet within a generation the upland cotton planter had skimmed the cream of fertility from the soil and the eastern part of the state was showing marked decay.[10]

The only considerable urban centers in the Southern states at the opening of the nineteenth century were the seaports of Baltimore and Charleston. Baltimore had a population of 26,111 people, slightly larger than that of Boston, and Charleston contained 20,473 whites and slaves. In both of these cities the merchants held high place in society. In Charleston, where they closed their businesses at four o'clock in the afternoon, they were fond of giving elaborate dinners and entertainments. Of this city President Washington wrote during his Southern journey of 1791: "The inhabitants are wealthy—Gay—and hospitable." The Carolina ladies of the upper class, observed Mrs. Nathanael Greene, widow of the Rhode Island Revolutionary general, who had been given a plantation by the grateful state of Georgia, spent half of their time making their toilets, one-fourth of the remaining time paying and receiving social visits, and another fourth in scolding and hitting the servants.[11] Not all the Carolina ladies, however, lived this vapid existence, for there were some like Eliza Lucas, the introducer of indigo

[9] Alfred G. Smith, Jr., *Economic Readjustment of an Old Cotton State* (Columbia, 1958), p. 2.

[10] Private Diary of Ed. Ruffin, "Agricultural Survey in S. Ca. 1843," January 29–31. MS. in Southern Collection, University of North Carolina Library.

[11] Archibald Henderson (ed.), *Washington's Southern Tour* (Boston, 1923), pp. 197, 232 n.

planting into South Carolina, who were active in managing the domestic affairs of the plantation.

Just as the country gentry of England maintained town houses in London, the Carolina planters lived in Charleston for a large part of the year. Fear of malaria caused many of them every summer to flee from their swampy and mosquito-ridden plantations to the more salubrious atmosphere of Charleston and Sullivan's Island, though many remained on their rice estates, sleeping at night in the pinelands. Their long sojourns in the city made these tidewater planters not only more sophisticated but also more closely-knit in their views. They went to Charleston because of their dread of fever and ague, but also because of their love of the fashionable life there; they all made sure of being in the city during race week in February.

The society of this opulent city practiced what Thorstein Veblen would have called conspicuous leisure, consumption, and display. The Duc de la Rochefoucauld, who traveled in the Southern states in 1795–97, noted that a Charleston gentleman seldom had less than twenty servants in his domestic establishment and that the children had Negro maids and body servants to wait upon them.[12] Abiel Abbott commented, some years later, "No coach moves in Charleston without a negro behind and a negro before." He also observed that house slaves were so numerous that "the Charlestonians are obliged to exercise their wits to devise sufficient variety to keep them employed."[13] Besides enjoying jockey clubs, eating clubs, card playing, and formal balls, some of the upper class organized golf clubs at Savannah and Augusta as early as 1800.

Although South Carolina lacked free schools and relatively few of its planters were masters of Greek and Latin, its capital city displayed such evidences of culture as the St. Cecilia concerts and balls, the Charleston Library Society, founded in 1748, good bookshops, and a small group of amateur naturalists and scientists. The Reverend Mr. Abbott attended dinners given by gentlemen of the city at which the conversation was cultivated and witty, although the guests used "expressions not quite pleasant to the ears of a minister or a lady." He visited the spinster daughters of Dr. David Ramsay, the noted historian,

[12] Duc de la Rochefoucauld-Liancourt, *Travels through the United States of America* . . . (London, 1799), I, 557.
[13] Abbott, "Journal," p. 33.

who three years earlier had been murdered on the streets of Charleston by an insane person. In their conversation with him these spinster ladies observed great formality, which he attributed partly to their consciousness of ancestry and partly to their occupation as school-teachers. The homes of some of the planters, such as Middleton House and Drayton Hall, reminded the Duc de la Rochefoucauld of the residences of ancient English country estates. The Carolina rice planters continued until the Civil War to be more affluent and to live with more style than the tobacco planters of the Chesapeake Bay country.

Another New England visitor to Charleston in 1818, a young clerk named W. Thacher, saw Charleston and the low-country society in a less favorable light than did the Reverend Mr. Abbott. The streets, he noted, were unpaved and shockingly muddy, the buildings black and dirty, "so unlike Boston and New York." He arrived with $4 in his pocket and had to room in the cheapest place, with a grocer. Unable to obtain a job in a mercantile house, he became a tutor on the plantation of a Dr. Jervey. Here he saw the extremes of slavery—great cruelty in hunting runaway Negroes, but kindness in dealing with tractable slaves. The servant assigned him slept in his room and was so kindly treated that he had never been whipped and had been permitted to learn to read and write. The planters, although they had a number of cattle, made little use of milk, which they believed to cause biliousness, except when used in tea and coffee. Dr. Jervey and his wife were agreeable, plain, and unaffected, "not like town folk." The young New Englander disliked Charleston, especially the merchants on King Street, who, he wrote, were all Jews and Yankees, practicing the low arts of lying, artificial smiles, and flattery—"the finesse of the drygoods trade."[14]

Quite different from the privileged and polished society of the lowland aristocrats were the people in the back or up country. Here were concentrated the descendants of non-English stocks who had emigrated from Pennsylvania by the Great Valley route. At the close of the eighteenth century, approximately one-third of the Southern people were descended from other than English stocks. While it is impossible to know with any certainty the racial ingredients in the South at the

[14] W. Thacher, Diary kept for his brother Davis in Vermont, July 14, 1816–December 31, 1818. MS. in South Caroliniana Library, Columbia.

close of the eighteenth century, a fair estimate is Scottish, 11 per cent; German, 8 per cent; Scotch-Irish (Ulster), 7.8 per cent; Irish, 5 per cent; French, 1.5 per cent.[15]

These people made notable contributions to Southern life. The Germans set an example of careful cultivation of the soil, established the Lutheran Church in the South, introduced the horizontal log cabin (first brought to this country by the Swedes on the Delaware), and their superior artisans made the Kentucky long rifle, the iron stove, and the Conestoga covered wagon. The Scottish element, the most numerous of the foreign stocks in the South, provided able merchants and teachers. The Scotch-Irish introduced the Presbyterian Church into the South and were active in founding academies and colleges. Especially remarkable was the contribution of this virile and turbulent group in producing frontier leaders and statesmen such as John C. Calhoun, Andrew Jackson, James K. Polk, and Woodrow Wilson.

Whether they were English in origin or German or Scotch-Irish, the people of the back country developed a strong feeling of sectionalism.[16] They had real grievances against the ruling classes of the tidewater. Not until 1835 in North Carolina and 1850 in Virginia were they given fair representation in the legislature. They believed that their interests were sacrificed in favor of eastern interests. When the residents of the up country visited Charleston, they felt that the people of this proud city regarded them as lacking in refinement and breeding. One of the greatest differences between the homespun society of the back country and the more urbane society of the tidewater was caused by the prevalence of slavery in the latter and free labor in the former.

[15] American Council of Learned Societies, "Report of the Committee on Linguistic and National Stocks in the Population of the United States," *Annual Report of the American Historical Association, 1931* (Washington, 1932), I, 118–124; see also Bureau of the Census, *A Century of Population Growth, 1790–1900* (Washington, 1909), p. 116.

[16] Carl Bridenbaugh in *Myths and Realities, Societies of the Colonial South* (Baton Rouge, 1952), pp. 156–161, maintains that political sectionalism did not develop in Virginia and Maryland prior to 1776, partly because of the quickness with which those colonies provided the back settlements with county government. Moreover, in North Carolina and South Carolina a belt of pine barrens long separated the Piedmont and coastal counties. At any rate sectionalism developed strongly in Virginia during the first half of the nineteenth century. See Charles H. Ambler, *Sectionalism in Virginia from 1776 to 1861* (Chicago, 1910).

Yet the Germans afforded a good illustration of how prejudices against slavery tended to disappear when economic conditions changed to make it desirable. The German settlers of the Shenandoah Valley and the Piedmont were for some years averse to the employment of slaves; they relied on the strong backs and arms of members of their own families. By 1820, however, many of them had overcome their reluctance to own slaves. Adam Hodgson, journeying through the Shenandoah Valley, noted that there was scarcely a family in this region without a slave. In contrast to conditions in the tidewater, though, few slave gangs were to be seen, and the German farmers worked side by side with their slaves in the fields.[17] The Moravians who settled in small villages in Piedmont North Carolina, notably Salem, set an early example of reliance on free labor. Nevertheless, by the decade of the 1850's, some of the more prosperous among them, such as the Fries family, pioneer textile manufacturers, had become slaveholders.

The distribution of slaves was a good indicator of economic and social status in the South throughout the ante-bellum period. At the close of the eighteenth century the planter class (those owning at least twenty or thirty slaves) was small in comparison to the great majority of plain farmers. South Carolina was probably the most aristocratic of the Southern states, but in 1790, although two-thirds of the lowland Carolinians were slaveholders, the majority owned less than five slaves, and in the Piedmont section only 30 per cent of the families held slaves. In North Carolina the greatest pretensions to aristocracy were to be found in a group of counties clustered around Albemarle Sound. Here in 1790 in the Edenton district 42 per cent of the heads of families owned thirty or more slaves and could therefore be considered as planters, but in the Piedmont county of Mecklenburg only 3 per cent held slaves and only two persons were reported as possessing thirty or more bondsmen. In tidewater Maryland a sample county, Prince George, contained a high percentage of slaveholders, approximately half of the heads of families; but in Frederick County in the western part of the state only 14 per cent were slaveholders and there were only nine planters among them.[18]

[17] Hodgson, *Letters*, I, 306–307.
[18] Bureau of the Census, *Heads of Families at the First Census of the United*

The census figures tend to rob the South of the early republic of some of its glamour, and the evidence of travelers and of contemporaries fills out the picture of an earthy and homespun society. Stephen Ravenel of South Carolina was impressed, during a journey through North Carolina and Virginia in 1803, by the slovenly farming, the unpainted houses, and the ignorance of the lower classes of those states. "The lower class of People here," he wrote, "differ very much from the same class of People in New England, there they are civil, well-bred, & it is rare to find one that can neither read or write—here it is the reverse, they are brutish in their manners and exceeding vulgar & as I remarked before very much addicted to profane swearing and in many instances can neither read or write."[19]

Some travelers noted such a difference between the upper and lower classes that they appeared to be almost two separate breeds of men. Elias Fordham, traveling through Virginia in 1818, wrote: "The gentlemen are fairer than Englishmen, their faces being always shaded by hats with extraordinarily broad brims."[20] The poorer people and the overseers, on the other hand, were burned by the sun and almost totally uneducated. The women withered early, their faces were wrinkled like a map, and one traveler thought that their sunbonnets "disfigured them amazingly." In North Carolina, Jeremiah Battle of Edgecombe County wrote to the editor Thomas Henderson of Raleigh in 1811 that fully half of the women and one-third of the men could not write their names.[21] "I had no idea that we had such a poor, ignorant, squalid population, as I have seen," commented the lawyer Archibald De Bow Murphey in 1819 after a survey of the eastern part of North Carolina.

States Taken in the Year 1790 (Washington, 1908), South Carolina, North Carolina, Maryland. The Virginia records are not extant.

[19] Diary of Stephen Ravenel, October 17, 1803–October 28, 1804. MS. in Archives of the South Carolina Historical Society.

[20] Elias P. Fordham, Personal Narrative of Travels in Virginia, Maryland, Pennsylvania, Ohio, Indiana, Kentucky; and of a Residence in the Illinois Country, 1817–1818 (Cleveland, 1906), p. 56.

[21] A. R. Newsome (ed.), "A Miscellany from Thomas Henderson's Letter Book, 1810–1811," North Carolina Historical Review, VI (1929). Thomas Oliver Larkin, a native of Massachusetts, who kept a store in Wilmington, 1821–26, estimated that about one-fourth of the population in eastern North Carolina could not write at all and about half could not write more than their names. Robert J. Parker, "A Yankee in North Carolina; Observations of Thomas Oliver Larkin, 1821–1826," North Carolina Historical Review, XIV (1937), 339–340.

"In the towns are found decent and well-informed Men in Matters of Business, Men who look well and live well. But the Mass of the Common People in the Country are lazy, sickly, poor, dirty and ignorant."[22]

The morals of the lower class in many parts of the South reflected the influence of a rough frontier. The journal of Charles Woodmason, an Anglican missionary, tells of widespread immorality, drinking bouts, card playing, disregard of the Sabbath, and crude fights in the back country of South Carolina toward the end of the colonial period.[23] Fifty years later Dr. Francis Joseph Kron, a native of Germany, reported a similar lack of morality in the Yadkin Valley of North Carolina, where he had settled. "Within a circle of eighteen miles where perhaps thirty families dwell," he wrote, "I could count as many as twenty illegitimate children, some the offspring of widows, others of single never married women, and others, too, intruders in lawful wedlock."[24]

The morals of the people varied greatly in different parts of the South and at different periods. When Christian Schultz visited Natchez in 1808, he observed the unchaste married gentlemen of this wealthy town who passed their time in the pursuit of three interests: "All make love; most of them play [gamble]; and a few make money. With Religion they have nothing to do."[25] A merchant from Steubenville, Ohio, who went down the Ohio and Mississippi rivers in a flatboat in 1839–40 was shocked by the immorality of the river towns. Of Louisville, Kentucky, he wrote in his journal: "I have never seen any Town or City that appear more loose in moralls than this one. Courtezans allmost flock the Streets. And the most profane language may at all times be heard, indeed the Language of some here would make the Devil stand aghast and wonder at their profanity. great quantities of

[22] Archibald D. Murphey to John Ruffin, April 25, 1819, in W. H. Hoyt (ed.), *The Papers of Archibald De Bow Murphey* (Raleigh, 1914), I, 138.

[23] Richard J. Hooker (ed.), *The Carolina Back Country on the Eve of the Revolution; the Journal and Other Writings of Charles Woodmason, Anglican Itinerant* (Chapel Hill, 1953), pp. 96–101.

[24] Diary of Dr. Francis Joseph Kron, November 14–December 17, 1835, typescript in W. K. Littleton Papers, 1791–1933. MSS. in North Carolina State Department of Archives and History, Raleigh.

[25] Christian Schultz, Jr., *Travels on an Inland Voyage* (New York, 1810), II, 134.

Liquor is drank which of course is well calculated to set every other evil afloat."[26]

The morals of the upper class in the old states of the South appear to have been higher than in the rough river towns of the Southwest. Joel R. Poinsett, an intelligent South Carolina planter and the first minister of the United States to Mexico, admitted to Alexis de Tocqueville that there was laxity of morals in the lower class; but in Southern society as a whole, he maintained, an excellent state of morals existed. "The marriage tie," he said, "is so prodigiously respected with us that the lover of a married woman dishonors himself even more certainly than she who yields to him. The road of preferment is closed to him . . . relatives of the woman think themselves bound to avenge the family honour on him." This exaltation of female chastity contrasted with the attitude of society in South America, where Poinsett had never known a woman faithful to her husband. "The notions of right and wrong are so reversed in this matter," he declared, "that a woman thinks it a disgrace not to have a lover."[27] The truth of Poinsett's observations concerning the jealous guarding of female honor in the South was demonstrated some years later in South Carolina, when Governor James H. Hammond, one of the largest planters of the state, was driven out of public life for years because he was accused of attempting to seduce one of Wade Hampton's daughters.[28]

Country gentlemen of the period of the early republic practiced their religion according to the Episcopal ritual. Some of them were deists and freethinkers as well, and on their library shelves could be found the works of Voltaire, Volney, Hume, Gibbon, and Tom Paine's *Age of Reason*. Washington was probably representative of the superior country squire in his religious attitudes. He attended the Episcopal church at Pohick and conformed to outward religious customs and usages; nevertheless, he was affected by deistic thought and referred to the deity not in anthropomorphic terms but as providence or a moral order in the universe.

[26] Journal of William Reynolds, September 5, 1839–March 4, 1840. MS. in private possession, p. 32.

[27] George W. Pierson (ed.), *Tocqueville and Beaumont in America* (New York, 1938), pp. 648, 655.

[28] James H. Hammond to William Gilmore Simms, August 13, 1857, James H. Hammond Papers, Library of Congress.

The Great Revival of 1800–1805 changed the religious atmosphere of the age. The upper classes, particularly the Episcopalians, tended to look down upon the extravagances of the camp meetings and the ignorance and uncouthness of the Methodist and Baptist exhorters. In such a critical spirit Ebenezer Pettigrew, son of a prominent planter of eastern North Carolina, wrote to his friend James Iredell at Princeton:

> On the 14th I was at what is called a Methodist camp meeting about 20 miles up the country. . . . While preaching they are tolerably orderly but immediately after, they get together as they call it to pray and be prayed for. There will be half a dozen praying at a time, some singing, some shaking hands, some laughing, some crying, some falling dead with what they call the spirit of conviction. They lay in an entire state of insensibility, and sometimes with their limbs so stiff that it is believed that they would break rather than bend, for 12, 24 and some 48 hours—they will have no medical aid used to recover them. They say he that struck them down will raise them again.[29]

Though the upper class frowned upon the religious enthusiasm that brought thousands of ignorant and irreligious farmers into the evangelical churches, they too were deeply affected by the revival movement. By 1830 there were few deists and freethinkers left in the Southern states. When Tocqueville visited New Orleans in that year, he was told by ex-Senator James Brown that the majority of Americans were not interested in religious dogma but looked upon religion as a respectable and useful thing in society. He declared that he was not acquainted with a single materialist; everybody had a firm belief in immortality and in the theory of rewards and punishments.[30] A decade later a Savannah mechanic wrote: "Had a long lecture from Ann on Religion—she was passing the mill this morning and just at the time I happened to be swearing at a negro who was helping me or rather hindering me—took me to task about swearing and not going to church —she says that all *Respectable* people here go to Church."[31] Indeed, a profound religious orthodoxy had settled upon the South.[32]

[29] Ebenezer Pettigrew to James Iredell, August 6, 1806, Pettigrew Papers, Southern Collection, University of North Carolina.

[30] Pierson, *Tocqueville and Beaumont*, pp. 486–487.

[31] William H. Garland to his wife, November 11, 1841, William Harris Garland Papers, Southern Collection, University of North Carolina.

[32] See "The Decline of Skepticism" in my *Freedom of Thought in the Old South* (New York, 1951), Chap. XI.

The planters, as a whole, were practical men who did not possess the culture and philosophic outlook of Jefferson or Madison. Henry Knight, a New England traveler, observed in 1824 that the planters lived an out-of-doors life and that the majority of them were surprisingly wanting in a knowledge of literature. Although an acquaintance with Latin was not uncommon among them, he reported, a knowledge of Greek was rare. The Virginians loved politics and the active life of hunting, but cared little for belles-lettres. They were socially minded and enjoyed visiting each other and gathering at the county seat on court days, or at barbecues, camp meetings, and fish frys, where "the talk is of slaves, crops, shooting-matches, and quaffing revels."[33] The novelist J. K. Paulding, who traveled in the upper South, was attracted by the nonchalant, hospitable demeanor of the tobacco planters. He observed that they were not "so debauched with the sordid money making spirit" as were his fellow Northerners. At the end of a day's travel, when he sought a lodging for himself and horse, he avoided applying at a neat, newly painted house, but sought some rusty, informal old mansion. "If I saw a broken pane stuffed with a petticoat," he wrote, "then I was sure of a welcome."[34]

The economic condition of the tobacco country during the first quarter of the nineteenth century showed little visible improvement over conditions in the 1790's. Robert Walsh, a Philadelphia editor, wrote of a trip through Virginia in 1817, "There is absolute desolation in the lower parts [of the state] and what is seen nowhere else in the U. S., something like despair of amelioration."[35] John Randolph of Roanoke wrote sadly of the improvident type of farming in Virginia which had led to gullied fields and rivers full of mud. Jefferson in his old age deplored "the impoverishment of our fields by constant culture without any aid of manure; and this cause [of Virginia's decline] will continue to increase. We must either attend to recruiting of our lands or abandon them & run away to Alabama, as so many of our countrymen are doing, who find it easier to resolve on quitting their country, than to change the practices in husbandry to which they have been

[33] "Arthur Singleton Esq." [pseudonym of Henry C. Knight], *Letters from the South and West* (Boston, 1824), p. 66.
[34] James K. Paulding, *Letters from the South* (New York, 1816), II, 125.
[35] Richard B. Davis, *Francis Walker Gilmer: Life and Learning in Jefferson's Virginia* (Richmond, 1939), p. 115.

brought up."[36] New England also suffered a great loss of population as a result of the westward movement, but its prosperity was recouped by immigration and the growth of industry.

The spirit of North Carolina at this time was particularly apathetic, so that the state was referred to as the Rip Van Winkle of the Union. With a coast almost landlocked and its arable land suffering from the same abuse that characterized Virginia and Maryland, the state during the first quarter of the nineteenth century was being depleted by the emigration of some of its most vigorous citizens. The lack of public spirit was shown in the neglect of the university at Chapel Hill, causing the treasurer to report in April, 1809, that the university did not have a cent of money on hand and that it could not even pay contingent expenses or the salaries of the professors. Archibald De Bow Murphey struggled in vain to get the people interested in keeping able young men from leaving the state by making needed reforms, particularly a system of internal improvements and an enlightened public-school system. "But I see clearly," he wrote in August, 1819, "that it is all idle Labour, at least for this Generation. Those who labor now will meet with nothing but Vexation, Chagrin, and Disgust. Another Generation will profit by their Labours. The Spirit of the present is radically mean and grovelling."[37] He himself resolved to leave his native state as soon as he could pay his debts, which, ironically enough, had been incurred in speculating in Western land.

The journal of Daniel W. Lord, during a trip from Baltimore to Savannah in 1824, shows that the seaboard Southern states were still in a stagnant condition. The cellar of William and Mary College sheltered cows and horses. Some slaveholders in Virginia lived meanly in log houses with stick-and-clay chimneys, no cellars, and ovens outdoors. Frequently homes and even taverns had wooden shutters instead of windows with glass panes. "If the Virginians can get Bacon and greens," he declared, "they are happy—they have also a great partiality for corn hoe cakes and ash cakes."

The bright oasis in his trip was Charleston, where he noticed that "the ladies have a more elegant and dignified gait than the Northern ladies." They were extremely fond of balls and the theater, but were

[36] Edwin M. Betts (ed.), *Thomas Jefferson's Farm Book* (Philadelphia, 1953), pp. 42–43.

[37] Hoyt, *Papers of Murphey*, I, 73, 141.

not so literary or well-informed as Northern women. Indeed, they exhibited that eternal characteristic of women—"their conversation savors of the trifling & commonplace."[38] He was informed that Charleston had more private carriages than any city in the Union and that it was considered "quite degrading" to ride in a rented carriage As he returned northward he saw a chicken fight at Warrenton, North Carolina, attended by all ranks of society, where the betting was heavy. In seventeen matches cocks from Virginia and North Carolina battled for the honor of the rival states. North Carolina won.

While the Atlantic seaboard society was languishing, the young states of Kentucky and Tennessee were flourishing. By 1820 the frontier conditions which had existed when they were admitted into the Union had to a considerable degree passed away. Although the Kentuckians raised corn, livestock, tobacco, and hemp, in middle Tennessee around Nashville cotton had been established as the money crop. Here Horace Holley, the president of Transylvania University, visited Andrew Jackson at the Hermitage and observed a style of life quite different from that of the older Southern states. This former frontiersman was now a cotton planter with interests in common with the one-generation type of aristocrats that were arising in the plantation areas of the new South. At the Hermitage, the "Old Hero" and his short, fat wife dispensed cordial hospitality; the ladies, Holley wrote, danced every evening in the hall of the mansion to the sound of a flute. The Tennessee planters may not have had the classic culture of the old Virginia society, but they had the vigor, directness, and heartiness of men who had built a new civilization in the wilderness. Holley commented in 1823 to his father in New England: "The people of Tennessee are much like the Kentuckians, showing the same influence of slavery and of an agricultural interior. Commerce makes a different sort of population from agriculture."[39]

The growth of Lexington as the "Athens of the West" was an example of the rapid changes taking place in the new society of the transmontane South. It lay in a rich agricultural region, the Bluegrass,

[38] Daniel W. Lord, "Journal of a Trip from Baltimore to Savannah & Return. February 12–May 20, 1824." MS. in Library of Congress, entries for February 12, April 8. John Palmer was served in Virginia with "hot short cakes called biscuit," *Journal of Travels in the United States . . .* (London, 1818), p. 125.

[39] Horace Holley to Luther Holley, August 14, 1823, Horace Holley Letters, Transylvania College Library.

to which many Virginia families of breeding had migrated; it was never the poor man's frontier. Lexington's primacy as emporium of Kentucky declined after the *Enterprise* made the first upriver voyage of a steamboat from New Orleans to Louisville in 1815.[40] But though Louisville and Cincinnati subsequently took away much of its trade, the capital of the Bluegrass compensated for this loss by its leadership in cultural achievements. Here the state's first newspaper, the *Kentucky Gazette,* founded in 1787, continued. The town supported the outstanding institution of higher learning in the West, Transylvania University. It had a public library and books were printed here. Silversmiths fashioned julep cups, bowls, and pitchers from "coin silver," melted silver dollars. In one of its fine homes, Ashland, lived the rising young statesman Henry Clay. Kentucky's leading artist, Matthew H. Jouett, also lived here and painted the portraits of the Bluegrass aristocrats.[41]

In this new society the Kentuckians, unlike the North Carolinians of the period, displayed great local pride. Charles Sealsfield, the German-American writer, traveling in the state in 1827, met a farmer who was bitterly prejudiced against Northerners. When the latter learned that Sealsfield was a resident of Pennsylvania, he declared that he liked the people of Pennsylvania better than those "God damned Yankees"; still, they were not Kentuckians. "The Kentuckians," he boasted, "are astonishingly mighty people . . . they are the very first people on earth!"[42]

The Kentucky farmer represented the rising of a new democratic force in the West. But in the older Southern states the country gentlemen continued to control politics and set the tone of society throughout the era of the Virginia dynasty of Presidents. Later, the structure of society in most parts of the South became essentially middle class. In the period of the early republic, on the other hand, the tone of society was more aristocratic; the psychology of the people led them to look up to the gentry and to vote for leaders of some culture and

[40] Bernard Mayo, "Lexington: Frontier Metropolis," in Eric F. Goldman (ed.), *Historiography and Urbanization* (Baltimore, 1941), pp. 32–36.

[41] Richard C. Wade, *Urban Frontier, 1790–1830* (Cambridge, 1959), Chaps. 5, 8.

[42] Charles Sealsfield, *The Americans as They are; described in a Tour through the Valley of the Mississippi* (London, 1828), p. 19.

breeding. Demagoguery was not completely absent, however, particularly outside of the plantation districts. Jeremiah Battle in a report on
social conditions in Edgecombe County, North Carolina, in 1810 described political campaigns in which the candidates used "the elec-
tioneering handshake," bought liquor for the voters, and flattered the
people.[43] Nevertheless, such expedients were not nearly as common as
they became in the 1830's and 1840's, when the suffrage was widely
extended. Indeed, the outstanding leaders of the South at this period
scorned such low appeals as unworthy of a gentleman and they displayed a more philosophical attitude toward politics than the sectional
leaders of the 1850's. The afterglow of the Revolutionary struggle
and of the constitution-making period lingered in Southern society to
give it more dignity, a greater sense of patriotism, and a broader nationalism.

Although the country gentry formed a distinct minority group, such
a large proportion of the people were uneducated that it was easy in
the first quarter of the nineteenth century for the gentry to dominate
their communities. Plural voting in some states, that is, voting in each
county where a man owned property, and *viva voce* voting (not abolished in Virginia until 1850 or in Kentucky until after the Civil War)
strengthened the hold of the aristocracy. The gradual removal of property qualifications for voting and holding office weakened their power,
but they retained other means of control, such as courthouse rings,
underrepresentation of the cities, and the apportionment of representation in the legislature on the basis of federal population instead of
the white-manhood basis; nor should intangible forces such as oratory,
economic power, and the support and prestige of family be discounted.
In North Carolina, a land predominantly of yeoman farmers, the
people did not have the right to elect the governor until the constitutional convention of 1835, and not until 1857 was the property quali-
fication for voting for state senators removed. Although the inequality
of representation between the western and eastern counties, as previously noted, was eliminated in 1835, representation in the House of
Commons (as the lower House was called) continued to be based on
federal population, and in the Senate on the amount of public taxes
paid. In Virginia a large proportion of the white population was ex-

[43] A. R. Newsome, "Twelve North Carolina Counties in 1810–1811," *North
Carolina Historical Review*, VI (1939), 89.

cluded from voting before 1830, and even after that date it has been estimated that one-fifth of the white males were disqualified from voting.[44]

The political power of the country gentry was also strengthened by the remarkable apathy of the people in exercising the suffrage when they possessed the right. This indifference was not confined to the Southern states, for there was no striking disparity between voting records both north and south of the Mason-Dixon Line. Especially notable was the political lethargy of the people during the administration of President Monroe, which has been called "the one-party period of American history."[45] In 1820 only seventeen persons in Richmond bothered to vote for presidential electors. Eight years later the real contest in the Jackson-Adams campaign, however, brought out a greater vote. Nevertheless, in Georgia the percentage of the white population that participated in the election was only 6.3—the exact percentage which obtained in Connecticut. Although more than 10 per cent of the white population of Alabama voted in this election, only slightly more than 5 per cent in both Virginia and Massachusetts and approximately 8 per cent in Tennessee participated in the election.[46] Moreover, it was a general rule both North and South throughout the ante-bellum period that the vote in presidential elections was larger than that in state elections.

The planter aristocracy was not aloof from the people as were most European aristocracies. During the period of the early republic many of the Southern political leaders identified themselves with the people, much as did Franklin Delano Roosevelt, a member of the Hudson Valley squirearchy, in the twentieth century. It is true that John Randolph disdained the rabble and scorned equality, but he was atypical. Jefferson, Madison, and John Taylor of Caroline, on the other hand, respected the rural folk and were solicitous for their welfare. Nathaniel Macon, who represented North Carolina in Congress for thirty-seven consecutive years, expressed a similar sympathy for "the people" in a letter of 1826: "The administration is gaining power & the people

[44] Ambler, *Sectionalism in Virginia,* p. 138.

[45] Charles S. Sydnor, "The One-Party Period of American History," *American Historical Review,* LI (1946), 439–451.

[46] Fletcher M. Green, "Democracy in the Old South," *Journal of Southern History,* XXII (1946), 3–24.

losing it; so that the people have all the taxes but none of the gains; with cross they do not win & with file they lose; it is always crow to them & never turkey."[47]

Southern society at this time, and even more so in the later ante-bellum period, afforded abundant opportunity for poor men to rise to the top. Take, for example, South Carolina, probably the least democratic of the Southern states. Abiel Abbott in his journal of 1818 cited striking examples of the fluidity of the Carolina social system, especially the case of Langdon Cheves, the son of an immoral Indian peddler. Despite his lowly origin Cheves became one of the most influential men of the state, president of the Second Bank of the United States, and a leading fire-eater. Also Mitchell King, a poor Scottish immigrant to Charleston, pursued many humble jobs until he published a poem in the city newspaper that attracted the attention of the president of the College of Charleston, who advanced his career so that King became a teacher in the college, an adept in the knowledge of Greek and Latin, a wealthy lawyer, a patron of the arts, and an honored member of the most aristocratic circles of the city.[48] Calhoun, the political dictator of South Carolina, arose from an unaristocratic up-country family. J. D. B. De Bow, editor of De Bow's Review, himself a poor boy from Charleston, pointed out in a pamphlet on The Interest in Slavery of the Southern Non-Slaveholder that the sons of nonslaveholders had always been "the leading and ruling spirits of the South," and he cited a long list, including George McDuffie, Langdon Cheves, Andrew Jackson, Henry Clay, James H. Hammond, James Orr, Christopher G. Memminger, Judah P. Benjamin, Alexander H. Stephens, Pierre Soulé, Alexander G. Brown, William Gilmore Simms, A. G. Magrath, William Aiken, and Maunsel White, who, he said, had not been made dema-gogues by their rise but were among the most conservative men of the region.[49]

Except in a few localities such as the rice district, the James River Valley, and the Northern Neck of Virginia, the country gentry were not a polished or urbane group. In some of the towns and cities one

[47] Nathaniel Macon to W. N. Edwards, May 20, 1826, Nathaniel Macon Papers, North Carolina State Department of Archives and History.

[48] Abbott, Journal, pp. 69–70.

[49] J. D. B. De Bow, The Interest in Slavery of the Southern Non-Slaveholder (New York, 1860), p. 10.

could meet cultivated groups of lawyers, physicians, teachers, and public men, as Jared Sparks did in 1826 when he journeyed South in quest of historical manuscripts. Of Columbia, South Carolina, he wrote, "Since leaving Boston, I have not found a more intelligent, literary, and hospitable society than in this place."[50] But in the country a homely simplicity distinguished the life of the squires, a certain informality and heartiness, though not folksiness or familiarity. There was a leisurely pace of life and a strong feeling of kinship among families. Plantation life nourished, as the novelist John Pendleton Kennedy observed, "an overflowing hospitality which knows no ebb."[51] Kennedy's description of country life in Virginia during the first quarter of the nineteenth century in *Swallow Barn* (1832), although it largely omits the common people, faithfully portrays the Virginia squires, who as a class were paternal masters and public-spirited citizens.

The hospitality of the country squires of this period was not merely the result of an evanescent state of Southern society when travelers and visitors were welcomed because of rural loneliness and when an abundance of servants and cheap food made entertaining easy. The lack of an adequate number of inns may have contributed somewhat to the practice of private hospitality.[52] But this kindly virtue arose also out of a sense of pride that disdained taking money for a service of courtesy, and out of a strong sense of kinship that led to frequent visiting of relatives. In the last decade of the ante-bellum period, "Southern hospitality" seems to have diminished. Frederick Law Olmsted in his travels in the South was often turned away when he asked for lodging. He reported that "Only twice, in a journey of four thousand miles, did I receive a night's lodging or a repast from a native Southerner, without having the exact price in money which I was expected to pay for it stated to me by those at whose hands I received it."[53]

The Southern planters were much like the landed proprietors of Russia before the Emancipation Proclamation of 1861. Hospitality was

[50] Herbert B. Adams (ed.), *The Life and Writings of Jared Sparks* (Boston, 1893), I, 440.

[51] John P. Kennedy, *Swallow Barn, or a Sojourn in the Old Dominion* (New York, 1929).

[52] Paton Yoder, "Private Hospitality in the South, 1775–1850," *Mississippi Valley Historical Review*, XLVII (1960), 424–425, 432, minimizes the practice of hospitality to strangers in the Old South, except to itinerant preachers; he maintains that lodging in private homes "as often as not" was paid for.

[53] Arthur M. Schlesinger (ed.), *The Cotton Kingdom by Frederick Law Olmsted* (New York, 1953), p. 550.

a virtue strongly cherished by both classes. Both classes had an exaggerated sense of self-importance produced largely by isolation and their history, so that the Russians thought themselves far above every other people and the planters regarded themselves superior both to the Northerners and to decadent Europeans. Mackenzie Wallace's description of Ivan Ivan'itch as a representative of the old landed proprietors would fit many Southern country gentlemen: "Though he had never been a cruel taskmaster, he had not spared the rod when he considered it necessary, and he believed birch-twigs to be a necessary instrument in the Russian system of agriculture." Like the more affluent Southern planters, the Russian gentry maintained a superfluity of house servants, who developed "an hereditary spirit of indolence and performed lazily and carelessly what they had to do." Yet Russian house servants, as the memoirs of Prince Kropotkin reveal, were often sincerely devoted to their masters in the same way that many of the household slaves were to the planters. The libraries of the Russian gentry resembled those of the Virginia and Carolina planters in being old-fashioned and little read, hereditary portraits hung on the walls, and the estates were generally untidy. The Russian landlords, like many wealthy planters, left the affairs of their estates to stewards or overseers, and the education of their children to tutors, while they hunted, fished, visited, engaged in duels, and accepted the world as they found it.

The fundamental differences between Russian and Southern country gentlemen seem to have arisen primarily from a difference between governments and the military origin of the Russian landed gentry. The Southerners loved politics, spoke their minds without fear of offending an autocrat, and enjoyed a free press during the period of the early republic. Variant economic differences between the two societies also produced different attitudes. In contrast with the settled condition of the Russian landlords, the Southern planters were on the move during the nineteenth century, migrating to the Southwest, and their market was largely international. Furthermore, the two labor systems could hardly be equated, for the majority of the serfs were in a position of half-freedom, or of being manorial dependents (although some serfs were virtually slaves). Nevertheless, the planters as well as the Russian proprietors looked upon their bondsmen as children and acted toward them accordingly. Wallace was told by a Russian landed proprietor that the serf was "a child—a foolish, imprudent, indolent child, who inevitably ruins himself when not properly looked after." The great difference that rendered Southern slavery harsher than Russian serf-dom was the existence of an impassable gulf between the white masters and the black bondsmen because of race.[54]

Ivan Ivan'itch did not have the sense of public responsibility or of *noblesse oblige* that distinguished many of the Southern country gentle-men of the early republic, such as Nathaniel Macon. This North Caro-lina planter and Jeffersonian leader was far more typical of the average planter than was Jefferson or Madison, who would be rare figures in any society. Thomas Hart Benton's description of him in his *Thirty Years' View* presents an appealing portrait of a representative country gentleman of the Old South. Dressed in a superfine navy-blue suit with a cambric stock, a beaver hat, and with the legs of his pantaloons stuck in his boots, he was perhaps neater in person and more dignified than most planters. Although he had a Princeton education, he was plain and countrylike in his speech. On his 2,000-acre tobacco plantation Buck Spring were ten blooded saddle horses and many hunting dogs, for he loved to chase the fox. On Sunday mornings he required his seventy slaves to appear before him in clean clothes; then he read a passage from the Bible, gave a homily, and had one of the old slaves lead in prayer. Macon cherished the simplicity and independence of the agricultural life in a community where no man lived so close to his neighbor that he could hear his dogs barking. Like Cincinnatus, according to Benton, he worked on occasion at the head of his slaves in the fields under the hot Carolina sun.[55] In the highest degree he exhibited a sense of patriotism and simple dignity that was characteris-tic of the better Southern planters. "He *actually believed in democ-racy,*" wrote his biographer William E. Dodd;[56] it was a democracy, however, in which gentlemen rather than demagogues led the people. Such a type of liberal democracy was destined to be outmoded in the rising Cotton Kingdom.

[54] William D. Lewis to Edward Coles, St. Petersburg, October 7, 1816, Ed-ward Coles Papers, Historical Society of Pennsylvania. This long and valuable letter on Russian society has been edited by Stanley J. Zyzniewski of the Uni-versity of Kentucky and will be published. See also Roger Dow, "Seichas: a Comparison of Pre-Reform Russia and the Ante-Bellum South," *Russian Re-view*, VII (1947), 1–5; Peter Kropotkin, *Memoirs of a Revolutionist* (Boston, 1930), Chap. 8; D. M. Wallace, *Russia* (London, 1877).

[55] Thomas Hart Benton, *Thirty Years' View* . . . (New York, 1875), I, Chap. XXXIX.

[56] William E. Dodd, *Life of Nathaniel Macon* (Raleigh, 1903), last sentence.

CHAPTER 2

The Rise of the Cotton Kingdom

T HE SUNDIALS in quiet Southern gardens registered the passage
of time in an unhurried civilization—until the rise of the Cotton
Kingdom. After the invention of the cotton gin in 1793, the tempo of
life in the South quickened. The Whitney gin was a technological
break-through that affected nearly every phase of Southern life, stimulating the growth of the materialistic spirit, a vast westward migration,
an unbalanced economy, and, most unfortunate of all, the revitaliza-
tion of the moribund institution of slavery. It resulted in a King Cotton
psychology, which James H. Hammond of South Carolina expressed
flamboyantly in the Senate in 1858: "What would happen if no cotton
was furnished for three years . . . England would topple headlong
and carry the whole civilized world with her save the South. No, you
dare not make war on cotton. No power on earth dares to make war
on it. Cotton is king."[1]

Hammond was speaking primarily of short-staple cotton, but the
first commercial cotton produced in the South was the long-staple or
sea-island variety. This variety had been introduced into Georgia in
1786 from seed sent by Loyalist refugees in the Bahama islands. Possessing a staple of two inches in length, approximately twice as long as
that of upland cotton, it was used principally in delicate laces and

[1] *Congressional Globe*, March 4, 1858, p. 961.

superfine cloth of a silky luster. The seeds were glossy and black and could be easily ginned or separated from the fibers by rollers. Upland cotton, on the other hand, had green seed to which the fibers tightly adhered, so that it took a slave a whole day to gin a pound of lint by hand. Consequently, before the invention of the Whitney gin, little upland cotton was grown in the American colonies and hardly any was exported. Sea-island cotton was always much more valuable than the upland variety, bringing in 1803 fifty cents a pound, while short staple cotton sold for approximately half that amount. The high price of sea-island cotton was owing partly to the excessive amount of labor involved in its production, which required ten or twelve pickings, while the short-staple variety could be harvested in three. Furthermore, sea-island cotton could be grown commercially only on the sea islands off the coast of Georgia and South Carolina and the adjacent littoral. After an enormous spurt in production during the latter part of the eighteenth century, sea-island cotton exports remained stabilized between eight or nine million pounds from 1805 to 1850, when production increased greatly because it was found that this prized variety could be grown successfully in the interior of Florida. In 1860 over fifteen million pounds were exported from the Southern states.[2]

By the close of the eighteenth century a great potential market for cotton fiber had been created by English inventions of spinning and weaving machinery. Only a practicable gin was needed, and this was supplied by the invention of young Eli Whitney, who after graduating from Yale College in 1793 took passage on a ship bound for Savannah, Georgia, to accept a position as tutor on a South Carolina plantation. On board ship he met the vivacious and warmhearted widow of the Revolutionary general Nathanael Greene, who was returning to her plantation near Savannah. Mrs. Greene invited Whitney to visit Mulberry Grove, and here he heard planters talking about the need for a cotton gin to separate the fiber from the green seed of upland cotton. He set to work to design a model, which he completed in ten days. It was a simple machine consisting of a roller equipped with wire teeth which tore the fiber from the seed as the spikes revolved between the slats of a hopper. The original Whitney gin, which was patented in

[2] Lewis C. Gray, *History of Agriculture in the Southern United States to 1860* (New York, 1941), II, 673–681, 731–739.

1794, was operated by a hand crank and could gin fifty pounds of cotton a day, as contrasted with one a day by the old method.[3]

Whitney formed a partnership with Phineas Miller, Mrs. Greene's manager and tutor, to manufacture gins in New Haven. They tried to maintain a monopoly on the use of the invention, but it was of such simple construction that a blacksmith could make it, and soon many gins were built that infringed the patent rights. Moreover, improvements were made by others, notably Hodgen Holmes of Augusta, Georgia, who in 1796 substituted circular iron saws for wooden rollers with wire teeth. Whitney and his partner prosecuted many suits against infringers, but with little success before Southern juries. Finally Judge Johnson of the Supreme Court of Georgia upheld Whitney's patent rights in the year before they expired. The South Carolina legislature appropriated a lump sum of $50,000 to pay Whitney and Miller for their rights in that state, and North Carolina and Tennessee levied a tax on each gin using the Whitney patent and paid the proceeds to the inventor. But having spent large sums in court litigation, the partners realized little from the epoch-making invention.

Short-staple cotton was almost ideally suited for cultivation in the South with its warm climate and its slave labor system. Early in the spring the seeds were planted in rows; as the plants grew, the grass grew too, and had to be kept down by frequent plowing and hoeing. Horace Holley, the Northern-born president of Transylvania University, described the flowering of the plant on Andrew Jackson's plantation near Nashville in a letter to his father: "The flower of this plant is white the first day of blooming, red the second, and falls the third."[4] Then green bolls developed, bursting open when the plants matured in August. Forty or fifty bolls grew on the ante-bellum plant; some luxuriant specimens contained as many as a hundred and fifty. After they burst, a good cotton field was a white carpet on the land.

Cotton was well adapted to the slave-gang system. The height of the plant was low enough not to hide the workers; they could be kept like an army marching across the wide fields in plowing, hoeing, and picking gangs. Since the slaves could cultivate twice as much cotton

[3] Jeannette Mirsky and Allan Nevins, *The World of Eli Whitney* (New York, 1952), Chap. 6.

[4] Horace Holley to Luther Holley, August 14, 1823, Horace Holley Papers, Transylvania College Library.

as they could pick, the acreage planted was limited by the picking capacity of the plantation force. Usually ten acres, together with eight or ten acres of corn, were as much as could be cultivated by a hand. Under favorable weather conditions, good soil produced a 500-pound bale or a bale and a half of ginned cotton per acre.[5]

The picking lasted from the latter part of August to early January. Women and small children as well as the male hands were used in this operation. Dragging a long sack tied to their waists to deposit the cotton in, they employed both hands to pluck the fleece from the open bolls. Since the bolls ripened unevenly, it was necessary for the field to be picked over at least three times. This unequal ripening was the most important reason for the failure until the 1930's to develop a successful mechanical picker. The yield of cotton was greatly increased after 1815 by the introduction into the lower South of the Mexican variety, whose bolls opened more widely and could be picked more easily than the upland cotton. Consequently the amount of cotton picked by a slave in a day doubled during the ante-bellum period. Full-grown hands were required to pick from 150 to 200 pounds of seed cotton per day. The seed cotton was taken to the planter's gin, which was usually driven by mules attached to a long sweep. After ginning, it was pressed into bales by means of a screw and covered with hemp cloth, or bagging, tied by ropes. In the ports it was reduced by steam presses into smaller bulk for shipment to Europe.

Three-fourths of the world's supply of cotton came from the Southern states, and the remainder from India, Egypt, and Brazil.[6] From the beginning of the cotton trade until the Civil War, the great port to which Southern cotton was shipped was Liverpool, the port of entry for Manchester, the textile center of Great Britain. The destination of Southern cotton exports in 1859–60 was divided as follows: Great Britain, 2,344,000 bales; continental Europe, 1,069,000; and the United States, 943,000.

Liverpool determined the world market price for cotton; consequently the Southern planters anxiously awaited the news from there of the varying prices paid for different grades of their staple. The

[5] An excellent description of the cultivation and picking of cotton is found in U. B. Phillips, *Life and Labor in the Old South* (Boston, 1939), Chaps. VI, VII.

[6] Gray, *History of Agriculture*, II, 692, 1026–1027.

main determinant in its price was whether there was a short crop or a bonanza yield in the Southern states, but other factors, such as disturbed conditions in Europe or a panic, also influenced the market. In the first decade after the invention of the gin, prices of short-staple cotton rose as high as 23 cents a pound, but the increased production that resulted from high prices led to a rapid decline; in 1812, largely because of the outbreak of war, the price in New Orleans descended to 7 or 8 cents a pound. After the conclusion of peace with Great Britain in 1815, prices became phenomenally good, rising in 1818 to 33 cents a pound. The panic of 1819 depressed prices to 8 cents, but in 1835 cotton rose spectacularly to 15 cents, then began a long decline, reaching a low point of 4 cents in January, 1844. The last five years of the ante-bellum period were a time of prosperity for the cotton planters, who in 1860 produced their greatest crop of over four and a half million bales. Yet the future for both cotton and slavery was clouded by the prospect of overproduction of this staple.

The Whitney gin opened up a vast kingdom for cotton. Upland cotton could be grown wherever there were two hundred frostless days. The western limit of cultivation was the ninety-eighth meridian of longitude, beyond which the minimum requirement of twenty-three inches of annual rainfall was not met. The northern limit excluded Virginia and Kentucky except for the western tip of the latter; before 1826, cotton was grown enthusiastically in the southeastern corner of Virginia and in Piedmont North Carolina, but crop failures caused both states to reduce their planting drastically after that date. In the decade of the 1850's, however, cotton brought such a high price that these states started growing it again.

In the Atlantic seaboard states the center of the production of short-staple cotton soon moved from the coastal plain to the Piedmont. Here in 1799 Wade Hampton I of Millwood, near Columbia, South Carolina, the first great cotton planter of the region, with his eighty-six slaves made a crop of six hundred bales worth $90,000. Thereafter he prospered so greatly from his cotton planting in South Carolina and his absentee sugar plantation in Louisiana (acquired in 1811) that when he died in 1835 he was reputed to have been the richest planter in the United States.[7] The expansion of cotton culture into the Pied-

[7] Charles E. Cauthen (ed.), *Family Letters of the Three Wade Hamptons, 1782–1901* (Columbia, 1953), p. xiii.

mont tended to unify the people of the state economically and politically.

At the same time a decline took place in the economy of the coastal plain. The competition of the fresh lands of the Piedmont and even more of the virgin soil of the Southwest drained population, both white and black, from this old region. When Edmund Ruffin made his agricultural survey of South Carolina in 1843, he was saddened by seeing the decay and desolation of the plantations of the tidewater. Goose Creek Parish, for example, once the seat of many wealthy planters, was now a scene of dilapidation and abandonment. Beautiful old houses, standing in groves of noble and venerable live oaks, such as Oak Forest, the former home of Sir James Wright, were deserted and falling into decay. Land values in the low country had declined enormously, and instead of producing crops some of the old plantations were valuable chiefly for their lumber, which was floated in rafts to Charleston. The countryside gave Ruffin the impression of "the former residence of a people who have all gone away, leaving the land tenantless."[8] Even more melancholy was the sight of the deserted towns of the low country, Dorchester, Jacksonborough, Pineville, and Purysburg; Beaufort, Ruffin remarked, was sustained by malaria, which drove people to it for refuge.

The typical cotton planter of the Piedmont was not the owner of many slaves and a large estate but rather a small planter, such as Moses Waddel. Waddel owned a cotton plantation near Abbeville in upcountry South Carolina, on which he had twenty-three slaves. Cotton planting was only one of his interests, for he was a preacher and a famous schoolmaster of the Old South. His diary shows that he visited his plantation often and was much concerned with the practical details of its operation and the management of the Negroes.[9] The largest amount of cotton picked by his slaves was twenty bales. He had his own gin, operated by mules attached to a long sweep, and a press which compressed the cotton into bales by means of a screw. The market for his cotton was Augusta, to which he sent his crop by boat, paying freight of one dollar a bale. He received good prices of 15 to 16 cents a pound, and his expenses were slight, chiefly the cost of shoes,

[8] Private Diary of Ed. Ruffin, January 29, 1843.
[9] Moses Waddel's diary covers the period January 24, 1822, to September, 1836. MSS. in Library of Congress.

cloth, and blankets. Besides cotton he raised oats, wheat, and corn. During the winter he kept his Negroes employed clearing new ground, splitting rails for fences, and pulling fodder. His slave women performed various tasks, including picking peaches and apples, cutting them into pieces, and preserving them by drying them in the sun.

Waddel's diary gives many interesting details of slave management on a small cotton plantation. He employed an overseer, who whipped the slaves for delinquent conduct, at the same time Waddel, the schoolmaster, was flogging his pupils. During the picking season, he "encouraged his hands much & sincerely with the promise of hats, blankets, etc." He recorded with satisfaction that two hands picked 836 pounds in one day, a fine performance. Waddel was apparently as strict a master of his slaves as of his pupils. He reproved his slaves for absence from prayers, for want of industry, and for untruthfulness. On July 8, 1834, he wrote that Dick had rebelled against the hard work of clearing new ground and that the other Negroes had refused to aid the overseer in subduing him. The recalcitrant slave then ran away, but, after being absent twelve days, was captured and whipped. Waddel seems to have been much more concerned than the average planter with the religious condition of his bondsmen, for his diary contains frequent references to his praying with them, catechizing them, and rebuking them for derelictions from virtue.

The expansion of the Cotton Kingdom into the Gulf region was facilitated by the passage of the Harrison Frontier Land Act of 1800, which fixed the minimum price of government land at two dollars an acre and permitted payment to be made in four annual installments. As early as 1804, cotton was cultivated in the wild territory of Mississippi, for in that year Abram Mordecai erected a cotton gin at the junction of the Coosa and Tallapoosa rivers.[10] Cotton planters began settling the rich Tennessee Valley of northern Alabama around Huntsville between 1805 and 1809, and a large migration to Alabama occurred after the war with England. James A. Graham of the Piedmont village of Hillsborough, North Carolina, wrote in 1817: "The *Alabama Fever* rages here with great violence and has carried off vast numbers of our citizens. I am apprehensive if it continues to spread as it has

[10] Charles S. Davis, *The Cotton Kingdom in Alabama* (Montgomery, 1939), p. 12.

done, it will almost depopulate the country."[11] The Treaty of Fort Jackson in 1816 had made available much agricultural land, but the full exploitation of the arable land of the state was not possible until the removal of the Creek Indians west of the Mississippi twenty years later.

The purchase of cotton lands in Tennessee and the Southwest was not confined to bona fide settlers but was eagerly made by speculators and land sharks. The acquisition by the federal government of rich cotton lands in western Tennessee from the Chickasaw Indians, the so-called Jackson Purchase of 1818, was a signal for North Carolina and Virginia farmers and speculators to rush to that area. Among the speculators were Andrew Jackson, Marcus Winchester, and John Overton, who in 1819 founded the town of Memphis.[12] Jackson and his friend General John Coffee also speculated in the lands of the Tennessee Valley in the Huntsville area. Coffee organized the Cyprus Land Company before 1819, acquired coveted land around Muscle Shoals, and founded Florence in northern Alabama. Federal land offices were opened at Cahaba, which became the early capital of Alabama, and at St. Stephens, where spirited bidding at auctions ran the price of fertile bottom lands far above the minimum of $2 per acre. Settlers flowed into Alabama lands not occupied by Indians by way of the Upper Federal Road, opened in 1811, which led from Athens, Georgia, through Columbus and Montgomery to St. Stephens (north of Mobile), or else by the Natchez Trace from Nashville to Muscle Shoals and then to St. Stephens. Many settlers, too poor to buy federal lands, squatted upon them. Cotton lands were also available to poor men in Georgia if they were lucky enough to win a farm in the Georgia land lottery, which was started in 1803 to dispose of the lands from which the Indians had been removed. Any man who had resided in the state for three years was entitled to a lottery ticket for himself as well as one for his wife and another for his children.

In 1819 speculation in Western lands received a severe jolt from the financial panic of that year. Much of this land had been bought

---

[11] J. G. de R. Hamilton (ed.), *The Papers of Thomas Ruffin* (Raleigh, 1918–20), I, 198.

[12] See T. P. Abernethy, *From Frontier to Plantation in Tennessee* (Chapel Hill, 1932).

on credit from banks that engaged in unsound practices. Also many purchasers of the federal land under the credit system of the Harrison Act had bought more than they could pay for. After the panic they put pressure on Congress to pass the Land Act of 1820, which abolished the credit system, reduced the minimum price of land to $1.25 an acre, and allowed those who had overbought to surrender part of their holdings and receive title to the remainder. The panic temporarily arrested the Western movement, but after a few years it was resumed with even greater force.

It expressed the overwhelming desire of many men to abandon exhausted land and get a fresh start on the rich virgin soils of the West. Land was getting "so pore" in the Southern uplands, the principal region from which the settlers of the Southwest came, that many farmers decided to move. They were further stimulated by letters, from friends and relatives who had ventured into the new lands, describing a soil that "it would do your heart good to look at." Timothy Flint, a New England schoolteacher who lived in the Southwest during the early 1820's, wrote: "Very few, except the Germans, emigrate simply to find better and cheaper lands." Rather they sought a mythical region where they would enjoy new and more beautiful woods and streams, a milder climate, wild game, and "the boundless license of a new region." They were led on by the restless hope of discovering in a new country a combination of delightful things, "something we crave and have not."[13] Also some men like Gideon Lincecum, who emigrated to the Tombigbee River country in 1818, delighted in freeing themselves from the restraints of civilization and settling in the "wildest, least trodden and tomahawk-marked country." An incarnation of the restless and resourceful spirit of the frontier, he was a jack-of-all-trades, wood sawyer, planter, teacher, storekeeper, explorer, founder of towns, manager of an Indian ball team, and a doctor specializing in herb remedies.[14]

In 1828 Captain Basil Hall of the Royal Navy observed emigrants from the older South camping by the road with their wagons, car-

[13] Timothy Flint, *Recollections of the Last Ten Years Passed in Occasional Residence and Journeys in the Valley of the Mississippi* (Boston, 1826), pp. 240–241.

[14] Gideon Lincecum, "Autobiography," *Mississippi Historical Society Publications,* VIII (1904).

riages, women, children, and slaves, lured by the same dream. He talked to one of the emigrants bound for Florida, who had never been to this El Dorado of the imagination, but who told the Englishman that it was the finest country in the world, with a delightful climate, rich soil, and "plenty of room." Although he had a good plantation in Maryland and did not want for anything, he had sold his land and with his family, furniture, and slaves started for Florida. His wife gave Hall this explanation for his irrational conduct: "It was all for the mere love of moving. We have been doing so all our lives—just moving —from place to place—never resting—as soon as ever we git comfortably settled, then, it is time to be off to something new."[15] The planter described the Southwest to the British traveler in terms of a dream: "It is a wide empty country, with a soil that yields such noble crops that any man is sure to succeed, go where he will."

Tyrone Power, the Irish actor, during his travels in the Gulf states in 1835 was impressed by the restless energy and acquisitive spirit of the recent settlers. They displayed much the same desire for quick wealth, the feverish energy, the speculative urge, the desire for change, that motivates the real estate developers of our era. Neither the climate nor the hard conditions of pioneer living slowed them down:

These frontier tamers of the swamp and forest are hardy, indefatigable and enterprising to a degree; despising and condemning luxury and refinement, courting labour, and even making a pride of the privation, which they, without any necessity, continue to endure with their families. . . . Their pride does not consist in fine houses, fine raiment, costly services of plate or refined cookery; they live in humble dwellings of wood, wear the coarsest habits, and live on the plainest fare. It is their pride to have planted an additional acre of cane-brake, to have won a few feet from the river, or cleared a thousand trees from the forest; to have added a couple of slaves to their family, or a horse of high blood to their stable.[16]

Emigration to the Southwest followed a time pattern that throws doubt on the validity of Frederick Jackson Turner's safety-valve theory. The heaviest emigration occurred during boom times, 1819, 1830–37,

[15] Basil Hall, *Travels in North America in the Years 1827–28* (Edinburgh, 1829), I, 130–133; see also Hodgson, *Letters from North America*, I, 113–114, 141.

[16] Tyrone Power, *Impressions of America during the Years 1833, 1834, and 1835* (London, 1836), II, 215.

and 1853–57. During hard times there was a notable diminution of westward migration—one must have cash or good credit to buy land even at the low prices of the public domain. The settler also required money for the trip and to finance himself until a crop could be grown and sold. Nevertheless, there were numerous poor people who emigrated to the Southwest like Ike and Betsy in the old ballad "Sweet Betsy from Pike."

> Oh, dont you remember Sweet Betsy from Pike,
> Who crossed the big mountains with her lover Ike,
> With two yoke of oxen, a large yaller dog,
> A tall Shanghai rooster and one spotted hog.

Thousands of these poor people became squatters on the public land.

The period of the 1830's until the panic of 1837 was what one of the Virginia emigrants called "flush times in Alabama and Mississippi."[17] It was a time of great inflation of bank notes, when it was easy to borrow paper money to pay for land. The new settlers endorsed one another's notes freely and grandly, for it was regarded as an insult not to do so. When James D. Davidson left his native Virginia for the lower South in 1836, he wrote from Vicksburg that the people were mad with speculation. "They do business," he reported, "in a kind of frenzy, largely on credit."[18] The most frequent question asked was what was the price of cotton and the next was the price of "niggers." In the 1830's settlers flocked to the Black Belt of Alabama, a strip of rich black soil, twenty to fifty miles wide, running across the south central part of the state into northeastern Mississippi. This region had been avoided by the early settlers because of its lack of trees, its thick canebrake, and its stiff soil. Yet it contained the richest soil of the state and became the seat of the finest plantations.

The spirit of the times in the Black Belt was reflected in the letters of Henry Watson, a young Northern tutor who settled in the village of Greensboro, Alabama, in 1834. He noted that the country in his neighborhood had been settled by people from Virginia and the Carolinas who brought their Negroes with them and bought lands from the original settlers at an advance of price. "They are," he wrote,

[17] J. G. Baldwin, *The Flush Times of Alabama and Mississippi* (New York, 1853).

[18] Herbert A. Kellar (ed.), "A Journey Through the South in 1836: Diary of James D. Davidson," *Journal of Southern History*, I (1935), 355.

"some of the nobility of the old states, the Randolph family, the Taylors, and the Bollings—first rate & intelligent men." Nevertheless the settlers lived altogether in log houses, had no tea, all commodities were outrageously high—corn four dollars a bushel, eggs 37 cents a dozen, $5 clocks sold for $40—everybody was in debt for land and Negroes, and materialism prevailed. So strong was the democratic spirit among the people that the politicians running for office sought to ascertain public sentiment and follow it—"the candidates would consider it madness to attempt to lead."[19]

The westward and southern flow of Southerners followed in general along isothermal lines. Emigrating farmers liked to settle in areas where there would be no abrupt changes in their mode of life. As a rule, if they were used to growing tobacco and had acquired skill in producing it, they had no desire to try a new crop. Grain and cattle farmers usually moved into regions like their old homes, where they could continue to raise wheat, corn, and livestock. They were even influenced in their selection of a site by whether the drinking water was like that of their old home, limestone or freestone. The women, with clothes of the family to wash, hated to move to an area where they had to contend with hard water. The emigrants also preferred a soil that was similar to but richer than the land to which they had been accustomed. They preferred, moreover, to locate, not on the fertile river bottoms, which were unhealthy, hard to clear, and subject to floods, but on the higher lands.

An interesting feature of the migrations was the tendency to make settlements in groups. Sometimes a whole congregation would follow their minister to the new country. Frequently a man was sent ahead to spy out the land and select a favorable location; then planters would send their overseers with a slave force to clear some of the land, plant a corn crop, and build a cabin in preparation for the emigrating family. Although economic considerations were the main impulse of the migrations, some Southerners were motivated by the desire to get away from slavery and to bring up their children in a free state.[20] Among

[19] Henry Watson to Julius Reed, February 12, 1834; to his father, February 10, 1834, December 15, 1836, Henry Watson Papers, Duke University Library.

[20] James W. Patton (ed.), "Letters from North Carolina Emigrants in the Old Northwest, 1830–1834, *Mississippi Valley Historical Review,* **XLVII** (1960), 263–277.

these were the Quakers of Guilford County, North Carolina, who in the 1820's emigrated to southern Indiana and Illinois.

The Census of 1850 enables us to trace movements of population from the different states to the West and Southwest which reveal a persistent drift of emigration along parallel lines. The expatriates of Maryland, for example, were living in the following regions: 54,310 in the Old Northwest; 30,000 in Virginia and Pennsylvania; 12,277 in Kentucky, Tennessee, and Missouri; and only 4,722 in the seven states of the lower South. North Carolina sent approximately as many settlers to Tennessee, Kentucky, and Missouri as it did to the lower South. One of these North Carolina emigrants, Samuel R. Ralston, settled in 1843 with his slaves on a hemp plantation near Independence, Missouri, where he represented an outpost of Southernism.[21] Kentucky sent many settlers to Missouri, including the famous proslavery leader David Atchison. South Carolina and Georgia were the main sources of population for the newer states of the Southwest. So many natives of Tennessee migrated to Texas, more than from any other state, that Texas was largely the child of the "Volunteer State."

Virginia, "the mother of states and statesmen," held a special status. It contributed more than 150,000 of its natives to the Old Northwest and 140,000 to Kentucky, Tennessee, and Missouri, but only 37,000 to the lower South.[22] Although the Old Dominion furnished relatively few white settlers to the lower South, many of the slaves there from this state spoke with nostalgia and pride of their birthplace. The Virginian emigrés to the Southwest regarded themselves as superior to the common run of settlers, and thereby often aroused resentment among the latter. A young Virginian who settled in Jonesboro, Texas, wrote to a friend in his native state in 1853 that "the name of F.F.V. is held somewhat in contempt all through the South, so many from that good old state, who have no pretensions to either refinement or education attempt to insinuate themselves into good favour and society by boast-

---

[21] W. D. Overdyke (ed.), "A Southern Family on the Missouri Frontier: Letters from Independence 1843–1855," *Journal of Southern History*, XVII (1951), 216–237.

[22] William O. Lynch, "The Westward Flow of Southern Colonists before 1861," *Journal of Southern History*, IX (1943), and F. L. Owsley, "The Pattern of Migration and Settlement of the Southern Frontier," *ibid.*, XIX (1945), 147–176.

ing that Virginia is their native land."[23]

The migration of the Lides from the Darlington district of South Carolina to the Black Belt of Alabama was typical of the experience of the better class of emigrants. They left the pleasant neighborhood of Society Hill in the fall of 1835. Their party formed a caravan of wagons pulled by oxen, carrying food, agricultural tools, and some of the Negroes. The ladies of the family rode in a carriage and a chaise. Traveling at the rate of fifteen miles a day, after five weeks they reached their destination of Carlowville, Alabama, where they had purchased a plantation of 490 acres at $4 an acre. They met with many hardships and dangers on the way—breakdown of wagons, leaky tents to sleep in, terrible roads, dangerous fords, and dread of the Indians as they passed through their territory. There were pleasures also, delight at the scenery, sociable calls from other families who were traveling to the Southwest along the same road, and an occasional treat of hearing preaching in the little villages along the route. Near Camden the Lides heard "a very good sermon" from a colored Methodist minister, whom they dignified by calling "Mister," an unusual occurrence in the South. Upon arrival at their homestead, the men went furiously to work to clear the land and prepare for planting the crops. The senior Lide, his daughter wrote, was "the most busy man you ever saw," all the time among his Negroes in the field; "he seems to have forgotten that he is old."

The impulse to move to greener pastures was not easily quenched among the cotton planters of the Southwest. The Lides, for example, although they were comfortably situated and raised good crops, were not satisfied. Ten years after they had settled in Alabama, Maria wrote to a brother at her childhood home, lamenting the restless spirit of "pa":

His having such a good crop seems to make him more anxious to move. I don't know why it is but none of them are satisfied here. I have no idea that we will stop short of red river; brother has seen that place and was so perfectly delighted with it that he can find no place to equal it. I have been trying my best to get brother into the notion of going to California, because I think he would be obliged to stop then for he could go no farther,

[23] Curtis B. Sutton to "Buck" Lyons, September 25, 1853, James and William H. Lyons Papers, Huntington Library.

and I think he would be far enough away from society to be satisfied to settle himself permanently. You have no idea how tired I am of hearing about moving; it is the subject of conversation every time pa and brother meet and that is very often. . . .[24]

The end of the story came in 1854, when the son had reached Woodville, Texas. There he died of cholera, which also killed several of his slaves, including "Old Grannie Sara," the nurse who had accompanied the family from their original home in South Carolina.

Though aristocratic planters from the tidewater formed only a small proportion of the emigrants to the Southwest, Thomas Dabney of Gloucester County, Virginia, was a distinguished example of the gentry who moved to the Southwest. He lived in a beautiful old plantation house, Elmington, in the Tidewater section, where he was surrounded by refined and aristocratic neighbors, and in 1835 decided to sell his plantation and remove to Hinds County, Mississippi. In Virginia he was a successful wheat and tobacco farmer, but his growing family (his wife bore him sixteen children) and his expensive style of living required an ampler income than his worn-out Virginia plantation could provide. Accordingly, he sold his pleasant estate and with his two hundred slaves set out for the Southwest. Before his departure his friends gave him a public dinner presided over by Senator John Tyler.[25]

Earlier he had made a trip through the Southwest to choose a suitable location for his family. Before moving, he gave his slaves the privilege of going with him or remaining in Virginia, choosing their own masters; but only two, feeble old people, elected to remain in Virginia. After three weeks of traveling, the family reached its future home in Mississippi, the plantation of Burleigh, consisting of the partially cleared farms Dabney had bought from half a dozen frontier farmers. The pioneer farmers of the region invited him to house-raisings and logrollings, and he helped neighbors whose crops were beset with grass; but when he came with a gang of Negroes and directed them from his horse while wearing gloves, they resented his aristocratic manners. So successful was he in the change from a wheat and

[24] Fletcher Green (ed.), *The Lides Go South and West* (Columbia, S.C., 1952), pp. 17, 35–36.
[25] Susan Dabney Smedes, *A Southern Planter* (New York, 1890).

tobacco farmer to a cotton planter that in the course of years his estate expanded to four thousand acres.

Many a planter in the old states of the South must have debated with himself, as did James Henry Hammond of Silver Bluff in South Carolina, whether to remain on a plantation of poor soil or emigrate to the West. On February 6, 1841, Hammond wrote in his diary of "the emigration to the West of nearly every one of the young men with whom I was brought up & with whom I was or might have been intimate." On March 31 he complained that the soil of Silver Bluff had become so poor that he was perplexed as to his future. He had "hung on here rather than go to a new state" because he had not wished to carry his family into "the semi-barbarous West." He was also detained by his political prospects and his desire to give his children "a certain rank in society."[26]

The removal to a crude frontier did indeed result in a temporary loss of some of the comforts and refinements of civilization. Usually the settler hastily built a double cabin with a passage or breezeway between its two rooms. Such a house often lacked windows, and at first the chinks between the logs were not sealed with mud. The Lides removed the door of their cabin at mealtimes to serve as a table. Frederick Law Olmsted observed in 1853 that the majority of the planters of Alabama lived in such log cabins. Twelve years after the Dabneys had emigrated to Mississippi, they were still living, despite their prosperity, in the old house with its leaky roof which Thomas had built when they first settled in the state. The deprivation that many of the emigrating families felt most keenly was the lack of preaching. To compensate for the absence of schools, mothers and fathers would teach their children. It was surprising, however, how quickly schools and churches were established in the new communities. The Lides, five months after reaching Carlowville, were able to enjoy preaching every Sunday, and two day schools and a singing school had been established in the neighborhood.

One of the flourishing cotton areas in the lower South in the 1840's was the Tallahassee region of Florida with its rich red soil. Here was located, according to Solon Robinson, a high-bred class of planters who made society in that region very agreeable. The planters averaged

[26] Diary of James Henry Hammond, February 6, 1841, Library of Congress.

six bales of cotton per field hand and raised sufficient food for their slaves, except for pork. The soil was plowed by primitive one-horse plows. Since land was cheap they wasted it recklessly. Solon Robinson, the agricultural reformer, observed, "They are real land destroyers," but at the same time they were money-makers.

The cotton planters who emigrated to the virgin lands of the Southwest carried on the same wasteful type of agriculture that had exhausted their old plantations. As a consequence, in the 1840's and 1850's farms in Alabama and Mississippi were being abandoned for fresher lands in Texas and Arkansas. Robinson found in 1845 that lands in Mississippi were being eroded because the farmers "skinned" the soil, or scratched the surface only two inches deep with their plows. He discovered that many of the farmers in Mississippi were not "fixed" but ready to sell out and move to Texas. In the fertile counties of Madison and Hinds in the delta country, he passed what he called "Gone to Texas" farms, abandoned and desolate-looking.[27]

Notwithstanding the youth of society in Alabama in the 1850's, there was constant and extensive emigration from the state. Part of this movement was caused by prosperous planters' buying the adjacent farms of poor men, who would then leave for land farther west. Senator Clement C. Clay, Jr., of Alabama explained this flow of population from the state: "Our small planters, after taking the cream off their lands, unable to restore them by rest, manures, or otherwise, are going farther west and south, in search of other virgin lands, which they may and will despoil and impoverish in like manner."[28] He pointed out that numerous farmhouses once occupied by yeoman farmers were at the time abandoned or occupied by Negroes, and that the once fertile fields were unfenced and covered with broomsedge and foxtail. Counties of Alabama were exhibiting the same signs of decay and exhaustion that had characterized Virginia and the Carolinas. He cited one county which in 1825 had cast 3,000 votes, but thirty years later cast only 2,300. In crossing Louisiana into Texas, Olmsted passed many abandoned farms on both sides of the Sabine River. Numerous emigrant trains going to Texas presented a melancholy picture: jaded

[27] Herbert A. Kellar (ed.), *Solon Robinson, Pioneer and Agriculturist; Selected Writings* (Indianapolis, 1936), II, 462–465.
[28] *De Bow's Review*, December, 1855, p. 727.

cattle, spiritless and ragged slaves, the men in homespun, silent and surly, the women bedraggled and forlorn.[29]

Of all the classes of Southern society, the nonslaveholding farmers were the most migratory, and many were propelled westward by the advance of the plantation. Jefferson County, Mississippi, was an example of an area where the emigration of the lower classes of the population was striking. Located on the lower Mississippi River, the county was one of the earliest settled areas of the state, but by 1850 its hilly lands of loess soil had become badly eroded. Partly because of this fact, between 1850 and 1860, 85 per cent of the nonslaveholders left the county.[30] Indeed, the number of small farms in the delta-loess area of Mississippi declined sharply in the decade, those having less than 50 acres of improved land from 17 to 7 per cent of the farms, and those having 50 to 99 acres from 13 to 8 per cent, while the percentage of plantations having over 500 acres of improved land rose from 11 to 22 per cent.[31]

Although much has been written of the part that the exhaustion of soils played in the westward movement, the story of farmers leaving their homes because of the washing away of the topsoil and the formation of gullies is still largely untold. In 1857 Micajah Clark made a sentimental journey from Kosciusko, Mississippi, to his old home in up-country South Carolina, which he had left ten years before. In his journal he tells how he found his Grandfather Clark's place dilapidated and the land almost worn out—his uncle's farm nearby was also worn out. The old man was living in a ramshackle house "destitute of the comforts of life yet had 4 likely stout young negro women and a gang of young negroes growing up and all not making a living"—some of his cousins were living on places that had been worn out thirty years. He visited his birthplace, now an old field covered with pine trees and saplings, with gullies all through it, the house untenanted for many years.

His Grandfather Webb's place was "a perfect waste, houses had all long since been removed, and the place cultivated where his houses and

[29] Frederick Law Olmsted, *A Journey Through Texas: or, A Saddle-Trip on the Southwestern Frontier* (New York, 1857), pp. 56–57.

[30] Fabian Linden, review of Herbert Weaver, *Mississippi Farmers, 1850–1860*, in *American Historical Review*, LII (1947), 339.

[31] Herbert Weaver, *Mississippi Farmers, 1850–1860* (Nashville, 1945), 36.

negro quarter once stood until it had worn out—washed into Gullies from 3 to 4 feet deep—now growing up in briars and pine saplings— it was prosperous in my boyhood—grandfather had a large river farm on the Seneca River." He then made a pilgrimage to the family grave- yard, which had been entirely neglected: "Gullies around the graves as deep as my horse."[32] Some of his cousins who had remained in South Carolina seemed to him to lack energy. Perhaps their initiative and spirit were broken by the small rewards obtained from their toil on wasted land.

The expansion of the Cotton Kingdom in the Southwest led to an unwholesome development of absentee plantations. Planters and busi- nessmen in the older Southern states who had surplus capital, or whose slaves had multiplied beyond economical use on their plantations, often invested in the ownership of fertile farms in the Southwest, which they managed from a distance. An example of the large absentee planta- tion was Wild Woods in Mississippi, owned by Wade Hampton III, an estate which in 1850 produced 433 bales of cotton and 5,000 bushels of corn. Hampton owned five other plantations in Mississippi, the whole containing 10,409 acres and a labor force of 900 slaves. The Carolina proprietor paid an annual visit to his Wild Woods plantation, where he hunted bears and conferred with his overseers. The greatest cotton planter of the South in the 1850's was probably Stephen Dun- can, a banker who lived in the beautiful Greek Revival mansion of Auburn near Natchez, owned eight plantations, 1,018 plantation slaves, and 23 house servants, and produced 4,000 bales of cotton.

A notable area of absentee plantations was Concordia Parish, Louisi- ana, across the river from Natchez. Here in 1860 lived a population composed chiefly of overseers and their families, 1,400 whites and 13,000 Negroes. The proprietors of the land were monopolists, described by a representative of the New Orleans *Crescent* as exercising "the au- thority of ownership over estates as broad as some German principali- ties, and yielding far greater revenues. But very few of these lords of the soil reside on their estates but have their residence across the river in Natchez or elsewhere."[33]

[32] Micajah A. Clark, Travel Journal, July 7, October 2, 1857, South Carolini- ana Library, 42–46, 48–49.
[33] Walter Pritchard (ed.), "A Tourist's Description of Louisiana in 1860," *Louisiana Historical Quarterly*, XXI (1938), 1176, 1212.

As new areas were opened to settlement in the Southwest, land speculation became incessant. In the undeveloped sections of Louisiana the speculators closely watched the government surveyors, spotted the richest tracts of land, and, as soon as they were put on the market, bought them. Human greed was constantly active.[34] J. W. Dorr of the New Orleans *Crescent*, who made a tour of Louisiana by horse and buggy in 1860, reported that the building of the Vicksburg and Shreveport Railroad was opening fertile prairie lands to settlement and that the small proprietors would soon be bought out by large ones. He observed that this process "promised to root out of all the most productive regions of the South the great body of small agriculturists."[35] The plantation organization had decided advantage over the small farm in the production of staple crops, so that the advance of cotton and sugar culture drove many of the small farmers from fertile soil either into the relatively poor lands of the vicinity or to westward emigration.[36] But many plantations were formed, not by consolidating the holdings of frontier farmers, but by buying large tracts directly from the federal or state governments, from land companies, or from speculators.[37]

The rapid advance of the Cotton Kingdom was registered in the admission of new states into the Union: Louisiana in 1812; Mississippi, 1817; Alabama, 1819; Missouri, 1821; Arkansas, 1836; Florida and Texas, 1845. The drain of population from the older Southern states was indicated by the fact that North Carolina, despite having one of the largest birth rates in the nation, remained virtually stationary in population during the decade 1830–40, and Virginia increased only 7 per cent. During the same decade the population of Alabama increased 76 per cent and that of Mississippi 154 per cent. The growth of the slave population in these states was even more spectacular, 114 and 197 per cent respectively. By 1830 the Gulf states had surpassed the Atlantic seaboard states in the production of cotton, and at the

[34] Southerners invested extensively also in Northern lands during a period of great sectional hostility. Paul Gates, "Southern Investments in Northern Lands before the Civil War," *Journal of Southern History*, V (1939).

[35] Pritchard, "Description of Louisiana," p. 1212.

[36] U. B. Phillips, "The Origin and Growth of the Southern Black Belts," *American Historical Review*, XI (1906), 798–816.

[37] Paul W. Gates, *The Farmer's Age: Agriculture, 1815–1860* (New York, 1960), pp. 140–141, lists a large number of prominent planters who thus founded their plantations.

outbreak of the Civil War were raising three-fourths of the cotton grown in the South. In 1850 the leading cotton-growing state was Alabama, but by 1860 it was surpassed by Mississippi. The last frontier of the Cotton Kingdom was the rich soils of eastern Texas and the alluvial lands of Arkansas.

Young men were especially attracted by the opportunities in this far Southwest. Curtis B. Sutton, a young Virginian who had emigrated to Texas, wrote to his friend William H. Lyons in Richmond:

I could not myself live in Virginia after seeing what I have and as to the advantages of a young man in a new country, I like a Southern life [in the lower South], there is an excitement in the Southern people that I admire. Old Virginia I shall never forget and what son of hers was ever known to forget her, God bless her. I can look back and appreciate her openness of character, liberality, and hospitality—Old Virginia, if I had money, forever is my motto, but she presents no encouragement to young adventurers.[38]

Sutton compared the easy living in Texas with the hard life of the poor people in his native state working from "sun to sun," too poor and too attached to Virginia to move. He noted the advantages of the "limy" black soil of Texas, "one of the best wheat countries in the world, producing 25 to 35 bushels to an acre." Its main crop, however, was cotton, and here one Negro hand could produce ten bales that would sell in New Orleans for $400, a net profit of $300 per hand. "Who can clear," he asked, "$300 on that poor land of the Slashes of Hanover?"

Emigration to Texas was so heavy in the decade of the 1850's that the population nearly tripled, and the number of slaves increased even more phenomenally. Cotton production in eastern Texas expanded from 58,161 bales in 1850 to 431,463 bales ten years later. Some of the plantations resembled old Virginia estates, with their worm fences, white-pillared mansions behind groves of trees, flower gardens, and gangs of slaves. In favorable seasons the rich soil produced three bales of cotton to the acre as compared with one bale in the old cotton states. So anxious were the Texans to give strangers a favorable impression of their country that they boasted grandiloquently of its superiority

[38] Curtis B. Sutton to William H. Lyons, September 25, 1853, James Lyons Papers.

and concealed its drawbacks.[39] Rutherford B. Hayes in December, 1848, visited his classmate of Kenyon College, whose family owned Peach Point Plantation on the Brazos River. He was charmed with the springlike climate, live-oak trees covered with Spanish moss, and the hospitality and the pleasant people he met. He marveled at the patience of the planters: "I don't think Job was ever 'tried' by a gang of genuine Sambos.' " He commented that "the haughty and imperious part of a man develops rapidly on one of these lonely sugar plantations where the owner rarely meets with any except his slaves and minions."[40] Not all of the Texan settlers became successful planters; Albert Sidney Johnston, the future Confederate general, worked heroically, assisted by a family of slaves, in plowing and hoeing cotton on his China Grove plantation in 1847–49; but, lacking capital to secure an adequate labor force, abandoned the plantation as a financial failure.[41] The widow of Horace Holley, who had land to sell in Texas, observed that the greatest part of the emigration to the state consisted of small farmers who arrived overland and sought to obtain small tracts of land in healthy situations. Speculators came by sea.[42]

Texas had a valuable German element in its population that cultivated cotton with free labor. At Mainz in the Rhine Valley a group of noblemen, headed by Prince Carl of Solms-Braunfels, formed the Adelsverein, or Society for the Protection of German Immigrants in Texas, which in 1844 sent over a large number of their countrymen to settle in western Texas. The idea of establishing a separate German state seems to have had the support of only a minority of the immigrants. They founded thriving villages, such as New Braunfels northwest of San Antonio, Fredericksburg, and Sisterdale, which was called a "Latin Colony" on account of its learned inhabitants.[43]

[39] Olmsted, *A Journey Through Texas: or, A Saddle-Trip on the Southwestern Frontier* (New York, 1857), pp. 235, 244.

[40] Charles R. Wilson (ed.), *Diary and Letters of Rutherford B. Hayes* (Columbus, 1922), I, 254–255; see also Abigail Curlee, "The History of a Texas Slave Plantation, 1831–1863," *Southwestern Historical Quarterly*, XXVI (1922), 79–127.

[41] William Preston Johnston, *The Life of General Albert Sidney Johnston* (New York, 1879), Chap. X.

[42] Mary Austin Holley to Harrietta Brand, March 21, 1839; Mary Austin Holley Letters to Mr. and Mrs. Wm. M. Brand, typescripts, University of Kentucky Library.

[43] Oswald Mueller (ed.), *Roemer's Texas, 1845–1847* (San Antonio, 1935);

These Germans were careful farmers who picked their cotton fields clean; they were literate and saw that their children became so; they were noted both for being good artisans and for loving music, which they cherished in their music festivals. They voted the Democratic ticket, and although a minority were militantly antislavery, the great majority wished to get along with the American element and accordingly discouraged antislavery agitation. When Dr. Adolf Douai made the San Antonio *Zeitung* an abolition organ, Germans as well as Americans withdrew their support and condemned his radical course. Frederick Law Olmsted tried to encourage him to stay in Texas and work for a West Texas free state by sending him money collected from prominent Northern abolitionists. But public opinion forced Douai to leave in 1856, and, furthermore, Olmsted's efforts to stimulate the emigration of free soilers from England and the Northern states also failed.[44]

San Antonio and the surrounding region were strongly influenced by Mexican civilization, since more than half of the population were Mexicans. The latter were regarded by many Texans as vermin to be exterminated. George Denison, a Northern teacher in San Antonio, was amazed upon his arrival in 1854 to see women and children smoking and ladies daubing their faces with chalk "an inch thick." He found that his pupils were more restless, less studious, and less easily controlled than Northern youth. In San Antonio there was much swearing, drinking, fighting, dancing, and carrying of pistols. At first he was delighted with the hospitality, frankness, and naturalness of the inhabitants. In April, 1855, he wrote to his sister: "All through this part of the South there is greater liberty of opinion and the expression of opinion than I ever knew of elsewhere. A man can state and advocate any opinion of the truth of which he is convinced and not be subject to abuse or ridicule or persecution therefor. Compared with these people the descendants of the Puritans are really intolerant." This favorable opinion changed during the next year, when Frémont was a candidate for President. Then the young teacher described slavery as being the Grand Golden Calf of the people, opponents of whom were denounced as traitors to the South. "Because Mr. Sherwood (a lawyer of Galveston)," he wrote, "in the Legislature advanced the ideas entertained by

R. S. Biesele, *The History of the German Settlements in Texas, 1831–1861* (Austin, 1930).

[44] Laura W. Roper, "Frederick Law Olmsted and the Western Texas Free-Soil Movement," *American Historical Review*, LVI (1950), 58–64.

Henry Clay and Jefferson, he is called all kinds of dreadful names and is regarded with abhorrence."[45] Sherwood was forced to resign. This episode illustrated a significant fact about the Cotton Kingdom; like the rising industrialism of the North, it placed material profits above human rights.

[45] George Denison to Eliza, April 6, 1855, January 12, 1856, George Denison Papers, Library of Congress.

CHAPTER 3

Profits and Human Slavery

IN 1839 James Silk Buckingham, an English traveler, recorded a
typical Southern scene which he saw near Fredericksburg, Virginia.
He met a slave gang being driven by Negro traders from the upper to
the lower South. The men were chained together in pairs to prevent
their escape while the women walked with their children in the melancholy procession carrying their possessions in large bundles. The slave
dealers rode on horseback, armed with long whips.[1]

This scene was symbolic of the revival of slavery, which resulted
from the invention of the cotton gin and the rise of the Cotton Kingdom. The rejuvenation of slavery is strikingly illustrated by a chart of
slave prices made by Ulrich B. Phillips, the historian of American
Negro slavery. In 1795 a prime field hand (a young man eighteen to
twenty-five years old) was worth less than $300 in Virginia or South
Carolina. In 1860 such a hand was worth $1,250 in Virginia and
$1,800 in New Orleans.[2] During that span of time there were fluctua-
tions in the price of slaves, depending on boom times or depressions,
but the general trend of prices was upward.

The slave trade was the darkest side of the peculiar institution.
Always there had been a certain amount of buying and selling of
slaves within local communities; but after the legal closing of the

[1] James Silk Buckingham, *The Slave States of America* (London, 1842), II,
552–553.
[2] Ulrich B. Phillips, *American Negro Slavery* (New York, 1929), p. 370.

49

African slave trade in 1808 and the opening of rich cotton lands in the West, a thriving trade developed in buying the surplus stock of slaves in the upper South and transferring them to the lower South. Slave traders made individual deals with planters or attended auctions of estates and sales by the sheriff of the slaves of bankrupts. Moreover, masters sometimes disposed of slaves because they were incorrigible runaways or drunkards or had vicious dispositions. Dr. John J. Cabell, a salt producer in western Virginia, sold a boy for the New Orleans trade because he kept running away and redeeming him had recently cost $84, plus jail fees.[3] When the state condemned a slave to death or transportation for a crime, it had to pay the owner his appraised value. Some states reimbursed themselves for such loss by selling criminal slaves in the lower South. Virginia, for example, sold more than 600 criminal slaves between 1800 and 1850. The practice of selling bad or criminal slaves became so notorious that states of the lower South, Mississippi in particular, required a certificate of good character for all slaves sold in the state, signed by two freeholders of the county from which the slave came.

Slave auctions were usually held in front of the county courthouse on sale days or on days of county court meetings, but some were held in the auction rooms of slave dealers and even, in New Orleans, in the lobby of the St. Louis Hotel. Buyers of slaves on the auction block carefully examined them, looking at their teeth, fingers, and especially at their backs to see that they were not scarred by whip marks, indicating an unruly character. Slaves were often spruced up for the occasion with new clothes, their skins oiled, and gray hairs blackened.

Many slaves were apparently not moved by the ordeal of being sold and were proud of the high prices that they brought. On occasion, however, harrowing and tragic scenes occurred involving the separation of families. William Reynolds, the itinerant merchant, witnessed in Memphis the sale of twenty-three slaves at auction, which he described in his journal: "One yellow woman was sold who had two children. She begged and implored her new master on her nees to buy her children also, but it had no effect, he would not do it. She then begged him to buy her little girl (about 5 years old) but all to no purpose, it was truly heart rending to hear her cries when they were taking her

---

[3] John J. Cabell to Richard K. Crallé, July 2, 1832, John J. Cabell Papers, Brock Collection, Huntington Library.

away."[4] Only Louisiana, and Alabama after 1852, prohibited the sale of a child under ten years of age from its mother.

Among the various causes for the sale of slaves were the settlement of estates after the death of the owner and the foreclosure of mortgages on slave property. Thomas B. Chaplin, a planter on St. Helena Island, South Carolina, wrote in his journal on May 3, 1845, that hospitality had caused him to live beyond his means and he was forced to sell ten of his slaves. "Nothing can be more mortifying and grieving to a man," he commented, "than to select out some of his negroes to be sold—you know not to whom, or how they will be treated by their new owners, and negroes that you find no fault with—to separate families, Mothers & Daughters, Brothers & Sisters—all to pay for your own Extravagance."[5]

Nevertheless, there were many efforts to ameliorate the cruelty of the slave trade. Owners frequently stipulated in wills that their slaves should be sold only in family groups or should not be sold out of the county in which they were born. Some, when they felt the necessity of selling a slave, sought to find a humane master for him, and there were innumerable cases of masters who endeavored to unite husband and wife living on different plantations by offering to sell or buy one of the couple. Some masters who sold their slaves did so reluctantly and with the reservation in their minds to repurchase them as soon as they could. Such a one was the Transylvania student William Little Brown, who sold his slave Abram in order to finance his education. In his diary he recorded: "Necessity compels me to sell Abram. I have told him so and he acquiesces. Justice forbids slavery and traffic in human flesh. The money, therefore, which I may receive for him I shall esteem so much borrowed from Abram. In consideration of which, I do promise should heaven prosper me at some future date to redeem him and give him his liberty."[6]

On the other hand, there were slaveowners who in their dealings with their bondsmen consulted their own interests to the limit that the law permitted. A poignant episode of the slave traffic is revealed in the

[4] Journal of William Reynolds, MS. in private possession, p. 96.

[5] Journal of Thomas B. Chaplin, January 12, 1845–September 14, 1860, Archives of South Carolina Historical Society.

[6] William Little Brown Diary, June 1, 1812, typescript in New York City Public Library.

diary of the Baptist minister William Moody Pratt of Lexington, Kentucky, in 1860. On County Court Day two sisters, seventeen and nineteen years old, were sold at auction by court order to satisfy creditors. Their father had formerly bought their emancipation, but their freedom papers had been obtained from their mother under false pretenses and they had nothing to show that they were free. Because of the pleas of their grandmother, Pratt bid for them. They were "handsome and active girls," and the bidding was spirited. After the minister had bid up to $1,500 for one of the girls, he felt that he could go no further, and a slave trader bought her for $1,700 and took her to his slave jail. Pratt commented in his diary: "Such scenes are shocking to our moral nature. Negro traders are the greatest curse of our society—should be driven out of Kentucky by prohibitive taxes."[7]

The slave-trading firm of Isaac Franklin and John Armfield, with headquarters at Alexandria (then in the District of Columbia), was the leading slave-trading business of the South in the decade of the 1830's. This firm had a model jail there which was displayed to visitors with pride. Its depot in the lower South for the sale of Virginia and Maryland slaves was located at the "Forks of the Road" near Natchez, Mississippi. Annually 1,000 to 1,200 slaves were sent there. Three ocean-going ships were used to transport their human merchandise; slaves were also driven overland in coffles.[8] That risk existed in the former method of transportation was demonstrated by the incident of the *Creole* in 1841, when the slaves seized control of the ship and took it to Nassau, where the British authorities liberated them.

Slave traders varied widely in character and reputation. Some of them, such as Lewis Robards of Lexington, Kentucky, who was involved in constant ligitation, were as cruel, coarse, and dishonest as the stereotype pictured them. The better slave dealers, however, were honest and courteous. They shunned the name of slave traders or "nigger traders," and advertised themselves as "agents," "brokers," "auctioners," or "commission merchants." Because of hostile public sentiment, the slave dealers in Lexington refrained from advertising in the newspapers until after 1848. One highly successful slave dealer, Isaac Frank-

---

[7] William Moody Pratt Diary, II, February 12, 1860, University of Kentucky Library.

[8] Wendell H. Stephenson, *Isaac Franklin; Slave Trader and Planter of the Old South* (University, La., 1938).

lin, a man of little education, made three-quarters of a million dollars from slave trading and planting, married a Presbyterian minister's daughter, and built one of the most beautiful estates of the South, Fairvue, near Nashville. Nathan Bedford Forrest of Memphis, son of a blacksmith, also made a fortune in slave trading; nevertheless he was highly respected by his fellow citizens, elected mayor of Memphis, and became a feared Confederate military figure. In Charleston the two leading slave traders, Thomas Gadsden and Louis de Saussure came from aristocratic families and lived in beautiful homes on the Battery, the fashionable residential section of the city.[9]

Despite the bad reputation of the slave trade, a considerable number of Southerners pursued it because of its high profits.[10] The *Directory* of Richmond in 1860 listed eighteen Negro traders, eighteen agents, and thirty-three auctioneers. In the 1850's Charleston surpassed Richmond as a slave market and had some fifty slave dealers. New Orleans was the greatest slave mart of the lower South and was known as "the Modern Delos"; it supported 200 Negro traders. In Montgomery during the period 1839–60, 164 dealers paid the license tax for engaging in selling slaves.[11] Many slaves were sold for credit, usually at 10 per cent interest. Although some slave traders made fortunes, the majority operated in a small way. The correspondence of a Virginia slave trader in 1834 indicates a practice of forming partnerships between dealers and Virginia planters for the venturing of joint capital in the business— buying slaves in Virginia, taking them to the lower South in the fall after the planters had sold their crops and had money, selling them as quickly as possible, and hiring out those that could not readily be sold until a favorable market occurred.[12]

Frederic Bancroft has estimated that Virginia exported annually an average of 9,371 and Kentucky 3,400 slaves. The receiving state of

[9] Frederic Bancroft, *Slave-Trading in the Old South* (Baltimore, 1931), and J. Winston Coleman, Jr., *Slavery Times in Kentucky* (Chapel Hill, 1940), Chaps. VI, VII.

[10] Daniel R. Hundley, *Social Relations of Our Southern States* (New York, 1860), Chap. III.

[11] James B. Sellers, *Slavery in Alabama* (University, Ala., 1950), pp. 155–156.

[12] A. H. Ryland, Mobile, to William S. Field of Culpeper Court House, Va., October 30, December 11, 1834; February 1, 10, 1835, William S. Field Papers, Huntington Library.

Mississippi imported approximately 10,000 annually. In the decades of early settlement of the Southwest the majority of the slaves transported there were taken by emigrating masters; but in the 1850's, Bancroft estimated, 70 per cent of those exported to the lower South were taken there by slave traders.

Prices of slaves were long closely geared to the selling price of cotton. In the last decade of the ante-bellum period, however, a veritable "Negro fever" carried the price of bondsmen above the old values based on the profits to be expected from cotton. Men speculated on the rising market for slaves, as they do in stocks today, and prices became artificially high, partly because of the prestige value of holding slaves. A considerable difference existed between the price of servants in the lower and the upper South, slaves selling for at least $300 to $400 more in Louisiana than in Virginia. Women sold usually at one-fourth less than the value of men, but "fancy girls" sold for $2,500 or more.

The demand for slaves in the expanding Southwest and the high prices paid for them led to a movement in the decade of the 1850's to reopen the African slave trade legally. In 1853, Leonidas W. Spratt, editor of the Charleston *Daily Standard,* began an agitation to repeal the constitutional amendment and laws prohibiting the African slave trade. Three years later Governor James H. Adams of South Carolina espoused the cause in a message to the legislature. The advocates of this measure proclaimed that it would enable the poor nonslaveholder to acquire slaves and thus be attracted more strongly to the proslavery cause; not only would it prevent Virginia and Maryland from becoming free-labor states, but it would enable slavery to expand into the West. The movement was supported by *De Bow's Review* in New Orleans and by a few extremists in the upper South, such as George Fitzhugh, author of *Sociology for the South* and *Cannibals All,* who reversed his former opposition to the revival of the traffic. The Southern commercial conventions voted the proposition down until 1859, when the states of the upper South were unrepresented. Even in South Carolina, Robert Barnwell Rhett and the *Mercury* and the ardent proslavery leader James H. Hammond opposed agitating the subject on the ground that it would divide the South. So strong was the opposition that Governor Adams himself became silent and was defeated for the U.S. Senate in 1858. Most of the advocates of the reopening of the slave trade seem to have been fire-eaters, motivated by a desire to agitate for the formation of a Southern confederacy.[13]

Smuggling of slaves into the lower South increased notably during the decade of the 1850's. A slaver with a large cargo of African slaves was captured in 1858, and the Africans were imprisoned in Fort Sumter until they could be sent back to their native land. D. H. Hamilton, the officer in charge of them at Fort Sumter, wrote Senator Hammond that twenty-five had died while in his custody and that he anticipated one hundred more would die because of the cruelties to which they had been subjected in the slave ship.[14] The British consul reported to his government on May 26, 1857, that some fifteen vessels had been dispatched from New Orleans on slave-trading expeditions within the past two months. Baltimore as well as New York ships were sold to slavers plying between the Congo and Cuba. In 1857 a trial in the federal court in Maryland of persons involved in fitting out and sending slave ships to Africa resulted in acquittal of the defendants. In 1858 Charles Lamar, member of an aristocratic Georgia family, imported 420 slaves from Africa into Brunswick, Georgia. Travelers, and advertisements for runaways, mentioned the presence of African slaves in the South with tattooed skin, marks of lion claws, and filed teeth.

With the increasing demand for labor, it is striking to note that on many plantations less than half of the slaves worked in the fields. On old plantations in the upper South and even in the Southwest, often only a third of the labor force were field hands. Captain Basil Hall in 1828 visited a sea-island plantation in Georgia containing 122 slaves, of whom forty-eight were children under fourteen years of age and four superannuates. The working hands, men and women, were classified as follows: thirty-nine full hands, sixteen three-quarter hands, eleven half hands, and four quarter hands.[15] On Bishop Leonidas Polk's plantation in Louisiana, only a third of his force of 396 slaves were effective field hands, thirty were entirely superannuated, and

[13] Harvey Wish, "The Revival of the African Slave Trade in the United States," *Mississippi Valley Historical Review*, XXVII (1941), 569–588; W. J. Carnathan, "The Proposal to Reopen the African Slave Trade in the South," *South Atlantic Quarterly*, XXV (1926), 410–429.

[14] D. H. Hamilton to James H. Hammond, September 1858, James H. Hammond Papers.

[15] Basil Hall, *Travels in North America*, I, 218.

nearly twenty were children under ten years of age. The new plantations of the lower South, however, bought a large proportion of prime
field hands. Solon Robinson described in his journal a sugar plantation in Louisiana on which 80 of the 139 slaves were field hands. But
on the other hand, Thomas Pugh, one of the great sugar planters, had
251 slaves on his plantation Madewood, of whom only one-third were
effective field hands; there were 98 children and 17 over fifty years of
age; 20 per cent of the men had partial or total disabilities.[16] In that
day of shortened lives there were relatively few aged "aunties" and
"uncles" whom the plantations had to support, since only 1.2 per cent
of the slaves lived to be over seventy years of age.[17]

A great distinction was made between the house servants and the
field hands. The former were much better treated than the common
field hands; ate better food, usually from the master's kitchen; wore
the castoff finery of the master and the mistress; and became more refined and intelligent as a result of close association with white families.
Frequently house slaves slept on a blanket on the floor at the foot of
the bed of the master and mistress. In the plantation hierarchy, the
driver, the house servants, and the skilled craftsmen ranked at the top;
also there was some feeling of superiority among the lighter-colored
Negroes over their darker brethren. The "mammy" Negro nurse ranked
highest among the female servants. Many of the house servants showed
deep affection for the white family in the "big house"; when the master
returned from trips, they welcomed him with demonstrations of joy.
The master would shake hands with the Negroes; this sign of respect
on both sides vanished later. The idealized legend of the plantation is
based largely on the relations between the planters and their house
servants rather than their field slaves.[18]

Nevertheless, a much closer integration of blacks and whites occurred
during slavery days than has existed in this century; indeed, strict segregation was largely a product of the 1890's and the early twentieth cen-

[16] Barnes Lathrop, "The Pugh Plantations, 1860–1865; a Study of Life in
Lower Louisiana," Ph.D. Dissertation, University of Texas, 1945, p. 50.
[17] Kenneth M. Stampp, *The Peculiar Institution: Slavery in the Ante-Bellum
South* (New York, 1956), p. 319.
[18] Bell I. Wiley, *Southern Negroes 1861–1865* (New Haven, 1939), pp. 19,
20, 21.

tury.[19] In the ante-bellum period Negro and white children played happily together. Slave women often nursed the master's children at the breast. Negroes belonged to the same churches as the whites, and joined with their masters in singing hymns. Only after the Civil War did they withdraw, of their own volition, from the white churches. Travelers recorded numerous instances of Negroes riding in stage-coaches and railroad cars with whites. E. S. Abdy, the Cambridge don, traveling in a stagecoach between Lexington and Frankfort in 1834, found that two of his fellow passengers were Negroes. The driver re-fused to eject them to make places for two white ladies.[20] The English-man Richard Cobden noted in 1835 that a Southern planter brought his slave, riding on top of the coach, inside the vehicle when it began to rain and squeezed him between the white passengers, and that the Negro ate in the tavern in the same room but at a different table as the master.[21] On some of the small farms the slave ate at the same table as the yeoman farmer.

The field slaves worked according to two main labor organizations, the gang system and the task allotment, or a combination of the two. The task allotment, by which a slave was assigned a definite amount of work to do by the overseer or Negro driver, was employed chiefly in the rice, sea-island cotton, and hemp regions. When a slave finished his task, he could go to his cabin and the remainder of the day was his own; since the tasks were adjusted to the slower slaves, an energetic worker often finished at three or four o'clock in the afternoon. The gang system was used in the cultivation of tobacco, sugar cane, and cotton fields. This system in the lower South employed a slave driver, usually one of the largest and strongest of the Negroes, who super-vised the work of the slaves under the direction of the overseer, and acted as a policeman in the slave quarters. The slaves were awakened at sunrise by the blowing of a horn or the ringing of the plantation bell; then they worked until sunset. In the summer they were usually given a two-hour rest period at lunchtime. They usually

[19] C. Vann Woodward, *The Strange Career of Jim Crow* (New York, 1955), Chap. I.

[20] E. S. Abdy, *Journal of a Residence and Tour of the United States* (London, 1835), II, 354.

[21] Elizabeth H. Cawley (ed.), *The American Diaries of Richard Cobden* (Princeton, 1952), p. 95.

received a week's vacation at Christmas, and they got Saturday afternoons off.

These gang slaves lightened their labor with music. William Cullen Bryant visited a tobacco factory in Richmond, where the foreman told him that sometimes the Negro hands sang all day with great spirit, but that on other days they were silent. Their tunes, he said, were all psalm tunes and the words were from the hymnbooks.[22] Bryant recorded a song that he heard at a corn shucking by a lightwood fire, in which jollity was mingled with a sad note:

> De cooter is de boatman
> Johnny come down de hollow
> > Oh hollow
> De mocking-bird is de lawyer
> Johnny come down de hollow
> > Oh hollow
> The nigger trader got me
> > Oh hollow
> I'm going away to Georgia
> > Oh hollow
> Boys good-bye forever
> > Oh hollow.

The Negro boatmen and firemen frequently sang in rhythm with their work, the leader improvising and the chorus repeating a phrase. Fanny Kemble noted the natural musical ability of the Negroes who rowed her boat between the rice islands and the mainland of Georgia, but she rebuked them for singing that "Twenty-six black girls not make mulatto yellow girl."[23] The spirituals had the same sadness and solemnity of the white spirituals sung by the mountaineers. They came largely from the same source, camp-meeting songs and hymns, and they spoke of the joys of Heaven, of escapes from Satan, of the troubles of this world, and of Judgment Day. The slave songs which William Francis Allen and Charles P. Ware collected among the Negroes of South Carolina at the end of the Civil War were with few exceptions religious songs such as "Roll, Jordan, Roll," "Blow your Trumpet, Gabriel,"

[22] Parke Godwin (ed.), *Prose Writings of William Cullen Bryant* (New York, 1884), II, 25.

[23] Frances A. Kemble, *Journal of a Residence on a Georgian Plantation in 1838–1839* (New York, 1863), pp. 218–219.

and "Jacob's Ladder."[24] Long after freedom came to the Negroes their songs generally had a high, plaintive air—even today such tunes are characteristic of Negro singing in rural South Carolina.

Perhaps the sadness in their music arose not only from mankind's common lot of trouble but also from the ever-present threat of the separation of families, rather than from any physical abuse. The food of the slaves, for example, was usually plentiful and nourishing, but monotonous. It varied little from the diet of poor white farmers, and it was better than the diet of the Russian serfs, who subsisted on black bread and cabbage and seldom enjoyed meat or milk products. On Sunday the overseer apportioned the week's rations to the slaves, consisting of a peck of cornmeal and three or four pounds of fat bacon to each. In the rice country they sometimes received broken rice as a substitute for cornmeal, and in the sugar country a quart of molasses and sweet potatoes. A large number of the slaves supplemented their standard rations by raising vegetables in garden plots assigned to them, chickens and hogs, and, on some plantations, nankeen cotton. "Bull Run" Russell noted that the Negroes of a South Carolina plantation mutilated their chickens by cutting the comb, removing one claw, or pulling out feathers to distinguish their property and prevent other slaves from stealing it. They also trapped rabbits, treed opossums, and fished. It was a common practice for them to sell their eggs and chickens to the master or to trade them in town with his permission and thus obtain money to buy little luxuries. Only one state, Louisiana, required masters to feed meat to their slaves.

The clothing of the field slaves and their living quarters represented minimum comfort. Little Negroes wore a shirt and nothing else. Men were issued two shirts of cotton and two pairs of cotton pants in summer, and in the fall a pair of woolen pants, a jacket, a hat, a pair of rough brogans, and every second or third year a blanket. The women received cloth to make long dresses and a kerchief or sunbonnet. The slaves were required to take a bath once a week and to appear in clean clothes on Sunday. Much of the Negro cloth was spun and woven by the slave women. On many farms and plantations the slaves presented a ragged and dirty appearance; but on Governor A. B. Roman's plan-

[24] W. F. Allen et al. (eds.), Slave Songs of the United States (New York, 1867).

tation in Louisiana, Russell reported, the Negroes danced every Sunday in the sugar house, and the Negro girls wore crinoline dresses and pink sashes.

Behind the big house lay the cluster of log cabins occupied by the slaves. On the large plantations these were frequently arranged along a street with the overseer's house at the end. Some planters, such as Henry Clay, built brick cottages for their slaves, but most of the cabins were made of logs or frame timber, whitewashed once a year. The cabins seldom had glass windows, but they were equipped with shutters. Inside, the furniture consisted of homemade chairs, beds, a chest, a table, and wooden pegs upon which to hang clothes.

The slaves could not enjoy much privacy. Jefferson Davis and his wealthy brother Joseph were model planters in their care of their slaves; there were 28 cabins for the 113 slaves at Brierfield, Jefferson's plantation, and 76 houses for the 355 slaves of his brother.[25] In Arkansas the average slave cabin contained only one room, which housed between five and six persons. However, many white families in this semifrontier state lived in the same crowded conditions.

Discipline on the plantations was maintained by the overseer, the driver, and the master himself. Some masters did without overseers and managed the Negroes and the plantations themselves. On Forest Rill, a Virginia plantation where Catherine Hopley, an Englishwoman, taught, there was no overseer. The master was a mild, courteous gentleman, who did not whip his slaves. She noted, ironically, that the happy slaves did about one-third the work of English or Irish laborers.[26] Edwin Hall, a tutor on the plantation of Dr. Mann Page near Charlottesville, Virginia, in 1837, wrote that the slaves were seldom flogged; the most effective punishment was to deprive a delinquent slave of his meat ration. He also observed that a slave on this Virginia plantation did less than a third of the work performed by a Northern laborer.[27] Miss Hopley later taught in the family of Governor Milton at Sylvania near Tallahassee, Florida, and here she observed that there

[25] Charles S. Sydnor, *Slavery in Mississippi* (New York, 1933), p. 43.

[26] [Catherine C. Hopley], *Life in the South: from the Commencement of the War. By a Blockaded British Subject* (London, 1863), I, 44–45; II, 248.

[27] Katherine M. Jones (ed.), *The Plantation South* (Indianapolis, 1957), p. 41. Olmsted, *Seaboard Slave States*, II, 65–66, estimated that the slaves did less than half of the work of a Northern laborer.

were few whippings of the slaves but that the white children were flogged often in accordance with the mores of the period.

Most planters felt that flogging was absolutely necessary to maintain discipline on the plantation. Bennet Barrow, who served as his own overseer on his plantation in West Feliciana Parish, Louisiana, obtained excellent service from his slaves; he was young and vigorous and whipped them often, especially when they picked "trashy" cotton. He also punished them by various humiliating devices that made the culprit look ridiculous to his fellow slaves, such as exhibiting him on a scaffold with a red cap on his head or making rascally buck Negroes wear dresses or wash clothes. On the other hand, he rewarded his slaves for faithful service by giving them frequent holidays throughout the year, treating them to a special dinner, giving outstanding workers an extra suit of store-bought clothes, providing them with whisky for a dance, and donating a money gift before Christmas.[28] Maunsel White on his Deer Range Plantation in Louisiana put Negroes who feigned sickness in the stocks, and when the gang did bad work deprived them of meat, giving them only dry bread. Many well-regulated plantations had a strict code governing the administration of the punishment of slaves. Whipping was never to be done in anger or to exceed twenty lashes. Usually the corporal punishment on large plantations was done by the Negro driver or headman under the supervision of the overseer.

Overseers were inclined to rely more heavily on the efficacy of whipping than did masters. Consequently, slaves on absentee plantations were more liable to harsh treatment than those living on plantations under the master's eye. George Noble Jones, who spent much of his time traveling in Europe or in the North, left the care of his plantations El Destino and Chemonie to overseers. John Evans, overseer at the latter, wrote to his employer in 1854 concerning the derelictions of the overseer of El Destino: "When he flogs, he puts it on in two Large doses. I think moderate Flogings the best . . . I always punish according to the crime, if it is a Large one I give him a genteel floging with a strop, about 75 Lashes I think is a good whipping. When picking cotton [failure to pick a sufficient amount] I never put on more than 20 stripes and verry frequently not more than 10 or 15. I find I git along

[28] Edwin A. Davis (ed.), *Plantation Life in the Florida Parishes of Louisiana, 1836–1846, as Reflected in the Diary of Bennet H. Barrow* (New York, 1943).

with this as well as if I was to give Larger Whippings."[29] James Tait had a rule on his Alabama plantation that the last slave to rise in the morning for work after the horn was blown should be whipped.[30]

Many masters had a high sense of responsibility toward their slaves, as the diary of Richard Eppes, owner of three plantations in eastern Virginia, shows. On June 9, 1858, he recorded that he gave a slave a few licks with a switch for disobeying orders of the overseer, in order to maintain the latter's authority. He "explained to the overseer that there were certain negroes of the estate that I never whipped for light offenses, preferring to punish them in some other ways as whipping did them more harm than good." He told the overseer that since he had had no experience in managing Negroes, he should report to him and he "would do the necessary punishment." When the dairymaid displeased him on one occasion, he "boxed Susan's jaws" and, another time, gave Jane "a few blows over her clothes."[31]

The preservation of the health of the slaves was a major concern of the plantation economy, especially after prices of prime slaves had arisen to $1,500 and $1,800. As compared to modern days, there was a fearsome amount of infant mortality among both whites and blacks. In the lower South, at the end of the ante-bellum period there were approximately 150 deaths to every 1,000 live births, or 15 per cent mortality; Negro infant mortality was twice that of the whites.[32] A pregnant slave woman worked, usually at light tasks, until the birth of her child, but it was standard practice to allow her a month of rest after the delivery of the child. When she returned to field labor, the baby was cared for on large plantations in a nursery, and the mother left her job in the field to nurse her child four times a day. Thomas Jefferson was greatly concerned by the infant mortality among the slaves on his Poplar Forest plantation in southwestern Virginia. He wrote to the overseer in 1819: "The loss of 5 little ones in 4 years induces me to fear that the overseers do not permit the women to

[29] U. B. Phillips and J. D. Glunt (eds.), *Florida Plantation Records* (St. Louis, 1927), I, 111.

[30] Davis, *Cotton Kingdom in Alabama*, p. 54.

[31] Richard Eppes, Plantation Journal, January 1, June 9, 1858, University of Virginia Library.

[32] William D. Postell, *The Health of Slaves on Southern Plantations* (Baton Rouge, 1951), p. 158: see also Stampp, *The Peculiar Institution*, p. 320.

devote as much time as is necessary to the care of their children; that they view their labor as the 1st object and the raising of their child but as secondary. I consider the labor of a breeding woman as no object, and that a child raised every 2 years is of more profit than the crop of the best laboring man. In this, as in all other cases, providence has made our interest and our duties coincide perfectly."[33]

When slaves became sick the overseer or master, or the master's wife, usually prescribed remedies. Many of the plantations were equipped with manuals of treatment for disease, such as Gunn's *Domestic Medicine*, *Poor Man's Friend*, Ewell's *Medical Companion*, or Sime's *Guide to Health*. In the 1850's, when the theory was promulgated that Negroes were of a different species from white persons, there was a demand for a manual devoted exclusively to Negro medicine, but the Civil War prevented publication of such a book. Some of the larger plantations paid a fixed sum to a physician for medical care of the slaves, and virtually all of them had a slave hospital and a nursery. Overseers on most of the plantations did not call in a doctor until the case had become serious. The overseer of El Destino in Florida described, in a letter to the absentee master, his treatment of slaves who had pneumonia: "My treatment has bin Calomill, Dove powders, Laudenum, Tartar Emetick and sault peter and flaxseed and also the blistering ointment." He was proud of his remedy for curing mules of colic, boasting that he had never lost a mule treated with his remedy, which consisted of two and one-half inches of plug chewing tobacco mixed with a gallon of water and "4 or 5 shovels of Hot Oak Ashes." He also exercised his medical skill in treating a slave, who had "come very near killing himself eating dirt," with "a preparation of Steeal dust, copras, Pruvian Barks and Salt peater and Whiskey."[34]

The most common of the ailments that affected slaves were various types of fevers, dysentery, pneumonia, hernia, and lockjaw. They appeared to be more susceptible to cholera than whites, but less so to malaria, yellow fever, and hookworm. But they were not altogether immune to these diseases, for plantation records show that many Negroes, particularly the young ones, suffered from malaria or ague. Venereal diseases were occasionally mentioned in reports of Negro

[33] Betts (ed.), *Thomas Jefferson's Farm Book*, pp. 42–43.
[34] Phillips and Glunt, *Florida Plantation Records*, p. 163.

sicknesses. Insanity seems to have been rare among the slaves.[35] The life span of slaves and of whites, according to Charles S. Sydnor, was approximately the same. The life expectancy of a twenty-year-old white in 1850 was 23.72 years; of a Negro, 22.30 years.[36] Southern Negroes, despite a slightly higher mortality than that of whites, increased at a rate of about 23 per cent each decade between 1830 and 1860.

Except for the havoc wrought among slaves by epidemics of cholera, the planters were not unduly harassed by the loss of labor on account of sickness. Chemonie Plantation in Florida had thirty-three field hands, of whom thirty lost time from working because of sickness in 1857, averaging for each slave an absence of twenty-four days from work. This record was unusual. Postell examined the sick records of fourteen plantations of the lower South during the 1840's and 1850's, and found that the average loss of time from work per slave was only eleven or twelve days a year, a lesser disability rate than among Negroes a hundred years later.[37] The health records, indeed, indicate that the physical abuse of slaves was not common.

Slave labor was usually protected from dangerous occupations. Irishmen were employed in posts of danger, such as handling the bounding cotton bales on steamboats as they descended the chutes from river bluffs. Masters hired out some slaves in the 1850's to help dig the Blue Ridge Railroad tunnel in Virginia, but refused to allow them to work near blasting. Most of this perilous work was done by a gang of Irish laborers. Planters often contracted with labor bosses of the Irish to dig ditches for drainage of the sugar lands. The overseer of the Louisiana plantation of Governor Manning of South Carolina told William H. Russell that the planters usually employed Irishmen to clear swampy land, for such hard work was "death on niggers and mules."[38] Planters reasoned that it was wiser to hire Irishmen than risk their own slaves in dangerous and unhealthy jobs, for the loss of an $1,800 slave was serious indeed, while the death of an Irishman was a small matter.

Negro slaves were frequently hired out in occupations in which

[35] Albert Deutsch, "The First U.S. Census of the Insane and Its Use as Pro-Slavery Propaganda," *Bulletin of the History of Medicine*, XV (1944), 469–482.

[36] Charles S. Sydnor, "Life Span of Mississippi Slaves," *American Historical Review*, XXV (1930), 566–574.

[37] Postell, *Health of Slaves*, pp. 164, 148–149.

[38] William H. Russell, *My Diary North and South* (Boston, 1863), p. 282.

there were only normal risks. The building of railroads and public works was a field peculiarly suited to the employment of hired slaves. They were also used extensively in the saltworks of western Virginia, the ropewalks and cotton bagging factories of Kentucky, the turpentine forests of North Carolina, the coal and iron mines, on steamboats, in hotels, and in domestic service. In the tobacco factories of Virginia in 1860, hired slaves constituted 52 per cent of the hands. So careless, ignorant, and inefficient was slave labor in general—although it could be made efficient under the right incentives and direction—that Southerners regarded the slaves as unsuited to the operation of machinery. The hundreds of slaves employed in the Richmond tobacco factories as well as in the hemp factories of Kentucky did mostly handwork that did not involve operating machines.

In agriculture the most frequent use of hired slave labor arose from the practice of trustees of estates hiring out the slaves of a plantation until a settlement was made. The unpublished census returns of 1860 indicate that the hiring of slaves was less prevalent in agriculture than in industrial enterprises and in domestic service in the cities. In Virginia, where the hiring of agricultural labor was more extensive than in other Southern states, some eastern counties, such as Accomac, reported that approximately 10 per cent of slaves were hired, but the more usual ratio was 5 or 6 per cent. On the other hand, Southern towns such as Louisville, Nashville, and Lynchburg had percentages of hired slaves of approximately 16, 25, and 50.

Slaves were hired through newspaper advertisement, auction at the courthouse on January 1, and through slave-hiring brokers or commission men. The hirer gave his bond to pay the sum of the hire at the end of the year, to feed and clothe the slave adequately, and to furnish medical services if needed. The courts decided that if a slave ran away during his period of service, the hirer, not the master, suffered the loss of time, but the death of a slave released the hirer from paying for the unfulfilled part of the contract. So remarkable an increase in hiring rates occurred during the latter part of the ante-bellum period that the annual rent for the labor of a hired slave was 10 to 15 per cent of his value.[39]

How efficient was the Negro worker under the conditions of slavery?

[39] Clement Eaton, "Slave-Hiring in the Upper South—a Step toward Freedom," *Mississippi Valley Historical Review*, XLVI (1960), 663–678.

Northern and European travelers, as has been pointed out, were in agreement that the Negro did about one-third or one-half of the labor of a Northern worker. Some observers, such as Catherine Hopley, said that they had never seen a Southern Negro in a hurry. Left to themselves, the majority of slaves did as little work as possible, and the free Negroes as a group followed the same course. Nevertheless, under the right incentives, the slaves on a plantation often became efficient workers. The slaves of Bennet Barrow in Louisiana, for example, often did what he called "a Brag day's work." Two men on his plantation in November 1837 picked 511 pounds of cotton each; eight of his hands averaged 431 pounds each. One of his slaves, Demps, picked 570 pounds in 1830, setting the plantation record. The average picking of all Barrow's hands on August 31, 1836, was 167 pounds and on October 1, 1842, it was 193 pounds. Barrow stimulated his slaves to this high record by offering rewards and by developing pride of work as well as a wholesome respect for his ready right arm.[40] The excellence of these Negroes' achievement should be compared with the average of 150 pounds of cotton picked per day by slaves as a whole during the ante-bellum days. Sydnor points out that in Mississippi this average was approximately the same as that of free Negro workers in the South in 1933, thus indicating that there was no overworking of the slaves there.

Obviously there was a great difference in the efficiency of slaves on different plantations. Likewise the profitability of slavery varied from plantation to plantation and fluctuated according to market conditions. Earlier writers, such as U. B. Phillips (1918), Charles S. Sydnor (1933), and Charles S. Davis (1939), have held that slavery was an uneconomical system of labor and that only planters of exceptional managerial ability occupying fertile land with good transportation facilities made much profit from plantation slavery. A considerable proportion of the planters were in debt, and Davis has pointed out that "Even the planters themselves were in agreement that a large part of the food supply had to be raised at home in order to preserve the slender margin of profit which inevitably resulted because of certain fixed charges which had to be met."[41]

Furthermore, Southerners as a whole believed that the Negro slave

[40] Davis, *Plantation Life in the Florida Parishes*, pp. 78–102.
[41] Davis, *Cotton Kingdom in Alabama*, p. 189.

was unsuited to the use of agricultural machinery and labor-saving tools. Olmsted was told by a Louisiana planter in 1854: "Such hoes as you use at the North would not last a negro a day."[42] An enterprising salesman for a Northern ax company wrote to his employer that in the back country, where the population was chiefly white, superior axes were appreciated, but in the slaveholding districts "the Slave holders accustomed themselves to considering any tool good enough for a Negro to use and spoil."[43] Consequently slavery hindered the South from exploiting its man power to the best advantage through the wide use of machinery and labor-saving tools.

On the other hand, recent writers have challenged the view of the general unprofitability of Southern slavery. Lewis C. Gray maintained that slave labor was efficient, even expert, on the well-managed plantations. (But how many were well managed?) Slave labor, under the system of incentive and punishments practiced on these plantations, he argued, was probably more productive than free Negro labor in the modern South. Competent observers in the ante-bellum South expressed the opinion that slave labor was more capable than free Irish labor or that of the available native whites. Slavery, moreover, had an advantage over free labor in that it provided a stable supply of workers, incapable of striking. Under competent plantation management, Gray contended, slave labor had an "irresistible ability to displace free labor" in competition for rich soils accessible to markets.[44] This competitive advantage of slave labor arose primarily from the low subsistence level of the slave—a melancholy evidence of human exploitation.

A recent study estimates a life expectancy of thirty years for a twenty-year-old male field hand. The total cost for his clothing, food, medical care, taxes (only 39 cents to $1.20), and supervision was estimated to have been only $20 to $21 a year. The conclusion is that slave labor engaged in raising cotton earned about 5 per cent on average lands, 12 per cent on rich lands, and 4 per cent on poor lands. Capital invested in New England cotton mills paid dividends of 16.76 per cent in the period 1844–48 and 5.75 per cent in the period 1848–53; railroad bonds and New England municipal bonds paid a return of 7 to 8 per cent and 5 per cent respectively. Southern slavery "was apparently

[42] Olmsted, *Seaboard Slave States,* p. 666.
[43] Clement Eaton, *A History of the Old South* (New York, 1949), p. 129.
[44] Gray, *History of Agriculture,* I, 474.

about as remunerative as alternative employments to which slave capital might have been put."[45]

The variables in computing the profitability of Southern slavery are extraordinarily difficult to assess. Planters' diaries and letters are full of complaints: only half or one-fourth of a crop raised because of adverse weather and pests; good crops produced, but the price of their staple too low to allow any profit. Moreover, a large part of a planter's labor force might suddenly be carried off by a cholera epidemic. Frequently he had to pay high interest rates on mortgages. He had to support his slaves during periods of no profit or even of loss, while a manufacturer could turn his employees off; he had also to take care of disabled and old slaves and children. Plantation slavery was affected by business cycles, the constant danger of overproduction, and the variability of world markets. The decade of the 1840's, when cotton sold at a very low price, was not a time of profit for the slave system. Southern people at that time began to turn to plans of manufacturing, or even to thinking of other crops. The decade 1850–60, when export markets were good, was a time when slavery seemed to be profitable, but it would be shortsighted to base an evaluation of the institution on this decade alone.

A comparison of the standard of living in the South with that in the North should throw some light on the question of the profitability of slavery. Slavery gave the Southern states a valuable exportable surplus, for the great bulk of the cotton, rice, sugar, and tobacco crops was produced by slave labor. It is improbable that free white labor would have produced the staple crops in the quantity that the gang system of slave labor did. Despite these rich exports only a small proportion of the Southern people lived with any degree of luxury. Travelers' writings agree that after they crossed the Mason-Dixon Line and the Ohio River from the North, they found a striking contrast between the neat, prosperous farmers of the Northern states and the thriftless, unprogressive ones of the slave-tilled country. Slavery was only partly responsible for the backward condition of large areas of the South;

[45] Alfred H. Conrad and John R. Meyer, "The Economics of Slavery in the Ante-Bellum South," *Journal of Political Economy*, LXVI (1958), 95–130; see also T. P. Govan, "Was Plantation Slavery Profitable?" *Journal of Southern History*, VIII (1942), 513–535; R. W. Smith, "Was Slavery Unprofitable in the Ante-Bellum South?" *Agricultural History*, XX (1946), 62–64.

soil exhaustion and erosion were a more important cause, to which slaveless farmers as well as planters had contributed.[46] In 1850 the average value per acre of agricultural land in the Southern states was less than half that of the Northern states. Furthermore, the average slaveholding farmer possessed little ready cash in comparison with the Northern agriculturist.

In the decade of the 1850's many of the slaveholding farmers had standards of living only slightly better than their grandfathers had had. They still lived in rough log houses, with few modern conveniences, and ate the same unvaried diet in the winter months. Frederick Law Olmsted, after extensive traveling in the South, wrote: "From the banks of the Mississippi to the banks of the James, I did not (that I remember) see, except perhaps in one or two towns, a thermometer, nor a book of Shakespeare, nor a pianoforte or sheet of music; nor the light of a carcel or other good centre-table or reading-lamp, nor an engraving or copy of any kind, of a work of art of the slightest merit. I am not speaking of what are commonly called 'poor whites'; a large majority of all these houses were the residences of slaveholders, a considerable proportion cotton-planters."[47]

One of the principal reasons for raising the question of the profitability of Southern slavery is its political bearing. Some students have maintained that slavery in the South, because of its inefficiency and unprofitableness to the majority of slaveholders, would have fallen of its own weight without the intervention of the Civil War. This view of the natural demise of slavery was propounded as early as 1837 by George Tucker, who predicted that slavery must expire when the lower South had used up its best lands, an eventuality, however, which would probably not take place for forty or fifty years.[48] It is perhaps ironic that recent exponents of the profitability thesis agree with Tucker that the maintenance of profits in the slave system depended upon the continued expansion of staple agriculture into the Southwest. To support

[46] See Robert R. Russel, "The General Effects of Slavery upon Southern Economic Progress," Journal of Southern History, IV (1938).

[47] Arthur M. Schlesinger (ed.), The Cotton Kingdom by Frederick Law Olmsted (New York, 1953), 520.

[48] George Tucker, The Laws of Wages, Profits and Rents (Philadelphia, 1837), Chap. III; The Progress of Population in the United States (New York, 1855), p. 17; see also Leonard C. Helderman, "A Social Scientist of the Old South," Journal of Southern History, II (1936), 158–174.

slavery's slender margin of profit it was necessary for productive slave labor to be continually transferred from lands of declining or low productivity (such as those of the slave-breeding states) to the richer soils of the Southwest.

Ramsdell has maintained that by 1860 slavery in the United States had reached its natural limits. Since this form of labor could not exist with any vitality or significance except on rich soils accessible to market, it was unsuited to the semiarid country of Utah and New Mexico, which were opened to the theoretical extension of slavery by the Compromise of 1850.[49] Here it could not compete successfully with cheap Mexican labor. On the other hand, Gray has held that there was no prospect of slavery being curbed at this time by a lack of fresh, fertile lands. Railroads were opening up new areas of rich soil suitable for exploitation by slave labor. Slaves may have been overcapitalized in 1860, he admits, but this was only a temporary phenomenon that would have adjusted itself just as stocks and bonds that are overvalued do today.[50]

The Ramsdell thesis of the natural limits of slavery expansion seems today to be on the whole a sounder view than the Gray thesis. According to the Census of 1860, despite the ten-year-old opportunity for slavery to advance into New Mexico, there was not a single slave in the territory. Only two slaves resided in Kansas and fifteen in Nebraska territory, which had been opened to the expansion of slavery by the Kansas-Nebraska Act of 1854. In Texas alone was slavery advancing appreciably in the West, and here it was held back from occupying the "black waxy" lands of the central part of the state by lack of wood for fencing materials (barbed wire was not introduced into Texas until 1878 or 1879), the fear of droughts, and the lack of railroads. It was possible for slavery to exist in southern California, but the question of its expansion into that area had been decided by the people of California in their constitution of 1850. Moreover, the northern boundary of the Cotton Kingdom remained virtually the same in 1890 as in 1860, slightly above the Arkansas line, and had not advanced westward in Texas beyond the 98th meridian.

Walter Prescott Webb has pointed out in *The Great Plains* that

[49] Charles W. Ramsdell, "The Natural Limits of Slavery Expansion," *Mississippi Valley Historical Review*, XVI (1929), 151.

[50] Gray, *History of Agriculture*, I, 476.

although the South won political victories in Washington that permitted them to carry their slaves into the western territories, they were debarred by nature from doing so beyond the 98th meridian. That the Southern people recognized this natural prohibition of slavery in the West was shown by their opposition after 1850 to the enactment of a homestead law that would facilitate the expansion of the free-labor farm but could not be utilized by the slave plantation. Nevertheless, Southern politicians and editors made a great political and emotional issue of winning the right to extend slavery into territory which they knew was not suited to its expansion.

After a hundred years it seems clear that the Southerners were short-sighted in permitting the Republican party to define the issue between the two sections as slavery extension and thus win for itself a moral advantage. It is understandable that they should have fought strenuously against the Northern attempt to exclude their human property from federal territories by political measures. The success of such an attempt would have placed a stigma on the holding of slaves and indirectly on the Southern people, who had a supersensitive spirit of honor and pride. It meant denial of the equal protection of the laws. Regardless of the question of legal right, their insistence on protecting their "peculiar institution" by seeking to extend it into a region where it did not fit the needs of the people was unrealistic statesmanship. Yet few of the Southern leaders (notable exceptions being John Bell, Thomas Hart Benton, and Sam Houston) saw that.

As to Northerners, probably the majority of them did not understand the economics of slavery and the unlikelihood of slavery expanding into the West. Furthermore, to Lincoln and to thousands of Northerners who were conservative constitutionalists and therefore willing to acquiesce in the existence of slavery in the states where it was protected by the Constitution, its expansion into the territories was not a pragmatic question but a great moral issue. Slavery was a national evil, and wherever the people through their government could strike a blow against it, it was their duty to do so.

CHAPTER 4

Danger and Discontent in the Slave System

FRANCIS J. GRUND, an Austrian who lived in the United States during the age of Jackson, thought that from their appearance, the Negroes were the happiest people in the Union. They laughed so easily and loudly.[1] Nevertheless, many of the bondsmen—certainly not the majority, however—lived under tension and in fear. There is much evidence to discredit the frequent assertion of Southerners that the slaves were content with their lot and to indicate, instead, the existence within the slave regime of danger for the whites and great bitterness among some slaves. The runaways, the hatred of overseers, the slave code, and the patrol system advertised the need for stern precautions on the part of the master class. The anguish of the separation of families by the slave trade, the melancholy of slave songs, and the frustrations of the free Negro class all pointed to the unhappy tensions of Southern slavery.

One of the most obvious manifestations of discontent among the slaves was the number of runaways. Slaves ran away to avoid punishment, to escape hard work, and to join relatives from whom they had been separated by the slave trade. The advertisements for fugitive slaves frequently called attention to a significant psychological characteristic of many fugitives: they stuttered and had a downcast look when a white man spoke to them. Great cruelty was often practiced in

[1] Francis J. Grund, *Aristocracy in America* (New York, 1959), p. 117.

the hunting and punishing of runaway slaves. Sometimes bloodhounds were employed by white men who made a profession of catching Negroes. Bennet Barrow of Highland Plantation in West Feliciana Parish, Louisiana, wrote in his diary, September 6, 1845: "The negro hunters came this morning. Were not long before we struck the trail of Ginny Jerry, ran and trailed about a mile, *treed* him, made the dogs pull him out of the tree. Bit him very badly, think he will stay home a while."[2] Usually fugitive slaves would hide in neighboring woods or swamps for a week or two until hunger and privation drove them back to the plantation and to a severe flogging.

Relatively few escaped permanently from their masters. The federal Census of 1850 recorded the escapes to free territory of only 1,011 slaves; in 1860 the number was 803. They came principally from the border states. An organization of Quakers and antislavery people in the border states and in the North aided some slaves to escape to Canada; however, their assistance has been vastly exaggerated in the legend of the Underground Railroad.[3] The most valuable aid given to escaping slaves was by free Negroes and fellow slaves, such as Harriet Tubman, who herself had escaped from bondage in eastern Maryland. They hid the fugitives during the daytime and gave food and directions to them.

The greatest bitterness that Southern slavery generated was directed against the overseer. He was the buffer between the master and the slaves. If he was too exacting, he would have the problem of runaways; if he was too lenient, the slaves would shirk their work. He must have a shrewd knowledge of Negro psychology to be able to distinguish when slaves were malingering or feigning sickness and when they were actually ill. The rules of the plantations strictly enjoined the overseer from familiarity with the Negro women; yet there were numerous mulatto babies fathered by overseers. William H. Russell, the British newspaper correspondent, portrayed the overseers whom he observed on Louisiana sugar plantations as stern, practical men, without much education. He noted the significant detail that they carried bowie knives

---

[2] Davis (ed.), *Plantation Life in the Florida Parishes,* pp. 370, 373, 376.
[3] Wilbur Siebert, *The Underground Railroad from Slavery to Freedom* (New York, 1898), *passim;* Larry Gara, "The Liberty Line: the Legend of the Underground Railroad," unpublished MS., University of Kentucky Press.

in their belts as well as whips.[4] Henry Stanley, the African explorer, visited a plantation in Arkansas whose overseer was a coarse, familiar fellow who gave a slave a cut on the bare shoulders with his whip because he was slow in answering.[5] Nevertheless, the majority of overseers seem to have been decent, unimaginative men, striving to succeed in an exceedingly difficult position. Some overseers, such as the one employed by the Dennards in Bienville Parish, Louisiana, in 1860, boasted that they had not given the slaves under their command a single stroke of the lash within the year.[6] Zachary Taylor's overseers on his Cypress Grove plantation in Mississippi were his relatives and were classed as gentlemen.

It has been generally held that the Negro was submissive in slavery. But slaves could and often did make the life of an overseer or master miserable. Richard K. Crallé, a journalist of Lynchburg, Virginia, who later was to edit Calhoun's works, found his Negro foreman to have a fiery and intractable temper. He wrote to Doctor John Cabell, "As soon as I got my Overseer at home, my head man, Anthony, cut some tremendous capers and cleared out—I have not heard of him since. He was pretty well armed with a cudgel and threatened quite bravely. He said to the overseer's wife as he went off, that he should hang himself and might be found by the buzzards. If so, the buzzards shall bury him, for I am resolved not to stop my hands to dig his grave. If I get hold of him again, I will make him acquainted with the climate of the West Indies."[7] Indeed, by passive resistance slaves were often able to force a master or overseer to modify the strictness of a regime. A master in Orange County, Virginia, in sending his slave to Richmond to be hired out by a slave-hiring broker, commented, "She is a perfect custer and I can do nothing with her here—at least I have to punish her so often or yield so often that I can't stand it no longer."[8]

The height of slave resistance was reached in servile insurrections. Although one student has found what he regards as over two hundred revolts by Southern slaves, many of these were labor strikes; only three

---

[4] Russell, *My Diary North and South,* pp. 277, 281.

[5] Stanley, *Autobiography,* pp. 148–149.

[6] Pritchard (ed.), "A Tourist's Description of Louisiana in 1860," p. 1189.

[7] Richard K. Crallé to Dr. John Cabell, September 11, 1831, John J. Cabell Papers.

[8] Edmund Taylor to Lewis Hill, June 29, 1853, Lewis Hill Papers, Brock Collection, Huntington Library.

revolts or plots in the nineteenth century really came off.[9] In 1800, Gabriel Prosser organized a plot to lead his fellow slaves on the plantations around Richmond to destroy the city, but was thwarted by the revelation of his design by a faithful slave. The fear produced by this dangerous incident led to the establishment of a guard, virtually a little standing army, at the capital, which continued through the antebellum period. In 1822 the people of Charleston were frightened by the discovery of a plot of insurrection planned by a free Negro, Denmark Vesey, who had read the debates in Congress over the admission of Missouri to the Union. Vesey had gathered crude arms and had enlisted the voodoo man Gullah Jack to provide charms for his followers against the weapons of the white man. The plot was revealed in time, again by a faithful slave, and, after a trial, thirty-five Negroes were hanged and thirty-four deported.

The greatest shock to the sense of security of the Southern people came from the Nat Turner insurrection in Southampton County, Virginia, in August 1831. Turner was a Negro preacher whose head had been turned by reading bloody prophecies in the Book of Revelation. He stirred his fellow slaves to strike a concerted blow for freedom by killing their masters. Before the insurrection was suppressed, the slaves, some of them maddened by brandy from the cellars of their victims, had killed sixty whites. The revolt alarmed the whole South, for no one could tell when some brooding Nat Turner might arise in his community.

After the Southampton insurrection no other serious slave outbreaks occurred in the Southern states. Nevertheless, Southern society was frequently disturbed by rumors of plots and insurrections, culminating in the great scares of the election years 1856 and 1860. In such crises the regular courts were by-passed, and frightened Negroes were tried and executed by vigilance committees. Many poor Negroes were tortured and hanged by these extralegal committees on the basis of unsubstantial evidence. Danger was far greater to the slaves than to their masters during recurring periods of panic set off by rumors of servile plots and of machinations by white abolition agents.[10]

[9] Herbert Aptheker, *Negro Slave Revolts, 1526–1860* (New York, 1939).
[10] Clement Eaton, *Freedom of Thought in the Old South* (Durham, 1940), Chap. IV; W. S. Drewry, *The Southampton Insurrection* (Washington, 1900);

Such a mass hysteria occurred in northern Alabama during the spring of 1861; it is vividly described in the manuscript diary of Daniel R. Hundley, the noted author of *Social Relations in Our Southern States.* On May 18 he recorded that a vigilance committee in the village of Triana had "ferreted out a most hellish insurrectionary plot among the slaves." As a consequence, he was out all night patrolling the countryside. On May 20 he became a member of the Committee of Public Safety of his community, which punished several slaves and "elicited" testimony that the whole servile population was disaffected by rumors. In this time of popular hysteria some planters tried to protect slaves under suspicion by sending them away; the master of Parson Peter Mud, one of the accused slaves, tried to save his life in this way, but the slave was caught, convicted by the vigilance committee, and summarily hanged after sundown. The revolutionary tribunal also tried a white man, who was given until Christmas to settle up his affairs and get out.[11] The remarkable fact about this flagrant flouting of the regular courts of law was that Hundley, a lawyer educated at the University of Virginia and Harvard College, and a devout Christian, should have participated in it.

It was under such influences of fear that the Southern states had earlier modified their slave codes drastically. The Nat Turner insurrection had accelerated a previous movement to regulate the slaves more strictly. In 1829 David Walker, a free Negro who had emigrated to Boston, published in that city a highly incendiary pamphlet entitled *Appeal to the Colored Citizens of the World.*[12] In the following year this pamphlet was discovered in the houses of Negroes in Savannah. So alarmed was the Georgia legislature that it enacted laws decreeing the death penalty for circulating publications designed to stir the slaves to insurrection, providing severe penalties for teaching slaves to read or write, requiring vessels that entered Georgia ports carrying Negro sailors to go into quarantine for forty days, and subjecting Negro sailors who stepped on shore to imprisonment. The Virginia House of

---

and Harvey Wish, "The Slave Insurrection Panic of 1856," *Journal of Southern History,* V (1939).

[11] Daniel R. A. C. Hundley Diary, May 24–31, 1861, Southern Collection, University of North Carolina Library.

[12] Clement Eaton, "A Dangerous Pamphlet in the Old South," *Journal of Southern History,* II (1936), 1–12.

Delegates passed by a one-vote margin bills forbidding the circulation of incendiary publications and the teaching of slaves to read and write; however, the Senate rejected them. At this time curiosity prompted the British traveler James Stuart to seek to buy a copy of the Walker pamphlet at a Richmond bookstore, but the dealer declared that "any man that would sell it should be gibbetted."[13] In North Carolina the legislature enacted laws prohibiting the circulation of publications that would tend to excite slaves to insurrection and forbidding the teaching of slaves to read or write. Liberals in the state, especially the Quakers, fought against the enactment of such harsh laws, but they were passed in the Senate by a vote of thirty-six to twenty-two. Victory for the conservatives was a gift from David Walker and his incendiary pamphlet.[14]

The coincidence of the founding of *The Liberator* in Boston in January 1831, and of the Nat Turner insurrection in August of that year, led to still further restrictive legislation against slaves and free Negroes. The Virginia legislature now enacted the laws against teaching slaves to read and write and against the circulation of incendiary publications that the Senate had rejected in 1830. Also it prohibited free Negroes from preaching to slaves unless a white man was present. When the African Church was organized in Richmond in 1841, it had to have a white preacher. After Nat Turner's insurrection, in all slave states except Maryland, Kentucky, Tennessee, and Arkansas it was against the law to teach a slave to read or write. Slaves were prohibited from leaving the plantation without a written pass; they must be in their houses by curfew, usually nine o'clock, which in the cities and towns was announced by the ringing of a bell. They could not legally assemble outside their own plantations in groups of more than five unless a white person was present; a slave could not own a horse or firearms (except that each plantation was allowed a huntsman), buy liquor, or trade without his master's permission. He was not permitted to work in a printing shop or a drug store, or to administer medicine to a white person. A white man must always be resident on a slave plantation, and it was illegal for a slave to hire himself out or live

[13] James Stuart, *Three Years in North America* (New York, 1833), p. 54.
[14] John S. Bassett, *Slavery in the State of North Carolina* (Baltimore, 1899), pp. 98–101.

independently as a freeman. Death was the penalty for insurrection, plotting a revolt, raping a white woman, administering poison, or committing arson.[15]

The legal status of the slave showed a curious conflict between regarding him as a person and as property. At times the slave was classified as real estate, notably in Louisiana and Kentucky until 1852, but his general status was that of personal property or chattel. It was deemed a trespass on property for a hirer to abuse or injure a slave that he had hired. It was a capital crime for a Negro to commit rape on a white woman, but it was only a trespass for a white man to rape a slave woman. The slave had legally no power to own property or make contracts, nor could he sue in the courts except in suits to obtain his freedom. Some states, moreover, provided that if his suit for freedom failed, he should receive corporal punishment.[16] There was no legal sanction to marriage between slaves. They were often married by the quaint ceremony of jumping over a broomstick together, though house servants frequently were given elaborate religious weddings and feasts, for which the bride and bridegroom were dressed in the castoff finery of the white folks.

The laws of the Southern states eventually made it a capital crime for a white person deliberately to murder a slave, South Carolina being the last state thus to humanize its code, in 1821. Southern laws, however, exempted a master or overseer from punishment if the slave died during the course of or after reasonable punishment. To what extent was a slave permitted by law to defend himself against cruel treatment or mayhem on the part of master or overseer? It was a difficult decision for the Southern courts to make. Could slaves be allowed to decide for themselves when they were entitled to resist excessive punishment? In a famous North Carolina decision in the case of *The State* v. *Will* (1834), the liberal Judge William Gaston said yes. He ruled that if a slave was endangered in life or limb by an overseer or master, he was justified in using sufficient force to defend himself, "even if in so doing he kills the aggressor."[17]

---

[15] See J. C. Hurd, *The Law of Freedom and Bondage in the United States* (Boston, 1858–62), 2 vols.

[16] T. R. R. Cobb, *An Inquiry into the Law of Negro Slavery* (Savannah, 1858), I, 247–249.

[17] H. T. Catterall (ed.), *Judicial Cases Concerning American Slavery and the Negro* (Washington, 1929), II, 2–3.

A recent study of Southern slavery observes that there were few convictions of masters for cruel treatment or the killing of slaves.[18] Courts did at times, such as in the case of Alpheus Lewis and wife in Kentucky in 1855, take slaves away from cruel masters and sell them at auction. Also they did sentence slaveowners to death for the murder of slaves, as in the case of Lilburne and Isham Lewis, grandnephews of Thomas Jefferson, who in 1811 during a drunken fit chopped a slave boy to pieces on their plantation in Kentucky.[19] Public opinion undoubtedly operated to a large extent to protect slaves from cruel masters. In one spectacular instance, a mob arose in New Orleans in 1834 to storm the house of a sadist, Madame Lalaurie, who had tortured her slaves, and forced her to flee to France.

The weakness of legal measures for the protection of slaves from abuse lay in the fact that slaves were prohibited from testifying in court against a white person. In all Southern states, also, except Louisiana and Arkansas, free Negroes were prohibited from testifying against a white person. The trial in 1852 of Baylor Winn for the murder of William Tiler Johnson, a free Negro barber of Natchez, turned entirely upon the question whether the defendant was a free mulatto or a white man; if he was proved to be a white man he could not be convicted by the Negro witnesses of the crime. It was finally determined that Winn, some of whose ancestors in Virginia had been free Negroes, was a white man, and he was acquitted.[20] The Southern states varied in their legal definition of a Negro: in Virginia, a person who had as much as one-quarter Negro blood was a Negro; in North Carolina, a person with one-sixteenth Negro blood. None of them took the position of Southern states today that the possession of a drop of Negro blood classifies a person as a Negro.

For grave crimes Negroes were tried by jury. In most states the jury consisted of slaveholders or at least a large proportion of slaveholders. The accused was entitled to counsel and to bail, except in capital cases, and to an appeal to the Supreme Court in such cases. The higher courts, moreover, protected him from intimidation by throwing out confessions made to master or overseer. Whenever a slave was sen-

---

[18] Stampp, *The Peculiar Institution*, pp. 221–222.

[19] Coleman, *Slavery Times in Kentucky*, pp. 252–261.

[20] William R. Hogan and Edwin A. Davis, *William Johnson's Natchez, the Ante-Bellum Diary of a Free Negro* (Baton Rouge, 1951), pp. 58–63.

tenced to death, the state governments, with the exception of Arkansas, paid the appraised value of the executed slave to his master. For lesser crimes the slave was tried by informal courts, consisting in Louisiana of one justice of the peace and four slaveholders, in Mississippi of two justices and five slaveholders, and in Virginia of five justices. Frequently criminal justice was administered on the plantation by the master whipping the slave without recourse to the courts. William Tiler Johnson, the Natchez barber, discovered one of his slaves committing sodomy with a duck, and merely whipped him. A white man convicted of this offense might have been hanged.

To protect the community from slave insurrection and to keep the slaves in proper subordination, the patrol system was created. A patrol usually consisted of a captain and three others, who were appointed for a period of three or four months either by the county court or at the militia muster. In Alabama every slaveholder under sixty years of age and every nonslaveholder under forty-five was held liable for patrol service.[21] Those who served on the patrol were freed from militia or jury service and from work on the public roads. They were required to patrol the roads of their precinct or "beat" one night every two weeks and to punish Negroes found away from the plantation, usually by administering twenty lashes on the spot. They also searched Negro cabins for guns or pistols and broke up unlawful assemblies. Patrol duty was considered so irksome that many men paid fines of $5 to $25 rather than serve.[22]

The Southern slave code was undoubtedly severe, but it was laxly enforced. The laws forbidding the teaching of slaves to read and write, for example, were constantly violated by masters and mistresses. Joseph A. Turner, editor of *The Countryman*, published on a plantation near Eatonton, Georgia, declared in 1862, at the time when there was some agitation to repeal the law prohibiting the teaching of Negroes to read, "the law is obsolete, and never has prevented a negro who desired it from learning to read. I have never known a case of punishment for its violation."[23] The patrols were often neglected until the people were

---

[21] Sellers, *Slavery in Alabama,* pp. 220–221.

[22] See H. M. Henry, *The Police Control of the Slave in South Carolina* (Emory, Va., 1915), pp. 28–52.

[23] *The Countryman,* Turnwold, Putnam County, Ga., November 17, December 1, 1862.

alarmed by rumors of servile insurrections. Some masters paid no attention to the laws forbidding a slave to hire out his time and others were careless about writing passes when they sent their slaves on errands from the plantation. Laws relating to the residence of free Negroes in the state often remained unenforced. Phillips has pointed out the habit of Southern legislatures of passing laws more for emergencies than for constant use.[24] Like pistols, they were to be brought forward only in time of danger. The courts by their decisions also moderated some of the draconic features of the slave code.

The stereotype that represents the treatment of slaves in the lower South as much harsher than that practiced in the upper South is exaggerated. Masters in the upper South often blackened the reputation of the lower South and used the threat of selling refractory slaves in the deep South as a bugbear to secure better discipline. Actually there does not seem to have been any greater cruelty or ill treatment of slaves in the lower South, except on absentee plantations, than in the upper South. Timothy Flint, a New Englander who taught and traveled widely in this region, commented in 1826: "I found the condition of the slaves in the lower country to be still more tolerable than in that above; they are more regularly and better clothed, endure less inclemency of the seasons, are more systematically supplied with medical attendance and medicine," and, he observed, were better protected from access to alcohol than in the upper South.[25] The Swedish traveler Carl David Arfwedson in 1834, the English geologist Sir Charles Lyell in 1846, the Northern agricultural writer Solon Robinson in 1849, and the Northern schoolteacher De Puy Van Buren in 1857 reported that the slaves on the plantations of both the middle and the lower South were well cared for and humanely treated.[26]

Often comparison is made between the paternalism on the Virginia tobacco plantations during the period of decline when the slaves did not have much to do and the "driving" of Negroes on the flourishing cotton and sugar plantations of the lower South in the 1830's and

[24] Phillips, *American Negro Slavery,* p. 484.
[25] Flint, *Recollections of the Last Ten Years,* pp. 345–346.
[26] Carl David Arfwedson, *The United States and Canada in 1832, 1833 and 1834* (London, 1834); Sir Charles Lyell, *A Second Visit to the United States of North America* (London, 1849); Kellar, *Solon Robinson;* A. De Puy Van Buren, *Jottings of a Year's Sojourn in the South* (Battle Creek, Mich., 1859).

1850's. It is true that on the sugar plantations during the grinding season, when it was imperative to get the cane cut and ground before frost, the slaves were worked hard. Despite the long hours of work, the slaves liked this time best of all seasons, for it meant better food, drams of whiskey and coffee, and the celebrations that followed the harvest. Normally the Negroes on the plantations of the lower South did only moderate amounts of work, as evidenced by the cotton-picking records.

Although slaves on absentee plantations were probably not as well treated as on those under the direct supervision of masters, the stereotype of general mistreatment on these plantations has been overdrawn. Sydnor found that half of the plantations of over fifty slaves in the delta region of Mississippi were owned by absentee landlords.[27] On the rice plantations of South Carolina and Georgia masters were absent during the sickly seasons. Here the slaves were under the control of the overseer, who did not have an owner's interest in taking care of them. When a citizen of Tallahassee, Florida, protested to George Noble Jones in 1855 that the slaves on his absentee plantation El Destino were being cruelly treated by the overseer, the master appointed two respectable planters to investigate the charge. They reported that there was no evidence of unnecessary punishment of his Negroes and that their general appearance was healthy; moreover, their natural increase, 10 per cent a year, in a gang of 120 Negroes indicated that they were not maltreated.[28] General Zachary Taylor's cotton plantation, Cypress Grove, near Rodney, Mississippi, was an absentee plantation where the slaves were well fed (a pound of meat a day and on Sundays coffee, butter, and flour for making pastry), well housed, and rewarded for good behavior ($500 was distributed to the eighty-one slaves at Christmas).[29] Lady Emmeline Stuart-Wortley described one of the slaves as having "Chesterfieldian manners."[30]

Was the slave more humanely treated on the farm or small plantation than on the larger plantations? The stereotypes of slavery are

[27] Sydnor, *Slavery in Mississippi*, p. 69.

[28] U. B. Phillips and I. D. Glunt (eds.), *Florida Plantation Records* (St. Louis, 1928), p. 123.

[29] Holman Hamilton, *Zachary Taylor, Soldier in the White House* (Indianapolis, 1951), Chap. III.

[30] Lady Emmeline Stuart-Wortley, *Travels in the United States . . . during 1849 and 1850* (New York, 1855), pp. 118–119.

derived mainly from the portrayal of the large plantation, for it is difficult to find records and accounts of slavery on the smaller agricultural units.[31] In 1860, approximately 47 per cent of all slaves were owned by men who held less than twenty. In the upper South the percentage was much higher, 61.7 per cent, but in the lower South only 38 per cent of the slaves belonged to small slaveholders. The advantages to the slave of belonging to a farmer or small plantation owner were that his work was likely to be more diversified, he came into more intimate contact with a white family, and he escaped the overseer system. Some small farmers who employed slaves, however, worked them to the limit and fed them poorly, while on large plantations slaves often had the protection of strict rules governing the overseer as well as the advantages of hospitals, nurseries, and plentiful food.

As the plantation matured and the westward movement slowed down, much of the harshness in the relations between masters and slaves disappeared. There is a constant reference in the correspondence and diaries of Southern slaveholders to "family negroes," those slaves who had been inherited and had belonged to the family for a long time. Toward these Negroes there was an especially fine feeling—they were members of the family. Also, after the rise of the abolition movement slaveholders seldom referred to the bondsmen as slaves, but called them "my people," "the servants," "boys," etc. Only the low-class whites referred to colored people as "niggers." Custom was more important than law, and custom determined standards in such things as allowances of food and clothing, the treatment of pregnant women and nursing mothers, medical services, and the amount of work to be expected from slaves. Planters learned the wisdom of not trying to overwork the slaves. (In fact the passive resistance of the slaves made it difficult to exact labor beyond the custom of the region.) Slavery as it actually worked out was undoubtedly a compromise between the master or overseer and the slaves.

The hiring system tended to enlarge the privileges and the liberties of the slaves. The practice of the tobacco factories of Richmond affords a good example. In order to secure the co-operation of the hired slaves, the factories adopted the task system and paid bonuses for overwork.

[31] Richard Hofstadter, "U. B. Phillips and the Plantation Legend," *Journal of Negro History*, XXIX (1944), 109–125.

During the ten-hour day the slave was required to do a task of forty-five pounds of processed tobacco. Most of the slaves did more than the task and received compensation of at least $5 a month and many over $20. If they were thrifty they could save money to buy their freedom, but the majority of the factory hands were improvident and spent their bonuses for pleasure. The tobacco hirelings also had many privileges, such as the allowance by the manufacturer of a small sum of money each week for meals and sleeping quarters, which made plantation Negroes eager to work in the factories. The practice of the tobacco factories was not exceptional, for in the iron, hemp, lumbering, and coal industries, hired slaves received various sums of money for working beyond the requirements of the tasks. Moreover, hired slaves were often given the privilege of selecting their masters and they learned to use this privilege to bargain for others.[32]

Despite the fact that the law did not recognize the right of slaves to hold private property or to keep any money they might earn, their masters in practice almost always let them do both. Many masters allowed their slaves to have garden patches and to raise chickens, to earn money by cutting and selling cord wood, by making and selling buckets and baskets, by retaining the tips which visitors gave to house servants, and by selling Spanish moss which they had gathered. Many masters, too, stimulated their slaves to vigorous efforts by offering prizes for competition in cotton picking or by rewarding them for good work by giving them privileges, a special dinner, or a suit of clothes. A few masters increased their slaves' pride and self-respect by establishing a type of jury system, notably James Hamilton Couper on his Georgia plantation, John McDonogh in Louisiana, and Jefferson Davis at his Brierfield Plantation near Vicksburg.

The slave system did provide room for the development of some remarkable Negro personalities. There were numerous instances in which a slave became the overseer on the plantation. De Puy Van Buren noted that planters often selected capable young slaves and apprenticed them to skilled artisans to learn trades. A good example of the skilled slave was Harry, the blacksmith who was hired out to various planters in Tennessee and Mississippi by his master, James K. Polk. In 1842 Harry wrote to his master reminding him that he had

---

[32] Eaton, "Slave-Hiring in the Upper South," *passim.*

been "faithful over the anvil for thirty years" and asking to be allowed to hire his own time. Polk refused, for Harry's services were too profitable. Ten years later the faithful blacksmith was working for the widow of the ex-President, earning for her nearly $500 annually from the jobs he did for planters.[33] In the papers of Ebenezer Pettigrew of eastern North Carolina are records of remarkable slaves. Such individuals were scattered throughout the plantations of the South—slaves who were so intelligent that their masters consulted them on plantation policies; slaves like George Washington's Negro overseer at his Muddy Hole Plantation, who became trusted foreman; slaves who acquired skills; slaves who had a passionate attachment to the plantation and a pride in the crops and in their masters.[34] U. B. Phillips was right in regarding the plantation as a school of vocational training for the American Negroes.[35]

Despite legal prohibition of teaching slaves to read and write, energetic individuals among the Negroes could certainly learn if they wanted to. Literacy was perhaps not much harder for them to come by than for many poor whites, such as Andrew Johnson and Abraham Lincoln. Some masters took pleasure in teaching them; some planters' children could not be prevented from teaching their colored playmates what they themselves were learning; lacking an indulgent master, Negroes could get other whites or fellow slaves to teach them. The estimate of Carter Woodson, the Negro historian, that 10 per cent of the adult Negroes in 1860 could read is an exaggeration.[36] A Presbyterian minister in the Chester District of South Carolina, however, reported that of the 213 slaves belonging to members of his congregation 23 were members of his church and almost all of the latter could read.[37]

---

[33] John S. Bassett (ed.), *The Plantation Overseer as Revealed in His Letters* (Northampton, Mass., 1925), pp. 56–57; 161–163.

[34] Jared Sparks (ed.), *Letters and Recollections of George Washington* (New York, 1906). Washington wrote (p. 156) that Davy, the overseer at Muddy Hole, "carries on his business as well as the white overseers and with more quietness than any of them."

[35] Phillips, *American Negro Slavery*, pp. 342–343.

[36] Carter G. Woodson, *The Education of the Negro Prior to 1860* (New York, 1915), p. 228; see also his volume, *The Mind of the Negro as Reflected in Letters* (Washington, 1927), p. 29.

[37] *Proceedings of the Meeting in Charleston S.C. May 13–15, 1845 on the Religious Instruction of Negroes* (Charleston, 1845), pamphlet in the University of Kentucky Library, p. 5.

The free Negroes were considerably more literate than the slaves; according to some statistics of free Negroes who emigrated from North Carolina to Liberia in the 1850's, 33 out of 152 were literate, or approximately 21 per cent.[38]

The testimony of the Negro himself, the most important witness, as to his treatment is so highly contradictory that valid generalizations from it are impossible.[39] The narratives of fugitive slaves, usually published under abolitionist auspices, are in general untrustworthy. During the 1930's, under the Federal Writer's Project, the department of social sciences of Fisk University and a group of students at Southern University in Louisiana collected a mass of testimony from ex-slaves.[40] Some of these old Negroes retained nostalgic memories of kind masters, good food, and simple pleasures; others remembered frequent whippings, poor food, overwork, miscegenation, cruel Negro drivers, and the nagging fear of being separated from their families by the slave trade. Hiram Revels, a free Negro of Fayetteville, North Carolina, the first member of his race to become a United States Senator, presented a favorable picture of the treatment of Negroes by ante-bellum Southerners. He observed in his brief autobiography that despite the increased restrictions that followed the Nat Turner insurrection, "so much of the former friendly generous feeling toward the free people of color remained that in many parts of the state, especially in the cities and the larger towns, colored schools were tolerated through the sympathy of the better class of the white people."[41] He noted particu-

---

[38] Franklin, *The Free Negro in North Carolina*, pp. 209–210.

[39] The most valuable of these narratives are Rayford W. Logan (ed.), *Memoirs of a Monticello Slave* (Charlottesville, 1951); Frederick Douglass, *My Bondage and My Freedom* (New York, 1855); David Wilson (ed.), *Narrative of Solomon Northrup* (Buffalo, 1853); Kate Pickard, *The Kidnapped and the Ransomed* (Syracuse, 1856); and Joseph Henson (reputed to be the original of Uncle Tom), *Father Henson's Story of his Life* (Boston, 1858).

[40] B. A. Botkin, *Lay My Burden Down, a Folk History of American Slavery* (Chicago, 1945); John B. Cade, "Out of the Mouths of Ex-Slaves," *Journal of Negro History*, XX (1935), 214–337; and Fisk University Department of Social Sciences, *God Struck Me Down* (Nashville, 1945). Professor H. C. Nixon told the writer that he had talked with old ex-slave women in northern Alabama, one of whom said that her master forced her when she was twelve years old to marry a slave she had never seen, and another who was promised her freedom if she bore twelve children.

[41] Autobiography of Hiram R. Revels, photostat in Carter G. Woodson Papers, Library of Congress.

larly that there were two "fine" colored schools in Fayetteville, one taught by a white woman and the other by a Negro, which he himself attended.

Southern churches sought in some degree to ameliorate the condition of the slaves, but in general they sided with the ruling classes. Slaves often belonged to the same church as the master and attended the same services, sitting in the gallery or on the back rows. Some masters employed white ministers to preach, but pious slaves on the plantations also preached to their brethren. Victoria Clayton, in her reminiscence of life on her father's plantation near Eufaula, Alabama, related that the Negro foreman, Uncle Sam, was a Methodist preacher who could read the Bible and who preached to the slaves. He had even enough education to record at the end of the day the weights of cotton that each Negro picked.[42] Slaves attended the white camp meetings and added fervor to these occasions with their shouts and their singing of camp meeting songs.

Religion was used by the slaveowners not only to elevate the slave spiritually but as a system of control. One method of control was by church trials, which excommunicated slaves for stealing, running away from their masters, impudence, and having illegitimate children. In the manuscript record book of Providence Baptist Church in Kentucky it is recorded that Frank, a slave, was excommunicated for the sins of lying, disobeying his master's commands, and "making too free with women." Also it is recorded that "Mr. Coleman's Archubel is excluded for refusing to hear the Church to answer for his conduct Shuch as Carnelly Singing, biting at a horse nose, and report sais that he Swore and Dancest."[43]

The Moravian Church and intermittently the Methodist and Baptist churches were active in establishing missions for the purpose of giving religious instruction and conducting services among the slaves.[44] The Presbyterian Church sponsored a work by Charles Colcock Jones of Georgia, published in 1847, entitled *Suggestions on the Religious*

---

[42] Victoria V. Clayton, *White and Black under the Old Regime* (Milwaukee, 1899), pp. 23–24.

[43] Minutes of the Providence Baptist Church, Kentucky, University of Kentucky Library.

[44] Chase C. Mooney, *Slavery in Tennessee* (Bloomington, 1957), pp. 96–98; Taylor, *Negro Slavery in Tennessee*, Chap. X.

Instruction of the Negroes in the Southern States, in which missionaries were urged to inculcate among the slaves not only good morals but the duty of obedience to masters. The Southern churches as a whole did not exert themselves, as did the Catholic Church in Latin America, to bring the Negroes into the fold. Some overseers and masters were strongly opposed to religious excitement among the slaves. Hugh Mc-Cauley, overseer on Isaac Ball's rice plantation, wrote to his employer: "We all seem to live in peace and quietness & by putting a stop to this pretended Religion the Negroes gits their Rest of nights."[45]

In May 1845 a meeting was held in Charleston, South Carolina, to consider the religious instruction of the Negroes. Attended by such prominent leaders as Robert Barnwell Rhett and Robert W. Barnwell, the meeting issued resolutions urging the oral instruction of the slaves in religion and published its proceedings and numerous letters from ministers and planters in South Carolina and Georgia. The most significant of these letters was one from the great rice planter Robert F. W. Allston, who observed that slaves who had grown up under religious instruction were more intelligent than other Negroes. "Indeed," he wrote, "the degree of intelligence which, as a class, they are acquiring is worthy of deep consideration."[46] He and other planters pointed out that not only the intelligence but the morals of Negroes who had received religious instruction had improved. One writer thought that the improvement in Negro conduct in South Carolina was owing to the fact that some of the worst Negroes had been sold to the Southwest. Another observed: "Plantations under religious instruction are more easily governed, than those that are not." The letters indicate that both masters and ministers used Charles Colcock Jones's published catechism for slaves, and that some slaves attended family prayer with the whites at the end of the day.

The paramount evil of Southern slavery was not that the slaves were mistreated physically, but that they were deprived of the opportunity to develop their capabilities fully. The experience of John Mc-Donogh with the slaves on his Louisiana plantation showed how the latent abilities of the slaves, the great untapped reservoirs of intelligence, good will, and industry, could be released by the introduction

[45] Hugh McCauley to Isaac Ball, June 2, 1814, Ball Family Papers, South Caroliniana Library.
[46] *Proceedings of the Meeting in Charleston,* p. 35.

of incentive and hope into the slave system. In 1842 he wrote a letter to the New Orleans *Commercial Bulletin* outlining his plan of self-emancipation by the slaves. He allowed his slaves to work for their freedom by using their free Saturday afternoons and by working an extra hour in the morning and another in the evening to accumulate money to pay their passage to Liberia. He acted as their banker and kept records of their earnings from extra work, and they accumulated sums which enabled them to finance their passage to Africa in approximately fifteen years of saving. After the adoption of his plan a remarkable change came over them; they became cheerful and industrious workers, devoted to their master. He employed no white overseer but selected a capable Negro leader, the "commander," to supervise the laborers. The jury system which he established worked so well that the master often had to reduce the punishment decreed. A number of the McDonogh Negroes became skilled mechanics, and he used some of them as clerks and rent collectors. Two of his slaves he sent to Lafayette College at Easton, Pennsylvania, from which they graduated, one becoming a missionary to Liberia and the other a successful physician in New York City.[47]

An important step that Southern society could have taken to improve the conditions of slavery and carry out its professions of Christianity was the revision of the slave code to protect elemental human rights. Francis Lieber of South Carolina College made some excellent suggestions of legal reform in letters which he wrote (but did not send) to Calhoun, apparently in 1849, urging him to support the Wilmot Compromise. His recommendations, which were in a sense a commentary on the most glaring evils of slavery, were (1) legalize marriage of slaves; (2) declare a quinteron, or person with four-fifths white blood, a white person and free; (3) allow a slave legally to own property; (4) permit him to buy his freedom by working for pay during his leisure hours; (5) grant land to a slave who had performed a certain number of years of service; (6) admit slave testimony against whites in courts, with certain limitations.[48] Lieber pointed out that the Roman law allowed slaves to own property and to buy their freedom, the Code

[47] W. T. Childs, *John McDonogh, His Life and Work* (Baltimore, 1939), Chaps. VII–IX.

[48] Tranquillas, "Letters to John C. Calhoun on the Present Slavery Question," Francis Lieber Papers, Huntington Library.

Noire of Louis XIV declared a quinteron white, and the Spanish law provided for the appointment of an officer for the protection of slaves, who could order a slave to be sold if his master treated him cruelly. Another reform that liberals advocated was the repeal of legislation prohibiting the teaching of slaves to read and write.

Judge Thomas R. R. Cobb of Georgia, in *An Inquiry into the Law of Negro Slavery in the United States of America,* published in Savannah in 1858, advocated revising the slave code to humanize it. The law should be changed, he thought, to prohibit the separation of husband and wife by sheriffs' sales and administrators' sales of estates. Slaves should be protected from the possible cruelty of masters by the state's paying large fees to people reporting such cruelty and requiring that the slaves of masters convicted of it be sold and the masters disqualified forever from owning or possessing slaves. Admitting that the exclusion of Negro testimony against whites in court might lead to the defeat of justice, he suggested that the law be modified to allow the testimony of Negroes in cases of cruel treatment of themselves and other Negroes by whites other than the master. A curious light on Southern society is seen in Cobb's suggestion of the reform of the code to make the rape of a colored female by a white man a criminal offense instead of the civil offense of trespass. This Georgia jurist wrote that the lascivious nature of Negroes was such, however, that actual rape by the master was almost unheard of in Southern society. Other thoughtful Southerners were as sensitive to the abolitionists' criticism of the slave code as was Judge Cobb, who proposed that unnecessary laws that furnished texts for the abolitionists should be expunged. The lawmakers in the Southern states, he wrote, should have regard for the "honor of the statute book" and should be guided by "Christian philanthropy."[49]

If one considers the legal code alone, he is likely to agree with a modern historian that "in 1860 the peculiar institution was almost precisely what it had been thirty years before."[50] This view, however, does not take into account the significant changes that practice had introduced. The hiring system, the customs that grew up outside of the law, the exposure of the Negro to city life, the lax segregation prac-

[49] Cobb, *Inquiry into the Law of Negro Slavery,* pp. 98–100, 246.
[50] Stampp, *Peculiar Institution,* p. 28.

tices (which contrast with conditions in our times), the advance of the Negro in skills and, to some degree, in bootleg education—all modified Southern slavery. Nevertheless, however much custom and adaptation softened the harshness of the peculiar institution, evidence is strong that the slaves were not content to remain in bondage. When the Civil War came they did not rise in rebellion; however, most of them, especially the field slaves, took the first opportunity to leave plantations and become free.[51]

In comparison with slavery in areas settled by Spain and Portugal, Southern slavery seems very severe. The Catholic Church, with its doctrine of the equality of man before God, and the prevailing Roman law, modified the harshness of slavery in the Latin American countries. Especially was this true of the law and practice of manumission. In the Southern states, emancipation by owners became increasingly difficult to obtain; in the Latin American countries it was easily accomplished by a money payment in installments, for manumission was encouraged by the Church as a meritorious act to be rewarded in Heaven. Furthermore, there the emancipated slave entered fully into the rights of citizenship and was not handicapped by the stigma attached in the United States to a person who had been a slave.[52] But in Latin America there was no strong and dangerous abolition movement, little irrational race prejudice independent of the institution of slavery, or anything like the aggressive and uncontrolled commercialism of the English and American development of slavery. Even before slavery was legally established in the American colonies in the 1660's, a strong prejudice existed against black men both here and in England, a prejudice against color that did not prevail in the Spanish colonies. Professor Degler has described slavery in the English colonies as "the institutionalization of a folk prejudice."[53] Prejudice against the Negro remained so strong among the masses of people in the North that the English travelers, Edward Dicey and David W. Mitchell,

[51] See Wiley, *Southern Negroes 1861–1865,* Chap. I.

[52] Frank Tannenbaum, *Slave and Citizen, the Negro in the Americas* (New York, 1947), pp. 48–64; Stanley M. Elkins, *Slavery, a Problem in American Institutional and Intellectual Life* (Chicago, 1959), pp. 63–80.

[53] Carl Degler, *Out of Our Past, the Forces that Shaped Modern America* (New York, 1959), p. 38.

found great discrimination against the free Negro above the Mason and Dixon line.[54]

The slave at least had the care and protection of his master; the free Negro had an insecure and unhappy position in Southern society. The black code determined the legal status of a Negro as derived from the status of his mother. The class of free Negroes arose principally from the manumission of slaves with children, a prominent motive in this emancipation being the desire of white masters to liberate their mulatto children. In his study of the free Negro in Tennessee, J. Merton England cites numerous cases of masters emancipating their mulatto offspring born of slave mothers, such as William Sanderlin of Shelby County, whose will stated that, in addition to having six white children, one of them illegitimate, he was the father of thirteen mulatto children whom he had emancipated.[55]

The free Negroes were concentrated in the upper South, the greatest number in Maryland, where half of the Negro population was free. Baltimore in 1860 had a free Negro population of 25,680 and New Orleans 10,689. In contrast, the state of Mississippi contained only 773 free Negroes. They usually gravitated to the cities and towns, though in North Carolina and Arkansas they remained rural. The free Negroes had almost a monopoly on the barber's trade, and some of them were skilled mechanics and petty tradesmen, but the majority were domestic and unskilled laborers.

The diary which William Tiler Johnson kept from 1835 to his death in 1851 reveals the remarkable life of this exceptional free Negro in a Southern community. In the 1830's Johnson made profits of $15 to $20 a day from his barber shop and accumulated an estate worth $25,000. He invested capital in two stores, which he rented out, made loans to white men, and purchased a farm, which he named Hardscrabble. He owned fifteen slaves and employed a white man to serve as overseer of his farm. He owned a gun and hunted; went to the theater, sitting in the colored gallery; attended races; and subscribed to five or six newspapers. He took a keen interest in city affairs, politics, the crimi-

[54] Edward Dicey, *Six Months in the Federal States* (London, 1863), I, 70–75; D. M. Mitchell, *Ten Years in the United States* (London, 1862), p. 227.

[55] J. Merton England, "The Free Negro in Tennessee," Ph.D. Dissertation, Vanderbilt University, 1941, p. 38.

nal court, militia musters, and firemen's parades; he was on terms of friendship with several of his patrons, but never tried to violate the taboo against dining or of drinking with white people. He belonged to the aristocracy of the free people of color and did not attend "darky dances and parties."[56]

The decade of the 1820's and the early 1830's seem to have been the best period for the free Negroes of the South; in 1830 more than 3,600 free Negroes owned slaves.[57] It was in this decade that John Chavis, a free Negro of North Carolina, conducted schools for white children at Hillsborough and Raleigh, teaching youths who later became eminent statesmen. Free Negroes voted in Tennessee until 1834 and in North Carolina until 1835.

The position of free Negroes in Southern society, however, deteriorated after the Nat Turner revolt of 1831. On account of their freedom of movement they were suspected of distributing incendiary publications and acting as agents of insurrection. Moreover, they were regarded as setting a bad example to the slaves, and were accused of selling liquor to and receiving stolen goods from them; they were criticized for being shiftless and disorderly; and white mechanics were bitterly opposed to them because of their competition in the skilled trades. In North Carolina, to take an example, the free Negro in the decade of the 1830's lost many of the privileges which he had previously enjoyed, such as the right to preach freely to Negroes, to peddle goods outside the county in which he resided without a special license, to own a shotgun without a license, and to vote. (He was disfranchised in the constitutional convention of 1835 by the close vote of 66 to 61.) In 1859, after several attempts in the legislature had failed, a law was passed prohibiting the sale of liquor to free Negroes except upon a physician's prescription.[58]

In all the Southern states free Negroes were prohibited from immigrating, and in most of them a slave was compelled to leave the state when he was emancipated. He was required to register with the county court, and in Georgia he had to have a white guardian. He had to obey the curfew law. In most states he was heavily taxed, and free-

[56] See Hogan and Davis, *William Tiler Johnson's Natchez, passim.*

[57] Carter G. Woodson, "Negro Owners of Slaves," *Journal of Negro History,* IX (1924), 41.

[58] Franklin, *The Free Negro in North Carolina,* pp. 79–81.

Negro testimony against whites was inadmissible in court. The height of hostility against this class was reached in 1859, when Arkansas ordered the expulsion of all free Negroes from the state.[59] The free Negroes, as Joel Chandler Harris's story "Free Joe and the Rest of the World" indicates, were less happy than the slaves.

To get rid of the free Negroes as well as to furnish an outlet for humanitarian sentiment, the American Colonization Society was founded in 1817 in Washington, with Bushrod Washington, a nephew of George Washington, as president. A law of Congress of 1819 authorized the appropriation of money for purchasing a territory in western Africa where free Negroes and Africans captured from slave ships could be sent. Two agents of the Colonization Society, who also represented the United States government, purchased an area next to British Sierra Leone, which was named Liberia. The first permanent settlement of American Negroes there was made in 1822. When the Colonization Society five years later tried to secure additional federal appropriations for its ambitious project of sending thousands of free Negroes and emancipated slaves to Africa, the cotton states, particularly Georgia, opposed such a diversion of federal funds to accomplish the "fanatical" object of diminishing their valuable labor force.[60]

The main support of the Colonization Society came from the Southern border states, with little help from the Northern states. The membership of the society was divided into two groups, those interested only in removing the free Negroes and thus strengthening the slave system, and those, like Henry Clay, who envisaged the colonization plan as a means of encouraging emancipation and carrying Christianity and civilization to Africa. The society sent out agents, among whom was James G. Birney, the future presidential candidate of the Liberty party, to found state and auxiliary societies and to collect money. In North Carolina, for example, the agents collected a total of nearly $24,000 before the Civil War. The legislature of Tennessee in 1833 appropriated $10 for each Negro sent to Africa. A number of planters freed their slaves on condition that they be transported to the Dark Continent, and some of them provided money for their transportation. A notable case was that of Captain Isaac Ross of Port Gibson, Missis-

[59] Orville W. Taylor, *Negro Slavery in Arkansas* (Durham, 1958), Chap. XIII.

[60] See E. L. Fox, *The American Colonization Society, 1817–1840* (Baltimore, 1919).

sippi, whose will in 1836 provided for giving his 170 slaves the choice of emancipation and transportation to Liberia or remaining in Mississippi in slavery. All but one elected to go to Africa.[61]

The state-rights spirit of the Southern people was shown curiously in the desire to partition Liberia into parts reserved for slaves from the separate states. Thus the Kentucky Colonization Society in 1847 paid $5,000 for a portion of Liberia, named Kentucky in Liberia, with its capital called Clay Ashland. There were also a Mississippi in Liberia, a Louisiana in Liberia, and a Maryland in Liberia. The Maryland legislature appropriated more money for colonization than any other state, providing in 1832 (after the Nat Turner insurrection) for the removal of all the free Negroes in the state and appropriating the sum of $20,000 the first year and $10,000 annually thereafter. Liberia became an independent republic in 1847, with a Virginia mulatto, Joseph J. Roberts as president. Maryland's colony remained separate, however, until 1857, when a war with the natives led to its joining the republic.

The dream of returning the American Negro to Africa was the white man's dream, not the Negro's. American Negroes as a whole dreaded going to Africa, where they would have to cope with tropical diseases, hostile natives, and unfamiliar conditions. Many of the Negroes that were transported died, and some of those who survived wrote discouraging letters to their former masters and brethren in the Southern states, describing the huge snakes, the small farms of five to ten acres, the almost total lack of draft animals, and the laziness and want of enterprise of most of the immigrants.[62] The American Negro was poorly equipped to be a pioneer and much of his failure may be attributed to the fact that he had been habituated by slavery to depend on the white man. Some of the colonists, however, discounted the physical discomforts of their new life and emphasized the fact that Negroes could enjoy freedom in Liberia. One of John H. Cocke's former slaves wrote that in Liberia "I can speak for myself like a man & show myself to be a man so far as my ability allows me."[63] John McDonogh's former

[61] R. R. Gurley to Philip R. Fendall, July 12, 1836, American Colonization Society Papers, Library of Congress.

[62] See a small collection of letters from emigrants to Liberia, 1846–48, Wilson Collection, University of Kentucky Library.

[63] Peter Skipwith to John H. Cocke, September 29, 1844, Bremo Slave Letters, University of Virginia Library.

slaves from Louisiana wrote many affectionate letters to this wealthy merchant praising Liberia and giving a favorable report of their condition; but they were religious slaves who had been trained to industry and self-help.

The method of gradually emancipating the Southern slaves by colonization proved to be totally impracticable. Congress refused a request for a million acres of public land to finance colonization. Northerners were suspicious of the movement as a proslavery design; only in the border states of the South was there any significant interest in it. Yet such notable figures as Henry Clay and Abraham Lincoln believed that the colonization of freed Negroes was the only solution of the race problem. The hostility of the native tribes of Liberia, the lack of transportation, and the invincible birth rate of the American Negroes made the plan of colonization appear fantastic. The American Colonization Society during its existence transported a total of over 12,000 Negroes, of whom a little over one-third were originally free.

Although the free Negro was regarded as an element of danger in the slave system, the greatest peril was apprehended from the effects of abolition agitators and abolition propaganda upon the slaves. Actually, the propaganda of the Northern societies was addressed to the white population and the Negroes were scarcely affected by it. The master of Forest Rill Plantation in Virginia told Catherine Hopley, "We entertain no fears about our Negroes as long as they are left to themselves."[64] A master's sense of security, however, applied only to his own slaves. George W. Mordecai of Raleigh, North Carolina, a prominent lawyer of Jewish background, expressed a prevalent attitude of Southerners to the danger of insurrection. "As to insurrection among our slaves," he wrote to a Northern Republican on December 28, 1860, "if the vile machinations of the abolitionists would allow them to remain in peace & quiet as they are, we apprehend no danger from that quarter. . . . I would much sooner trust myself alone on my plantation surrounded by my slaves, than in one of your large manufacturing towns when your laborers are discharged from employment & crying for bread for themselves & their little ones."[65]

The danger and discontent within the slave system had far-reaching

---

[64] Hopley, *Life in the South*, p. 81.
[65] George W. Mordecai to [a Northern Republican], December 28, 1860, Mordecai Papers, Southern Collection, University of North Carolina.

effects which have never been adequately investigated. The effect on the legal system is obvious, resulting in a draconic slave code. Active discontent and a rebellious disposition do not seem to have been characteristic of the majority of the slaves, but a minority were certainly dangerous in their smoldering resentment and desire to be free. The more daring, intelligent, and fortunate individuals escaped to free territory, thus lessening the danger of violence in the slave system. The most serious consequence of the repressions of the slave regime was not the periodic outbreaks of fear of servile plots and insurrection that led to the formation of vigilance committees and a complete disregard of legal processes. It was the suppression of freedom of thought and expression in Southern society and the creation of a profoundly conservative attitude toward social reforms.

CHAPTER 5

The Maturing of the Plantation
and Its Society

T HE PLANTATION has come to stand for the characteristic element in the civilization of the Old South. Nevertheless, there were only 46,274 persons out of a white population of approximately eight million people in the slave states in 1860 whom the census officials classified as planters, i.e. owning as many as twenty slaves. In this privileged class slightly less than three thousand persons held as many as one hundred slaves, and only eleven individuals possessed over five hundred slaves. Despite the fact that the vast majority of Southern families lived on small farms rather than on plantations, the plantation type of life set the tone of Southern society, provided the leadership, and was one of the most important forces differentiating rural life in the South from that of other regions.

The Southern plantation had a life cycle of youth, maturity, and old age. In its youth the plantation exhibited many of the characteristics of the frontier. So rapid was the growth of the plantation in the lower South, however, that in the lifetime of the original owner much of the crudeness of its early origin disappeared; log cabins were either boarded over or replaced by dignified frame houses with white pillars supporting the veranda roof; stumps were removed from the fields, and rail fences were built around the arable fields. As planters attained wealth they replaced the rough frontier furniture of their houses with polished mahogany tables, chairs, and chests.

Yet there remained many incongruities even in the well-established plantation homes of the lower South. De Puy Van Buren observed in 1857, during a visit among the wealthy country gentlemen of the Yazoo Valley of Mississippi, "A clock, a almanac, and a good fire are hard things to find in a planter's house."[1] He noted also that one planter whom he met had purchased a carriage in Philadelphia for $600, but the roads were so bad that he had not ridden a rod in it. The Choctaw chieftain and Mississippi cotton planter, Greenwood Leflore, ordered from France furniture for one room of his mansion at a cost of $10,000, consisting of Louis XIV period chairs, ottoman, and sofas, covered with gold leaf and crimson brocade.[2]

The plantation entered upon old age when its arable fields became exhausted from ruthless exploitation. Many of the planters then abandoned their plantations, selling at a sacrifice and moving farther west. Others, the majority, remained and sought to readjust their lives to changed conditions. The rice plantations of the Carolinas and Georgia had a more stable existence than the cotton and tobacco plantations because the topsoil was renewed every year by controlled flooding. Consequently they grew old gracefully and maintained their prosperity almost to the end of the ante-bellum period. But according to the census of 1850 they were relatively few, only 551 plantations raising as much as 20,000 pounds of rice compared with 74,031 cotton plantations producing more than five bales, 15,745 tobacco estates raising as much as 3,000 pounds of tobacco, 8,327 hemp plantations, and 2,681 sugar plantations, inclusive of the smallest (by 1860 the number had declined to 1,308).[3]

The plantations varied in size, but a middle-sized one consisted of a thousand to fifteen hundred acres of land. Its size was limited by the walking distance of an hour or so from the slave quarters to the most distant field. Accordingly, owners of great acreage usually had a number of scattered plantations. Since the plantations were engaged prin-

[1] A. De Puy Van Buren, *Jottings of a Year's Sojourn in the South* (Battle Creek, Mich., 1859), p. 89.

[2] Florence R. Ray, *Chieftain Greenwood Leflore and the Choctaw Indians of the Mississippi Valley* (Memphis, 1936), pp. 62–64.

[3] J. D. B. De Bow, *Compendium of the Seventh Census* (Washington, 1854), p. 178.

cipally in producing crops for foreign export, it was essential that they should be so located as to have easy transportation facilities (usually rivers) to market and that their soil be relatively fertile. During the course of time planters learned to adapt agricultural procedures to their Negro labor; they improved the quality of their seed and of their draft animals, they learned to make the best use of the soil and to correct the mistakes of their ancestors; and many of them developed efficient units of production. Thus, if one thinks of the plantation as an organic development, in many parts of the South it had matured by the eve of the Civil War. The hand of tradition, or custom, lay heavy upon the operation of the plantation partly because of the cultural isolation of the South and partly because of the nature of Negro slave labor. It rested heaviest upon the isolated rice plantations of the Carolina and Georgia coast.

The rice country was limited to a narrow belt of land near the coast by the need for using the tides to flood and drain the fields. At the same time the fields had to be located above the reach of salt water, which killed growing plants. One of the favored rice districts of South Carolina was along the Waccamaw River, west of Georgetown, where in 1850 there were eighteen or twenty plantations, extending no farther than twenty-four miles from the mouth of the river. The rice planters built an elaborate system of dikes, floodgates, and drainage ditches that enabled them to flood and drain their fields at proper intervals. The fields were flooded by opening the floodgates as the incoming tide raised the level of the fresh-water rivers. The gates were closed as the tide ebbed, and the trapped water was allowed to stand on the fields for several weeks, accomplishing the twofold purpose of killing the grass and irrigating the rice plants. When the time came to drain the ground, the floodgates were opened as the tide ebbed and the level of the river fell. The difference between high and low tide south of Cape Hatteras was five to seven feet, a differential that was needed to flood and drain the rice fields properly with fresh water.

The rice plantations were cultivated by rather primitive methods on the whole. Hoes were used almost entirely, even in breaking the land, and the rice was threshed—except on the most prosperous plantations after 1850—by the Negroes beating the stalks with a flail on threshing floors. The rice lands were subdivided by embankments into fields of twelve to twenty-two acres in size. The seeds were sown in the spring, in trenches four feet apart. After they had sprouted, the fields were periodically hoed and irrigated. Formidable enemies menaced the rice crop, particularly flocks of yellow ricebirds and the severe storms of the South Atlantic coast, which destroyed dikes and temporarily ruined fields by flooding them with salt water. The golden-yellow fields of rice were cut late in August or early September by sickle; the rice heads, called paddy, were pounded in mortars to separate the grain from the husks; and finally the grains were polished, usually in mills in Charleston.[4]

The task system of labor was the normal practice in the rice fields. Each full hand was assigned from a fourth to a third of an acre to cultivate during a day. Almira Coffin of Maine, who visited relatives in the Georgetown district, wrote in 1851: "Their tasks are only half day ones if they are ambitious, & then they can cultivate land for themselves, raise poultry, pigs & and on some places cattle, catch fish, dig oysters or whatever they please. . . ."[5] Olmsted observed in 1854 that some slaves finished their tasks by two o'clock. But Solon Robinson, the Northern agriculturalist, on his travels in the South in the middle of the century, saw some slaves hoeing in the rice fields so slowly that he commented such slow work would give a Yankee convulsions.

One of the largest of the rice planters in 1850 was the Charleston banker and politician, ex-governor William M. Aiken, whose father had emigrated from County Antrim, Ireland. This self-made gentleman had a capital investment of $380,000 in his plantation and slaves on Jehossee Island. He cultivated 1,500 acres of rice land and 500 acres of corn. His average annual sales of rice during the 1840's (a period of low prices) were $25,000, and his expenses, including the salary of $2,000 paid to his overseer, were approximately $10,000. Despite his wealth and great prestige, he was plain and unostentatious in manner, living in a simple house. He treated his slaves paternally, but they must have lived in crowded quarters, for there were only eighty-four

---

[4] Albert V. House, *Planter Management and Capitalism in Ante-Bellum Georgia: the Journal of Hugh Frazer Grant, Ricegrower* (New York, 1954); Arney R. Childs (ed.), *Rice Planter and Sportsman: The Recollections of J. Motte Alston, 1821–1909* (Columbia, 1953), pp. 42–47; and Charles Lyell, *A Second Visit to the United States [1845–46]* (New York, 1849).

[5] Jones, *Plantation South*, p. 189.

double frame cabins for his seven hundred slaves.[6] Captain Basil Hall described a rice plantation that he visited as having 140 slaves, of whom sixty were children, all living in twenty-eight huts.

The Allston and Heyward families were good examples of paternal rice planters. Robert F. W. Allston, educated at West Point, was in personality as well as in lineage a gentleman. He was active in politics, becoming governor of the state. On his plantation near Georgetown he raised two and a third to two and a half barrels of rice (600 pounds to the barrel) to the acre, which he marketed in Charleston through a factor.[7] Unlike Allston, Nathaniel Heyward did not participate in politics but stuck closely to the task of managing his seventeen plantations and two thousand slaves. He kept amassing plantations and slaves, so that when he died in 1852 his estate was worth one million dollars in slaves and another million in land, stocks, and bonds, making him "the largest planter of his day."[8] Fanny Kemble, the English actress who married Pierce Butler, owner of a rice plantation in Georgia, and Fredrika Bremer, the Swedish traveler, have left contrasting pictures of slave life on the rice plantations. Fanny Kemble depicts a scene of great cruelty and immorality on the plantation of her absentee landlord husband. Fredrika Bremer, on the other hand, found the slaves well treated on the plantation of Joel Poinsett on the Great Pedee River in South Carolina and on the admirably run rice plantation of James Hamilton Couper on the Altamaha River in Georgia.[9]

The diary of John Berkeley Grimball, extending from 1832 to 1864, reveals the daily life of a great South Carolina planter more faithfully than any other available document.[10] At the age of thirty-two, when Grimball began his diary, he owned six rice and cotton plantations in lowland South Carolina. Slann's Island, his "home plantation," had

---

[6] *De Bow's Southern and Western Review,* IX (1850), 201–203.

[7] See James H. Easterby (ed.), *The South Carolina Rice Plantation as Revealed in the Papers of Robert F. W. Allston* (Chicago, 1945).

[8] D. C. Heyward, *Seed from Madagascar* (Chapel Hill, 1937), Chap. 8.

[9] Fredrika Bremer, *The Homes of the New World: Impressions of America* (New York, 1853), I, 285–287; II, 480–490; Frances Anne Kemble, *Journal of a Residence on a Georgian Plantation in 1838–1839* (New York, 1863).

[10] The manuscript diary is in the Southern Collection of the University of North Carolina Library, but there is a typed copy in the Charleston Library Society.

thirty full hands, nine one-half hands, twenty-five children, a nurse, and a cook. During the malarial season he and his family resided in a town house in Charleston. He commented that long and melancholy experience had abundantly proved that it was impossible to inhale the miasma from the swamps (believed to be the cause of malaria) with impunity. Yet he was ruthless in insisting that his white overseer remain on the plantation during the sickly season. When North, the overseer at Dawho, refused in November 1834 to sign a contract for the following year unless he and his family could spend the sickly season in the pinelands, Grimball refused this permission and they parted. Yet the diary records that North, not finding another place, surrendered and signed a contract to oversee for another year for $325.

The diary lists the various expenses of using slave labor, such as doctors' bills, clothing, food, and so on. In the fall he distributed to each slave five yards of cloth with which to make clothes. One of his slaves, Cudjo, who was hired out, gave his master $6 a month as his hire, from which Grimball handed him $1 for summer clothing. At the rice harvest time he ordered the overseer to kill a beef for meat for his people at Antwerp Plantation. In July 1833, he purchased two hundred bushels of corn at 85 cents a bushel, fifteen pounds of bacon, and one hundred pounds of tobacco for his people at Slann's Island. He gave them also fish and molasses. His plantation force apparently raised enough sweet potatoes for their use. During residence in Charleston, he hired a Negro nurse for his child, paying a monthly wage of six dollars. When she asked for a raise in wages to eight dollars, which all the nurses in Charleston were getting, he refused her request, but finally compromised by giving her $7.

Grimball seems to have been hard up for money whenever there were requests for charity. Jehu Jones, a Negro tailor in Charleston, called on him as well as his other customers to contribute money to transport himself and his father to Liberia. Grimball declined on the ground of lack of money; he also refused to give more than twenty dollars for the founding of a Southern Theological Seminary. Yet he could find money for his own pleasures and interests. He ordered one-half pipe of Madeira wine at a cost of $127 and a set of white china for $110. After serving on the jury for five days he invested the $5 of pay that he received in a lottery ticket. He gave a dinner for eight of his aristocratic friends that cost $27. It was an elaborate feast of turtle soup, ham, boiled mutton, trout, scalloped oysters, roast turkey, a haunch of venison, plum pudding, apple pie, floating island, blanc mange, English cheese, fruit, sherry, and Madeira and claret wines.

His relations with his slaves were apparently friendly and tolerant. On March 20, 1834, he began planting rice. When he found that his Negroes, who were exceedingly superstitious, believed that it was ill luck to plant on Friday, he indulged them by putting off planting. Bacchus, who acted as confidential messenger, would bring to his master letters and reports of the overseer; the slave himself would report on conditions as he had observed them at the plantations. Occasionally a slave would complain to the master about the conduct of the overseer or the driver; when a slave came from the plantation to complain of the injustice of Adam, the Negro driver, Grimball supported the authority of the driver and had the complaining slave punished. Grimball had to deal with another vexing problem of discipline when Richard, the driver at Slann's Island Plantation, came to his master to report that the overseer had deprived him of his office. The overseer had become angry because the driver had reported his misconduct, particularly the fact that he had been feeding his own five slaves at Grimball's expense. The master restored the faithful Richard to his position.

By the time of the Civil War Grimball was living in baronial style. He had a fine house in the aristocratic part of Charleston with twelve slaves. He owned 133 field slaves, and his net annual income from rice alone was $15,148.69. Of his twelve children, one son was studying medicine in the office of a doctor in Charleston, another law in a lawyer's office, a third had completed his study of law and was the assistant bookkeeper in a Charleston firm, and a fourth was attending the College of Charleston. One of his sons belonged to the exclusive St. Cecilia Society. He rented a pew in St. Michael's for the summer for $30. Despite his ample income he was heavily in debt, owing $45,109 on June 1, 1860.

An ardent state-rights man, Grimball supported the nullification and secession movements. On December 17, 1860, he wrote: "The prospect before us in regard to our Slave Property, if we continue to remain in the Union is nothing less than utter ruin." His conservative mind was indicated by his remark, concerning corruption in the election of 1860 in Charleston, that the principle of universal suffrage was clearly demonstrated to be wrong. During the war four sons fought for the Confederacy. Grimball himself volunteered for patrol duty at the age of sixty-two, contributed money to equip an infantry company, bought Confederate bonds with the produce of his plantation, loaned his boat to the cause, and furnished corn and fodder for the cavalry. On March 1, 1862, one of his overseers sent word that nearly all the slaves, eighty in number, had fled from the plantation. A year later he sold the remainder of his slaves, keeping only his house servants and ten field slaves to cultivate food crops. He invested the proceeds in Confederate bonds, which became a complete loss at the end of the war. When the Union army invaded St. Paul's Parish, his plantation there was abandoned, the residence was burned, and the trunks and floodgates of his rice fields destroyed. In his despondency he joined the Episcopal Church.

Among the many unsuccessful planters of the older regions of the South, William Gilmore Simms, the South Carolina novelist, was perhaps the most interesting. His intimate friend, James H. Hammond of Silver Bluff, an outstanding example of the successful planter, wrote to him in 1857: "I dont know whether it is lands, negroes, or management, or all combined but certainly your planting for many years has been all—pardon the word—a farce. It is perfectly absurd to plant unless you can make 1200 lbs. of ginned cotton to the hand & an abundance of provisions, to thrive one must make 2000 lbs."[11] Simms had begun the life of a cotton planter in 1836, when at the age of thirty he married Chevillette Roach, daughter of a large planter of the Barnwell district, and moved to Woodlands, the home plantation of his father-in-law. At this time Woodlands was a cotton plantation of two thousand acres and had a labor force of approximately seventy-five slaves. Here the Simms family lived in style during the decade of the 1830's, the lush period of his life. Sixteen of the slaves were house or yard servants. The plantation mansion with its twelve rooms was filled with children and guests; Simms had fifteen children, all but six of whom died before he did in 1870. Every May the family moved to a town house in Charleston, owned by the father of his wife, in order to escape malaria. Thus he, like most of the Carolina planters, enjoyed a

[11] Hammond to Simms, December 30, 1857, James H. Hammond Papers, Library of Congress.

combination of city and rural life.[12]

Simms's financial affairs illustrate the chronic shortage of money and frequency of debt characteristic of many planters. In 1841 a crop failure at Woodlands reduced the cotton crop from a normal two hundred bales to seventy-two. In seeking to borrow money at this time from the actor Edwin Forrest, Simms enumerated his assets: Woodlands Plantation, valued at $15,000; Oak Grove, a plantation of four thousand acres in Orangeburg District, valued at $20,000; a brick town house in Charleston, valued at $6,000; and ninety slaves, valued very low at $300 each.[13] Furthermore, he supplemented his income from agriculture by writing and lecturing. In the 1830's he earned $6,000 a year from royalties on his novels, but in later years he received as little as $1,500. In 1848 he wrote to a Northern friend that "our planting interests barely pay expenses."

Simms tried to make his plantation largely self-sufficient. Cotton and rice were the money crops, but he also raised quantities of corn, wheat, black-eyed peas, sweet potatoes, and sugar cane for molasses. He reared sheep and converted the wool into homespun cloth. He tanned the hides of cattle slaughtered on the plantation, and his slaves made shoes; they also made candles and soap. Yet often he did not succeed in producing enough food to supply the needs of the slaves and the white family. On January 15, 1845, he recorded that he had killed fifty hogs, but two years later he was forced to buy two hundred pounds of bacon as well as flour and corn. Part of his failure to attain self-sufficiency was owing to the many vicissitudes of farming, such as losses from droughts, ravages of caterpillars and other pests, rust, sickness of slaves, storms, and bad luck.

A kind and indulgent master, he wrote in 1850 that a partial explanation of why he was always in debt was "an undue indulgence to the slaves" on the plantation. Each Negro cabin on his plantation had its garden, and, like many Southern planters, he bought some of the produce raised by the slaves, such as chickens, eggs, and vegetables. He permitted five of his slaves to keep guns in their possession for the pur-

[12] The only biography of Simms—William Trent, *William Gilmore Simms* (Boston, 1892)—is brilliant but prejudiced, overemphasizing especially the lack of appreciation of Simms by Charleston society.

[13] Simms to James Lawson, January 1, 1841; Mary C. Simms Oliphant *et al.* (eds.), *The Letters of William Gilmore Simms* (Columbia, 1854), I, 210.

pose of hunting. At times without the services of an overseer, Simms himself supervised the operation of the plantation with the aid of Negro drivers. Not only did the master care for the physical well-being of the slaves, but he delighted in affording them entertainment. On one occasion in 1848, he staged a *tableau vivant* at Woodlands with costumed queens, princes, sultanas, and sylphs; Simms himself, dressed as a Comanche Indian, let a vigorous damsel, "a Texas Hunter," throw him to the floor. "The whole plantation," he wrote to a Northern friend, "gathered to the Spectacle. You should have seen our negroes— our piazza was crowded with them, leaping over each others heads & much more delighted than you and I have ever been at Niblo's."[14] Charles Lanman, the painter and author, visited Simms at Woodlands in 1848 and was much impressed with the polite and happy slaves on the plantation, especially with the black and white children "frolicing [together] under the trees."[15]

Although he often complained of financial difficulties, he and his family lived well. In addition to enjoying a rural plenty of good food, he made frequent trips to the North. He was constantly buying books. When Sherman's army burned the mansion at Woodlands, its library contained 10,700 volumes. Simms spent much time hunting and he entertained lavishly. He belonged to the St. Cecilia Society of Charleston. He indulged in the luxury of politics, serving in the legislature and running for election to the office of lieutenant governor, which he lost by one vote.

The kind of life that Simms led represented the maturing and mellowing of plantation society. The maturing of the plantation brought a greater sense of order, a more paternal treatment of the slaves, and an improvement in agriculture. One of the most appealing personalities in the Old South, who illustrated the fulfillment of the plantation ideal and protested against the nomadic life of the cotton planters, was Thomas Spalding of Sapelo Island in Georgia. On this sea island, before his death in 1851, he had developed a spacious long-staple-cotton and rice plantation employing 250 slaves. He built his mansion for permanence with thick walls of tabby to stand against the frequent hurricanes of the Georgia coast. Here he collected a fine library, cre-

[14] Simms to James Lawson, April 30, 1848, *Letters of Simms*, II, 409.
[15] *Ibid.*, II, 404 n.

ated a beautiful garden, and maintained a patriarchal attitude toward his slaves. He advocated a work day of six hours except in cotton-picking time and seasons requiring unusual effort. He sought to make his slaves more self-reliant and advocated that, like the serfs of Europe, they should be attached to the land and not sold away from it. He himself supervised his plantation without the services of white overseers, using as foremen talented Negroes such as Bu Allah, a Mohammedan slave brought from Africa, who kept a journal in Arabic.

Spalding tried to stop emigration of farmers and planters from the Atlantic seaboard. In speeches before agricultural societies and articles in agricultural periodicals, he pointed out the advantages of cherishing one farm or plantation for keeps. He thought that one way to stop the flow of emigrants to the West was to diversify crops, and he himself became a great experimenter. In 1806 he introduced the cultivation of sugar cane in Georgia; he planted mulberry trees for silk culture, olive groves, vineyards, different kinds of grasses, including Bermuda grass, and various fruits. He sought to popularize scientific agriculture, particularly the rotation of crops, and the promotion of agricultural societies and fairs which offered prizes. Indeed, one of the best aspects of the maturing of the plantation was the movement by people like Spalding to improve farms and conserve the topsoil. These gentlemen farmers developed a ripened philosophy of life, a rural wisdom, a love of nature and of their own communities that ennobled the Southern way of life despite its basis in slavery.[16]

The planters who emigrated from the Atlantic seaboard states to the virgin lands of the Southwest were able to establish thriving plantations in a remarkably short time. The Taits, Charles and his son James A., for example, moved in 1819 from Georgia to the Alabama River Valley, where with the same labor force they raised twice as much cotton as they had in Georgia. Charles brought with him to his new home twenty-five working hands; by the time of his death in 1835 he had increased his holdings to 115 slaves. He fed and clothed his servants well, provided them with good medical attention, and even made it easy for some of them to learn to read and write. He bought young Negro girls from twelve to fifteen years old who would make

[16] See E. Merton Coulter, *Thomas Spalding of Sapelo* (University, La., 1940).

fruitful wives, so that fifty-eight Negroes were born on his plantation. Indeed, there were five generations of slaves owned by him, one of whom had been in the family for seventy-eight years. Variously skilled slaves—a blacksmith, a tanner, a cobbler, a millwright, a gunsmith, a carpenter, and seamstresses—made many articles for the plantation use. Like most of the Alabama planters, the Taits did not raise sufficient food for all their slaves.[17]

A large number of the planters of the lower South increased their acreage by buying on credit. Hugh Davis's plantation Beaver Bend on the Cahawba River in Alabama was a good example of such expansion. By 1850 Davis had acquired 5,462 acres of land on the edge of the black belt, much of which had been bought on credit. Starting with eighteen slaves in 1848, he had increased his force to seventy-eight when he died in 1862. Davis cultivated only a small portion of his estate, never more than a thousand acres, of which a little more than half was planted in cotton and the rest in food crops, especially corn. He sought to raise enough food for the plantation, but in no year was he successful. Although he killed approximately forty hogs annually, they did not produce enough meat for his slaves, and often he had bad luck when his hogs ate the infant pigs. He bought his plantation supplies from his factor in Mobile or from stores in a nearby village, usually on credit, for which he was charged high interest, a markup price, and a commission of 2½ per cent. His yield of cotton varied from 51 to 196 bales, and the price fluctuated in 1848–60 from 4⅞ cents to 14½ cents. When his cotton brought high prices, he usually bought more slaves. On occasion, he was completely devoid of cash and, like many planters owning large estates and slave gangs, borrowed sums as small as 25 and 50 cents from storekeepers. Nevertheless, he was a successful planter and found slavery a profitable system of labor.[18]

The management of Beaver Bend showed that a well-run plantation could secure co-operation and efficient service from slaves. Davis was more methodical than most Southern planters. He established written rules for the conduct both of the overseers and the slaves, which were strictly enforced. One of the most important was that the overseer must

[17] See Charles H. Moffat, "Charles Tait, Planter, Politician and Scientist of the Old South," *Journal of Southern History,* **XIV** (1948), 206–233.

[18] Weymouth T. Jordan, *Hugh Davis and His Alabama Plantation* (University, Ala., 1948).

write detailed reports about the work on the plantation in the farm book each day. He fed his slaves well (the food being prepared by the plantation cook); provided twenty-three cabins for them, which were whitewashed every year; and encouraged them to work zealously by offering prizes and rewarding them with gala dinners and dances. If they did extra work, he paid them small sums. Despite his good treatment only sixteen babies were born on the plantation in twelve years, and of these only seven lived. But he was troubled by remarkably few runaways; from 1848 to 1861 there were only fifteen fugitives, and they stayed away only a few days. Although the slaves were whipped on occasion, it was seldom that they needed such drastic punishment, and, on the other hand, their master often commended them for their good work. Davis was fortunate in having some reliable and highly respected leaders among his slave force. During the years 1855 and 1856, having become disgusted with overseers, he supervised the plantation himself, using two intelligent and reliable slaves as foremen. He trusted them so implicitly that he would leave the plantation completely in their charge during visits to distant Mobile. Indeed, after the Civil War, his son found that the freedmen did not pick nearly as much cotton or work as well as they had in the days of slavery.

After the first exploitation of the virgin soil was over, the planters began to realize the need of conserving the soil and practicing a more careful husbandry. Agricultural reform in the cotton belt was led by a group of planters and farmers in the Georgia Piedmont, particularly in Hancock County.[19] The reform began partly as a result of low prices for cotton in the decade of the 1840's. Moreover, Georgia had suffered seriously from the emigration of its young men and from the depletion of its soil by erosion and exhaustive methods of agriculture. Sir Charles Lyell gave a graphic example of the ruin caused by erosion, describing in 1846 a ravine near Milledgeville which in the course of twenty years had widened to 180 feet in breadth, 55 feet in depth, and 300 yards in length. Furthermore, the Georgia land lottery, by which thirty million acres of land taken from the Indians were presented free to the citizens of the state, had encouraged people to abandon land instead of trying to improve it.

The reformers of Hancock County, organized into a Planters Club,

[19] J. C. Bonner, "Genesis of Agricultural Reform in the Cotton Belt," *Journal of Southern History*, IX (1943), 473–500.

determined to stay on their farms and increase their value. Accordingly, led by David Dickson, they developed improved strains of cotton seed; checked erosion; bred quality livestock; introduced new crops, such as grasses, peaches, and strawberries; and adopted more intelligent methods of utilizing slave labor. In 1844, when the price of cotton sank to the lowest point that it had ever reached, a Georgia planter, Dimos Ponce, proposed a crop-control plan of reducing cotton acreage quite similar to the New Deal plan of the 1930's. Unfortunately, he could not secure the co-operation of the individualistic farmers of the South to work out his proposals.

Nevertheless, cotton planters' conventions were held during the 1840's and 1850's for the purpose of co-operation in the marketing of their crop. One of these, which met at Macon on October 27, 1851, with delegates from nine states, considered the "Florida Plan" of chartering a cotton planter's association to erect warehouses to store cotton and sell it only at the minimum price of 10 cents a pound. Another plan, presented by Colonel John R. Gamble, was to organize county agricultural societies throughout the South that would report each year to a central executive committee the extent of the cotton crop. If production was larger than demand, the committee would determine how much cotton should be withheld from the market and would fine violators of quotas $1 a bale for excess amounts that were sold. At the Montgomery Convention of May 1853 it was proposed that every state establish an agricultural college "with a model farm attached," that the Southern universities appoint professors of agriculture, and that the legislatures should provide for geological surveys. Although eloquent speeches were made and resolutions adopted, no practical action resulted.[20]

One of the signs of the maturing of farm life in the lower South was the publication of agricultural magazines and newspapers.[21] In 1828 the *Southern Agriculturalist* was founded in Charleston and had a successful career. In Augusta, Georgia, Dr. Daniel Lee, a New

[20] Weymouth T. Jordan, *Rebels in the Making: Planters' Conventions and Southern Propaganda* (Tuscaloosa, 1958), Chap. II.

[21] A. L. Demaree, *The American Agricultural Press 1819–1860* (New York, 1941); Weymouth T. Jordan, *Ante-Bellum Alabama, Town and Country* (Tallahassee, 1957), Chap. VI: Herbert Weaver, *Mississippi Farmers, 1850–1860* (Nashville, 1945).

Yorker, founded in 1843 a flourishing agricultural periodical, *The Southern Cultivator,* which by 1852 attained a circulation of 10,000. He became the first professor of agriculture in the South at Franklin College (the University of Georgia), holding a chair established in 1854 by a philanthropist. *The Soil of the South,* published in the decade of the 1850's in Columbus, Georgia, was so valued by progressive Georgia planters that one of them, Joseph Bond of Hancock County, subscribed to it for each of his six overseers. Dr. Noah B. Cloud, a native of South Carolina who had studied medicine at Jefferson Medical College in Philadelphia, emigrated to Alabama to become a planter and the editor of the *American Cotton Planter,* published at Montgomery. Cloud was an ardent advocate of raising food crops and more livestock, of the humane treatment of slaves, and of establishing textile factories. His periodical, after it was combined with *The Soil of the South,* reached a circulation of over 10,000.[22]

The planters of Mississippi had by 1830 developed a new variety of cotton which has been described as a contribution to cotton growing second only in importance to the invention of Eli Whitney's cotton gin. By crossing Mexican cotton with the Georgia Upland or Green Seed cotton and the Creole Black Seed variety, they produced a variety that was much easier to pick and was resistant to the "rot disease." It was the devastation caused by this disease that led the eastern planters after 1834 to abandon the Green Seed variety and substitute the much superior Petit Gulf cotton. Henry W. Vick (for whose family Vicksburg was named) became the greatest cottonseed breeder of the South. He developed a system of sending his most intelligent Negroes into the fields ahead of the regular pickers to gather the seed cotton from the largest and most productive plants. Thus, by carefully selecting and breeding only the superior specimens, he developed in the 1840's a notable strain which he called 100 Seed cotton; other highly productive varieties, such as Banana, Pomegranite, and Jethro were developed, all refinements of the Petit Gulf cotton.[23]

Among the most progressive of the Mississippi agriculturists were Dr. Martin W. Phillips of Log Hall and Thomas Affleck, a Northerner

[22] Weymouth T. Jordan, "Noah B. Cloud's Activities in Behalf of Southern Agriculture," *Agricultural History,* XXV (1951), 53–58.

[23] See John H. Moore, *Agriculture in Ante-Bellum Mississippi* (New York, 1958), Chaps. II, VIII.

who had settled in the delta town of Washington. Phillips was a notable experimenter and propagandist of scientific agriculture. His periodical, the *South-Western Farmer*, of Raymond, Mississippi, urged farmers of his region to diversify their crops and to plant pedigreed cotton seed as well as to improve the minds and character of the slaves by oral instruction in religious truths. An unusual method of urging agricultural reform was adopted by Thomas Affleck, who had established the Southern Nursery. He published *Affleck's Southern Rural Almanac*, in which he not only advertised his nursery but used the almanac as a medium for agitating for such reforms as diversification of crops and the keeping of businesslike records of farm operations. Affleck designed and published the *Cotton Plantation Record and Account Book* to aid planters to develop efficient methods.

Solon Robinson in 1848–49 found a considerable number of "improving planters" in the Gulf states who practiced scientific agriculture, raised adequate food for their plantation force, and subscribed to agricultural papers.[24] One of the progressive planters of this region was Eli J. Capell of Pleasant Hill, in Amite County, Mississippi. Capell's father, who had been a squatter in southwestern Mississippi, left his son a section and a half of land, which the latter expanded into 2,500 acres, also acquiring ninety slaves. Capell was constantly experimenting, and he kept careful records of his agricultural operations. He used his mulatto headman Tone as his overseer, and conferred with him at the end of the day's work. By writing articles for agricultural papers he tried to encourage the planters and farmers of the state to follow his example of improvement. In 1845 he wrote to the editor of the New York *American Agriculturalist*, "We are about one hundred years behind you in improvement." Showing little, if any, sectional bias, he advocated the immigration into the South of farmers possessing "northern enterprise."[25]

The maturing of the plantation led not only to a more scientific management of the crops and the soil but to cultivation of the mind. The upper class held an attractive ideal of education derived from the eighteenth century when Fithian taught in the home of Colonel Carter

[24] Kellar, *Solon Robinson*, I, 455, 474–486.
[25] Wendell H. Stephenson, "A Quarter-Century of a Mississippi Plantation: Eli J. Capell of Pleasant Hill," *Mississippi Valley Historical Review*, XXIII (1936), 363.

at Nomini Hall in Virginia—a Renaissance ideal of all-round cultivation. The planters believed that the Southern gentleman should be accomplished in riding, hunting, dancing, conversation, and manners. He should also have a practical knowledge of law, agriculture, and military science. But the indispensable ingredient of a gentleman's education was a knowledge of the ancient classics. Latin and Greek, therefore, became the most valued subjects taught by the tutors in plantation homes, by the academies, and by the colleges.

The plantation tutor was employed only by the wealthy families. Frequently the tutors were young Northerners, such as William Ellery Channing, Virgil Maxcy, and William H. Seward, who came South to earn money by teaching until they could establish themselves in other careers. Such a person was Edwin Hall, a graduate of Bowdoin College, who in 1837 accepted a position as tutor in the home of Dr. Mann Page of Turkey Hill in Albemarle County, Virginia. He taught the three Page boys and six other youths from neighboring families—languages principally, Latin, Greek, and French. He noted that the boys and girls in the South were educated in separate schools. To a friend in Maine he wrote enthusiastically, "I am in the very best of Virginian society, as the Doct. has a great many visitors."[26] He was faithfully waited upon by slaves, ate with the family, and was treated as an equal by the aristocratic Virginia society in which he was placed.

One of the richest of the South Carolina planters, James H. Hammond of Silver Bluff, wrote in 1847 to Professor Gibbes of the College of Charleston, asking his aid in finding a tutor for his six children. He was willing to pay $400 a year for a classical tutor and $500 for a French tutor to instruct his children and four others. The tutor would be expected to teach the classics, French, mathematics, and English. He would be provided with board, laundry, and the use of a horse, and given a month's vacation.[27] Although an ardent Southern nationalist, Hammond employed a Yale man to teach his children.

The letters of Henry Watson of Connecticut, who after graduating from college set out in 1831 to start a career in Alabama as a teacher,

[26] Larry Gara (ed.), "A New Englander's View of Plantation Life; Letters of Edwin Hall to Cyrus Woodman, 1837," *Journal of Southern History*, XVII (1952), 347.

[27] James H. Hammond to Lewis R. Gibbes, November 5, 1847, Lewis R. Gibbes Papers, Library of Congress.

throw much light on education in the lower South. He reported that in the rich black belt around Greensborough, Alabama, few private tutors were wanted and these rarely paid more than $250 or $300 a year. It was a more common practice for several families to unite their resources and pay $450 or $500 for a teacher to conduct a subscription school. In nearby Demopolis, for example, a subscription school had been started which obtained twenty-five pupils at $16 a head. Watson concluded that the cotton planters thought more of making money than of education. Schools in this region, he wrote, taught only the rudiments of learning, and they were generally conducted by such dunces or blockheads that he was ashamed to admit he was a school-teacher.[28]

Most Southern youth were educated not by private tutors but in academies and "old field schools." In 1850 the Southern states led the nation in the number of academies in operation, possessing 2,700 as compared with 2,100 in the Middle States and approximately 1000 in New England.[29] The most famous academy in the South was Moses Waddel's school at Willington, South Carolina, which educated such prominent leaders as John C. Calhoun, William H. Crawford, George McDuffie, Augustus B. Longstreet, Hugh Legaré, and James L. Petigru. The son of immigrants from County Down, Ireland, Waddel was educated at a famous academy in North Carolina, Clio's Nursery, and at Hampden-Sydney College. Deeply religious, he believed in a stern adherence to duty, with little tolerance for fun, such as dancing, or wasting time. His diary reveals a narrow, ascetic outlook on life, with little display of imagination. Although he ceaselessly taught the classics, his Calvinism made him incapable of appreciating their sensuous joy in the physical life and in the beauty of nature. He seems to have lacked any spark of humor, yet he was tremendously successful in training students to become eminent political leaders.

The academy at Willington was conducted on Spartan principles. The pupils lived in log cabins, arose at daylight, made their own fires, ate simple meals, and were kept hard at work reciting numerous lessons and studying in their rooms. Waddel's journal for 1830 records

[28] Henry Watson to Julius Reed, January 8, February 28, 1831; February 12, 1834, Henry Watson Papers.

[29] Edgar W. Knight, *The Academy Movement in the South* (Chapel Hill, 1919), and *Public Education in the South* (New York, 1923).

recitations in Virgil, Horace's *Satires,* the Greek Testament, and English grammar. Every day he opened and closed his school with prayer, maintained strict discipline by whipping and by his awesome personality, and taught forensic eloquence.[30]

Although girls did not have the opportunity to attend college—except the Moravian College in Salem, North Carolina, and Wesleyan College for Women at Macon, Georgia, founded in 1836—the education of females of the upper class was not neglected. When James Atherton of New Hampshire was traveling through the South in 1832, he was surprised to find how well educated the females in the Bluegrass area were; better educated, he thought, than were the girls of Boston. He talked with a teacher from New England who had visited a female academy in Lexington, and who told him that the system of education in this academy was much better than that pursued in New England schools.[31] John R. Gwathney, a teacher in Green Academy for young ladies at Huntsville, Alabama, commented in a letter of 1856: "There are a great many young ladies in this place and the greatest attention is paid to their education, far more than that of the young men."[32] Certainly Locust Dell Female Academy, taught by Nicholas and Caroline Hentz at Florence, Alabama, must have been superior to most Northern schools for girls.[33] Professor Hentz had taught at George Bancroft's famous Round Hill School in Northampton, Massachusetts, and the University of North Carolina, and Caroline Hentz, a native of Massachusetts, was a brilliant woman, the author of romantic novels. Fredrika Bremer, the Swedish traveler, described in glowing terms the school for young ladies near Macon kept by the cultivated Bishop Stephen Elliot, Jr. The school was located on the Bishop's delightful plantation and nearly all the teachers came from the North.[34] Unfortunately, early marriage, often at sixteen

[30] Moses Waddel, Diary, 1822–36; also Augustus Baldwin Longstreet, *Master William Mitten* (Macon, 1864).

[31] James H. Atherton to Hon. Charles H. Atherton, January 1, 1830, James H. Atherton Letters, University of Kentucky Library.

[32] John R. Gwathney to ——, September 10, 1856, Brock Collection, Miscellaneous, Huntington Library.

[33] Charles A. Hentz, "My Autobiography," describes his parents' activities as teachers in the South. Typescript of MS., Southern Collection, University of North Carolina.

[34] Bremer, *Homes of the New World,* I, 328–329.

and seventeen years of age, put an end to the formal education of many Southern girls.

A discerning picture of female education in the South was drawn by Catherine C. Hopley, who was teaching in Virginia when the Civil War came. The planters, she found, were eager for their daughters to be taught "the ornamentals"—French, playing the piano, singing, and drawing and painting. They also wished them to be instructed in Latin, mathematics, and algebra. Instruction in the schools and academies, she thought, was too largely a matter of memorization. Miss Hopley taught music in a Baptist College for Ladies at Warrenton, Virginia, where she found that the girls were far more interested in learning popular music than the great classics.[35] Notwithstanding the emphasis on the ornamentals, such hard subjects as natural science and mathematics were also taught in their academies and seminaries to the "sweet Southern girls."[36]

The letters of Sue Buckner, who was attending a popular school for girls in Lexington, Kentucky, in 1856, indicate that Southern maidens of the upper class had a lively interest in politics. At this time Sue was studying arithmetic, algebra, Latin, chemistry, and the history of England. Two of her teachers she described as old maids from New York and Ohio. During the presidential campaign she wrote that "Politics are running high in Lexington." A Fillmore flagpole had been raised and a torchlight procession and a grand illumination were held. "The girls here," she wrote, "are all great politicians and have some of the greatest disputes you ever heard." Of seventy-five "scholars" at Sayre Academy only seventeen were Democrats.[37]

Academies such as Sue Buckner attended existed for the upper and middle classes; the poor were largely without schools in many parts of the South. The only Southern states that had respectable public-school systems in 1860 were North Carolina and Kentucky, where two great educational leaders, Calvin H. Wiley and Robert J. Breckinridge, conducted a crusade for popular education.[38] Elsewhere the common

[35] Hopley, *Life in the South*, II, 98–102: 46–47, 60–61.
[36] Thomas Cary Johnson, Jr., *Scientific Interests in the Old South* (New York, 1936), Chap. IV, "Sweet Southern Girls."
[37] Sue Buckner to her brother, Sayre Institute, October 21, 1856, Buckner Family Papers, University of Kentucky Library.
[38] See C. W. Dabney, *Universal Education in the South* (Chapel Hill, 1936), 2 vols.

schools were in reality charity schools for poor children and orphans. The poverty and frequent indignity that beset the teacher of a poor school are revealed in the letters of Samuel B. Sweat of Georgia to his mechanic friend William H. Garland. In the autumn of 1843 Sweat was teaching in the Lightwood Knot Ridge Academy in South Carolina, in which sixteen pupils were enrolled, but in which on a cold, cloudy day in November only eight students were present. The community in which he taught was very crude; nearly everything used there was of home manufacture, including shoes and clothing. The people ate cornbread almost exclusively since little wheat was raised in that region. When his school was over in June he was not paid, because there was not "Enough of the chink in the Treasury of the poor school fund—the money being loaned out it cannot be collected in 3 or 4 weeks." During the following year he taught in Pebble Hill Academy, having fourteen pupils in the poor school and receiving a salary of $25 a month for three months. No wonder Sam considered "starting a farm among these crackers." In 1852 he was teaching thirty-four "scholars," aged from six years to twenty-two, in a school in South Carolina. The last news heard from Sam was dated 1867 from Savannah, where he was engaged as a timber factor and at the same time preaching to a country congregation.[39]

Although the Southern states neglected the education of their poor people, they gave great attention to the training of their upper class. Virginia, for example, was credited by the Census of 1850 with having twelve colleges, enrolling 1,343 students and 73 teachers; while Massachusetts, though its white population was approximately 100,000 larger than that of Virginia, had only 1,043 college students and 85 teachers. North Carolina was the first state in the Union to found a state university, which opened its doors in 1795. South Carolina College was probably the most liberal institution of higher learning in America during the presidency of Dr. Thomas Cooper, 1820–34.[40] The University of Virginia with its elective system, beautiful campus, and freedom from clerical influence during its early years, was also one of the most attractive and enlightened colleges in the nation. In the latter part of

[39] Sam Sweat to William H. Garland, November 23, 1842; January 14, 1843; July 16, 1852, Garland Papers.

[40] See Dumas Malone, *The Public Life of Thomas Cooper, 1783–1839* (New Haven, 1926).

the decade of the 1830's, South Carolina College was more advanced in the field of social studies than was Harvard; it had a chair of history held by the able professor Francis Lieber, while Harvard did not have such a professorship. In 1856, 558 students were attending the University of Virginia and Harvard had an enrollment of 361 students.

Sending a son to college was a sign of success and prosperity, but the building of an imposing mansion to replace the original log house on the plantation was even more an indication of wealth. The prevailing taste in architecture for these mansions was Greek Revival, which, though a national style between 1820 and 1860, flourished especially in the South.[41] The enthusiasm for Greek independence in the early part of the period; the emphasis on the classics in a gentleman's education; the fact that the Greek temple form was a symbol of Grecian democracy, which bore some resemblance to democracy in the slave states; and the adaptability of the high portico of the Greek temple to a warm climate combined to make the style popular in the Southern states. There were few professional architects in this region, but the planters used architectural books, particularly those of Asher Benjamin and Minard Lafever, to find classic designs for their houses, to be executed by carpenters. The planters and master builders adapted the outward forms of the buildings of Periclean Athens to the practical needs of the nineteenth century, so that, as Oliver Larkin has phrased it, "under their colonnades and pediments they had created something which the Greeks never knew."[42] The introduction of steam planing mills in key cities made possible the mass production of joiner's work with classic details. Doorways and windowframes, mantelpieces, sections of stairways, entablatures with dentils and modillions, and whole columns with carved capitals were manufactured by these mills and sold to the planters.

The Southern states developed what has been called the "plantation Greek" style, full of variations.[43] The most original and charming was

[41] Rexford Newcomb, *Architecture in Old Kentucky* (Urbana, 1953), and Talbot F. Hamlin, *Greek Revival Architecture in America* (New York, 1944); before the Greek Revival style became the vogue, the Regency or Federal style produced charming and dignified works, such as the City Hall and the Manigault house in Charleston, designed by Joseph Manigault, and residences in Savannah by William Jay.

[42] Oliver Larkin, *Art and Life in America* (New York, 1949), p. 166.

[43] See Joseph Frazer Smith, *White Pillars, Early Life and Architecture of the Lower Mississippi Valley* (New York, 1941).

the Louisiana Classic, which combined the classic design with traces of the old Creole building. In this style, the house was surrounded on all sides by a two-story piazza, supported by tall white pillars. French windows shaded by green blinds gave on to both floors of the porch, dormered windows opened from the roof, and often there was a cupola. Since the planters entertained often, some of the Louisiana estates had *garçonniers,* small classic buildings separate from the mansion, which provided quarters for the boys and girls and guests. In the James Galliers, father and son, Louisiana produced architects who were able to combine tastefully the classic with French colonial influences. The names of some of the most beautiful of these houses suggest aristocracy and romance: Shadows on the Teche; Asphodel; Woodlawn, home of the mighty Pughs; Houmas House, owned by the Hamptons of South Carolina and later by the great merchant John Burnside; Belle Grove, Rosedown, and Ellerslie.

A little later than the Greek Revival style came the vogue for the Gothic Revival. In the Virginia and Maryland tidewater still stood some of the Gothic buildings that had been built before the rise of the Georgian style, notably Bacon's Castle. During the last two decades of the ante-bellum period, the Gothic Revival constituted a minor trend in Southern architecture. The chief exponent of this style was John McMurtry, a Kentucky architect who had been taken to England by a wealthy iron foundryman of Lexington to study the homes of the English gentry, particularly those built in the Tudor style. Upon his return to Lexington he designed striking residences for two families that had made their wealth in commerce, Loudon (1849) and Ingleside (1852).[44] The most impressive monument of the Gothic Revival style was the abbey of the French Trappists in Nelson County, Kentucky, begun in 1851. Although Gothic was commonly used in the design of arsenals and prisons, the only state capitols built in this style during the ante-bellum period were at Baton Rouge and Milledgeville, Georgia. A striking Gothic Revival house was erected in Columbus, Mississippi, the Elias Fort House, with a portico of flattened Gothic arches supported by tall octagonal pillars. Another notable Gothic house was Afton Villa, home of the planter David Barrow in West Feliciana Par-

---

[44] Clay Lancaster, *Back Streets and Pine Trees; the Work of John McMurtry, Nineteenth Century Architect Builder of Kentucky* (Lexington, 1956).

ish, Louisiana, which, in addition to a Gothic façade, had an elaborately carved Gothic stairway.

Most of these fine mansions of the Gothic and Greek Revival styles were built in the 1840's and 1850's after the masters had acquired wealth from their exploitation of slave labor. A realistic student of Southern society has observed that they were frequently symbols of absenteeism. They were located usually in villages or towns, such as Natchez, which is today almost a museum of exquisite Greek Revival houses. In ante-bellum days these houses were occupied by planters and lawyers, who drank mint juleps and danced away the hours while their overseers managed the slaves on their outlying plantations. Classic houses in the country were relatively rare, except in favored regions like the Bluegrass sections of Kentucky and Tennessee, the black belt of Alabama, and the delta counties of Louisiana and Mississippi. Well-to-do planters often lived in plain farmhouses with no pretensions to architecture. Their houses had evolved from the double log cabin with its breezeway or "dog run," to which a porch in the back and the front had been added. An important influence in deterring planters and farmers from constructing more substantial and tasteful houses was their unsettled feeling; they were always ready to sell out and move. In the agricultural magazines and newspapers between 1830 and 1860, J. C. Bonner found, none of the editors or their contributors who wrote concerning rural architecture proposed "anything remotely resembling the Greek Parthenon"; instead they advocated the adoption of a practical, indigenous style.[45]

Many of the owners of imposing Greek Revival mansions had been born in log cabins or had come from humble parentage. One of the most beautiful homes of the upper South, Fairvue near Nashville, was built by the great slave trader Isaac Franklin. In 1832 he erected this mansion with profits from the sale of human flesh; his widow, the daughter of a Presbyterian minister, after remarrying built an even more magnificent house, Belmont, in Nashville. Andrew Jackson remodeled The Hermitage in 1831 with imposing Corinthian columns made of wood and a façade that concealed a tin-covered pitched roof. The hallway with its grand staircase was covered with wallpaper of classic motif, the search of Telemachus for Ulysses.

[45] J. C. Bonner, "Plantation Architecture of the Lower South on the Eve of the Civil War," *Journal of Southern History*, XI (1945), 370–388.

A surgeon in the Union army which invaded northern Virginia commented on the incongruity often to be found in imposing Southern mansions. "In this portion of Virginia," he wrote, "lived many of the old proud families of the state—the Weavers of Weaverville, the Schumates, a branch of the Washington family, etc. Folks say they were, however, 'on their last legs' as a rule, the young men dissipated and worthless, the elders incompetent. The houses, though often presenting a stately appearance at a distance, reveal poor taste and a total lack of finish on closer inspection. . . . It is in reality the same flash and love of show that one sees in many other places."[46] The ante-bellum traveler in the South noticed also that the spacious colonnaded porches were often cluttered with saddles and bridles, piles of loose cotton, agricultural implements, and a washstand, wash bowl, pitcher, towel, and wash bucket.

Although the plantation houses, on the whole, were wooden structures of unsophisticated style, many of them possessed the charm of fragrant gardens and splendid trees. Gunston Hall, George Mason's home in the Potomac Valley, had a garden bordered by ancient box bushes. When Sir Charles Augustus Murray, a grandson of Lord Dunmore, visited Brandon on the James River, he praised it for its magnificent elms and its beautifully laid-out lawn, whose design resembled that of English manors of the old time.[47] Traces of colonial formal gardens, with flower beds bordered with box, could be seen on old estates in the upper South, but the style of gardens changed in the nineteenth century to fit the romantic temper of the period. Instead of regular formal walks, flower beds of geometric design, clipped hedges, and the prim, highly civilized look of the eighteenth century, Southern gardens and landscapes of the ante-bellum period took on informality, expressed in serpentine walks, irregular grouping of trees, and romantic vistas. There were also small summerhouses shaped like Greek temples, embowered in trees, where one might read a Sir Walter Scott novel, idly watch the hummingbirds sipping nectar from flowers, or drink a mint julep and converse with visitors.

In 1857 De Puy Van Buren, a young tutor from the North, described the grounds of Oak Valley, home of the Barksdales in Yazoo

[46] Journal of Dr. Daniel G. Brinton, August, 1863. MS. owned by Professor Brinton Thompson of Trinity College.

[47] Charles Augustus Murray, *Travels in North America during the Years 1834, 1835, and 1836* (London, 1839), I, 406.

county, Mississippi, as follows: "In the front ground, you see magnificent China-trees. The orange myrtle, with its glossy green foliage, trimmed in the shape of a huge strawberry; the crape myrtle with its top hanging thick with long cone-shaped flowers of a peach-blow color; the cape jasmine, with its rich polished foliage spangled all over with white starry blossoms . . . and that richest and sweetest blossom of tropical shrubs—the japonica."[48] The Canadian traveler, William Kingsford, observed that some of the gardens in and around Natchez had shrubberies "cut into quaint figures as was the fashion of the last century."[49] In the deep South many of the plantations were approached through avenues of live-oak trees with gray Spanish moss hanging from them. The magnolia, with its large waxlike white blossoms and its intoxicating fragrance, became almost an emblem of Southernism.

Fredrika Bremer in 1850 visited Joel Poinsett on his South Carolina plantation Casa Bianca on the Pedee River and was charmed by the beauty of the grounds. She reported that Poinsett had planted his trees and shrubs according to the advice of Andrew Jackson Downing of Newburgh, New York, who in 1841 had published *A Treatise on the Theory and Practice of Landscape Gardening Applied to North America*. She heard Poinsett say, "Mr. Downing has done much for this country, so universal is the influence of Mr. Downing here in the improvement of taste, and the awakening of a sense of the beautiful, as regards buildings, the cultivation of gardens, and laying out of public grounds."[50] Poinsett embellished his estate with exotic trees and shrubs which he had imported from other parts of the world. From Mexico, where he was minister from 1825 to 1829, he introduced the poinsettia plant named after him. Miss Bremer was especially delighted with the "deliciously odoriferous *Olea fragrans* from Peru." Henry Clay also imported foreign trees and shrubs, particularly the Oriental gingko, a "living fossil" among trees, some of which still stand on the grounds of Ashland. Southern agricultural journals encouraged farmers to beautify their grounds with flowers and shrubs; especially notable were the writings of Charles Alfred Peabody, horticultural editor of *The Soil of the South*.

[48] Van Buren, *Jottings of a Year's Sojourn in the South*, pp. 133–134.
[49] William Kingsford, *Impressions of the West and South during a Six Weeks' Holiday* (Toronto, 1858), p. 46.
[50] Bremer, *Homes of the New World*, I, 286.

The Greek Revival mansion with its slave quarter was a symbol of the maturing of plantation society. It was a recent maturity, though, that beneath the surface contained elements of violence and crudity. The roads, for example, were so wretched as to lead travelers to marvel that the South had attained as high a culture as they saw. In contrast to the miserable state of the roads and to the dirty, uncomfortable inns, however, were the homes of the planters with their Greek Revival porticos, fragrant gardens, and gracious hosts. The image of these, preserved in romantic novels such as *Gone with the Wind,* still evokes feelings of nostalgia for a vanished way of life that seems to have been serener, more unhurried, and closer to nature than our own age. Actually the letters, diaries, and plantation records that have survived do not indicate that the occupants of those lovely old homes lived happier or more romantic lives than the people of our own time. They show rather a great concern for practical affairs, money, crops, weather, the management of labor, disease, debts, gossip, and petty frustrations interspersed with simple pleasures, camp meetings, courtship, love, children, visiting, and hunting and fishing. To a far greater degree than today, religion played a significant role in their lives, a faith that imposed on them an acceptance of the inscrutable ways of Providence. The serenity of the big mansion was in thousands of cases troubled by the infinite vexations of slavery. The great shadow on Southern lives, aside from personal sorrows and worries, was the approaching storm over slavery that, certainly after 1846, most thoughtful men foresaw.

CHAPTER 6

The Creole Civilization

ONE HAS only to read the diaries of two young Creoles of fashion, Lestant Prudhomme and Placide Bossier, to realize that the world of the Creoles in Louisiana was quite different from that of the Anglo-Americans. It was not simply because the Creoles spoke French and were Catholics, but the two groups were separated by different traditions and by a different sense of values. Although some Anglo-Americans, such as the Whig Senator Alexander Porter, Edward Livingston the great merchant, Maunsel White, and Judah P. Benjamin, married Creole women, the Creoles and the Anglo-Americans lived to themselves. The Prudhomme and Bossier diaries mirror a gay life of parties, hunting, fishing, dancing, serenades, and constant visiting. But seldom does an English name intrude in the pages of these Creole diaries; they tell of the belles of *la côte joyeuse* in the Red River Valley, of Odalie, Desirée, Julie, Celestine, Nizilda, and Attala, and of their carefree companions Achille, Narcisse, Felix, Hippolyte, Antoine, and Serdot.[1]

The Creoles occupied the lower part of Louisiana from Baton Rouge to the Gulf Coast; there were also oases of French-speaking natives in

[1] P. Lestant Prudhomme Diary, January 29, 1850–November 24, 1852, 3 vols., courtesy of the owner, Mrs. Irma Sompayrac Willard, and of Eugene P. Watson, Librarian of Northwestern State College of Louisiana, Natchitoches; Placide Bossier Diary, January 1 and February, 1861, owner, Miss Carmen Breazeale of Natchitoches, microfilms loaned by Northwestern State College of Louisiana.

eastern Missouri and in the area around Mobile, Alabama. The languorous climate of their home and the known willingness of Latin colonists to mingle their blood with other races might provide some basis for a popular picture of the Creoles as a mixture of French and Negro blood. Such a conception, however, was manifestly incorrect and was greatly resented by them. According to George Washington Cable, the New Orleans novelist, the term Creole applied only to the descendants of French and Spanish colonial stock of Louisiana who had no Negro blood in their veins.[2] A modern student, on the other hand, has concluded that the word was used in the early decades of the nineteenth century to designate a native of Louisiana regardless whether he was black or white or of mixed blood or of Spanish, French, or English stock.[3] In the later ante-bellum period, and in common usage, the term was applied chiefly to the French-speaking natives of Louisiana, Alabama, and Missouri.

Despite its outward charm, Louisiana was a land of many drawbacks and contrasts. The climate was exceedingly hot and humid; the average rainfall during the year was sixty inches as compared to forty-five or forty-six in the upper South. The lagoons and bayous produced a plague of mosquitoes. A French traveler to Louisiana in the summer of 1831, invited to dinner in a Creole home, was disturbed by movements and noises under the table. Thinking that they came from a dog prowling under the table, he kicked the moving object and discovered that he had hurt a little black boy who had been stationed under the table to chase away "mosquitoes from under the marbled petticoats of our hostess."[4] Moreover, the prevalence of malaria and the recurrent epidemics of yellow fever, cholera, and smallpox sapped the energy of the people and made life precarious. Tremendous effort, also, had to be exerted to keep the levees and dikes of the treacherous Mississippi standing firmly; even then, crevasses and floods during many months of the year imperiled the property and lives of the Creole country.

[2] George Washington Cable, *The Creoles of Louisiana* (New York, 1884). In his novels, particularly *Old Creole Days* (1879), Cable romanticized Creole civilization, yet he was bitterly attacked by Creole aristocrats for falsely portraying the Creoles by representing them as poor and ignorant.

[3] Joseph Tregle, Jr., "Early New Orleans Society: a Reappraisal," *Journal of Southern History*, XVIII (1952), 20–36.

[4] George J. Joyaux (ed.), "Forest's Voyage aux États-Unis de l'Amérique en 1831," *Louisiana Historical Quarterly*, XXXIX (1904), 465.

On the other hand, there were many advantages to living in this opulent land. The visitor in early spring was charmed by the bright flowers and semitropical vegetation; the orange, lemon, and banana trees; exotic birds, such as the parakeet and hummingbird; and the romantic vistas of lagoons and bayous bordered by magnificent live-oak and cypress trees. Gray Spanish moss hung in long festoons from the trees. For some visitors, such as actress Fanny Kemble, the sight of it produced feelings of melancholy and aversion, but to others the graceful drooping strands appeared romantic; to Thomas Rodney of Delaware they looked like a "Dunker's beard and makes the wood look very Venerable."[5] Certainly the Spanish moss softened the sleep of many a slave who used its pliant fibers for mattresses and to sell for pin money.

Travelers admired the vast fields of waving sugar cane which they saw from the Mississippi steamboats growing on plantations "level as a billiard table." Especially pleasing were the gardens of the sugar planters with their Cherokee rose hedges and flowers that did not grow in the North, such as oleanders, camellias, purple bougainvillea, tuberoses, the sweet-smelling cape jasmine, and pink crepe myrtle. After the heat of a summer day it was pleasant for a traveler to sit on the veranda of a planter's house and sip mint juleps (which were often served before breakfast) and engage in quiet conversation, watching the innumerable fireflies glow in the darkness and breathing the magnolia-scented air. William H. Russell, the London *Times* correspondent in America in 1861, enjoyed the utter silence and peacefulness of the planters' homes, interrupted only by the song of the mockingbird and the tolling of the plantation bell at noon and at sunset.

Indeed, Louisiana was a colorful part of the South, not only because of its sugar plantations and beautiful perfumed gardens, but because of the variety of its population. Dominant were the descendants of the early French settlers who founded New Orleans in 1718 and of the Spaniards who ruled Louisiana from 1766 to 1803. There were also descendants of the Germans who had settled on the "German Coast" of the Mississippi above New Orleans in the time of John Law. To the original French settlers, mostly humble people, including some prostitutes like "Manon Lescaut" and some virtuous "casket girls," there had

[5] Arthur P. Hudson, *Humor of the Old Deep South* (New York, 1936), p. 57.

been added several later infusions of French blood. In 1764, ten years after the expulsion of the Acadians from Canada, the first group of these French-speaking exiles arrived in Louisiana. They settled in the southwestern part of the colony around St. Martinville, along Bayou Teche and Lafourche. Mostly poor peasants, they were far different from the sentimental picture of them in Longfellow's *Evangeline*. Although some of them became substantial yeoman farmers, and one of their number, Alexander Mouton, became governor, these so-called Cajuns were looked down upon by the old French population. Preserving the dialect of Normandy, modified by the incorporation of English and Creole words, they formed as a whole an illiterate and unprosperous people comparable to the poor whites of the sandhills.[6] The Cajuns of southern Alabama continued in the twentieth century to be a backward people, characterized by xenophobia, resentful of any imputation that they had Negro blood in their veins, but admitting some admixture of Indian blood.[7]

Another important French element which joined the old population was the Santo Domingo planters. In 1791 the mulattoes of this island, influenced by the French Revolutionary movement, arose in revolt, stirred up the black slaves, and established a reign of terror in the island, during which many of the planters who survived fled to Charleston, Norfolk, and Louisiana, bringing their slaves with them. It is estimated that over ten thousand of these refugees entered the United States. Some of them were people of cultivation; they were responsible for starting the French theater in New Orleans. They also had an important part in establishing the sugar industry in Louisiana. Among the Santo Domingans were teachers of the French language, musicians, pastry makers, fencing masters, and wigmakers who contributed to the art of pleasant living in the South.[8] At the same time it is probably true that they increased the fear of servile insurrection wherever they settled.

The Revolutionary movement in France and the disturbances of the Napoleonic period resulted in a number of political exiles settling in Louisiana. These émigrés were usually much better educated and more

[6] See Arthur G. Doughty, *The Acadian Exiles* . . . (Toronto, 1916).

[7] Carl Carmer, *Stars Fell on Alabama* (New York, 1934), pp. 255–269.

[8] Howard Mumford Jones, *America and French Culture* (New York, 1927), p. 134.

sophisticated than the native population, and they regarded themselves as superior to the provincial Creole; one of these immigrant Frenchmen, Étienne Mazureau, was called "the eagle of the Louisiana bar." After the purchase of Louisiana by the United States these émigrés became formidable contenders for the political leadership of the territory and state.[9]

Besides the French element, there was a considerable contingent of the offspring of the Spanish settlers and the Islenos from the Canary Islands. A large number of Cubans and natives of the West Indies emigrated to Louisiana, particularly around the year 1810. Always the port of New Orleans was receiving numerous European immigrants, some of whom continued their journey up the Mississippi River, but others who remained to become citizens of the state. Cheap passage to New Orleans could be obtained on the cotton ships returning from Liverpool and Le Havre, which usually were in ballast. The census of 1860 reported 80,975 foreign-born persons in the state, constituting 22.6 per cent of the white population. Of this group the Irish ranked first in numbers, the Germans second, and the English third.

Nowhere in the world, perhaps, was there such a mixture of Negroes with other races and nationalities. On the streets of New Orleans one could see fair-skinned, blue-eyed octoroons, griffes, mulattoes, and particularly quadroons (three-fourths white). On Congo Square on Sundays some of the Negroes danced voodoo dances. The "Red Bones" of the Natchitoches area were a mixture of French, Indian, and Negro.

The Creole myth has exalted the French-speaking inhabitants of Louisiana as superior in culture to the Anglo-Americans, as aristocrats above the undignified pursuit of money. The Creole historian Charles Gayarré, Grace King, Lafcadio Hearn, and, in more recent times, Lyle Saxon, have portrayed the Creoles as a people who had learned the art of gracious living. The elite of their society had courtly manners and an Old World charm, but they were not the great patrons of art and culture which the Creole myth makes them out. Joseph Tregle, Jr., has removed much of the reputed glamour from this picturesque minority in the lower South. He has shown that it was the Anglo-

[9] Dunbar Rowland (ed.), *Official Letter Books of W. C. C. Claiborne* (Jackson, Miss., 1917), 6 vols.; Henry M. Brackenridge, *Views of Louisiana* (Baltimore, 1817); Vincent Nolte, *The Memoirs of Vincent Nolte, or Fifty Years in Both Hemispheres* (New York, 1934).

American element that supported the theater, education, newspapers, and libraries. The Creole women, on the other hand, had undoubted charm that impressed the travelers; Louis Tasistro, the actor, for example, commented that the perfection of female beauty and dress was to be seen oftener among the Creole circles of New Orleans than anywhere else in America. To see these captivating ladies with lustrous dark eyes and hair, he wrote, one should go to the French theater on opera nights.[10]

The Creoles, to a greater degree than the Anglo-Americans, lived a life of sensation and careless enjoyment. They loved to dance, gamble, fish, attend feasts, play on the fiddle and to live without much thought of the morrow. Often beautiful and vivacious when they were young, the Creole women became fat and domesticated early; most of them were completely lacking in intellectual qualities. The men, dressed in crude, ill-fitting pantaloons of blue cottonade, whiled away the hours smoking cigars, playing dominoes, and gossiping long over a glass of wine. The Creoles seldom joined the westward movement to better their condition or prospects in life. Consequently, as their sons grew up, they subdivided their farms into small acreages to accommodate the expansion of their families. On these diminutive farms they raised perique tobacco, rice, and small quantities of sugar cane for juice, using antique and inefficient plows. Their homes were cottages made of cypress logs, with steep roofs and galleries or verandas around them.[11]

These generalizations apply only to the lower and middle classes, for there were many refined and aristocratic Creole planters and professional men, such as Pierre Beauregard, Governor Roman, and the planter Valcour Aimé. A representative of the New Orleans *Crescent* wrote, in an account of his visit in 1860 to the sugar parish of St. James, that the planters almost to a man belonged to "the old Creole-gentleman type, who were hospitable, chivalrous, and high-spirited."[12]

After the United States' purchase of the colony in 1803, Americans flocked to this land of new opportunity. Previously, the French popula-

[10] Louis F. Tasistro, *Random Shots and Southern Breezes* (New York, 1929), Chap. VII.

[11] H. I. Priestly, *The Coming of the White Man, 1492–1848* (New York, 1929), Chap. VII.

[12] Pritchard (ed.), "A Tourist's Description of Louisiana in 1860," p. 1119; see also Grace King, *Creole Families of New Orleans* (New York, 1921).

tion had formed an unfavorable opinion of the Americans because they had seen chiefly the crude boatmen, "the half-horse, half-alligator" type, who had brought the produce of Kentucky, Tennessee, and the Ohio Valley to New Orleans in flatboats. After the purchase, a new American type appeared, planters seeking rich land; lawyers, doctors, professional men, and businessmen seeking money. These Americans were in general better educated than the French colonials, more enterprising, energetic, and resourceful.

Many of the newcomers were New Yorkers, businessmen and professional men. In 1860 5,538 New Yorkers lived in the state, while there were only 2,986 natives of Virginia. Among the Anglo-Americans who came to New Orleans with an urge to make profits was Simon Cameron, later to become a political boss in Pennsylvania and Lincoln's first Secretary of War. Cameron arrived in New Orleans in 1831 and was delighted with its balmy climate and hospitable people. He was quick to note that although New Orleans had an immense business of shipping and commerce, it was sadly lacking in manufacturing enterprises. To Governor J. A. Schulze of Pennsylvania, he wrote, "Everybody here makes money, at every business. . . . It would be a great place for a brewery—not one within 1,500 miles. A tallow chandler could make a fortune soon. Tallow 3½¢ a pound—candles 20¢. Everything is the same way. Raw materials very cheap—manufactures very high. The reason is that nobody likes to work. All depend upon the negroes."[13] Many lawyers emigrated to New Orleans, the most notable being Edward Livingston, the recently resigned mayor of New York, who arrived in 1804, and James Brown of Kentucky, Henry Clay's brother-in-law, who became attorney general of Louisiana and in 1812 United States senator.

With their close-knit family feeling and Catholic affiliation, the Creoles tended for many years to keep apart from the Americans. They spoke a different language, had a different religion, different customs, and a different philosophy of life. In contrast to the Anglo-Americans they had little conception of the value of time. In New Orleans they lived in a separate section called the Vieux Carré, which seemed to visitors like a foreign city. At the beginning of the War of 1812 the

13 Simon Cameron to Governor J. A. Schulze, November 28, 1821, Simon Cameron Papers, Historical Society of Pennsylvania.

Creoles displayed complete indifference to the American cause; it was difficult to raise troops among them. A young Harvard graduate, John Winship, who had come to New Orleans to practice law, observed that the Creoles were discontented with American rule and wished to be reunited with France. The French-speaking inhabitants voted as a national group, and even on jury service they displayed their national prejudice in favor of men of French descent. But in 1814 Governor Claiborne reported that public sentiment had changed in favor of loyalty to the United States, and many of the French inhabitants, including a Creole battalion of free Negroes, fought with Jackson to repel the English invasion.[14]

The legal system of the Creoles was another point of difference between the Anglo-Americans and the old inhabitants. It was based on the Roman law as codified by Napoleon—the Code Napoléon. In 1822, the legislature appointed three jurisconsults, headed by Edward Livingston, who had married a Creole and become one of the principal leaders of the Creole faction against the Americans, led by Governor Claiborne. The work of the jurisconsults resulted in the adoption in 1825 of the Civil Code and the Code of Practice in Civil Cases, as well as a commercial code. Approximately 80 per cent of their provisions were taken from the Code Napoléon and most of the remainder from commentaries of French jurists. The law of Louisiana, therefore, was different from that of any other state, representing as it did an amalgam of Roman and French and Spanish elements with the common law of England. In the courts and in the legislature, both French and English were used as official languages.[15]

The conflict between the Creoles and the Anglo-Americans was settled in favor of the Americans by the rapid spread of cotton and sugar culture. Until 1830, observers believed that the Creoles constituted the majority of the population. Between 1810 and 1820, the greatest increase of the population of Louisiana occurred, over 100 per cent. There was a let-up in immigration in the decade of the 1820's, but from 1830 to 1840 population increased again, over 63 per cent. The

---

[14] Rowland, *Letter Books of Claiborne*, VI, 285–289; Everett S. Brown (ed.), "Letters from Louisiana, 1813–1814," *Mississippi Valley Historical Review*, XI (1925), 560–579.

[15] William B. Hatcher, *Edward Livingston, Jeffersonian Republican and Jacksonian Democrat* (University, La., 1940), Chap. XI.

proportion of French-speaking Creoles to the other elements of the population can be roughly measured by the proportion of Catholics in the state, for the Creoles were stanchly Catholic. It is likely that the majority of the immigrants from Europe, notably the Irish, were Catholic too, but the French-speaking Creoles formed the bulk of the membership of the Catholic Church. The Census of 1850 reported that the Roman Catholic churches had accommodations for 37,780 persons out of a total of 109,615 accommodations for all denominations; that is, a little over one-third of the people presumably were Catholics. In 1860 the proportion estimated to be Catholic had declined to approximately one-fourth of the population.[16]

The distinctive crop of the Creole country in the nineteenth century was sugar cane. Small quantities of cane had been cultivated for syrup in the middle of the eighteenth century, but the money crop at that time was indigo. In the early 1790's, however, the ravages of insects and declining prices threatened to ruin the Creole indigo planters. Then, after the slave uprising in Santo Domingo in 1791, sugar planters from that island fled to Louisiana, stimulating an interest in the cultivation of sugar cane. In 1795 Étienne de Boré, a Creole planter who had been educated in France, experimented with raising sugar cane and granulating its syrup into sugar. He succeeded brilliantly in his pioneering attempt and sold his first crop for $12,000. In thus leading the way to economic revival he has rightly been called "the savior of Louisiana."

Growing sugar cane in Louisiana was somewhat hazardous; an early frost could ruin the crop. Consequently the parishes of the Sugar Bowl extended no farther north than Baton Rouge, a hundred miles from New Orleans. The planters waited to the last practicable moment in October before cutting the cane, so that it would be as fully matured as possible. In the West Indies, where there was no danger of frost, the cane did not require replanting for a dozen years, so it had time to mature fully. In Louisiana, on the other hand, for lucrative returns the cane had to be replanted every three years. Louisiana sugar could compete with the West Indies product only because of the protection of the American tariff and the remarkably fertile soil of the delta region. The introduction in 1817 of ribbon cane, which had a stronger

---

[16] J. D. B. De Bow, *The Seventh Census of the United States: 1850* (Washington, 1853), pp. 490–491.

resistance to cold weather, gave greater security to the Louisiana planters and enlarged the area of the sugar country.[17]

Sugar cane was ordinarily planted, not from seed, but by laying the stalks in furrows, six feet apart, and covering them with soil. From the joints of these stalks the new cane sprouted in early spring. By late summer the stalks had grown higher than a man's head. After the cane was cut in October it was transported to the sugar mill, where the juice was pressed out by machinery operated by steam engines or on small plantations by horse power. The grinding season, two months long, was a period of intense activity; the slaves often worked eighteen hours a day. During the early period of cane culture the syrup, tempered with lime to purify it, was boiled in open kettles. This inefficient method made the cost of fuel one of the large expenses on sugar plantations. Accordingly, during slack seasons, the Negroes were frequently employed in retrieving driftwood from the Mississippi River. In 1843 a brilliant Creole Negro, Norbert Rillieux, who had been educated in France, developed a process of boiling the cane juice in vacuum pans and using the vapor from one pan to heat another. Judah P. Benjamin was one of the earliest planters to introduce this process; by the eve of the Civil War it was being widely adopted. After the juice of the cane had been reduced to a thick syrup, it was poured into hogsheads of 1,100 pounds capacity, where it granulated; the part that did not granulate drained from the hogshead through cane stalks placed in holes in the bottom; this by-product formed molasses, and amounted to 600 gallons per hogshead of sugar.

Running a sugar plantation required much capital. Land for sugar raising cost twice as much as cotton land, partly because of the need of numerous ditches to drain the soil. A sugar mill with its steam engine was costly, too, involving a capital investment of $40,000 or more. Usually, planters had to employ a sugar maker, a skilled white man, to supervise the making of sugar during the grinding and boiling season. The planter often had to buy coal or cordwood to supplement his fuel supply of bagasse, that is, the dry pressed-out stalks of cane. His labor force had to be strong adult Negroes, who usually cost more than the land. Because of the need of capital and the limitations of the

---

[17] See J. Carlyle Sitterson, *Sugar Country, the Cane Sugar Industry in the South, 1753–1950* (Lexington, 1953), Chaps. II, VI.

climate, the number of sugar plantations was small, the highest being 1,536 in 1850; this number declined to 1,308 in 1860, partly because the small plantations using horse-power mills had been absorbed by the more efficient larger units. Because of the need for extensive capital to operate sugar plantations, 28 per cent in 1859 were owned by partnerships. Besides the production of the Louisiana plantations, an average of 300,000 hogsheads of sugar annually during the decade of the 1850's, Texas produced approximately 8,000 and Georgia around 1,000 hogsheads a year. Nevertheless, the Southern states provided less than half of the sugar consumed in the United States. Louisiana sugar was sold largely in the Western states. Only 20 to 25 per cent was disposed of in the East.

Solon Robinson has left in his journal accurate descriptions of some of the great sugar plantations that he visited during an agricultural tour in 1849. One of the largest was the Houmas estate, which had originally been purchased by Wade Hampton of South Carolina in 1811, but at the time of Robinson's visit was managed by John S. Preston, son-in-law of Wade Hampton II.[18] It consisted of 2,000 arpents of land (an arpent being one-seventh less than an acre). The labor force on the three plantations into which it was divided was 750 slaves, of whom over half were field hands. Each adult slave normally cultivated nine or ten acres of sugar cane, which yielded usually a hogshead or a hogshead and a half per acre.

Houmas Plantation was sold in 1857 to John Burnside, an immigrant from North Ireland who had made a fortune as a merchant in New Orleans. He acquired five plantations, valued at $1,750,000, and 937 slaves, valued at $500,000; these constituted the largest holding in sugar land in the South. His sugar production annually exceeded 3,000 hogsheads, together with a vast quantity of molasses. Sugar sold for five or six cents a pound during the last decades of the ante-bellum period. The Negroes on the Burnside plantations received five pounds of pork a week, as much Indian cornbread as they could eat, with a portion of molasses, and occasionally fish for breakfast, and were allowed to raise poultry and cultivate garden patches. The children seemed to be happy and healthy; they increased by about 5 per cent each year.[19]

Robinson also described in detail Madewood, near Napoleonville,

[18] Kellar, *Solon Robinson*, II, 166, 179.
[19] Russell, *My Diary North and South*, pp. 257–259.

the plantation of Thomas Pugh, one of the most successful of the sugar planters. The Pugh brothers moved in 1820 from North Carolina, where the soil of their plantations was exhausted, to southern Louisiana. Here they continually bought land and Negroes by borrowing money. By 1849 Thomas Pugh had accumulated 3,000 arpents of rich land and over 250 slaves. Each of his field hands produced about seven hogsheads of sugar. To his adult slaves he issued five and one-fourth pounds of pork a week and one and a half pecks of cornmeal as well as fresh vegetables. He raised a sufficient supply of corn for the plantation needs, but he bought his meat supplies. To take care of the health of the slaves, he paid a physician a fixed sum of $1.75 per slave for the year. His overseer, who was a Yankee, received a salary of $1,200 a year and living expenses. He also hired an engineer to operate his sugar house and a sawmill. His taxes were $2,000 a year on an assessed value of land and slaves of $206,265. His profits were considerable, for his sugar crop sold for $30,000 to $40,000.

Although there were great fluctuations in the price of sugar and numerous hazards, the cultivation of sugar cane was a profitable enterprise for many planters. One of the unsuccessful planters, however, was Bishop Leonidas Polk of the Episcopal Church. A native of North Carolina and a graduate of West Point, Polk had first settled in Maury County, Tennessee, where he managed a cotton plantation and served as a clergyman. After being appointed bishop of Louisiana, in 1841 he purchased a plantation on the Bayou La Fourche, to which he transported the 400 slaves which he and his wife owned. His plantation, Leighton, represented a large investment. He had superior sugar-making equipment, valued at $75,000, housed in a building 290 feet long. In good years his plantation produced five hundred hogsheads of sugar, bringing in an income of $27,500; his expenses amounted to approximately $10,000. Of the 2,500 arpents of land in his plantation, about a thousand were in cultivation. Polk was described by Solon Robinson as an "improving planter" who believed in good tillage and in manuring his fields. Although he bought his meat supplies for his slaves, he raised all the corn and hay needed for the plantation.[20]

Polk treated his slaves with paternal kindness. He fed them well, giving each adult slave a ration of four pounds of meat a week. Every

[20] Kellar, *Solon Robinson,* II, 201–204.

family had a chicken house and a garden. There was a nursery for the children and a hospital for the sick; Mrs. Polk personally attended to the welfare of sick slaves. In addition to the long Christmas holiday the master gave others to the slaves on church festivals. He paid a clergyman $300 annually to preach to them, and himself often read the Bible to them and prayed with them.

At Leighton the Polk family lived an idyllic life for a few years. A visitor in 1850, Mrs. Hilliard of Arkansas, was greatly impressed with the refinement and comfort in the life of the family. Mrs. Polk, she wrote, had a faithful Negro nurse, "to whose care she abandons her babes entirely. Only when she has a fancy to caress them does she see them. Eight children and cannot lay to their charge the loss of a single night's sleep." Also she had a housekeeper, "who gives out, regulates, and is everything she ought to be." An Irish woman trained in music served as a governess for the older daughters. Mrs. Hilliard was charmed by the Bishop's extensive and rare library. "I could linger forever," she wrote, "over the Books of prints collected in Italy." The garden also was charming with its orange trees, "pyramids of picayune roses," and other fragrant flowers.[21]

Yet this Southern idyll came to an end in 1854 when the Bishop was forced to surrender Leighton and its slaves to his creditors. Possibly he had been too indulgent a master. He would allow no work on the plantation on Sundays even during the critical grinding season. Sugar planting, especially at the time of sugar making, required the presence of the master, but Polk was frequently absent on his episcopal duties. He was a generous and noble man who gave freely of his time to serve humanity and refused to take a salary for his work as bishop. But he had bad luck, for in 1849 he lost seventy of his valuable slaves during a cholera epidemic. In the following year a severe storm damaged his plantation to the amount of $100,000 loss. Confronted by these misfortunes, he had to sell the plantation and move to New Orleans.[22]

The story of the expansion of sugar and cotton culture in Louisiana after the coming of the Americans is largely the story of enterprising

[21] Mrs. Isaac H. Hilliard Diary, 1849–1850, typed copy, Department of Archives, Louisiana State University.

[22] William M. Polk, *Leonidas Polk, Bishop and General* (New York, 1915); Vera L. Dugas, "The Ante-Bellum Career of Leonidas Polk," M.A. Thesis, Louisiana State University, 1943, Chapter V.

men, who had moved in from other states and had made fortunes in planting. Such was the career of Claudius Le Grand, who sold his plantation in Maryland in 1836 and emigrated to the delta country of Louisiana, where he established a cotton plantation. Although there were some fine houses in this region, he noted that it was no uncommon thing to see a planter who raised from 600 to 1,000 bales of cotton live in a house so open that he could not keep a dog out by shutting the door. "They laugh if you say anything about the uncomfortable way in which they live," he wrote, "and point with pride to the fields which bring them in this yearly fortune." He reported that one of his crops of cotton was worth the entire sum he had received from the sale of Portland Manor in Maryland. He treated his slaves well and observed that they were hearty and much pleased with their situation. He gave them the privilege of chopping wood from the plantation and selling it to the passing steamboats (for $3 a cord). He permitted his body servant, John, to follow his inclination and work at a hotel in Vicksburg, refunding to his owner $25 a month and receiving a considerable sum for his own use.

At this time credit was easy in the Southwest. Colonel Le Grand observed that it was easier to get a loan of $20,000 to $30,000 without any security but one's word than to borrow $5,000 on a mortgage on the best property in Maryland from the "cold-hearted" Marylanders. The Le Grands lived with considerable luxury and refinement. Their daughter, Julia, became one of the South's most charming ladies, a writer and intellectual. But after the death of the master the Le Grand fortune was lost, and Julia and her sister supported themselves by establishing a "select school" for young ladies in New Orleans.[23]

The Creoles and American farmers in the prairie region of Attakapas and Opelousas raised cotton and entertained themselves by all-night dancing at weekly balls. The Creole girls would arrive at the small villages in *calèches* made entirely of wood, the wheels having no tires. The young men, instead of working, hunted and frequented taverns where they dissipated their lives in drinking and gambling. Judge Thomas C. Nicholls, whose family was among the earlier American settlers in this region, described how he was led into habits of intemperance as a young lawyer at Opelousas because of a lack of employ-

[23] Lyle Saxon, *Old Louisiana* (New York, 1929), Chap. XII.

ment and "the taunts, gibes and entreaties of my dissolute companions."[24]

The diary of a young Creole of fashion who lived on a cotton plantation in the Cane River Valley, fifteen miles from Natchitoches, reveals how enervating life on a slave plantation could be to the sons of the planter. Lestant Prudhomme was twenty-two years old in 1850; he had finished his career at college in New Orleans and had come home to live on his father's plantation and study law. His record of his daily routine shows that he spent his time largely in a round of pleasures—simple pleasures as a whole—visiting his numerous relatives; playing cards; hunting snipe, bullfrogs, and deer; fishing; feasting on good food. The chief excitement of the day came when the steamship stopped at the landing, or when he went to Natchitoches to attend a dance or mass, to visit his cousins in the convent school, or to see a circus. Occasionally, there were minor misfortunes, such as when the cotton crop had to be replanted, or when he was sick with breakbone fever, or when he bruised his hand and sprained a thumb in whipping a slave.

He seems to have had little ambition or to have been much concerned with the affairs of the outside world. He began his diary on January 29, 1850, on the day that he commenced to read Blackstone. He had intended to begin his study of the law the day before, but was diverted by vast flocks of wild pigeons passing over, and he must go out to shoot them. Later, beautiful and demonstrative girls, billiards, cards, dances, and dinners lured him constantly from his studies. Nevertheless, he rode at intervals into Natchitoches and took an oral examination on what he had read.

He had a bodyservant whom he scarcely mentions; indeed, his diary contains few references to slavery. One April morning he visited his old nurse, who had been freed by his grandfather, and later he sent her some delicacies. When the overseer became sick, he gave out rations to the slaves and weighed the cotton of each picker at the end of the day. He seems to have had no class feeling in regard to overseers, for his journal mentions supping with the overseer, going fishing with him, and even attending a wedding in the company of two overseers; the guests danced all night to a fiddle played by a Negro boy.

[24] *Ibid.,* p. 119.

His diary reveals the indifference of the Creoles to public education. Lestant records that Mr. Harris, the common schoolteacher of the neighborhood, had received no pay for his trouble, and that he had become a victim of malaria and was so destitute that he was a subject for charity. Yet aristocrats like the Prudhommes did not neglect the education of their children; a brother of Lestant was sent to the Western Military Institute in Kentucky and an English governess was employed for the younger children, while his cousins attended the convent school in Natchitoches. Lestant and some of the younger Creoles thought that the American system of raising children was better than the Creole way, for he commented that sending young girls to the convent school was a cruel and unnatural separation of children from their families.

Lestant seems to have been morally an exemplary young man, dutiful to his parents, often assisting at Mass. His mind was almost completely orthodox; he was a strong believer in property and the natural inequality of man; an admirer of Clay and Webster, he rejoiced when the Compromise of 1850 was adopted. Despite his gay flirtations and his many praises of the Creole maidens, he never married; and his study of Blackstone seems to have been fruitless, for he never practiced law. Outstanding in his diary, however, are the revelations of warm family feeling among the Prudhommes and their numerous kin.

Ten years after Lestant began the study of law while the wild pigeons were flying, another young law student of the Natchitoches area, Placide Bossier, kept a brief diary. Like Lestant he found the study of Blackstone so tedious that he would doze away in a rocking chair. His mind was centered upon gay parties, playing billiards and euchre, enjoying oyster suppers, and hunting ducks on the lake. Though he delighted in visiting many young ladies and singing with them, he was madly in love with one. His young manhood was spent in a different period from that of Lestant; the shadows of the approaching war fell upon him, for he drilled with a cavalry company. Lestant had been a Unionist, but on January 7, 1861, Placide voted for the independence of Louisiana.[25]

The Louisiana planters varied widely in culture and background.

[25] Both the Prudhomme and Bossier diaries were written in English; the Prudhomme diary, according to its present owner, was corrected by the governess of the younger children of the family.

Frederick Law Olmsted (1822-1903), critic of the Old South and pioneer landscape gardener. Portrait at Biltmore Estate, N.C., by John S. Sargent. (*Photo by
Neune Glenn, Jr.*)

2. Carter's Grove, near Williamsburg; a Georgian house where young Jefferson courted Rebecca Burwell—unsuccessfully. *(Courtesy, Library of Congress)*

VIRGINIA SPLENDOR

3. Bremo, Piedmont, Virginia (1815-1819), designed partly by Jefferson; home of the Southern reformer John Hartwell Cocke. *(Courtesy, Library of Congress)*

4. Nathaniel Macon of North Carolina, Speaker of the House of Representatives, 1801-1807. Painting in Speaker's Lobby, U.S. Capitol, by Robert David Gauley

COUNTRY GENTLEMEN

5. Joel R. Poinsett of South Carolina (1779-1851). (*Courtesy, Library of Congress*)

6. Edmund Ruffin (1794-1865), Virginia agricultural reformer and secessionist. (*Courtesy, Alderman Library, University of Virginia*)

7. Cotton picking on a Southern plantation. (*Courtesy, Library of Congress*)

8. Salon mantel, Belnemus, Powhatan County, Virginia, eighteenth century.

(*Courtesy, Library of Congress*)

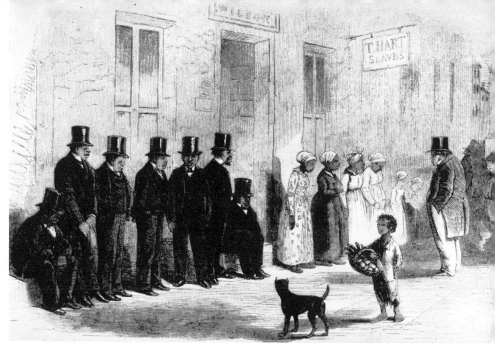

9.   Slaves for sale on a street in New Orleans, as drawn for *Harper's Weekly*.

10.   A slave auction as sketched by Theodore R. Davis for *Harper's Weekly*.

11. Thomas Roderick Dew (1802-1846), president of William and Mary College and pioneer pro-slavery writer. Painting attributed to G.P.A. Healy, at William and Mary College (*Frick Art Reference Library*)

12. William H. McGuffey, textbook writer, professor of moral philosophy and leader of the movement to Christianize Jefferson's university from 1845 to 1873 (*Courtesy, Alderman Library, University of Virginia*)

PROFESSORS OF THE OLD SOUTH

13. Francis Lieber, professor of history and political economy, South Carolina College, from 1835 to 1856. (*Courtesy, South Caroliniana Library*)

14. Beverley Tucker (1784-1851), professor of law at William and Mary College, romantic novelist and early secessionist (*Courtesy, Alderman Library, University of Virginia*)

15.   Ante-bellum public market.

Congregation Beth Elohin
).

17.   City Hall, designed by Joseph
Manigault.

18. Double log house with breezeway in Alabama. (*Courtesy, Library of Congress*

HOMES OF THE YEOMAN FARMER AND OF THE WEALTHY PLANTER

19. Belle Helene, Ascension Parish, La., home of Duncan Kenner, sugar planter and Confederate diplomat. (*Courtesy, Library of Congress*)

20. A rice field in the South.   (*Courtesy, Library of Congress*)

STAPLE CROPS OF THE OLD SOUTH

21. The sugar harvest in Louisiana.   (*Courtesy, Library of Congress*)

22. Judah Touro (1775-1854), merchant and philanthropist of New Orleans. Redwood Library and Athenaeum, Newport, R.I. (*Frick Art Reference Library*)

23. Leonidas Polk (1806-1864), Bishop of Louisiana and Confederate Lieutenant General. (*Courtesy, Library of Congress*)

EXTRAORDINARY SOUTHERNERS

24. William Gilmore Simms (1806-1870), writer, planter and devoted Southerner. (*Courtesy, South Caroliniana Library*)

25. George D. Prentice (1802-1870), Connecticut Yankee, first biographer of Henry Clay, editor of the Louisville *Journal*, Unionist. Louisville Free Public Library. (*Frick Art Reference Library*)

26. Shadows on the Teche, New Iberia, La.

THE GREEK
REVIVAL STYLE
(Courtesy, Library of Congress)

27. Melrose Plantation, near Natchitoches, La., home of a Mulatto planter.

28. Dunleith, Natchez, Mississippi.

29. Sherwood Forest in Tidewater, Virginia, John Tyler's last home.

HOMES OF THE UPPER SOUTH
(Courtesy, Library of Congress)

30. The Grange, Bourbon County, Kentucky, home of a slave trader killed by h
slaves.

31. Cottage on Pauger Street.

NEW ORLEANS
ANTE-BELLUM HOMES
(Courtesy, Library of Congress)

32. Dr. Lemonnier's house,
Royal Street.

33. Cottage on Bourbon Street.

34. An ante-bellum rice mill in Charleston. (*Courtesy, The News and Courier*)

35. William Gregg's cotton factory at Graniteville, S.C. (*DeBow's Review*)

36. Montgomery, Alabama, in 1861. *(Harper's Weekly)*

37. The *J. M. White,* fastest boat on the Mississippi. In 1844 this ship ran from New Orleans to St. Louis in three days and twenty-three hours. *(Courtesy, E. G. Sulzer, University of Kentucky)*

38. Colonel Richard M. Johnson (1781-1850), of Kentucky, Vice-President in the Van Buren administration, and reputed slayer of Tecumseh.
Painting by John Neagle, (*Courtesy, The Corcoran Gallery of Art*)

39. Henry Clay (1777-1852), hemp planter, advocate of gradual emancipation of the slaves, Union leader in the Senate.
Portrait by James Reid Lambdin, Huntington Library

STATESMEN OF THE UPPER AND LOWER SOUTH

40. John C. Calhoun (1782-1850) as a young man, then an American nationalist.
Portrait by John Wesley Jarvis (*Courtesy of Yale University Art Gallery*)

41. James H. Hammond (1807-1864) notable South Carolina planter and sectional leader.
(*Courtesy, South Caroliniana Library*)

There were, for example, a number of free Negro planters like Alexander Durnford, who owned the plantation Sainte Rosalie in Plaquemines Parish. Durnford formed a strong friendship with the New Orleans merchant John McDonogh, whose plantation apparently adjoined his. In the McDonogh correspondence are letters from Durnford which show that the possession of economic power by Negroes tended to break down some of the race barriers between colored and white men. The colored planter and the white capitalist exchanged gifts and rendered mutual services. McDonogh gave the Negro planter a gold watch, and the latter endorsed notes for McDonogh to the amount of $26,666. On one occasion in 1844, Durnford sent fifty-two of his slaves to McDonogh's plantation to plant five and a half acres of cane.[26] Durnford was only an outstanding example of the Negro Creole planters, many of whom lived on Cane River, a tributary of the Red River. Some were well educated, lived in handsome houses, employed tutors, spoke both French and English, and were respected for paying their debts and living sober and respectable lives. They were reserved in demeanor, and seldom associated with the whites.[27]

One of the highly cultivated Anglo-American planters was Samuel Walker, who named his plantation Elia because of his fondness for the writings of Charles Lamb. Here he lived in style, sending his children off to good schools rather than employing a tutor. In his diary he wrote that he had an ideal Negro woman to preside over the plantation nursery, which contained twenty little blacks. She had a mild, gentle voice and was never out of humor. Walker's benevolent attitude toward his slaves was expressed in a notation in his diary, "Let the Southern gentleman stay at home and treat his slaves well."[28] Walker read widely in the British reviews and in such works as those of John Selden and Jeremy Taylor. He had a critical attitude toward religion, a low opinion of Southern politicians, and a strong prejudice against Yankees. His wealth and assured social position as a large planter tended to deprive him of driving energy and ambition. In 1856 he was engaged in writing a novelette, but there was little likelihood of

[26] Alexander Durnford to John McDonogh, letters, 1842–44, John McDonogh Papers, Tulane University Library.

[27] Olmsted, *Seaboard Slave States,* pp. 633–634.

[28] Samuel Walker, "Diary of a Louisiana Planter—Elia Plantation," Feb. 10–March 11, 1856, Tulane University Library.

his enduring the drudgery of finishing and revising it, for he confessed that his besetting sin was "literary idleness"—he was a dreamer—he did not complete literary projects, because there was no necessity for it.

The sugar planters, whose sugar houses appeared almost like factories, were engaged in a capitalistic enterprise. Consequently they were inclined to be conservative men, members of the Whig party and supporters of a protective tariff and federal aid for internal improvements. Despite their wealth many of the sugar planters lived in unpretentious frame houses. Charles Daubeny of Oxford University, who visited Judge Alexander Porter on his plantation on Bayou Teche in 1838, wrote that it was rare "for the planters to aspire to anything beyond a cottage on their country estates."[29] He frequently saw "mean dwelling houses" on the borders of the Mississippi River connected with large Negro quarters and expensive sugar houses. Judge Porter had left northern Ireland as a penniless young man and had acquired a plantation of over 2,000 acres, 160 slaves, and a fine library. Like Judge Porter, the McCollam brothers, who had emigrated from New York to Louisiana, were relatively poor men who became large planters. They borrowed money to buy slaves and land, frequently at 8 per cent interest, and became rich.[30] Indeed, mortgages and loans were common in the lives of the sugar planters, for the risks were great; several bad crops, cholera among the slaves, floods and crevasses, fluctuations in the price of sugar, would bring bankruptcy.[31]

The stereotype of ante-bellum Louisiana portrays it as a land predominantly of large landowners, but this image is far from the truth. In 1860 approximately two-thirds of the agricultural property in the state were farms containing less than one hundred acres. In the Sugar

[29] Wendell H. Stephenson, *Alexander Porter, Whig Planter of the Old Louisiana* (Baton Rouge, 1934), p. 121.

[30] J. Carlyle Sitterson, "The McCollams: a Planter Family of the Old South," *Journal of Southern History*, VI (1940), 347–367.

[31] J. Carlyle Sitterson, "The William J. Minor Plantations: a Study in Ante-Bellum Absentee Ownership," *ibid.*, IX (1943), 59–74; "Magnolia Plantation 1852–1862; a Decade of a Louisiana Sugar Estate," *Mississippi Valley Historical Review*, XXV (1939), 197–211; "Lewis Thompson, a Carolinian and his Louisiana Plantation 1848–1888, a Study in Absentee Ownership," in Fletcher M. Green (ed.), *Essays in Southern History* (Chapel Hill, 1949), pp. 16–27; P. S. Postell, "John Hampden Randolph, a Louisiana Planter," *Louisiana Historical Quarterly*, XXV (1942), 140–223.

Bowl three-fourths of the agriculturalists were small farmers. Louisiana contained a vast amount of unimproved land; out of a total acreage of 26,461,440, only 2,707,108 were cultivated, but most of the arable land in the delta was cultivated and purchased at a high price. The value of land in the sugar parishes increased 93 per cent during the last decade of the ante-bellum period, while the production of sugar increased only about 21 per cent. Louisiana had a relatively large proportion of land devoted to livestock grazing, chiefly the prairie country of the southwest and the pine-belt district, where the owners of slaves were few in number. Between 1850 and 1860 the relative number of landowners increased in Louisiana, as in the other Southern states, so that in the latter year over 80 per cent of the agricultural operators in the southern alluvial district of Louisiana, the sugar parishes, owned their lands; while in sample counties of the northern alluvial districts, the cotton-producing area, 92 per cent owned their lands. In the oak uplands of Louisiana only 68 per cent of the agricultural operators owned their farms in 1850, but ten years later between 70 and 80 per cent had become landowners.[32]

Of the white population of Louisiana, 357,629 people in 1860, approximately 45 per cent lived in New Orleans and its suburb across the river, Algiers. The city was divided into three municipalities, the First, where the French-speaking Creoles lived; the Second, which was divided from the French quarter by Canal Street, where the Anglo-Americans dwelt; and the Third, inhabited by the Spanish and West Indian group. The divisions had been made in 1836 because the Creoles usually elected a majority of the council and the English-speaking group resented this control.[33] By this arrangement there was a common mayor, but each of the municipalities elected its own council and controlled its own affairs. Since this system resulted in extravagance and corruption, it was abolished in 1852 and a central government was adopted. New Orleans was the capital of the state until 1844, when the state government was moved to Baton Rouge.

New Orleans impressed travelers as a French city in America. Its

[32] See H. L. Coles, "Some Notes on Slave Ownership and Land Ownership in Louisiana, 1850–1860," *Journal of Southern History,* IX (1943), 380–394, and F. L. Owsley, *Plain Folk of the Old South* (Baton Rouge, 1949), pp. 549–561, 167–170, 205–209.

[33] William W. Howe, "Municipal History of New Orleans," in *Johns Hopkins Studies in Historical and Political Science* (Baltimore, 1889), VII.

architecture, however, was Spanish, for disastrous fires in 1788 and 1794 had swept a large part of the old French city away. Some of the public buildings, notably the Cabildo (the municipal building), and St. Louis Cathedral on the Place d'Armes (now Jackson Square), were rebuilt through the generosity of Don Andreas Almonaster y Roxas, a wealthy Spanish citizen. The shops and houses, with their stucco walls painted every pastel shade, patios, and the lacelike iron grillework of their porticoes and balustrades, preserved an Old World flavor. Patios, gay with semitropical flowers and plants, provided a touch of nature in the crowded city.

The great sight in New Orleans was the levee, a broad dike of earth along the Mississippi River where the ships docked. Here at the river bank were moored hundreds of flatboats, bringing the produce of the upper Mississippi and Ohio valleys—hams, whisky, flour, tobacco, butter, skins, hemp, etc. For four miles along the levee ships of all kinds were docked, often in five or six tiers. The number of steamboats that arrived in New Orleans in 1860 was 3,566. Because of the lack of proper warehouses, the levees for many years were crowded with the miscellaneous produce of the upper Mississippi Valley and with thousands of hogsheads of sugar and bales of cotton. At the close of the ante-bellum period, however, cotton bales overwhelmingly dominated the scene. The city's commerce grew astonishingly despite the serious drawbacks of its port. The city lay seventy-five miles from the multiple mouth of the Mississippi. The great river washed tons of soil into the Gulf, making a formidable bar across the principal channel, so that by 1830 the largest cargo ships could not reach the city. Moreover, after the completion of the Erie Canal in 1825, much of the produce of the Middle West was diverted from the Southern port.[34]

New Orleans was regarded by many of the visitors as "the Southern Babylon." One of the reasons for this reputation was the Creoles' conception of Sunday. After attending Mass in the morning they regarded the rest of the day as a holiday. When young Henry Benjamin Whipple, the future bishop of Minnesota, visited New Orleans in the spring of 1844, he was shocked by the worldly manner in which the Sabbath was

[34] Harold Sinclair, *The Port of New Orleans* (Garden City, 1942), Chaps. 11, 13; Wendell H. Stephenson, "Ante-Bellum New Orleans as an Agricultural Focus," *Agricultural History*, XV (1941), 161.

kept. His catalogue of the violations of the sacred day on Sunday, March 24, will serve as a list of amusements enjoyed by the citizens:

1st, three companies of military were out parading the streets and destroying the solemnity of the day by their music and show. 2nd, Horse race of seven horses and this attracted many. 3rd, a duel with small swords between a Mr. Richardson & Dubeyes. 4th, a match fist fight for a $300 bet between two boxers. 5th, A cock fight opposite the St. Louis. 6th, Masquerade ball at the Orleans ball room. 7th, Two theatres open. 8th, French opera ballet dancers. 9th, two circuses. 10th, Exhibition of wax works, etc. 11th, German magician. 12th, Organ grinders playing in the corners of the streets. 13th, Stores, grog shops open. 14th, Ten pin alleys, billiard rooms, & other gambling amusements. 15th, Several parties of pleasure to the lake, Carrollton, etc. 16th, Italian Fantoccini. 17th, Kentucky minstrels. 18th, Ordinary ball. 19th, Dinner parties. 20th, Rides on horseback, in carriages, etc., besides one or two lectures on subjects of such a nature as would be only made on a week day at the North.[35]

The highest point in revelry in New Orleans was reached in March just before Lent began, when the Mardi Gras festival with its street processions and masquerade balls was held, but this did not begin as an organized institution until about 1837.

Another feature of New Orleans life that served to blacken its reputation was the institution of quadroon mistresses. Harriet Martineau showed great curiosity in ferreting out and exposing this institution, which was chiefly confined to the French-speaking population. A businesslike arrangement would be made between the mother of the quadroon girl and the white suitor. The mother would inquire into his financial resources; if they were sufficient, provision would be made for supporting the quadroon mistress in proper style and, if the liaison should be broken, for providing a proper sum for support of the mistress and the children. James Davidson, a young Virginia traveler, reported that to maintain such a mistress cost from $1,500 to $2,000 a year, a sum that only the wealthy could afford.[36] Olmsted described the quadroons as practically a separate class of people, "far above the negroes and will not associate with them."[37]

[35] L. B. Shippee (ed.), *Bishop Whipple's Southern Diary 1843–1844* (Minneapolis, 1937), p. 119.
[36] Kellar, "Diary of James Davidson," pp. 358, 361.
[37] Olmsted, *Seaboard Slave States,* II, 243–248.

The quadroon balls were also a New Orleans feature, and much glamour has been falsely attributed to these masquerades. No Negro men were allowed to enter the ballroom, and the white men were searched for weapons before being admitted. Although some of the quadroon girls were refined and dressed with taste, and a few were educated in France, many were crude and promiscuously licentious. Davidson in 1836 saw two females promenading in their nightclothes at one of the balls. An Ohio merchant who visited New Orleans four years later noted that the most beautiful of the quadroon girls did not wear masks, for their charms were for sale, and that there were no virtuous women at these balls.[38]

The two centers of Creole social life in the gay metropolis were the French Opera and the St. Louis Hotel. The French Opera was built in 1816, an elaborate structure in classic style with parquet, two tiers of boxes, a gallery, and even grilled loges on the side for those in mourning. It was looked upon as the center of Creole social life, not to have a subscription being tantamont to being outside the pale of society. Patrons wore full formal evening dress. So popular were operas such as Meyerbeer's *Les Huguenots* and *Robert le Diable* that it was virtually impossible to buy seats.[39] In 1823 James H. Caldwell, an English actor, built the New American Theater in the American quarter of the city, which became a great success and a rival of the French Opera. The rivalry of the Creole and the English-speaking population was exhibited also in the hotel life of the city. The Creole St. Louis Hotel was a huge, ornate structure, where elaborate society balls were held; it contained gambling rooms and the finest bar in the city. In its rotunda slaves were auctioned and business was transacted. The chief hotel patronized by the English-speaking people, on the other hand, was the St. Charles, a building in the classic revival style, where the wives and daughters of the planters displayed the elaborate dresses and jewelry that advertised the wealth of their husbands.[40]

New Orleans had a kaleidoscopic population, with more transients

[38] William Reynolds, Journal of a Trip from Steubenville Ohio to New Orleans by Flatboat, September 5, 1839–March 4, 1840.

[39] [William H. Coleman], *Historical Sketch Book and Guide to New Orleans and Environs* (New York, 1885), pp. 136–138, 71–78, and Saxon, *Fabulous New Orleans*, pp. 280–281.

[40] See Matilda C. F. Houston, *Texas and the Gulf of Mexico, or Yachting in the New World* (Philadelphia, 1845), pp. 63–64, 83–84.

than any other city, at least one-third of the people leaving the city
during the summer. Being an immigrant port, the city had a plentiful
supply of cheap white labor. Irishmen and Germans took the place of
the Negroes in many occupations. Most of the cabmen were Irishmen
and the best hotels both in New Orleans and in Mobile used mainly
Irish labor. Indeed, New Orleans lost a considerable proportion of its
slaves during the decade 1850–60, a loss of 3,626, or over one-fifth of
its number. Also a large proportion of the Negroes in the city were
free, approximately 45 per cent. In New Orleans both the slaves and
the free Negroes seemed to have enjoyed a freer life than elsewhere in
the South.[41]

The Creole civilization was not confined to Louisiana; sporadic
islands of French influence existed in the Mobile area and in Missouri.
Whipple described Mobile in 1844 as a town of "about 15,000 inhabitants in the winter and 2,500 in the summer." A large part of its population was of French and Spanish descent, many of its streets had
French names, and the architecture of its houses was influenced by
French and Spanish styles. Gamblers infested Mobile as well as the
Mississippi River towns, and lotteries were a characteristic passion of
the Creole inhabitants. The Sabbath was observed as a day of pleasure.
"The tone of society in Mobile," Whipple wrote, "is very gay and to
a certain extent dissipated, although there are many here who prefer
literature and its rational enjoyments to the theatre and gay revels."[42]
Mobile grew rapidly as the cultivation of cotton expanded in Alabama,
and at the close of the ante-bellum period it was the second greatest
cotton-exporting port in the Southern states.

In Missouri, the Creole influence in the Mississippi River towns contended with the rough elements of the Anglo-American frontier. There
were four principal settlements of the French in the Missouri country,
St. Genevieve, founded in 1735; St. Louis, founded in 1764; and the
lesser towns of St. Charles and Cape Girardeau. The American settlement began with the founding of New Madrid on the Mississippi River
by George Morgan in 1789. Henry Marie Brackenridge visited the
Missouri country in 1811 and reported favorably on the genial and
gay character of the "ancien habitants." They lived mostly in one-

---

[41] A. L. W. Stahl, "The Free Negro in Ante-Bellum Louisiana," *Louisiana Historical Quarterly*, XXV (1942), 301–396.

[42] Shippee, *Whipple's Southern Diary*, pp. 85–86, 90.

story log cottages built perpendicularly rather than in the horizontal style of the American frontiersmen. The roofs extended over the galleries, giving shade to the houses. He observed there a village culture without much education or material wealth. St. Genevieve was the shipping port of a lead-mining district which employed primitive methods in mining and smelting the lead.[43] When Thomas Hart Benton emigrated in 1815 to St. Louis, a town of 2,000 white inhabitants and 300 slaves, he found that political affairs were still dominated by a small class of French aristocrats possessing good libraries and reading the works of the French freethinkers, in fact being better educated than the Americans. "The Junto," composed chiefly of the leading French merchants and fur traders, particularly the Chouteau family, controlled the city.[44]

The coming of the Americans after the Louisiana Purchase wrought a revolution in the civilization of old Missouri. The 6,000 Creoles and Negroes reported by the Spanish census of 1799 were overwhelmed by the rush of American settlers, which by 1820 increased the population of the territory to 66,586, of whom 10,200 were slaves. French geographical names were corrupted or displaced; the Gallic Sunday with its gaiety was frowned upon by the intolerant Anglo-Americans; the American spirit of enterprise seized the territory and there were many lawsuits over Spanish grants and titles to land.[45] In 1808 the *Missouri Gazette,* the first newspaper of the region, was published in English. Ten years later Benton became editor of a rival paper, the St. Louis *Enquirer,* which vigorously supported the old French leaders and advocated the interests of the small farmers, a hard-money currency, and the admission of Missouri into the Union without slavery restrictions. By the time Missouri became a state, much of the old French culture had been erased and the Creoles were rapidly being assimilated by the American civilization.[46] When William Kingsford visited St. Louis in 1857, he saw only a few traces of its former French culture, particularly

[43] H. M. Brackenridge, *Views of Louisiana* (Baltimore, 1817), Chap. VI.
[44] See William N. Chambers, *Old Bullion Benton, Senator from the New West* (Boston, 1956), Chaps. IV, V.
[45] Harvey Wish, "The French of Old Missouri, 1804–1821; a Study in Assimilation," *Mid-America,* XXIII (1941), 167–189.
[46] J. F. McDermott (ed.), "Diary of Charles De Hautt De Lassus from New Orleans to St. Louis 1836," *Louisiana Historical Quarterly,* XXX (1947), 359–438.

green jalousies, and the city gave little indication that it supported slavery.[47]

The Creoles made important contributions to Southern civilization and American life. Many useful words from the Creole language have enriched the American vocabulary, such as bayou, levee, crevasse, chute, bureau, depot, picayune, and lagniappe, the latter referring to the pleasant custom of tradesmen giving their customers something extra beyond their purchases—an additional yam or fig or flower—as a sign of good will. The French of the Missouri country were noted fur traders; they, as well as French settlers from the North, gave us such words as prairie, bateau, pirogue, rapids, portage, voyageur, cache, gopher, and brave for Indian warrior. The Roman law instead of the common law of England, owing to Creole influence, became the basis of the law of Louisiana.

They developed a type of architecture that spread up the Mississippi River and affected the style of domestic architecture in towns hundreds of miles away from New Orleans. They made valuable contributions to the development of lead mining and the fur trade. Creole cuisine— such foods as gumbo, bouillabaisse, frog legs cooked in wine, *poulet Creole,* orange wine, and pralines—added variety to American cookery. The Creole celebration of Sunday, the French opera, the Creole folksongs, also added gaiety to the life of the lower South. Finally, the Creoles of Louisiana, although they themselves contributed little toward creating a Southern literature, provided rich material for the school of local color that arose after the Civil War. Writers such as George Washington Cable, Kate Chopin, Grace King, and Lafcadio Hearn have re-created in their novels and short stories the life of the Creoles in the picturesque Latin quarter of New Orleans and in the dreamy bayou country.

[47] Kingsford, *Impressions of the West and South,* p. 34.

CHAPTER 7

Discovery of the Middle Class

FIRMLY entrenched in literature and the popular image of the South has been the legend of an aristocratic society. The legend has had a long history, starting at least as early as the 1830's, when John Pendleton Kennedy, Beverley Tucker, and William Alexander Caruthers published novels of plantation society. The abolitionists helped to distort the image of the South by portraying a three-class social structure of arrogant, aristocratic planters, "mean" or "poor" whites, and cruelly treated Negroes. After the Civil War the impoverished Southerners cherished the romantic legend as a compensation for their low estate. During the depression decade Americans in general found an escape from the tensions and frustrations of a machine-dominated age by reading Stark Young's *So Red the Rose* and Margaret Mitchell's immensely popular novel *Gone With the Wind,* which gave a particularly appealing version of the romantic stereotype of the Old South.

Yet as early as 1910 critical-minded historians had begun to attack the legend. Thomas Jefferson Wertenbaker published his realistic studies which did much to destroy the myth that Virginians were all descended from Cavaliers.[1] Francis Pendleton Gaines in *The Southern Plantation, a Study in the Development and Accuracy of a Tradition*

[1] Thomas Jefferson Wertenbaker, *Patrician and Plebeian in Virginia* (Charlottesville, 1910), and *The Planters of Colonial Virginia* (Princeton, 1922).

(1924) showed that the stereotype of the Old South had been created by exaggerating certain features of its society and by ascribing to the whole section the characteristics of privileged regions. Moreover, the stately image of colonial society was imposed on that of the society of the Cotton Kingdom, which had recently emerged from a crude frontier environment. The publication of the secret diary of William Byrd of Westover in 1941–42 showed, however, that even the elite of the colonial planters did not live the carefree and luxurious existence depicted by romantic writers.[2] The legend of the Old South represented a process of simplification and generalization that ignored the infinite variety of Southern society.

The discovery of the true nature of Southern society had to wait for a careful study of the manuscript census returns of 1850 and 1860. These records, located at Duke University and in Washington, were either unknown or their value had not been appreciated by scholars until the decade of the 1940's. Here in the agricultural and slave schedules are found the names of the landowners, the number of slaves they held, the amount of livestock they possessed, the number of improved acres in each holding, and the different kinds of crops they raised. When this material was supplemented by an examination of county records, such as wills, deeds, tax books, inventories of estates, a realistic picture of Southern society before the Civil War began to emerge. Such a study was hardly possible until a technique of sampling had been devised and the invention of mechanical computing devices enabled scholars to assemble and classify the vast amount of detail obtained from the unpublished census returns and county records. Frank L. Owsley of Vanderbilt University and his students were the first to study these records, which enabled them to revise the conventional picture of Southern society and slavery. Their researches have resulted in greater recognition of the role of the middle class of the ante-bellum South and its true role in Southern society.

Actually there were no hard-and-fast lines drawn between classes in white Southern society. The ante-bellum South possessed a relatively fluid social structure. Colonel Richard Mentor Johnson of Kentucky

[2] Louis B. Wright and Marion Tinling (eds.), *The Secret Diary of William Byrd of Westover for the Years 1709–1712* (Richmond, 1941); Maude H. Woodfin and Marion Tinling (eds.), *Another Secret Diary of William Byrd of Westover for the Years 1739–1741* (Richmond, 1942).

presented this view when he told the Senate of the United States in 1820 that there was no privileged class in his state. He related that when he first arrived in Washington he experienced mingled emotions of surprise and horror to see white servants in livery driving coaches and acting as footmen for Northern congressmen. "I could not reconcile it [such a practice]," he declared, "with my ideas of freedom; because in the state where I received my first impressions, slaves alone were servile. All white men there are on an equality; and every citizen feels his independence. We have no classes—no patrician or plebeian rank."[3]

Colonel Johnson was a living demonstration of this democratic cult. Born at Beargrass, Kentucky, in a log cabin, he acquired a large plantation at Great Crossings near Georgetown and represented Kentucky for many years in the House of Representatives and in the Senate. The most popular man in his state, more popular than Henry Clay, the Colonel owed much of the adulation of the crowd to the fact that he was credited with having killed Tecumseh in the battle of the Thames River.[4] A follower of Andrew Jackson, he represented the common man in Congress and is notable for championing a federal law abolishing imprisonment for debt. He was a humanitarian, a lover of mankind, who founded an academy on his plantation for the education of the Choctaw Indians. He had two mulatto daughters, whom he openly acknowledged as his children and educated to be refined ladies. Indeed, he utterly disregarded convention. Harriet Martineau on her visit to this country in 1835 observed that Senator Johnson disdained wearing a cravat. Even if he had no use for superfluous apparel, he was conspicuous in Washington because of his practice of wearing a red waistcoat.[5] While serving as Vice-President during the administration of Martin Van Buren, he conducted a tavern and health resort at White Sulphur Springs on his plantation. The irrepressible colonel saw no incongruity in presiding over the Senate as Vice-President and between sessions performing the duties of a tavernkeeper,

[3] Clement Eaton, "Class Differences in the Old South," *Virginia Quarterly Review*, XXXIII (1957), 357.

[4] See Leland W. Meyer, *Life and Times of Colonel Richard Mentor Johnson of Kentucky* (New York, 1932).

[5] Gaillard Hunt (ed.), *The First Forty Years of Washington Society, Portrayed by the Family Letters of Mrs. Samuel Harrison Smith* (New York, 1906).

"even giving his personal superintendence to the chicken and egg purchasing and watermelon selling department."

The fluidity of Southern society in the ante-bellum period was demonstrated by the careers of many members of the yeoman class. Governor David L. Swain of North Carolina, son of a Massachusetts hatter who had settled in Buncombe County as a small farmer, was an example. Swain attended the University at Chapel Hill briefly, studied law, became a judge, governor of the state, and served for thirty-three years as president of the University of North Carolina. His diary tells the story of another self-made man, in the eastern part of the state, who started propertyless but by great industry and thrift acquired the farms of ten or twelve small owners and became the greatest landed proprietor of his country. He built a fine house, but Swain observed that, "with Gothic rudeness," he used the tombstone of a person who had died in the colonial period for his doorstep.[6] The history of the Old South is full of these success stories of hard-driving, horse-trading farmers who became plantation owners. Overseers who could barely write a letter, such as Ephraim Beanland, overseer for James K. Polk, attained their ambitious goal of managing their own plantations. By sheer will power, industry, and practical judgment this representative of the yeoman class acquired slaves and a section of land in the Southwest, and so elevated his family that one son became a physician and others became persons of recognized standing in their communities.[7] From the yeoman class principally came the industrial leaders of the New South.

The travelers in the Old South did not appreciate the significance of the large middle class of farmers. They were looking for the picturesque and unusual, not the representative aspects of Southern life. Many of the English travelers, such as Sir Charles Lyell, the geologist, were entertained in the homes of the planters and did not investigate the life of the yeoman farmers. Moreover, they were misled by superficial appearances, for the farmers often lived in log cabins and their farms presented a rude frontier appearance. Accordingly, many farmers in the lower South who owned good land and were hardworking

[6] Diary of David L. Swain, April 21, 1832, Southern Collection, University of North Carolina.

[7] Bassett, *Southern Plantation Overseer*, p. 93.

and respectable citizens were confused with the shiftless class of "poor whites."[8] Furthermore numerous farmers owned considerable property in herds of cattle and droves of hogs that grazed in the woods or on the public land which were not apparent to the passing traveler. The cattleman's frontier existed throughout the ante-bellum period, particularly in northern Florida, the mountains of the Appalachian region, and the pinelands of Mississippi, Alabama, southern Louisiana, and Texas.

In some areas cowboys herded the cattle, but for the most part farmers managed their herds with the aid of shepherd dogs. On public land in the pinelands or on the prairie numerous livestock frequently grazed, rendered half-tame by salt licks placed for them in the neighborhood of the house. Cattle were branded and the ears of the hogs were notched to distinguish ownership. The yeoman farmers owned thousands of hogs that subsisted primarily on acorns in the woods and by rooting. They were so lean and wiry that they were called razorbacks.

The most common agricultural unit in the South was the farm, not the plantation. A large proportion of the agricultural holdings contained less than two hundred acres of improved land. In North Carolina only 2 per cent of the heads of agricultural families owned in excess of five hundred acres, the minimum number of acres for a plantation, while over two-thirds of the agriculturists occupied farms of less than a hundred acres. In Kentucky 76 per cent of the farmers in 1850 and 72 per cent in 1860 cultivated less than one hundred acres of improved land; even in the rich Bluegrass region the great majority of the agriculturists were small farmers.[9] In Tennessee approximately 62 per cent of the heads of agricultural families lived on farms containing less than a hundred acres. In Mississippi, which may be regarded as typical of the lower South, approximately one-fifth of the heads of families owned no improved lands, while nearly half of the proprietors held less than two hundred acres; persons owning five hundred or more acres of improved land constituted less than 9 per cent of the landowners.[10]

[8] Owsley, *Plain Folk of the Old South*, Chap. II.

[9] Richard Troutman, "The Social and Economic Structure of Kentucky Agriculture, 1850–1860," Ph.D. Dissertation, University of Kentucky, 1958, pp. 114–115.

[10] Weaver, *Mississippi Farmers*, p. 36.

A revised profile of the society of the Old South shows a considerable intermingling of small farms with plantations. The Owsley school, interpreting the unpublished census returns of 1850 and 1860, has maintained that there was no segregation of farms and plantations, that both types of agricultural units existed side by side, that the yeoman farmer ploughed as rich soil as the planter, and that there was little difference in the productivity per acre between the farms owned by the yeoman farmers and by the planters. Owsley's *Plain Folk of the Old South* illustrates this point by citing the 1860 census reports of acreage of farms of two communities within Hinds and Bolivar counties, Mississippi. Although these were among the richest agricultural counties in the South, the census taker, listing property as he came to it, recorded the existence of small farms, middle-sized farms, and plantations side by side. In one of the communities, consisting of thirty-three properties, only half of the agricultural holdings contained more than two hundred acres, and six had less than one hundred. All except one of the owners of these properties were slaveholders, but a third did not possess more than ten slaves and less than half could be classified as planters.

These bold generalizations run counter to the thesis held by U. B. Phillips and Lewis Gray. These scholars have envisaged the plantations as absorbing the farms in the favored land areas of the South.[11] Many plantations in the lower South were acquired by buying out small frontier farmers and consolidating their holdings into plantations. Men with money and slaves, such as the Taits of Georgia and Alabama, could afford to purchase the richest of the public lands at a premium, even as high as $20 an acre, while the yeoman had to buy the cheaper lands at the minimum price of $1.25 an acre. When the plantation economy developed in an area, there was frequently a movement of many of the yeomen out of the country, so that, step by step with the advance of slaves to cultivate the rich land, the white population significantly declined. Since there were great variations in the soil value in the same region, and since some farmers would not sell their landholdings to competing planters, any pattern of segregation of plantations and farms had many exceptions. Although the planters did not

[11] Gray, *History of Agriculture*, I, 474; U. B. Phillips, "The Origin and Growth of the Southern Black Belts," *American Historical Review*, XI (1906), 798–816.

monopolize the good lands, they tended to congregate in the rich soil areas, the black belts, and the yeoman farmers to occupy the areas that were not well suited to the production of staple crops.

The yeomen were engaged in producing crops primarily for subsistence—corn, wheat, oats, black-eyed peas, and livestock. Many of them, however, did raise small quantities of cotton or tobacco as a money crop to enable them to buy tobacco, lead, powder, snuff, sugar, and small luxuries. The lion's share of the staple crops was raised by slave labor. Herbert Weaver has shown that less than 7 per cent of the cotton grown in the state of Mississippi was raised by nonslaveholders.[12] In Virginia slaveless farmers produced only 5 per cent of the tobacco grown in that state.[13] Hemp in Kentucky was described as almost exclusively a "nigger crop." Few farms in Louisiana or Texas containing less than one hundred acres produced sugar, although in Georgia and Florida hundreds of farmers raised cane for domestic use to make brown sugar and molasses, grinding the cane in horse-driven mills and boiling the juice in cast-iron pots. It was the planter class that produced the exportable surplus of the South which raised the standard of living of the section.

It is difficult to find journals and letters of nonslaveholders which give a realistic picture of the life of the yeoman farmer. One of these rare records is an account by his son of Newton Knight, leader of the Unionists of Jones County, Mississippi. Jones County is in the pinelands belt of southern Mississippi, a region of small slaveless farmers in which a movement arose during the Civil War to detach the county from the Confederacy and, according to popular legend, establish the "Free State of Jones." Knight, a poor farmer boy, worked hard on his father's farm and received no schooling in his youth. When he was nineteen years old he married, erected a log cabin, and cleared some land for cultivating corn and sweet potatoes. The people of his community marketed their produce, chickens, wool, and grain, at Shubuta, Mississippi, transporting them by oxen, whose slow progress consumed six days going and coming.

Newton Knight was a primitive Baptist, who seems to have had the strong streak of Puritanism characteristic of the yeoman class of the

[12] Weaver, *Mississippi Farmers*, p. 100.
[13] Emmett B. Fields, "The Agricultural Population of Virginia, 1850–1860," Ph.D. Dissertation, Vanderbilt University, 1954, p. 168.

Old South. Quiet in demeanor, "strictly business," a person who "did not believe in any kind of foolishness," he had a grim and violent side to his nature which led him to kill a Negro.[14] Despite his lack of education (he was finally taught to read and write by his wife), he was a natural leader in his community. Since he resolutely refused to fight against the Union in the Civil War, he was made a hospital orderly by the Confederates.

Knight did not own slaves, but a considerable number of yeoman farmers did. Such a person was James Burroughs, the master of Booker T. Washington, who was born on a farm near Roanoke, Virginia, in 1858 or 1859. Burroughs lived with his wife and thirteen children in a two-story log house. He owned two female slaves, forty and forty-one years of age, a man twenty-two years old, and four children. Booker's mother was the cook for the farm and lived with her three children in the log kitchen. Booker and his brother and sister slept on a bed made of rags on the dirt floor. Booker's only garment was an uncomfortable flax shirt, but this was not unusual; indeed many of the pickaninnies ran about the plantations naked. The farmers and his sons worked with the slaves in the fields, cultivating the crops of wheat and corn. Although the slaves do not seem to have been well fed or clothed during the war period, there was a friendly feeling between them and the white family, and a whipping was a rare event.[15]

The life of the slaveowning farmer was illustrated also by the family of Jacob Eaton, who lived on a farm of 160 acres near the Piedmont village of Mocksville, North Carolina. The family, with eight children, dwelt in a three-room log house which had been covered with weatherboarding and had a loft where the boys slept. They owned, according to the Census of 1860, seven slaves, a woman aged twenty-seven, a man aged twenty, and five small children.[16] Their large barn was built of round logs, undaubed, with a shingle roof. Near the house clustered a granary, a slave cabin, and a spring house in which the butter and milk were kept fresh by the cool water of the spring. The fields were

[14] T. J. Knight, "Short Sketch of the Life of Newton Knight," Department of Archives, Louisiana State University.

[15] Samuel R. Spencer, Jr., *Booker T. Washington and the Negro's Place in American Life* (Boston, 1955), pp. 13–16; Booker T. Washington, *Up from Slavery, an Autobiography* (New York, 1902), Chap. I.

[16] Manuscript Census of 1860, Schedule II, "An Enumeration of Slave Population," Davie County, Jacob Eaton.

enclosed by fences of split rails laid in a zigzag pattern. Homespun clothing was made by spinning wheels, particularly a small ornamented one brought from North Ireland in colonial days, and a hand loom. The Eatons were devout Methodists with a strong feeling for kinship, expressed in the family graveyard, where the Eatons and Clements for generations were buried. What differentiated this family from thousands of others in the South was that the head was a schoolteacher as well as a farmer and taught an "old field school" in a log cabin on the farm.

Although the more prosperous of the farmers owned several slaves, the majority did not. In 1860 over 72 per cent of the white population of North Carolina and 65 per cent of Tennessee did not own slaves. Slaveholders constituted only a third of the agricultural population of Kentucky and 41 per cent of that of Virginia. Even in Mississippi the majority of the agricultural population, 51 per cent, owned no slaves. Although the black belt of Alabama contained one of the great slaveholding areas of the South in 1860, approximately 40 per cent of the agricultural population did not own slaves. There were marked differences in the proportion of slaveholding within different sections of a state. In Tennessee, for example, only 3.5 per cent of the white families of the eastern counties held slaves, while 43 per cent in West Tennessee and 53 per cent in Middle Tennessee were slaveholders.[17]

In the Southern states as a whole social discrimination against nonslaveholders was not common. South Carolina had something of a caste system, but this was not characteristic of the slaveholding class in most parts of the South. Although all classes, even the Negroes, looked down upon "poor white trash," this disdain arose not because the latter were slaveless but because of defects of character. When John Trotwood Moore was the state librarian of Tennessee, he sent questionnaires to surviving veterans of the Civil War in his state, asking them questions concerning the social status of the nonslaveholders. Blanche Henry Clark, author of *The Tennessee Yeoman*, analyzed these replies and concluded that there was much intermingling socially of slaveholders and nonslaveholders, and that it was not considered degrading for white men to work in the fields. Large slaveholders

---

[17] Chase C. Mooney, *Slavery in Tennessee* (Bloomington, 1957), p. 111; Weaver, *Mississippi Farmers*, p. 39.

themselves worked at times in the fields during emergencies, and their sons in many instances labored there during vacations from college. Southern yeomen disdained menial work, not manual labor. The Moore questionnaire indicated that nonslaveholders rarely held positions of political leadership, although in areas where there were few slaves nonslaveholders were elected to county positions, such as that of sheriff. In old communities family influence often counted much in social prestige and in politics.[18]

Whether a farmer was a slaveholder or nonslaveholder, he derived a sense of independence and self-respect from the ownership of the farm which he cultivated. Owsley and his students have demonstrated from the unpublished census returns that approximately 80 per cent of Southern farmers, except in Virginia and the Carolinas, owned their farms. Such a high proportion of proprietorship contrasts greatly with conditions in the South ninety years later, when 57.3 per cent of the farmers were tenants; in Georgia and Mississippi the percentage of tenants in 1930 was 65.6 per cent and 66.1 per cent.[19] During the prosperous decade of the 1850's there was a significant increase in land ownership and in general prosperity, and many nonslaveholders acquired farms. Contrary to the usual notion of the structure of Southern society, the unpublished census returns of 1850 and 1860 reveal that there was little difference in the proportion of yeoman farmers in the upper and lower South. (In South Carolina, however, the farmers were a smaller part of the agricultural population than in other Southern states.)

In portraying the yeoman farmers of the Old South, the writers of the period of the New Deal tended to exaggerate their prosperity. In the "century of the common man" hailed by the New Dealers, some students of Southern history reacted so strongly against the previous glamorization of the planter class that they went to the other extreme of romanticizing the life of the common man of the Old South. They idealized the farmer somewhat in the strain of Thomas Jefferson's glorification of the agricultural class. With gusto they described the large measure of self-sufficiency, the delicious country food and pure

[18] Blanche Henry Clark, *The Tennessee Yeomen, 1840–1860* (Nashville, 1942), pp. 11–15.
[19] Rupert Vance, *Human Geography of the South* (Chapel Hill, 1932).

water, and the wholesome amusements of the yeoman—the corn shuck-
ings, quilting parties, singing schools, log rollings, hunting and fishing,
church, camp meetings, gatherings at the courthouse during court week,
country dances, practical joking, and folk lore. Absent from this picture
was the low standard of living of most yeomen, a monotonous diet of
hog, hominy, and coffee in the winter, the provincialism and lack of education of the majority, the dipping of snuff and the chewing tobacco,
the rude fights in which gouging sometimes occurred, the lack of conveniences that Northern farmers enjoyed, and the chronic lack of
money.[20]

Moreover, the census reports of 1850 and 1860 showed that although
the Southern states were far behind New England in literacy, they
were not seriously backward compared with some of the states north
of the Ohio where overwhelmingly rural conditions prevailed. The
superintendent of the federal Census of 1850, J. D. B. De Bow, reported that the Southern states had an illiteracy rate among the white
population of 20.3 per cent, the Northwestern states nearly 10 per
cent, the Middle States 3 per cent and New England 0.42 per cent.[21]
In some parts of the South illiterates equaled one-third of the white
inhabitants. The abolitionists and some later writers have attributed
the large amount of illiteracy in the Southern states to slavery, but
undoubtedly that was only a minor factor. Many of the yeomen who
made their mark instead of signing their names were not lacking in
native ability but only in the opportunity to learn. Whipple observed
in 1844 that some of the Georgia upcountry farmers were sharp-
witted and intelligent. "They have a high estimation of their own
qualities," he wrote, "& look on book 'larning' as superfluous."[22]

The middle class in the ante-bellum South included not only the
large body of yeoman farmers but also the mechanics, tradesmen, and
overseers. The latter were very seldom poor whites. A considerable
number were sons of planters, and as a rule they were young men.
Zachary Taylor's overseers on his Cypress Grove Plantation in Missis-

[20] See Fabian Linden, "Economic Democracy in the Slave South; an Appraisal of Some Recent Views," *Journal of Negro History,* XXXI (1946),
140–189.

[21] J. D. B. De Bow, *Compendium of the Seventh Census* (Washington,
1854), p. 153.

[22] Whipple, *Southern Diary,* p. 77.

sippi were his relatives and were classed as gentlemen. A study of Hancock County, in the Piedmont region of Georgia, found that of the 139 overseers of the county twenty were sons of planters and forty-two lived with the planter's family.[23] Yet a social line was drawn between the overseer and the female members of the planter's family and visitors to the plantation. An overseer on the Hugh Davis plantation in Mississippi made this notation in the farm book concerning a female visitor: "Miss Marshall is a nice young lady. Was at the table with her today twice & in the Parlor tonight & received no introduction to her."[24] Some planters, such as George Washington, believed that in dealing with overseers it was the best policy "to keep them at a proper distance for they will grow upon familiarity in proportion as you will sink in authority."[25]

Most plantation owners expected too much from their overseers and placed so many restrictions on their liberty that they could not enjoy a normal life. They were forbidden, for example, to leave the plantation without permission, and were dismissed if they had too much company. Many masters judged their success by the number of bales of cotton that they produced. Maunsel White, the great New Orleans merchant and plantation owner, wrote to one of his overseers in 1847, "You ask for more salary—that depends on what you produce."[26] At the close of the ante-bellum period, overseers were paid $500 or $600 a year, better than the pay of teachers and tutors, and those who superintended large plantations received as high as $1,200. A considerable number owned a few slaves and hired them out, often to their employers. A majority of the overseers were stubbornly opposed to any variation from the traditional procedures of agriculture and reluctant to follow orders for scientific experimentation. The letters and diaries of planters are full of complaints against overseers, and many dismissed the old and hired a new overseer nearly every year. The insecurity of their tenure explains much of their failure.[27]

[23] J. C. Bonner, "Profile of a Late Ante-Bellum Community," *American Historical Review*, XLIX (1944), p. 677.

[24] Jordan, *Hugh Davis and His Alabama Plantation*, p. 50.

[25] Sparks, *Letters and Recollections of George Washington*, p. 153.

[26] Maunsel White to James P. Bracewell, October 4, 1847, Maunsel White Papers.

[27] See J. C. Bonner, "The Plantation Overseer and Southern Nationalism,"

The mechanics and tradesmen have been virtually ignored in the study of the structure of Southern society. Yet in 1860 this class constituted over 16 per cent of those gainfully employed in Virginia, 14 per cent in North Carolina, 26 per cent in Louisiana, and nearly 10 per cent in Georgia. In the latter state the carpenters were by far the most numerous among the skilled labor group, followed in numerical rank by the mechanics, blacksmiths, railroad men, millers, and shoemakers. Many of the artisans and skilled laborers in the South had come from the North or were foreign-born. In Hancock County, Georgia, thirteen of the 116 tradesmen had emigrated from Ireland, and they dominated the stonemason trade.[28]

The Southern states attracted immigrants from the North and from Europe by the high wages paid skilled labor. In 1860 the national average wage for a carpenter was $1.85 a day, but in Alabama he was paid $2.15 a day and in Mississippi $2.47.[29] In New Orleans skilled labor was paid over $2 a day and unskilled labor $1 a day without board. The main reason for the relatively high wages of skilled labor in the South was its scarcity, a condition explained partly by the agrarian ideal of the South. Some farmers, nevertheless, pursued a skilled trade along with their main occupation of farming. Such a jack-of-all-trades was Joseph Walker, who raised crops of wheat, rye, and corn in the Pennyroyal region of southern Kentucky and also manufactured wagons. In the early 1820's he had great difficulty in collecting payments for his wagons, and accordingly he constantly thought of emigrating to the West, but never reached the point of taking the risks involved.[30]

The economic status of the tradesmen was above that of the overseer, farm laborer, or factory worker. In Hancock County, Georgia, for example, nearly 14 per cent of them owned real estate and approximately 8 per cent owned slaves. In Virginia a plasterer named Evans owned at least twelve slaves in 1860, whom he generally hired out.[31]

Agricultural History, XIX (1945), 1–11, and Bassett, *The Plantation Overseer, as Revealed in his Letters.*

[28] Bonner, "Profile of a Late Ante-Bellum Community," p. 676.

[29] U.S. Bureau of the Census, *Statistics of the United States (Including Mortality, Property, etc.) in 1860*, p. 512.

[30] U. B. Phillips, *Life and Labor in the Old South* (New York, 1939), pp. 86–87.

[31] Catterall, *Judicial Cases*, I, 251.

Another skilled laborer who acquired a measure of property was John Robert Shaw, a well digger, who after a life of many vicissitudes, including military service, splitting rails, working with drovers, and digging wells, finally settled down in Kentucky, freed himself from thralldom to liquor, became a shouting Methodist, and wrote a racy autobiography.[32] Martin Marshall, a blacksmith, weaver, and farmer, emigrated from South Carolina in 1815 to Fort Claiborne, Alabama, where he rose to the planter class. He kept a remarkable daybook over a period of years in which he gathered a large store of empirical information about treatment of disease, weaving, farming, and practical household information.[33]

Some of the characteristics of the artisan class are illustrated by the career of the papermaker, Ebenezer H. Stedman. Stedman's father was the foreman of a paper mill in Massachusetts who had been induced by two Lexington, Kentucky, bankers in 1815 to come to Lexington to set up a paper mill. The mill failed just before the panic of 1819, and the Stedman family moved to nearby Georgetown, where both father and son, a boy of twelve years of age, worked in a paper mill. Stedman worked long hours for wages of $2 a week. He slept in his clothes on a pile of rags in the mill and arose before dark to begin his task. After working some years in the paper mill in Georgetown, Stedman learned the potter's trade, and then obtained employment in a wool-carding factory in Lexington. Borrowing a small amount of capital, he established a paper mill in Georgetown, and later bought Amos Kendall's paper mill near Frankfort, which he operated successfully until the Civil War. He manufactured newsprint, book paper, banknote paper out of linen rags, and wrapping paper out of hemp tow, which he marketed principally in Louisville. He was successful in rising from the mechanic class into the business class.[34]

The insecure position of many mechanics in the Old South is revealed in the correspondence of William Harris Garland, an Englishman of some education who had emigrated to Beaufort, South

[32] John R. Shaw, *The Life and Travels of John Robert Shaw, the Well Digger* (Lexington, Ky., 1807).

[33] Weymouth T. Jordan (ed.), *Herbs, Hoecakes and Husbandry, the Daybook of a Planter of the Old South* (Tallahassee, 1960).

[34] Frances Dugan and Jacqueline Bull (eds.), *Bluegrass Craftsman: Being the Reminiscences of Ebenezer Hiram Stedman, Papermaker, 1808–1885* (Lexington, 1959).

Carolina. In 1839 he was living in Savannah, variously employed as an engineer on steamboats and in repairing ships and working in railroad shops. Like many of his class, he moved from city to city, seeking opportunities for work. Although he received wages of $3 a day, he was paid in depreciated paper money worth only two-thirds of its face value. For considerable intervals he was not paid, and at times complained of having no money even to buy tobacco or obtain a letter from the post office. In 1841 he secured a job on the steamboat *Comet* because "the old engineer has the chills and fever and being a Northern man he got scared and quit." One of his fellow mechanics who had gone to New Orleans looking for work wrote: "Your branch of business is very dull here. I have enquired at every place I could see and no hands is wanted. Mechanicall Business of all kinds is dull & 100 hs. out of employ."[35] Garland later secured a job tending the machinery of a saw mill in Beaufort, but in a few months the mill failed and he was forced to look for other employment. At last he was able to establish a machine shop in Savannah in partnership with another mechanic. This enterprise ended in bankruptcy and he returned to working for wages. In this nadir of his fortunes his wife tried to cheer him by offering to sell her bracelet and breastpin to help him.

The correspondence Garland carried on with his wife and with fellow mechanics tends to corroborate Thoreau's observation that the mass of men lead lives of quiet desperation. His mother wrote, "we must not expect pleasure in this world, this is not our resting place." For Garland and his insecure fellow mechanics, membership in the Masonic lodge offered some consolation and aid. Among the last letters in the collection is one from his son Willie, who was in the Confederate army. Disturbed by the recent law that had extended the draft age to sixty years, he wrote to his father, "you cannot stand it, let alone being ordered about by every Pupy that comes along that happens to have a commission." In 1870 the last letters disclose that the old man was working, despairing of God's mercy, in a planing mill which was about to close.

The Garland letters also tell of one of his friends, John Evans, a boatbuilder, who had moved from Savannah to Baltimore. In April, 1846, Evans wrote Garland that he had abandoned his trade and had

[35] William H. Garland to Harriet Garland, Darien, Ga., June 9, 1841, William Harris Garland Papers, Southern Collection, University of North Carolina.

rented a small farm at Frog's Neck near St. Mary's. Here, with the aid of "a green dutchman" whom he had hired, he was raising potatoes. In the autumn he moved back to Baltimore, his family sick with the ague, convinced that farming was not profitable except to those who owned a gang of Negroes. After his failure at farming, his wife kept a small fruit and grocery shop and he went back to his trade, but he was gloomy over the prospects of mechanics in the city and thinking of returning to Savannah or going West. "Baltimore is getting worse every year for the laboring Classes," he wrote on August 6, 1847. "So much so that in a few years they will have to be under as much subjugation as they are in most parts of Europe. What mechanics are in this place are from the eastern and northern States, few of our young men stay long after their term of apprenticeship has expired for they will not become as subservient as those from the east. Their was a time when the people had some Hospitality about them, but their god of money has so changed their disposition that they do not exchange any friendship except with those whose purses is as large as their own."[36]

As early as the 1790's, Mechanics' Associations were organized in Southern towns. Their primary purpose was to provide decent burials for the members, to aid destitute members, and to provide for the education of orphans. Workingmen were greatly handicapped in forming true labor unions. The common law and the individualistic traditions of an agrarian society frowned upon strikes. Not until 1842 did Massachusetts, the most advanced industrial state, by the famous decision of Chief Justice Lemuel Shaw, free labor organizations from the danger of prosecution for engaging in strikes. In the Southern states strikes of workingmen were sporadic and generally unorganized. William Johnson, the Negro barber of Natchez, recorded in his diary on September 24, 1838, "The Journeman Quit the office and no paper was Issued for One Day," and William Gilmore Simms wrote to James H. Hammond, June 20, 1853, that a strike by the printers had held up the publication of the *Southern Quarterly Review*.[37] The white deckhands of the Mississippi steamboats were so greatly exploited and harshly treated that they frequently struck. In 1858 the Louisiana legislature outlawed the stoppage of work on ships or freight

---

[36] John W. Evans to Garland, August 6, 1847, *loc. cit.*

[37] Hogan and Davis, *William Johnson's Natchez*, p. 237; Oliphant, *Letters of William Gilmore Simms*, III, 238.

wharves by strikers, and thereafter strike leaders were arrested for "tampering" with the crews.

In 1847 the white mechanics in the Tredegar Iron Works of Richmond struck because the company had imported mechanics from the North to teach slaves the skilled processes of puddling and rolling. When the strikers demanded that slaves should not be used in these processes, Joseph R. Anderson, president of the company, replied that he would not relinquish his constitutional right to employ or discharge anyone at his pleasure and announced that the strikers had discharged themselves.[38] Such strikes, declared the Richmond *Times and Compiler*, attacked the foundations of the institution of slavery by maintaining the principle that "the employer may be prevented from making use of slave labor."[39] Not only were strikes, especially of Irish laborers on canals and railroads, put down by legal authorities, but a form of white bondage existed in the Southern states in respect to vagrants, men convicted of bastardy, and absconding seamen.

The two most powerful labor unions in the South were the Typographical Society and the Screwmen's Benevolent Association of New Orleans. Founded in 1835 by the printers of the city, the Typographical Society was disbanded and reorganized several times before it was firmly established in 1852 as a local of the International Typographical Union. Its leader, Gerard Stith, was elected mayor of New Orleans in 1858 by the Native Americans. The Screwmen's Benevolent Association was an organization of the stevedores of New Orleans who stowed the cotton bales in the oceangoing ships. This union was able to keep the wages of its workers relatively high—over $4 a day in 1858 —without resorting to a single strike. Furthermore, the organization paid members incapacitated by sickness $3 a week and provided for their burial as well. One of the stevedores on the levee, John Monroe, a relative of President Monroe, was elected mayor of New Orleans in 1860 by the Native American party.[40]

On April 15, 1853, representatives from twenty skilled trades met at Frankfort, Kentucky, to organize for the purpose of improving working

[38] Bruce, *Virginia Iron Manufacture in the Slave Era*, 224–227, 235.

[39] Richard B. Morris, "The Measure of Bondage in the Slave States," *Mississippi Valley Historical Review*, LXI (1954), 219–240.

[40] Roger W. Shugg, *Origins of Class Struggle in Louisiana* (University, La., 1939), 114–115.

conditions. Among the trades that were represented were the seamstresses, milliners, and mantua makers. The meeting resolved that wages should be raised 10 to 25 per cent; that employers should pay all their journeymen at least twice a week; that the ten-hour day be established; that citizens should patronize the local lawyers, merchants, and doctors as well as the mechanics as far as possible; and that the wages of all branches of female industry should be increased in the same proportion as that of male skilled labor. In the same year a meeting of steamboat engineers from nine states, particularly from the cities of Mobile, New Orleans, St. Louis, Nashville, and Louisville, was held in Louisville. After electing officers they passed resolutions for co-operating in a strict union of sentiment, for fixing wages, and for establishing a library of scientific and engineering works in Louisville.[41] Moreover, such group activities as the Louisville Stove and Hollow Ware Moulders' Ball of 1859 contributed to the growth of the union among skilled workers in the Southern cities.

The greatest grievance of the white mechanics of the South was the competition of slaves and free Negroes. Many of the plantations possessed skilled mechanics, who were often hired out to neighboring farmers and planters and in the towns. Some planters apprenticed promising Negro youths to mechanics in order that they might be taught a skilled craft. An example of the competition that white mechanics received from slaves was the practice of James S. Guignard I of Columbia, South Carolina, who owned a number of artisans whom he hired out to do jobs of bricklaying, plastering, and carpenter work.[42] In seeking to eliminate such competition the mechanics again and again petitioned the legislatures of the Southern states to pass laws forbidding the employment of slaves in the mechanic trades. In Arkansas the white mechanics of Little Rock in 1858 held a meeting presided over by a blacksmith, a German immigrant, to protest against the use of slaves, free Negroes, and convicts in the mechanic trades.[43] Earlier the Mechanics' Society of Baton Rouge protested against leasing the convicts of the penitentiary to private manufacturers. The kind of competition

[41] Louisville *Daily Courier*, August 16, 1853; Frankfort *Commonwealth*, April 20, 1853.

[42] A. R. Childs (ed.), *Planters and Businessmen, The Guignard Family of South Carolina, 1795–1930* (Columbia, S.C., 1957).

[43] Taylor, *Negro Slavery in Arkansas*, pp. 111, 251.

which the mechanics met from prison labor is indicated by an advertisement of Joel Scott, the keeper of the Kentucky Penitentiary, in the Frankfort *Argus of Western America,* July 22, 1826, announcing the sale of prison-made woolen textiles, wool hats, Windsor chairs, boots and shoes, and blacksmith work.[44] The protests of the mechanics against the employment of convicts and slaves in the skilled trades were made in vain, for the legislatures were under the control of the owners of slave labor, and the use of prison labor in manufacturing reduced taxation. Sometimes, however, the white mechanics would beat up a slave competitor; they did this to Frederick Douglass, who was working in 1836 as a calker in a Baltimore shipyard.[45]

The Southern states had a large number of unskilled laborers, of whom little is known. Although many were free Negroes, the great majority undoubtedly were white men. In Virginia the Census of 1860 reported 30,518 farm laborers and 108,958 farmers, or a ratio of nearly one farm hand to every three farmers; approximately the same ratio prevailed in Georgia, Louisiana, and Kentucky, while the proportion was one to four in North Carolina and Tennessee. In Mississippi, Arkansas, and South Carolina the ratio was about one to six, but in the border states of Maryland and Missouri more farm laborers were reported than farmers. In addition to such laborers the Census listed another class of manual workers as "laborers," who in South Carolina, Mississippi, Arkansas, and North Carolina were about equal in number to the farm laborers. In Virginia, Maryland, and Louisiana these workers were much more numerous than the farm hands. Many of these laborers were Irish immigrants who dug ditches and built railways and died in large numbers as the result of unhealthy and dangerous work. The Irish gangs were easily managed by their bosses through a plentiful supply of whisky. The priests were their only comfort, wrote Tyrone Power.[46]

Indeed, whisky and tobacco were potent factors in hiring white labor. Olmsted spent the night with a German farmer who hired out his four male slaves in Natchez, receiving $30 a month for one of them, and replacing his labor on the farm by hiring a white man at $10 a

[44] *Argus of Western America,* July 22, 1826, University of Kentucky Library.
[45] *Life and Times of Frederick Douglass, Written by Himself* (Hartford, 1882).
[46] Tyrone Power, *Impressions of America,* II, 239–243.

month who was content with his wages as long as he was kept in whisky and tobacco. In northern Alabama he met an illiterate miner whose son drove a cart for a forge, receiving as compensation "tobacco for both on 'em (himself and wife), and two people uses a good deal of tobacco you know; so that's pretty good wages—seven dollars a month besides their keep and tobacco."[47]

The lowest class in the white society of the South was that group variously called "poor whites," "piney woods folks," "sandhillers," "tackeys," "crackers," and "peckerwoods." They were the poverty-stricken, slaveless group that lived on the poor soil areas. Many were squatters, although some owned small pieces of low-quality land. The slaves looked down on them and called them poor white trash, while the planters laughed at their uncouthness and ignorance without feeling any sense of responsibility toward them. The old theory of their origin—that they were descendants of indentured servants and criminals brought to America in the colonial period—has been to a great degree discredited. Also the abolitionist theory that the institution of slavery caused the development of this class is largely erroneous. They became poor whites principally because of their environment and because of enervating diseases, such as malaria, hookworm, and pellagra.[48]

It is a mistake to equate the landless group among the rural population with the poor whites. Although the lack of property was a characteristic of the poor whites, there were many among the landless class who could not properly be so classified. Among these were renters or tenants who had slaves but no land, and vice versa. Sharecroppers, woodcutters, agricultural laborers, and overseers belonged to the landless group; some of them were poor whites, others were not. Miss Henry estimated that tenants formed from one-fourth to one-half of the landless class in Tennessee. Lucius Polk rented some of his large acreage in that state to tenants, but he concluded from his experience with them that they were "a curse."[49] A considerable number of the landless were squatters on the public land who were in process of acquiring title. The largest proportion of landless farmers seems to have been in

---

[47] Schlesinger, *The Cotton Kingdom by Frederick Law Olmsted*, pp. 426–427, 385–386.

[48] A. N. J. Den Hollander, "The Tradition of 'Poor Whites,'" in W. T. Couch (ed.), *Culture in the South* (Chapel Hill, 1935), pp. 403–431.

[49] Mooney, *Slavery in Tennessee*, p. 159.

the mountain counties; in east Tennessee they constituted 40 per cent of the farmers in 1860.

It is difficult to find adequate definition for this class in Southern society which has been compared to the slum element in the big Northern cities. An economic definition of status omits an important psychological difference between the poor whites and poor yeoman farmers. The latter had pride and respectability, even if they were poor, and regarded themselves as part of the "soveri'gn people." The poor whites, on the other hand, suffered from a feeling of inferiority as a class. Nevertheless, they had a striking personal pride. They would not deign to engage themselves to the planters to do menial work, for example; to wait on tables, carry water, bring wood, black boots, cut hair, drive a coach—such was "niggers' work," as they phrased it.[50]

The poor whites were primarily hunters and fishermen and not agriculturalists. They usually "squatted" upon the land, and their wives, rather than themselves, cultivated patches of corn or potatoes. Their log cabins were teeming with towheaded children and lean hound dogs. Olmsted reported that in the hilly region of northern Alabama they lived in rude log huts of one room "unwholesomely crowded." He noted one log cabin not more than fifteen feet square which housed five grown persons and as many children. In North Carolina he talked with a gentleman of Fayetteville who had under oath appraised the whole household property of some families of this class as worth less than $20. In order to gain a little money, they would sell game, fish, eggs, poultry, and corn meal. Some of them would work a few days for a farmer or planter for fifty cents a day, but they were unreliable and inconstant workers. Planters much preferred to hire Negroes rather than the poor whites.

The typical poor white was lean and gaunt, with yellow skin, sunken eyes, and poor teeth. The women looked old prematurely. Both men and women generally had a serious and melancholy expression on their faces. The men dressed in long homespun coats and wore slouch hats; the women wore calico sunbonnets. The whole family went barefooted in summer.[51] The men often went on drunken sprees on corn liquor, which they distilled in crude homemade stills. Their language was

[50] Olmsted, *Seaboard Slave States,* pp. 413–416, 506.
[51] See descriptions of poor whites in Bremer, *Homes of the New World,* I, 365–366; Smedes, *Memorials of a Southern Planter,* p. 113.

full of quaint Elizabethan pronunciations and expressions. Usually irreligious, they believed in witchcraft and "spirits" or "hants." An agent of the American Bible Society, distributing Bibles in Georgia, told Buckingham that in many of the ninety-three counties of the state more than half of the families lacked Bibles.[52]

A Northern soldier during the Civil War, C. W. Clifton, wrote a vivid description of some of the poor whites of eastern Tennessee in a letter to his sweetheart:

I tell you people of the North have very little idea of the ignorance and degradation of the citizens of the South, not one in ten can read or write. And they are about as ignorant in regard to their work. Our boys can beat these Southern women cooking all to pieces. And as a general thing they are very slack in their housekeeping, in fact perfect slovens. But very few ladies of the North would associate with them. The habit of chewing tobacco is very common with the women here. I have seen that which I would not have believed, had I not seen it. That is little girls ten years old chewing tobacco.[53]

The Georgia crackers from the pine woods and wiregrass country were somewhat different from the poor whites of the hill and mountain country. On court days they would come into the somnolent villages of the South, driving two-wheeled carts pulled by mules, bony horses, or oxen guided by a rope around the horns. In the morning the men seemed harmless, but toward noon, after they had drunk heavily of "bald-face whisky," provided gratis by storekeepers to their customers, a transformation took place. "Then might be seen," William Tappan Thompson relates, "the cadaverous-looking wiregrass boy in his glory, as he leaped out into the sand before the door, and tossing his linsey jacket into the air proclaimed himself the best man in the county. Then, too, might be seen the torpid clay-eater, his bloated, watery countenance illuminated by the exhilarating qualities of Mr. Hartley's rum, as he closed in with his antagonist"—cursing, biting, gouging, and, after victory, jumping upon a stump and crowing like a cock.[54]

The mountain whites were often classed with the poor whites, but

---

[52] Buckingham, *Slave States*, II, 64–65.

[53] C. W. Clifton in camp, fifteen miles from Chattanooga, to Julia Sanderlin, Grand Rapids, Mich., July 1, 1864. MS. in private possession.

[54] William T. Thompson, *Major Jones' Chronicles of Pineville* (Philadelphia, 1845), pp. 20–21.

the majority belonged to a different category, though there were some poor whites among them. They have been aptly described as "stranded frontiersmen" who remained in their isolated mountain valleys while the westward movement passed around them. The mountaineers as a whole were brave, manly, and self-respecting. Cherishing their kinship of clan, they believed in the right of private war or feud. Most of the highlanders owned their farms, upon which they raised corn, potatoes, and livestock in small quantities. In their patriarchal families a Spartan way of life was observed; their mountain home has been called the "land of do without."[55] Like the pine-woods poor whites, they had a prejudice against the Negro and showed little enthusiasm for freeing him, but they also disliked the lowlanders, "the furriners"; during the Civil War they resisted the draft and many of them supported the Union cause.

Charles Lanman's delightful *Letters from the Alleghany Mountains* (1849) tend to modify the stereotype that has been formed of the mountain people. He encountered various types of inhabitants of the Appalachian Mountains, ranging from families living in such squalor and ignorance that they fled with their dogs at the approach of a stranger to a "mountain aristocracy." Those were people who dwelt in fertile valleys, while the ignorant and "more barbarous" people lived up the creek on poor lands. The mountain aristocracy enjoyed a comfortable existence in good houses, their principal occupation being the raising of livestock, which were driven to market to Charleston, Savannah, and Baltimore. The mountain diet consisted of bacon, cornbread, game, and milk, and the chief luxury was honey. Lanman reported that not one white man in twenty in the mountains was sufficiently wealthy to own a slave, but that those who did treated their servants as "intelligent beings and in the most kindly manner."[56]

The most important cultural contribution of the Appalachian folk was their music. The isolation and primitive life of these people preserved not only old English speech but Old World ballads and songs, such as "Barbary Allen," "Lord Randall," "Frog Went a-Courtin," and "Weevily Wheat." The mountain fiddles played such lively tunes as "Money Musk," "Arkansas Traveler," "Old Joe Clark," "Leather

[55] Horace Kephart, *Our Southern Highlanders* (New York, 1913).
[56] Charles Lanman, *Letters from the Alleghany Mountains* (New York, 1849), p. 454.

Breeches," and "Sally Good'n." These plain people of the South fervently sang "white spirituals" and camp-meeting songs concerned with Heaven and the salvation of the soul.[57] Amateur singing masters taught these songs to the church "singing schools," using a songbook and a tuning fork. Two of the most popular songbooks in the Southern states were *The Sacred Harp*, compiled by B. F. White of Georgia, and *The Southern Harmony* arranged by "Singing Billy" Walker of South Carolina. The notes of the early songbooks in the South had four different shapes instead of dots so that they could easily be read by the rural folk.

Hardly anything was done in this era of laissez faire to improve the condition of the poor whites. Ridding them of the curse of hookworm and malaria had to wait until the twentieth century, when the causes of and remedies for these diseases were discovered. Little also was accomplished in the ante-bellum period for the education of these isolated people. Colporteurs at times visited them carrying Bibles and religious literature. A great step was taken toward improving their economic position when William Gregg began his propaganda campaign to utilize poor-white labor in the development of textile mills in the South. Yet it is questionable whether the creation of the mill villages with their long hours of unhealthy work and child labor brought any improvement in the condition of these people.

Although the poor whites were illiterate, after the Jacksonian movement they voted, usually the Democratic ticket; the mountain counties of North Carolina and Tennessee, however, were Whig strongholds. Politicians assiduously cultivated the poor whites. Franklin Plummer, a New England emigrant to the pineland belt of Mississippi, built up a political machine by appealing to the illiterate voters. With his New England school education, he was regarded as "a walking encyclopedia." He won the votes of the poor whites by visiting them in their log cabins and taking their children upon his lap and searching for redbugs, lice, and other vermin in their hair. Governor Hamilton of South Carolina also courted the vote of the people of the sandhills.[58] The

---

[57] G. P. Jackson, *White Spirituals in the Southern Uplands* (New York, 1913); H. C. Nixon, *Lower Piedmont Country* (New York, 1946), Chap. 7.

[58] See Paul H. Buck, "The Poor Whites of the Ante-Bellum South," *American Historical Review*, XXXI (1925), 44–46.

poor whites voted for candidates who upheld the slave regime, for they hated the Negroes and had no desire to free them.

Hinton Rowan Helper, a member of the yeoman class of North Carolina, tried to arouse the farmers and poor whites of the South to organize politically against the planter class. His book *The Impending Crisis of the South,* published in 1857, contained a savage attack on slavery, but he had no love for Negroes. In an autographed copy, dated 1870, he wrote in pencil: "For proof that this book was not written in behalf of negroes—as has been erroneously stated—but in behalf of the whites rather, See pages . . ." and he lists numerous references.[59] His book was banned from the South, particularly after it was reprinted in large numbers as a campaign document by the Republican party. Even if the nonslaveholders could have read it, there is little likelihood that it would have had any effect on them, for the more ambitious hoped to acquire slaves and they feared the consequences of liberating them. The society in which they lived was flexible enough for the talented and energetic to rise into the ruling class; thus many of the leaders of the plain people were absorbed in it.

After the Jacksonian movement there were sporadic manifestations of resentment against the planters in those states where they dominated. Professor Porcher of the College of Charleston tells in his memoirs of such a rebellion in 1844, when some of the farmers in his parish in the low country became dissatisfied because the members of the legislature were always selected from the planters. They were led by Dennis, a former overseer of Dr. Edmund Ravenel, who had become so successful that he had purchased his employer's plantation. This shrewd man of the people would not himself become a candidate for office, but he exerted himself to set up candidates in opposition to the planter class. Porcher, a planter at that time, though an unsuccessful one, sided with the rich and voted against the people's candidates, explaining, "I could not and would not desert my class."[60] The rumbling of discontent was also heard in the election for mayor in Charleston two years later. A communication in the *Mercury* appealed to the lower

[59] Autographed copy, addressed to R. A. Shotwell and owned by Professor Thomas D. Clark, University of Kentucky.

[60] Samuel G. Stoney (ed.), "Memoirs of Frederick Adolphus Porcher," *South Carolina Historical and Genealogical Magazine,* XLVII (1946), 105.

classes to vote for John Schnierle, the son of an adopted citizen, a fireman, and a mechanic. "Will you suffer," exclaimed the writer, "your brother to be trampled on by the silk stocking gentry, who wish to have a *gentleman* in office?"[61] On the eve of the Civil War the nonslaveholders in North Carolina found leaders in Moses Bledsoe of Wake County and John Pool to agitate (unsuccessfully) for the ad valorem taxation of all property, including slaves.

The prevalent notion that the Old South was dominated by the planter class, propagated by abolitionists, is inaccurate in many respects. By 1860 planters were not dominant politically in the South as a whole, for the Jacksonian movement and the constitutional reform movement of the 1850's had made most Southern states technically democratic. Planters were most powerful in the old Southern states and in Louisiana. In the newer states beyond the Appalachian barrier, the common man had become a formidable political power and here the planters fought many losing battles with the yeomanry. Clanton W. Williams observes that after 1822 the planter aristocracy in Alabama failed to control state politics on large issues: "The Montgomery planter constituency suffered one defeat after another in their political battles."[62]

The Jacksonian movement, however, was slow in bringing about change in the undemocratic practices of the older states of the South. In North Carolina, Georgia, and Maryland (before 1852) representation in the legislature was based on the federal ratio of population; in Louisiana and Maryland (after 1852) total population was the basis, the most undemocratic arrangement of all since Negro slaves were counted at their full number in the apportionment of representatives to the legislature. Virginia beat down the movement for the white basis of representation in the constitutional convention of 1850, led by Henry H. Wise and delegates from West Virginia, and adopted a compromise. Representation in the legislature was based on both white population and the amount of taxes paid; South Carolina also followed this system. In Alabama, Mississippi, Tennessee, Texas, and Missouri, all lying west of the Appalachian Mountains, the white-manhood basis for representation in the legislature had been won.

[61] Charleston *Mercury*, September 5, 1846.

[62] Clanton W. Williams, "Early Ante-Bellum Montgomery: A Black Belt Constituency," *Journal of Southern History*, VII (1941), 522–524.

Nevertheless, in all the Southern states the planters were able to secure very light taxation for their slave property and to protect slavery from all assaults. In 1849, after an agitation for the emancipation of the slaves in Kentucky, the constitutional convention went to the extreme lengths of placing the protection of slave property in the Bill of Rights, declaring: "the right of property is before and higher than any constitutional sanction, and the right of the owner of a slave to his property is the same and as inviolable as the right of the owner of any property whatsoever." Silas Woodson, a young lawyer from eastern Kentucky, vehemently opposed the adoption of this clause, maintaining that it was the act of a slavocracy which placed the peculiar institution beyond the control of a majority of the people.[63] But the people evidently did not think so, for they ratified the constitution by a majority of 51,351, though seven-eighths of the voters were nonslaveholders. Indeed, no clear political line could be drawn between slaveowners and nonowners. The nonslaveholders were linked to slaveholding families by ties of kinship, business and professional relationships, and church affiliations—not to speak of the hope and opportunity in an expanding agrarian society to become slaveholders themselves.

---

[63] *Kentucky Constitutional Convention of 1849, Debates and Proceedings* (Frankfort, 1850), pp. 867–70.

CHAPTER 8

The Renaissance of the Upper South

THE STORY of the revival of agriculture in the upper South after a period of decline is one of the bright pages in Southern history. The first era of reform in agricultural practices was initiated by enlightened planters who studied the works of contemporary English reformers. Washington read Jethro Tull's *The Horse-Hoeing Husbandry* and attempted to improve the tillage of Mount Vernon by practicing crop rotation and introducing new crops, such as lucerne and turnips. He imported an Arabian stallion to improve the breed of horses; the King of Spain gave him a pedigreed jack, Royal Gift, and Lafayette sent a jack from Malta to breed mules for draft animals. All his efforts availed little, for he had neglected Mount Vernon during his long period in the public service. Twenty-five years after his death a neighbor, describing the condition of the former regal estate, said that "a more widespread and perfect agricultural ruin could not be imagined."[1]

In 1784 John A. Binns of Loudon County in northern Virginia began to experiment with the use of gypsum, or plaster of Paris, as a fertilizer and with clover as a legume to improve the soil. Jefferson invented a superior moldboard for a plow and experimented with crop

[1] Mount Vernon was sadly neglected by Washington's heir, Bushrod Washington, Justice of the Supreme Court, who lived there until 1829; the Mount Vernon Association purchased it in 1860 and restored it. Paul Wilstach, *Mount Vernon, Washington's Home and the Nation's Shrine* (Garden City, 1916).

rotation. Other reformers of this period were Fielding Lewis (who had married Washington's sister), a pioneer in applying lime to Virginia's soil, and Thomas Mann Randolph, Jefferson's son-in-law, who managed Monticello during Jefferson's later years and is remembered for introducing contour plowing, which aided in checking erosion.[2] The most significant of these early agricultural reformers was John Taylor of Caroline, "the American Physiocrat."

This Virginia aristocrat loved agriculture more than he did his profession of law or politics, yet much of his energy was devoted to politics and to writing political tracts in order to protect the agrarian interests of the South within the federal government. He sought to make farming a gentleman's profession, a life of dignity. In 1813 he published *Arator*, an influential collection of essays on agriculture which he had previously contributed to newspapers. In this book he advocated deep plowing, a four-field system of crop rotation that gave each field a two-year rest, the restoration of worn-out fields by allowing them to lie fallow without grazing, and turning the weeds and grass under the soil with the plow. This pioneer work was widely read by the gentleman planters of Virginia and Maryland.[3] One of Taylor's disciples in North Carolina, George W. Jeffries, published in 1819 *Essays on Agriculture & Rural Affairs*, in which he advocated maintaining a balance on the farm between crops and livestock.[4]

Nevertheless, the isolated efforts of Taylor and Jeffries and a few planters to reform agricultural practices in Virginia, Maryland, and North Carolina had little permanent effect. The shifts of the currents of trade and markets during the Napoleonic Wars, on the other hand, resulted in far-reaching changes. An active market for American wheat was created in Europe, resulting in a large substitution of cereals for tobacco as the staple crops of the tidewater. Since wheat was not so exhausting to the soil as was the tobacco crop, its culture marked a step forward in Virginia and Maryland farming.

[2] Craven, *Soil Exhaustion as a Factor in the Agricultural History of Virginia and Maryland*, and Kathleen Bruce, "Virginian Agricultural Decline to 1860: A Fallacy," *Agricultural History*, VI (1932), 3–13.

[3] John Taylor, *Arator, Being a Series of Agricultural Essays, Practical and Political* (Petersburg, Va., 1818); see Avery Craven, "John Taylor and Southern Agriculture," *Journal of Southern History*, IV (1938), 137–147.

[4] C. C. Cathey, *Agricultural Developments in North Carolina, 1783–1860* (Chapel Hill, 1956), pp. 37, 42.

The second agricultural reform movement started in the 1820's with the experiments of Edmund Ruffin. Ruffin had inherited a run-down plantation on the James River, which he tried unsuccessfully to restore by the methods of John Taylor. In 1818 he read a copy of Davy's *Experimental Agricultural Chemistry*, which stated that acidity in soils could be counteracted by the use of lime. He concluded that the worn-out lands of eastern Virginia were suffering from vegetable acids and that the deposits of fossil shells, or marl, in the eastern part of the state could be used to reduce their acidity. His experiment of applying marl to restore the fertility of his own plantation was so highly successful that in 1821 he reported the results in John Skinner's *American Farmer* of Baltimore. In 1832 he published *An Essay on Calcareous Manures* which marks the beginning of an epoch in Southern agriculture. In order to propagandize the new gospel of marl, he founded in the next year an agricultural periodical, *The Farmer's Register*, printed in Petersburg. It was successful for ten years, until the zealous crusader began to use its columns to advance a hobby of bank reform.[5]

At first Ruffin's reforms were scoffed at by practical farmers, but gradually in the 1830's the more enlightened planters began to follow his example. His work had an important effect in producing a renaissance of agriculture in Virginia, Maryland, and the Carolinas. He and other progressive farmers of the upper South realized that their salvation lay not only in restoring exhausted soils but in adopting general farming instead of reliance on the old tobacco economy. His influence was enlarged by invitations from North and South Carolina to make agricultural surveys of these states. His report to Governor James H. Hammond of South Carolina in 1843 described the locations of extensive marl beds, and gave data concerning the operation of twenty-two plantations in eastern Virginia which had profited enormously from the application of marl. Some of the Virginia planters, he wrote, had begun to use marl on their lands as early as 1820, and in the 1830's the majority had adopted the practice. As a result, these plantations increased their yield of corn and wheat threefold to fourfold. In South Carolina, he observed, the amount of land that had been treated with marl before 1843 fell short of five hundred acres. A valuable part of his report was its inclusion of the answers of agricultural societies to questionnaires that he had sent out concerning crops and agricultural practices.[6]

There was indeed a renaissance in the older agricultural regions of the upper South. Ruffin's soil-improvement projects were only a part of it; the better planters began to drain lowlands and swamps, to replace the slow-moving oxen with tough and long-lived mules for pulling and plowing, and to abandon the scythe in favor of the more efficient cradle in reaping grain. Many progressive planters adopted contour plowing and terracing to check erosion and began to dismiss overseers and to direct the work on their plantations themselves with the aid of trusted slave foremen like Ruffin's Jem Sykes. They founded agricultural societies and fairs, where prizes were given for the best farm products and even for the prettiest quilts and other needlework and the best-preserved fruits. They subscribed to agricultural periodicals such as Ruffin's *The Farmer's Register* and John Skinner's *The American Farmer* and *The American Turf Register and Sporting Magazine*, which encouraged the improvement of the breed of American horses.

After 1845 the more progressive planters began to import guano from South America. Willoughby Newton, a prominent lawyer and politician of the Northern Neck of Virginia, was a pioneer in introducing this fertilizer in the state. The main source of guano used in the South was the islands off the coast of Peru; Baltimore became the principal port of entry of this fertilizer. Then in the late 1850's ex-Governor James Adams of South Carolina introduced guano from California on his Live Oaks Plantation at little more than half the price of Peruvian guano. He wrote to James H. Hammond, "guano is the only salvation for those of us who have worn lands and can't get rid of them."[7] The Virginia and Maryland planters seem to have been the most extensive users of this fertilizer, which worked like magic on their exhausted fields. When Solon Robinson visited Willoughby Newton's plantation in Westmoreland County, Newton told him that the introduction of guano in Virginia was "an interposition of Providence to save the country from total ruin, as most of the land had

[6] Edmund Ruffin, *Report of the Commencement and Progress of the Agricultural Survey of South-Carolina for 1843* (Columbia, 1843), Appendix.

[7] James H. Adams to James H. Hammond, August 23, 1858, James H. Hammond Papers.

become so utterly exhausted as not to be worth cultivating."[8] Some Southern railroads, notably the Georgia Central, helped spread the use of guano by transporting it at cost.

An important event in the rejuvenation of Virginia was the immigration of Northern farmers who bought worn-out lands cheaply and began general farming on them. Shortly after 1841 some Yankees from New Hampshire and Connecticut bought farms in Fairfax County in northern Virginia for $5 an acre. They tilled these lands with free white labor, and as a result of intelligent farming and thrift their properties increased greatly in value.

The Yankee colonists were at first welcomed by their Southern neighbors. The Richmond *Enquirer* commented on the agitation started by the Agricultural Society of Petersburg to persuade Northern farmers to settle in Virginia: "An infusion of a little Yankee industry and capital into the arteries of Virginia will produce a beneficial effect. We have seen it done successfully in the County of Fairfax."[9] The *Enquirer* attributed the success of these farmers to the fact that they were hard workers while the sociable nature of Southerners led them to congregate at the courthouse and country store to smoke, chew, talk politics, and, in general, waste time.

During the latter part of the ante-bellum period the antislavery controversy tended to make Southerners suspicious of the Northern immigrants. John M. Daniel of the Richmond *Examiner* wrote of this colonization as "the Vandal Invasion of Virginia," and opposed the movement of "fragrant hordes of adventurers fresh from the codfisheries of the Bay State," who would convert "lower Virginia into a paradise of onions, squashes, string-beans and 'liberty.' "[10]

The transformation of the old colonial estate of Sabine Hall, with its magnificent mansion on the Rappahannock River, might be taken as a symbol of the agricultural renaissance in the tidewater. Under Landon Carter, on the eve of the Revolution it was a flourishing tobacco plantation, one of the showplaces of Virginia. Nearby at Nomini Hall Fithian taught and kept his journal depicting the charm of a colo-

[8] Kellar, *Solon Robinson*, II, 373.
[9] Richmond *Enquirer*, June 26, 1845.
[10] *Ibid.*, May 22, 1857.

nial estate.[11] After the Revolution its tobacco lands became exhausted and reverted to old fields covered with pine trees. In 1851 when Solon Robinson visited Sabine Hall, he found that Robert W. Carter, a descendant of "King" Carter, had by the use of lime and guano and deep plowing restored the plantation. No longer did it produce tobacco, but it raised bountiful crops of wheat and corn. Robinson was enchanted with the new vitality of the aristocratic old estate, which still preserved its fine mansion, its lodge house at the gate, and its avenue of majestic trees. The proprietor was a hospitable gentleman of the old Virginia school, a natural nobleman, who literally made "the wilderness to blossom like the rose."[12]

The most prosperous part of the upper South in the late ante-bellum period was the Piedmont, whose soil was more durable and fertile than that of the coastal plain. In Virginia the northern counties of the Piedmont were predominantly grain-growing, where agricultural units tended to be much larger than the tobacco plantations. Indeed, the average Virginia tobacco grower in 1860 produced only about 3,500 pounds of tobacco, cultivated on five or six acres. The southern Piedmont contained the main tobacco counties of Virginia, and here the slaves of the state were concentrated. A recent study of the unpublished census returns of 1850 and 1860 shows that for every large plantation in Virginia there were three small plantations, four large farms, and seven small farms. Two-thirds of the agricultural properties in Virginia in 1860 contained less than two hundred acres of improved land each. Virginian agriculture by the end of the ante-bellum period had become far more diversified than it had been at the beginning of the nineteenth century. In 1850 the Old Dominion ranked fourth among the states both in the value of livestock and the production of wheat. Garden crops were being cultivated around Norfolk and shipped to New York. Fruit was being shipped northward by some farmers, notably William Sayre, son-in-law of Edmund Ruffin, from Sunnyside Farm near Portsmouth. The state also exported oysters and fish.[13]

[11] H. D. Farish (ed.), *Journal and Letters of Philip Vickers Fithian, 1773–1774* (Williamsburg, 1943).
[12] Kellar, *Solon Robinson*, II, 493–494.
[13] Fields, "Agricultural Population of Virginia, 1850–1860."

The typical Virginia or Maryland plantation combined tobacco growing with general farming. The cultivation of tobacco required a great amount of labor, so that a slave could tend only two or three acres of tobacco whereas he was able to cultivate twenty acres of wheat and an equal acreage of corn. The tiny seeds of the tobacco plant were planted in long beds of rich soil which were protected by cheesecloth, and in May the plants were set out in the fields at about three feet apart. After the plants had attained a height of several inches, the tobacco rows had to be frequently plowed and hoed, and a constant fight waged against insects and green tobacco worms. Men, women, and children did the fighting. The tobacco had to be "suckered," that is, the superfluous sprouts removed; topped, that is, the upper part of the plant must be cut off to prevent it from going to seed; "wormed," that is, the tobacco worms had to be removed; and primed, by pulling off all the coarse lower leaves, leaving only eight or ten to the stalk. After the stalks were cut in August or early September, they were left in the fields for the sun to wilt the leaves, which were then taken to the log tobacco houses to be cured or dried. By the 1830's the introduction of flues and thermometers enabled the crop master to control the process of curing more accurately than in colonial times. When the curing process was completed, the leaves were stripped from the stalk and "prized," or pressed into large hogsheads containing from 1,000 to 1,400 pounds.

In the early 1850's a new variety of tobacco, Bright Yellow, which sold for four times the price of ordinary dark tobacco, was developed in North Carolina. Stephen, the slave blacksmith and overseer on the farm of Abisha Slade in Caswell County, had accidentally discovered in 1839 a method of curing his master's tobacco by the use of charcoal as fuel, which produced a bright color in the leaf. It was later found that this variety grew best not on rich bottom lands but on the poor siliceous soil that half-starved the growing plant. This tobacco needed semistarvation; it also required curing by the use of flues and a thermometer to regulate the heat. Thus in the last decade of the ante-bellum period a new variety of tobacco had been developed, which was first used as an ornamental cover for plug tobacco but after the Civil War became the basis of the Southern cigarette industry.[14]

[14] N. M. Tilley, *The Bright-Tobacco Industry, 1860–1929* (Chapel Hill, 1948), pp. 24–25.

During colonial days and until 1805 in Virginia and 1817 in North Carolina, all tobacco had to be inspected, and rejected tobacco had to be burnt. Official inspection of tobacco for export continued through the ante-bellum period. In the decade before the Civil War two-thirds of the crop grown in Virginia and North Carolina, instead of being exported as formerly, was manufactured into chewing and smoking tobacco by the Virginia factories. A change came also in the method of marketing the crop that led to the abandonment of the tobacco note or inspection receipt which had served as currency in colonial days. Now the farmers transported their crop to the three principal markets, Richmond, Lynchburg, and Petersburg, where the buyers inspected its quality and bought at auction in the tobacco warehouses. In 1858 the Richmond Tobacco Exchange established centralized buying at auction through samples.

The style of life of the planters of eastern Maryland and the Old Dominion varied greatly. Relatively few owned luxurious establishments such as Westover, former home of the Byrds, and Wye House, the seat of the Lloyds on the Eastern Shore of Maryland, where Frederick Douglass spent his youth as a slave. Shirley in the James River Valley also belonged to this category. Here Henry Barnard of Hartford, Connecticut, visited in 1833 and left a pleasant account of its daily life. At this time Shirley had abandoned tobacco culture and had become a large wheat and corn plantation. Its 900 acres of improved land, tilled by a force of 100 slaves, yielded an annual income of $10,000. Hill Carter, the proprietor, a descendant of one of the most aristocratic colonial families, lived in rustic splendor. He kept twenty horses for domestic use and was lavish in hospitality. Barnard described a single day at Shirley. It began with a servant coming into his bedroom in the morning to build a fire, polish his boots, and brush his clothes. At eight o'clock he had breakfast with the family—tea, coffee, ham, hot muffins, and corn batter cakes served on a rich mahogany table. After breakfast visitors were on their own; they rode, read in the fine library, or strolled in the garden. (The master and mistress in Virginia were not expected to entertain guests until just before dinner at three o'clock.) The dinner was "princely"—the guests drank porter out of silver goblets, as well as fine Madeira wine. Barnard described the hostess as a lady from a high and wealthy family, yet "one of the plainest most unassuming women you will meet anywhere."[15]

Catherine Hopley's journal portrays life on a middle-sized plantation on the Rappahannock River, Forest Rill, where she taught. She found the master to be a gentleman of great dignity of character, mild and courteous. He employed no overseer, superintending himself the work of his slaves. There were no whippings of "my people" by the master. Miss Hopley was impressed by the lack of hurry in the South, both among the slaves and the whites, and the lack of tidiness in the houses and in the operation of the plantations. She also noticed the Virginians' insistence on family status, their pride in gentility. She tutored children on another plantation owned by a Baptist preacher, the Reverend Mr. Quence. The Quences would associate only with people in their own rank of society.[16] The Virginia families she encountered talked often of ancestors, and they made much of kinship—of "kissing cousins." The Virginia mind, as Miss Hopley saw it, was a mixture of pride, often quixotic, of paternalism in regard to their slaves, of hospitality, and of fanatical devotion to Southern institutions. They thought their own way of living was the world, because most of the plantations were largely self-sufficient, with some of the characteristics of feudal villages.

There was not so much aristocratic pretension on the slave plantations in North Carolina as in Virginia or South Carolina. North Carolina was a land of yeoman farmers. Its economic development and contact with the world were retarded by the lack of good harbors; most of its tobacco was shipped by the Dismal Swamp Canal to Norfolk or transported overland to Petersburg. Approximately two-thirds of the landowners had farms of less than a hundred acres. Nevertheless, in favored river valleys aristocratic plantations developed, such as the rice plantation of Orton near Wilmington or the large tobacco plantations in the Albemarle Sound region. Still, of the 34,658 slaveholders in 1860 only 611 owned between fifty and one hundred slaves and only 133 owned over a hundred slaves. Slavery was declining in North Carolina at the end of the ante-bellum period.[17]

[15] Bernard C. Steiner, "The South Atlantic States in 1833, as seen by a New Englander," *Maryland Historical Magazine,* XIII (1918), 310.

[16] Hopley, *Life in the South,* I, Chaps. III, VI.

[17] Cathey, *Agricultural Developments in North Carolina,* Chap. III.

Solon Robinson has described the cereal-growing plantations in the Roanoke Valley of North Carolina operated by the Burgwyn brothers. When they inherited their plantations in 1840, the Burgwyns had liberal sentiments about emancipating their slaves. But after losing considerable money as the result of hiring Irish labor, they gave up their sentiments and became highly successful planters by the use of slave labor. Their three plantations were so extensive that they had to maintain thirty miles of worm fences *"to keep out other folks' cattle."* (The Southern states retained the open range for cattle.)[18] When the Burgwyns acquired their plantations, cotton culture had largely exhausted the soil. Instead of continuing the old culture, they converted their lands into thriving wheat and corn plantations. They transformed the infertile fields by the use of lime. They forced their reluctant and tradition-bound overseers to practice scientific agriculture, especially to plow deep with "new fangled plows." They raised herds of cattle, numerous hogs, and huge crops of wheat, corn, and clover. Moreover, they used modern agricultural machinery, employing, for example, nine Hussey reapers, and threshing their wheat by steam power.

Contrary to the usual notion, the leading crop of the ante-bellum South was corn, which furnished food for both man and beast. This crop dovetailed into the cultivation of cotton, for labor in raising cotton decreased during the period when the greatest labor was required in corn production. In 1850 the Southern states raised 60 per cent of the nation's corn, a proportion that declined to 52 per cent in 1860. The most productive corn area was the upper South, but even the lower states raised a large amount of this cereal, producing 28 per cent of the South's total crop.[19]

In the pineland region of the coastal plain, farmers and planters were engaged principally in producing naval stores. During colonial days this industry had been nourished by bounties from the British government, which wanted to free the Empire from dependence on Swedish naval stores. The pine trees were slashed with an ax and, below the gash, boxes were placed, or cavities were cut, holding about a quart. Into these the sap flowed, which was collected and distilled by

[18] Kellar, *Solon Robinson*, II, 227, 359.
[19] Donald L. Kemmerer, *Agricultural History*, XXIII (1949), 236–239.

copper stills into turpentine, leaving a by-product of rosin. Tar was made by slowly burning pine logs covered with turf in a kiln, and pitch was derived as a concentrate by boiling the tar. Despite frequent hacking of the trees, a turpentine orchard lasted about fifty years. In 1850 North Carolina, with its vast forests of long-leaf pine, produced 87.6 per cent of the naval stores of the United States, and smaller amounts came from South Carolina, Georgia, and Alabama.

The turpentine planters practiced a highly specialized industry, buying most of their food, although they raised a little corn. A very few large proprietors combined growing cotton with exploiting their long-leaf pine forests. Many of the turpentine producers were small farmers, owning several slaves, but living in almost as primitive conditions as the poor whites. The task system was generally employed. Many slaves were hired in the turpentine industry; these were able to make $5 over their wages a month for their own use.

The planters in the turpentine region as a rule lived isolated and lonely lives. The letters of Sarah Williams, a New York girl who married a doctor and planter of Green County, North Carolina, vividly portray the society of the turpentine planters. Her description of their way of life is a refutation of the glamorous legend of the Southern plantation. She found that the mistresses of the plantations around her often worked harder than any Northern women she knew—sewing clothes for the Negroes, doctoring them, supervising the garden, and taking care of the chickens. A Southern lady, she wrote, received a number of slaves as dowry, and Sarah's mother-in-law was accordingly displeased that her son had married a Northern girl without any "niggers." She noted that Southern households were run without much system—"Wash, bake, or iron, just as the fit takes." Nor did the planters pay much attention to comforts that Northerners cherished. Many wealthy planters lived in crude frame houses. Sarah was disturbed also by seeing women, not only of the poor-white class but also of the upper classes, dip snuff. She feared that her small daughter, seeing ladies indulge in this habit, would seek to imitate them, and also that she would learn bad habits from little Negroes.[20]

Clifton Grove, to which she came in 1853 as a young bride, contained two thousand acres and thirty-seven slaves. Sarah belonged to

[20] J. C. Bonner (ed.), "Plantation Experiences of a New York Woman," *North Carolina Historical Review*, XXXIII (1956), 384–417, 529–546.

an abolitionist family, and therefore she was surprised to see the kind treatment of the slaves in her neighborhood. Her husband regarded slaves as "the most unprofitable property a person could possess." Instead of investing his profits from turpentine and cotton in more slaves, he bought railroad stocks that paid 7 per cent dividends. But at the close of the ante-bellum period he moved to Georgia to start a new turpentine plantation, and in order to obtain labor was forced to buy slaves. In her new home Sarah lived a lonely existence; she wrote on May 25, 1859, that she had not been a mile away from the plantation for six months.

Living on the cotton plantation of Looking Glass, also in the eastern part of the state, Catherine Edmondston recorded in her journal the manifold activities of a Southern lady who had a strong sense of responsibility. She cultivated in her garden tuberoses, dahlias, and cape jessamine. She made blackberry wine and brandied peaches, and on one occasion put fifty hams in bags to hang in the smokehouse. She vaccinated all the little pickaninnies, twenty-six of them, tried to prevent them from eating dirt, and taught them the catechism. She read romantic poetry and Shakespeare, and knitted socks. When the overseer was conscripted during the Civil War she took over the task of weighing the meat allowance for the eighty slaves—a half-pound of bacon a day for everyone over ten years of age.[21]

The plantation system that Catherine Edmondston and her husband knew changed somewhat, because of the nature of the crops, when it was transplanted across the mountains into Kentucky. Although hemp was cultivated principally by slaveholders and was known as "a nigger crop," it did not lead to the growth of large slave plantations since the crop required little labor as compared with cotton or tobacco (three slaves could cultivate fifty acres). Consequently the largest slaveholder of Kentucky, Robert Wickliffe of Fayette County, the "Old Duke," owned only two hundred slaves. The growing of hemp on a commercial scale was confined largely to the Bluegrass counties; here it was the money crop of the ante-bellum period, to be superseded after the Civil War by burley tobacco.

The hemp plant grew in slender stalks from six to ten feet high. In August it was cut and allowed to lie on the ground to be rotted

[21] Diary of Catherine Ann Edmondston, May 2, 18, 1861; May 8, 1862, North Carolina State Department of Archives and History.

by the dew. Although it required rich soil, its cultivation depleted the land only slightly, mainly because the dew-rotting process returned fertilizing elements to the soil. The fibers of the hemp plant were separated from the glutinous material of the stalk by a crude hemp brake, usually operated by a strong slave—many inventors tried to make a practical hemp-breaking machine, but none succeeded.

The hemp growers faced dangerous competition from foreign fibers, such as Indian hemp, and from Scottish-manufactured bagging. As early as 1816 hemp and cordage received tariff protection, and in 1824 a tariff act championed by Henry Clay raised the duties, especially on hemp bagging, to give adequate protection from foreign competition. Throughout the ante-bellum period the hemp manufacturers were protected by tariff legislation. Since the principal market for Kentucky hemp products—bagging for cotton bales and ropes for plows and wells and for tying cotton bales—was in the cotton-planting states, those states put up a strong opposition to a high tariff on these products. Moreover, the prosperity of the hemp industry fluctuated with the fortunes of these cotton planters.

The congressmen from the hemp-growing states, particularly Henry Clay, sought to require the Navy to buy American hemp rather than the Russian product. The latter, instead of being rotted by dew, was decomposed in pools and was much superior to Kentucky dew-rotted hemp. Efforts to persuade the Kentucky hemp growers to change to the water-rotted method, which was more laborious and disagreeable, proved unsuccessful. Clay tried the water-rotting process at Ashland, but after a brief trial returned to the older method. David Myerle, a cordage manufacturer of Louisville, engaged in an unsuccessful campaign to persuade Kentuckians to adopt the water-rotted process. In 1852 the government built a navy yard and a modern rope factory at Memphis; but, unable to secure high-grade water-rotted hemp from Kentucky, Missouri, and Tennessee, it abandoned the attempt to make cordage for the Navy from the native product and in 1854 donated the naval hemp establishment to the city of Memphis.[22] In the late 1840's and early 1850's the Kentucky planters began to abandon hemp for wheat and livestock. Nevertheless, in 1850 over half of the hemp grown in the United States was raised in Kentucky, her nearest com-

[22] James F. Hopkins, *A History of the Hemp Industry in Kentucky* (Lexington, 1951).

petitor being Missouri, where hemp plantations had been established in the Missouri River Valley.

Oxmoor, a plantation nine miles from Louisville, presented a good example of the larger hemp plantations in Kentucky. It was owned by the Bullitts, a cultivated and able family descended from French Huguenots. The plantation consisted of 1,028 acres, tilled by approximately one hundred slaves. Until 1849 the plantation had no overseer, and the Bullitt sons worked with the slaves during summer vacations from college. The crops of the plantation were hemp, corn, and wheat, and much livestock was raised, particularly Southdown sheep and short-horn Durham cattle. The task system was employed in the raising and processing of hemp; the task of a slave for breaking hemp was one hundred pounds, and for each pound over that amount he was paid one cent; some slaves broke three hundred pounds a day. The mother of the family was deeply religious and the Bullitts lived a simple and unostentatious existence in a small and plain house. Mrs. Bullitt sold butter, turkeys, and hams in Louisville to obtain pocket money.[23]

On such plantations as Oxmoor slavery appears to have been a kindly patriarchal institution, which dignified the life of the planters. Yet the general effects of slavery on the white population were unfortunate. William Reynolds, the flatboat merchant, in his journal compared the people of Kentucky with those of Indiana. He observed that the inhabitants of the Southern states were very polite to each other and to strangers, and that they had a "more fiery, ambitious spirit" than the homespun-clad people of southern Indiana. The upper-class Kentuckian, because of his ownership of slaves, developed an attitude that "God has made him a little better than those who have the misfortune to be born poor." Reynolds asserted that the Kentuckians were looser in morals than the natives of Indiana, and much more extravagant. Eastern merchandise sold from 15 to 20 per cent higher in the slave state than in Indiana, because "slaveholders are more spendthrift because they live on the labor of slaves & have not learned the economy of those who work." In virtually every town that he visited on the Kentucky side of the Ohio River he found people absorbed in horse racing and gambling; one could hardly engage a Ken-

[23] Thomas W. Bullitt, *My Life at Oxmoor; Life on a Farm in Kentucky before the War* (Louisville, 1911).

tuckian in conversation without hearing "I'll bet you."[24]

Tobacco was the staple crop of the central Kentucky counties along the Ohio River and of a section in the southern part of the state around Hopkinsville. Tobacco was also grown extensively in the Nashville basin and around Clarksville, Tennessee, and immigrants from the older tobacco country carried the culture of the "royal weed" to the Missouri Valley. The principal market of the Western tobacco was New Orleans; but after the Baltimore and Ohio Railroad reached Wheeling in 1853, a notable diversion from the river port to Baltimore occurred. The westward movement of population resulted in a severe competition between Virginia, Carolina, and Maryland tobacco and Western tobacco. In 1836 a London merchant wrote to Samuel Miller of Lynchburg that "Kentucky tobacco of all sorts is certainly obtaining a very great preference over Virginia" and had almost entirely driven Maryland tobacco out of the market.[25] In 1860 the Western states produced more tobacco than the old Eastern tobacco states, although Virginia still remained the leading tobacco-growing state, Kentucky ranking second. Twenty years earlier Virginia had produced only slightly more tobacco than she had in colonial days, and Maryland even less than her colonial production. But in the last decade of the ante-bellum period, when prices were good, a notable increase in the cultivation of tobacco occurred in Virginia and North Carolina, mainly in the Piedmont counties.[26]

The life and economic interests of a tobacco planter of Kentucky are vividly mirrored in the diary of Augustus Woodward of Graves County. According to the unpublished census returns of 1860, he owned thirty slaves, of whom nineteen were less than fifteen years old and eleven were working hands. His plantation consisted of 275 acres of improved and 200 acres of unimproved land. Most of the agricultural operators around him owned approximately 50 acres of improved and 100 acres of unimproved land. He raised considerably more tobacco than any of the other thirty-nine farmers listed with him on the manuscript census page. The average farmer of his community raised about 2,000 pounds of tobacco and 500 bushels of corn; his crop con-

[24] William Reynolds, Journal of Travel, pp. 61–63.
[25] Brock Collection, Huntington Library.
[26] Joseph C. Robert, *The Story of Tobacco in America* (New York, 1949), p. 61.

sisted of 28,000 pounds of tobacco and 3,000 bushels of corn. He also raised wheat and oats, and his forty swine probably provided enough meat for his slaves and family. His livestock in 1860 included four milk cows, eight horses, twelve mules and asses, and six working oxen.[27] He marketed his tobacco in Paducah, where it was probably shipped down the river to New Orleans.

Woodward was a Whig in politics, a Mason, and apparently a good Christian, for he notes in his diary going to church and reading the Bible on Sunday. He varied the monotony of farming by riding on court days in his buggy to Mayfield, the county seat, where he purchased such luxuries as cake, figs, candy, pecans, crackers, sardines, and ice cream. His main amusements were hunting, attending singing school, and barbecues. He also went to the meetings of the Sons of Temperance. He caught the Texas emigration fever in 1856 and proceeded to trade a horse and a black mule for 120 acres of land in that state. In 1860 he visited Texas, but died on the return journey in Arkansas at the age of thirty years.[28]

Increasingly, Kentucky and Tennessee raised livestock. Henry Clay and Lewis Sanders of Grass Hills were pioneers in bringing blooded cattle from England. In 1817 Clay introduced the Hereford breed into Kentucky, and Sanders imported the blooded short-horn bulls Tecumseh and Sam Martin. In the 1830's the Herefords lost their popularity and Kentucky stock raisers, instead, imported pedigreed Durham cattle from England.[29] Kentucky stock breeders organized associations and sent agents to England to buy breeding stock. Beef cattle were driven in large herds across the mountains to markets on the Atlantic seaboard. Cassius Marcellus Clay made large profits by buying cattle from farmers in his county and having them driven to market in Cincinnati.[30] Here and at Louisville beef was packed in barrels and shipped by steamers to New Orleans.[31] The Kentucky planters were particu-

[27] U.S. Census, 1860, Agriculture, Schedule IV, p. ii, No. 14, microfilm, University of Kentucky Library; Original in Duke University Library.

[28] Diary of Augustus Woodward, February 22–April 4, 1856, University of Kentucky Library.

[29] Lewis Sanders to Edwin G. Bedford, May 2, 1853, Bedford Papers, University of Kentucky Library.

[30] Olmsted, *Journey through Texas*, pp. 12–13.

[31] Paul C. Henlein, *Cattle Kingdom in the Ohio Valley, 1783–1860* (Lexington, 1959).

larly interested in raising fine mules, the draft animals of the ante-bellum South. Clay imported jacks from Malta, Spain, and France, notably the famous jack Magnum Bonum.[32] The Kentucky breeders sent droves of mules through the Cumberland Gap to be sold in the Atlantic seaboard states. In 1860, 90 per cent of the mules in the United States were in the Southern states.

Kentucky, and to some degree Tennessee, specialized in breeding race horses. Henry Clay was among the stock breeders of his region who imported Arabian stallions to improve the native breed of racers descended from English stock. Often several breeders would pool their resources to acquire blooded stallions from abroad. Andrew Jackson was a prominent breeder of race horses on his Hermitage Plantation, thirteen miles from Nashville. The Reverend Hardy Cryer, a Meth-odist minister, was a connoisseur of race horses and at times acted as agent for Jackson in selling his blooded horses and advised him in regard to their training. Jackson had a race track on his plantation; in 1830 there were at the Hermitage three brood mares, eight colts and fillies from noted sires, and his own stallion Bolivar.[33]

Southern planters also paid attention to improving the breed of sheep and hogs. In the 1840's the planters in the Nashville limestone basin began to shift from growing cotton and tobacco to raising live-stock. Mark Cockrill was the most successful of these livestock breeders. On his 5,000-acre plantation near Nashville, 2,300 head of sheep and approximately 700 horses, mules, and cattle grazed during the decade of the 1850's. He won a prize at a world's fair in London for the finest specimen of Saxon sheep. Less attention was paid to the improvement of the breed of hogs; nevertheless in the 1850's planters were importing from England Berkshire boars, such as the famous boar Ne Plus Ultra brought over by Doctor Shelby of Nashville.

An important stimulus to the improvement of livestock was the agri-cultural fairs, where prizes were awarded for the best livestock. Mrs. Isabella Trotter, an English traveler, was much impressed by the huge amphitheater at Lexington, Kentucky, capable of seating 12,000 spec-

[32] See Clement Eaton, *Henry Clay and the Art of American Politics* (Boston, 1957), Chap. V; G. G. Van Deusen, *The Life of Henry Clay* (Boston, 1937), p. 272.

[33] John S. Bassett, *The Correspondence of Andrew Jackson* (Washington, 1926–35), III, 401.

tators at the annual cattle shows.[34] Enlightened and prosperous planters were the chief promoters of livestock breeding for quality, for the
farmers were either too poor or too unconcerned to do much toward
raising blooded animals.

Andrew Jackson's letters give valuable information concerning Tennessee agriculture. The Hermitage combined raising livestock and growing cotton. Of its 640 acres, only 130 to 200 were planted in cotton;
approximately 300 acres were planted in corn, and smaller fields were
sown in wheat, oats, rye, and clover. Of his slave force of eighty Negroes, approximately half were working hands. During much of his
life he was an absentee planter and had to depend on ignorant and
careless overseers. Nevertheless he tried to hold them to high standards
of cultivation; he wrote on July 9, 1825, that his cotton had been
plowed eight times and that it was in splendid condition despite the
drought.

Jackson sought to make the Hermitage self-sufficient. He had little
trouble in raising enough corn and other grain for the plantation, but
he was constantly worrying about producing enough pork. He raised
from two hundred to four hundred hogs, but many of them got stolen
by the Negroes, particularly from adjoining plantations. Other efforts
at self-sufficiency were more successful. Spinning and weaving were
done by those of the female slaves who were not fitted for field work,
and shoes of the slaves were made on the plantation. He owned a
blacksmith and understandably was annoyed when his overseer once
bought a plow instead of having it made on the plantation. His slaves
also manufactured bricks and cut timber for sale.

Although Jackson was a good practical farmer, he does not seem
to have been a student of scientific farming or an experimenter. His
gin was homemade except for the running gear, and he appears to
have been content with crude homemade plows and to have used
horses and slow-moving oxen as draft animals rather than the more
efficient mules. Nor does he seem to have been careful in selecting
the seed for planting his cotton fields. In breeding his race horses, on
the other hand, he paid careful attention to pedigree.

The cotton plantations of Tennessee were concentrated in the middle and western parts of the state. Among the great planters of the

[34] Isabella Trotter, *First Impressions of the New World* (London, 1859),
pp. 244–252.

state were the Polks, who came from North Carolina and established a cluster of plantations in middle Tennessee, especially Rattle and Snap in Maury County, with its magnificent mansion. The Polks were agriculturists representative of Tennessee planters in general, who raised cotton, corn, hogs, and cattle. Despite their ability and energy, they had trouble with overseers and the management of distant plantations.[35] Floods, late frosts, and the ravages of disease and pests often drastically reduced the yield of the Tennessee plantations. When there was a bumper crop the prices were usually low, but the greatest loss came, Jackson believed, from bad overseers. Normally his crop of cotton was fifty bales of five hundred pounds each, but some seasons the Hermitage produced only half a crop. Like many planters he was often in debt and had little ready cash.

The upper South in the 1850's was fairly prosperous. The period of the "rural depression" in the old tobacco country, 1800–32, lay in the past; the depression in the cotton country that began in 1837 was over by 1850. The agriculture of the upper South had become more diversified, and more farmers had acquired land. On the eve of the Civil War slavery had declined slightly in this region from the peak of 1850. Emigration from the upper South, which had slackened during the decade of the 1840's, had been resumed, but the course of emigration was now to Missouri, Arkansas, and Texas. The upper South was building railroads and canals; developing tobacco factories, textile mills, ropewalks, and bagging factories; and mining its resources of coal and iron. Indeed, its people had lost the apathy and discouragement of the older generation, for a renaissance had occurred in economic and spiritual life.

---

[35] Mooney, *Slavery in Tennessee,* Chap. VII.

CHAPTER 9

The Colonial Status of the South

THE MOST striking characteristic of Southern economy was that although the colonial connection with England had been broken, a new colonialism arose with respect to Northern business. Southern trade in the first half of the nineteenth century came increasingly under the control of Northern men and particularly under the dominance of the port of New York. Credit was a vital need of the Southern farmers and planters; the North furnished this credit on its own terms. The protective tariff policy, moreover, contributed toward the dependence of the South on the North. The colonial status of the South was underlined by the highly unfavorable balance of trade of the Southern ports. They exported far more than they imported, and European goods destined for Southern consumers were channeled through the port of New York. Northern businessmen were largely the middlemen, the shippers, the bankers, the insurers, that took a lion's share of the profits of Southern agriculture. Every spring and autumn the trek of Southern merchants to Northern mercantile centers dramatized the colonial status of the region below the Potomac.

This analysis of the colonialism of the South has been disputed by a Southern scholar on the ground that the exchange of services between the two sections was equitable.[1] It was equitable only if skilled business-

[1] Charles S. Sydnor, *The Development of Southern Sectionalism, 1819–1848* (Baton Rouge, 1948), pp. 24–25.

men are entitled to higher profits from their labor and management than skilled agriculturists are from theirs. The Southerners of the ante-bellum period were in much the same position as exploited factory workers are before they organize powerful labor unions. They had to take what was given them for their crops. They did not organize to obtain a parity with industry, and their credit situation was so precarious that they could not withhold their crops from the market. Albion has shown clearly that in respect to trade and commerce Southerners failed to utilize their opportunities and defaulted to more aggressive Northern businessmen.[2]

The story of the Southern ports illustrates the commercial dependence of the ante-bellum South. The only port south of the Mason and Dixon line that did not have a colonial status lay on the perimeter of the region, Baltimore, Maryland. Much of this city's trade was derived from the exports of the Susquehanna Valley, flour, cereals, whisky, lumber, and iron. Indeed, this Southern town waged a strenuous fight with Philadelphia for this trade by building competing canals and railroads. The completion of the Baltimore and Ohio Railroad to the Ohio River at Wheeling in 1853 gave a tremendous boost to Baltimore's trade and population.[3] This city on the Chesapeake Bay was now able to monopolize the handling of the Ohio tobacco crop. And although the greater proportion of Kentucky tobacco was floated to New Orleans, about 1,500 hogsheads of it were yearly shipped by rail to Baltimore.

The city had a more diversified commerce than any other Southern port. Virtually all of the tobacco crop of Maryland was exported through its harbor. In 1857 the flour mills of the city produced 240,-000 barrels of flour, valued at $2,500,000, and it received an even larger number, 270,557 barrels, from Pennsylvania for export. Vast quantities of flour were shipped to South America, and in return the port received large consignments of hides and coffee. Considerably more than half of Baltimore's trade was with South America. But there was a good deal of trade with the lower South. In 1857, 35,000 bales of cotton were received from there, most of which was used in

[2] Robert G. Albion, *The Rise of New York Port 1815–1860* (New York, 1939), Chap. VI.

[3] Edward Hungerford, *The Story of the Baltimore and Ohio Railroad* (New York, 1928), I.

Baltimore's factories. The lower South also proved a good customer for the rye and corn whisky of the Baltimore distilleries.

Moreover, the city was not dependent on New England for its ships, for it was the most important shipbuilding center in the Southern states, famed for its Baltimore clippers. It was the only Southern port where there was no great disparity between exports and imports; in 1840 these were approximately even; in 1856, at the height of its prosperity, the ratio of imports to exports was roughly 10 to 13; after the panic of 1857 there was again a virtual equalization of imports and exports. The commercial activity of the port was indicated by the fact that in 1857 over four thousand coastwise vessels and over a thousand foreign vessels cleared its harbor.[4]

Norfolk in the colonial period seemed destined to become the great port of the Chesapeake Bay country. But her prosperity depended on the West India trade; and when Great Britain closed or severely restricted this trade, 1815–31, the Virginia port languished. In 1820 the town had a population of 8,608, which by 1850 had increased to 14,326, but during the last decade of the ante-bellum period the city's growth practically stopped. Norfolk suffered greatly from the fact that New York secured a virtual monopoly on European goods destined for the Virginia market. Although Virginia exports in 1837 were valued at $11,259,539, its direct imports from Europe amounted to the paltry sum of $816,887.

The introduction of steam navigation resulted in oceangoing ships proceeding directly to Richmond instead of, as in earlier days, transshipping their cargoes at Norfolk. The city did gain some prestige by the establishment of the Gosport Navy Yard near it, but its efforts to attract Western trade by building railroad lines connecting with the Kanawha and Ohio rivers were defeated by the powerful influence in the legislature of the fall-line towns of Richmond and Petersburg, which feared that the seaport would develop at their expense.[5] Norfolk was unable to obtain a railroad connection with Richmond until 1854 and with Petersburg until 1858. Its chance to become the terminal for Western exports was destroyed when the state-supported James River and Kanawha Company, chartered in 1832, made the grievous mistake

[4] J. C. Gobright, *The Monumental City, or Baltimore Guide Book* (Baltimore, 1858), p. 54.

[5] Thomas J. Wertenbaker, *Norfolk, Historic Southern Port* (Durham, 1931).

of deciding to build a canal instead of a railroad to connect the James with the Kanawha River.[6]

The shipping of cotton was the major business of the ports of the lower South. New Orleans ranked first in exports, Mobile second, and Charleston third, with Savannah close behind, and in the last decade of the ante-bellum period Galveston, Texas, became an important cotton port. Although Charleston ranked third as a cotton port in 1860, the city had declined from its proud position on the eve of the Revolution, when it ranked third among all American ports in volume of trade. Its prosperity was still high as late as 1815, when it was the leading cotton as well as rice exporting port. With the spread of cotton culture to the Southwest, however, it sank rapidly in relative importance as a port.

New Orleans far exceeded any other Southern port in commercial activity, for it shipped huge quantities of cotton, sugar, tobacco, and other products of the Mississippi Valley. Indeed, in 1860 it ranked second only to New York in the value of its exports. But its imports were far below those of the great Northern metropolis, not equal to even one-tenth in value. The principal imports into the various Southern harbors ranked in the following order: coffee, textiles, and iron products. A major reason why textiles bulked so large among Southern imports was the requirements of feminine fashion. Because of the yardage used in the hoop skirts and petticoats of the 1850's, one writer has estimated, a lady of the period used enough cloth to clothe fourteen women in the 1920's.[7]

Unlike the natural exchange of goods with the mother country in colonial days (which incidentally brought valuable cultural contacts with Europe), Southern commerce of the ante-bellum period was directed largely to the port of New York. In 1822, Southern products—cotton, tobacco, naval stores, and rice—represented 55 per cent of New York's exports to Europe. Thus early New York had developed an astonishing cotton triangle, which meant a detour through the port of New York of Southern cotton bound for European markets. The triangle worked as follows: cotton would be shipped to New York; from there it was exported to Europe; then the ships returned to New York

---

[6] See W. F. Dunaway, *History of the James River and Kanawha Company* (New York, 1922).

[7] Albion, *Rise of New York Port*, p. 55.

laden with foreign goods and immigrants. To carry on the cotton trade, New York established regular sailing packets to the Southern ports. The demands of the trade, however, were seasonal. Most of the shipping of cotton, sugar, and rice took place in the fall and winter. During the slack period of the summer there was little freight shipped from the South, chiefly lumber, hides, furs, flour, and tobacco. The large packets usually sailed a hundred miles a day, taking three weeks between New Orleans and New York. Furthermore, one of the disadvantages of the detour of cotton to New York was the hazards of the coastal voyage, which made insurance rates between New Orleans and New York higher than between New York and Liverpool.

Accordingly, during the last decade of the ante-bellum period there was a great diminution in the shipment to New York of cotton destined for Europe. Instead, merchants and speculators in New York purchased Southern cotton by samples and bills of lading, and the cotton was sent directly from the Southern ports to Europe. Some of this cotton was sold "in transit" to Liverpool. In 1859 only 28,800 bales were sent to New York, which was less than one-third the amount shipped thither in 1850. In the same year 310,400 bales were sent by Southern factors to other Northern ports, chiefly to New England for the expanding textile industry, while 1,866,000 bales were shipped directly to foreign ports.[8]

The key figure in Southern foreign trade and, in fact, of Southern economy, was the factor. He was the planter's agent, usually located in a port city, who sold the staple crops, provided credit, and sent supplies for the operation of the plantation. He has been often portrayed as the villain of Southern economy who kept the planter in a species of economic slavery. Actually, he performed a valuable and necessary role in plantation economy. He specialized in the knowledge of business practices relating to the sale of the staple crops, thus freeing the planter to devote his energies to production and the management of the plantation.

Since the crops were sold in a distant market, the planter needed the services and advice of the factor, who could provide him with up-to-date information on the state of the market and give him advice on when to sell. Because of the fluctuation of the market this knowledge

[8] *Ibid.,* p. 116.

was very important to the planter. The New Orleans *Price Current* published the daily prices of staple commodities; but the planter and his factor had to determine just when to sell, basing this decision on the prospects of a large or small crop and on the conditions of business. Hunt's *Merchant's Magazine,* published in New York, and *De Bow's Review,* published in New Orleans, also furnished the planters with valuable economic news. The factors often sent letters to individual planters forecasting prices, and some of them maintained crop-reporting systems and sent out circulars.

The factor charged a standard commission of 2½ per cent for selling the crops. In addition, there were numerous charges that the planter had to pay to market his crops, such as insurance, amounting from one-eighth to 1 per cent on the Mississippi River and 1 per cent between New Orleans and New York; storage, costing in 1830 36 cents per bale of cotton per annum; and drayage, wharfage (handling on the wharf), mending, and cooperage. Altogether it usually cost the planter of the lower South from 6 to 9 per cent of the sale price of his cotton to defray these various charges.[9] Besides selling the crop, factors furnished a variety of services to their clients, some of them gratis. They purchased and forwarded the plantation supplies, charging usually 2½ per cent commission. They bought and sold slaves for their clients, did errands in the seaports, placed children in school, and so on. Frequently such cordial relations existed between the factor and the planter that they exchanged gifts or visited each other. Maunsel White, for example, sent to his factor in Richmond a present of a tame deer and doe from the park on his Deer Range sugar plantation in Louisiana.

A draft on the factor was the principal method of borrowing money used by the planters. For such advances factors charged the current rate of interest, usually 8 per cent. Some required the indebted planter to send his whole crop to them.[10] The crop lien became a notorious form of exploiting farmers after the Civil War, but the practice of a

---

[9] See Ralph H. Haskins, "The Cotton Factor, 1800–1860, a Study in Southern Economic and Social History," Ph.D. Dissertation, University of California, 1950.

[10] See A. H. Stone, "The Cotton Factorage System of the Southern States," *American Historical Review,* XX (1915), 557–665, and Ralph H. Haskins, "Planter and Cotton Factor in the Old South: Some Areas of Friction," *Agricultural History,* XXIX (1955), 1–14.

merchant lending money on the basis of a mortgage on the growing crop was well established before the Civil War. In 1855, at the Southern Commercial Convention in New Orleans, resolutions were introduced that commission merchants should stop the practice of making advances to planters in anticipation of their crops, since it tended to establish the relation of master and slave between the merchant and planter.[11] Nevertheless, the practice continued. Indeed, so many planters went in debt in order to purchase land and slaves that often they were in desperate need of credit. Until their crops were harvested and sold, they had little cash. The factors, therefore, acted as bankers to finance them, frequently for a period of twelve months, until their crops were sold. Furthermore, factors furnished exchange or currency to planters to send to distant cities.

Many complaints were made by planters against the factors and especially against the buyers of staples in the ports. A. Durnford, a well-to-do free Negro planter, was outspoken in his criticism of the chicanery of some of the New Orleans sugar buyers. Durnford sent his sugar to New Orleans to be sold by the merchant John McDonogh. On one occasion the factor frankly told him that his last consignment of sugar was "dreadful stuff," and the latter apologized by blaming "the rascally negroes that I have around my kettles." On June 6, 1844, Durnford wrote to McDonogh that he would not sacrifice his sugar by selling cheaply to the buyers on the levee: "I don't care if one half of it melts away, so these rascally loafers on the Levee make nothing out of me. I have heard so much of their schemes that I am like an enrager against them all, some making 70,000 $ in one year out of the poor hard-working planters."[12]

Nevertheless, in general, good relations existed between the planter and the factor, as is illustrated in the papers of Maunsel White, who for many years operated the counting house of Maunsel White and Company in New Orleans before he retired to become a sugar planter. White was the factor both of Andrew Jackson and Zachary Taylor. His relations with these two eminent men were those of warm personal friendship. In 1845, the year of Jackson's death, the master of the Hermitage wrote two letters of protest to White regarding the management of his business. In the first place, Jackson felt that his cotton had

[11] Olmsted, *Seaboard Slave States*, II, 309–310.
[12] A. Durnford to John McDonogh, June 14, 1844, John McDonogh Papers.

been valued too low in regard to quality and he asked White to examine it personally. At this time White was living on his sugar plantation below New Orleans, leaving the direction of the cotton brokerage firm to his partners. Nevertheless, he examined Jackson's cotton by samples and reported that the bales recently sent to his firm from the Hermitage were the worst that he had ever seen from Jackson's plantation—the cotton was trashy and had been baled in damp condition, which had materially injured the color. To support his report he asked two experienced cotton men to grade Jackson's cotton, and in a second letter enclosed certificates from those experts, who had graded it by Liverpool classification as "ordinary," worth only 4½ cents a pound. Jackson also complained that the firm had sold his cotton too hastily, for cotton rose in price after the sale. On account of his complaint White credited Jackson's account with the difference between the sale price and the current market price, which was three-eighths of a cent higher, the amount equaling $136.60. Shortly thereafter Jackson sent White a letter testifying to his friendship for him and to the honorable character of the New Orleans merchant, which White treasured as a memento of the regard of the old hero for him to be transmitted to his grandchildren.[13]

Indeed, a remarkable trust was often established between the planter and his factor. Drafts were accepted by the factor because of his confidence in the honor of the planter. Some factors, particularly those who speculated in the commodities that they sold for others, exploited their clients, but as a whole they do not seem to have unduly taken advantage of their strategic position. Rather, the planters took advantage of the factor perhaps as often as the latter exploited his client. Some dishonest planters increased the weight of their bales by putting rocks in the center, or cheated by "plating" bales of inferior cotton with an outside layer of high-grade cotton.[14] Especially did factors lose money from making advances to unreliable persons.

A high percentage of these businessmen, frequently operating on a small capital, went into bankruptcy. Ebenezer Pettigrew, a prominent wheat and corn planter of eastern North Carolina, employed twenty-

[13] Maunsel White to Andrew Jackson, January 28, March 12, 1845, Letter Book, Papers of Maunsel White, Southern Collection, University of North Carolina.

[14] Haskins, "Planter and Cotton Factor," pp. 2–3.

five factors over a period of fifty years, of whom nine went into bankruptcy and another gave up "commission" to operate a distillery. There was a great turnover in the employment of factors by the planters, partly because of the dissolution of factoring firms, partly because of dissatisfaction with the service, and partly because of a tendency to hope for higher profits by changing factors. Instead of the factor being the exploiter of the planter, however, one student maintains that the carrier was the villain. From Pettigrew's papers he cites numerous examples of freight charges amounting to between 12 and 20 per cent of the gross sale price of wheat and corn. The cost to Pettigrew of shipping and marketing cypress shingles in New York was even greater, as illustrated by a shipment in 1821 of 74,000 shingles which sold for $243.31; charges were $171.16, leaving him $73.15 for his effort.[15] Finally he purchased a schooner, *The Lady of the Lake*, to carry his staples to market.

The factor dealt mainly with the well-to-do planter, while the country storekeeper usually served the needs of farmers, Negroes, and poor whites. The country stores, therefore, were least numerous in the rich plantation districts and most frequent in the Piedmont region. There were many types of such stores, some of them log cabins at a crossroads, called groceries or doggeries and carrying a scanty supply of goods and a barrel of whisky, and others occupying substantial frame or brick buildings, especially in the towns. Store boats also plied the rivers, and the commissaries of the planters often provided supplies for poor farmers. The planters, in turn, to some extent patronized the village stores, where they could secure long-term credit.[16]

The South seems to have possessed an adequate number of stores for its scattered population, especially since the poor whites, Negroes, and yeoman farmers consumed relatively small quantities of store-bought goods. In Virginia in 1850 there were 4,584 merchants, or approximately one for every 300 people, black and white; in North Carolina, one for every 450 people; and in South Carolina, one for every 400 people. Louisiana, with its great commercial metropolis of

[15] See Bennett H. Wall, "Ebenezer Pettigrew, an Economic Study of an Ante-Bellum Planter," Ph.D. Dissertation, University of North Carolina, 1947, Chap. VIII.

[16] See Lewis E. Atherton, *The Pioneer Merchant in Mid America* (Columbia, Missouri, 1939), and *The Southern Country Store 1800–1860* (1949).

New Orleans, had a merchant for every 130 people. Indeed, many villages and towns had a surplus of stores, such as the upland village of Hillsborough, North Carolina. Here a prominent merchant wrote in 1848 that although the Holt store had the largest patronage of the twelve stores in the village, it did not sell many goods and was a poor investment.[17]

The country stores carried a general line of goods suited to a rural population. Dry goods were a prominent feature of their merchandise, and they also sold such varied items as agricultural implements, coffee, salt, powder, lead, patent medicines, schoolbooks and books for adults, pork, flour, guano, and shoes.[18] Often merchants would treat their country customers to a dram of whisky; some of them, too, had perfected the art of flattery to promote sales.

The country stores were operated almost entirely on credit. Every fall or spring the substantial merchants would travel to New York or Philadelphia to buy their goods from jobbers. They were given a credit of from six to eight months. In order to aid the Northern wholesalers in determining the reliability of their Southern and Western customers, Lewis Tappan, the great silk jobber and abolitionist leader, in 1824 established a Credit Agency in New York, which sent agents into the South and West to ascertain the credit standing of merchants. When the merchants advertised their wares in their local newspapers, they almost invariably stated that they had purchased their goods in New York or other Eastern cities. The Danville, Kentucky, merchant, John H. Caldwell, for example, advertised that he was "now receiving from the Eastern cities a large and fashionable stock of Dry Goods, both Staple and Fancy. All kinds of Barter taken in exchange for Goods."[19]

Indeed, it was necessary for the merchants to take country produce in exchange for merchandise, since the farmers were in chronic want of cash. Consequently, they accepted beeswax, feathers, gingseng root, butter, wheat, corn, tobacco, hides, tallow, and knitted socks in exchange for goods. After the panic of 1819 the country customers of the merchant firm in Baltimore in which young Johns Hopkins clerked offered whisky in payment for debts. When the Quaker firm refused

[17] Alfred Holt to ———, April 5, 1848, Edwin Michael Holt Papers, Southern Collection, University of North Carolina.

[18] See Thomas D. Clark, *Pills, Petticoats, and Plows, The Southern Country Store* (Indianapolis, 1944).

[19] Danville *Kentucky Tribune*, April 15, 1853.

to accept this kind of payment, Hopkins started an independent business which received whisky in exchange for groceries and dry goods, and sold it under the brand of "Hopkins' Best." He was excommunicated by the Quaker Church on account of these transactions, but was later reinstated. He became one of the wealthiest men of the South, and left a great fortune to found a university.

Because of the vicissitudes of agriculture, the merchants had to charge a high markup on goods bought on credit, usually 100 per cent, for often they could not collect debts. Always they had to wait to receive payment until the farmers sold their crops in the autumn. The ledger of William Smith, who owned a store at Smithville, South Carolina, reveals a typical record of few cash purchases; in May 1841, the ledger showed a total of $455.41 sales, of which only $37 were in cash; and in August, out of total sales of $604.27, only $82.10 were paid in cash. It was a rare customer who did not buy some form of alcoholic beverage from his store.[20]

Southern commerce expanded greatly as a consequence of the transportation revolution. In 1812 the steamboat was introduced into the Southern states by the voyage of the *New Orleans* from Pittsburgh to New Orleans, and upstream navigation was inaugurated three years later when the *Enterprise,* commanded by Henry M. Shreve, arrived in Louisville from New Orleans. Steamboat navigation on the Southern rivers, however, was uncertain and full of hazards. Frequently the steamboats could not operate in summer because of low water. The Ohio River was obstructed by the falls at Louisville, around which a canal was constructed in 1831. The Tennessee River was practically unnavigable at Muscle Shoals and was very difficult of navigation at the narrows below Chattanooga, where the Boiling Pot and the Suck wrecked many watercraft. Furthermore, the navigation of the Mississippi was dangerous because of the numerous "planters," "sawyers," and snags in the river, which was constantly changing its course. In 1826 the federal government appointed Henry M. Shreve superintendent of Western river improvements. He invented a steam snag boat, called "Uncle Sam's tooth-puller," with which he made navigation on the river much safer, and ten years later he broke the great log jam that blocked the navigation of the Red River above Natchitoches.

The steamboats did not drive the thousands of flatboats on the Mis-

[20] Store Ledger of William Smith, the University of Kentucky Library.

sissippi out of business, but supplemented them as freight carriers. The cost of insurance of the steamboats was high, largely because of the frequent explosions of their high-pressure boilers, often caused by reckless racing. Freight insurance rates on the rivers amounted to approximately 1 per cent for a thousand miles, which was equal to marine insurance on cotton transported from New Orleans to Liverpool. The hazards of river transportation were so great that the average Mississippi steamboat lasted only about five years.[21]

Canals played a minor role in the development of Southern commerce. The Dismal Swamp Canal, connecting Albemarle Sound with the seaport of Norfolk, became a valuable artery of commerce after its enlargement in 1828. The Muscle Shoals Canal, for the construction of which the state of Tennessee received a donation of public lands, was so poorly designed that it was abandoned shortly after its completion in 1836. Inspired by the success of the Erie Canal, Maryland in 1828 began digging the Chesapeake and Ohio Canal to connect Baltimore with Cumberland at the big bend of the Potomac River. This was completed twenty-three years later. Virginia spent millions of dollars on the James River and Kanawha Canal, beginning construction in 1832; however, the canal was never completed to its destination; it stopped at Buchanan, fifty miles beyond Lynchburg.

In 1830, the era of railroads began in the South and in the nation with the opening of the thirteen miles of track between Baltimore and Ellicott's Mill. The strongest motive for this adventure in a new type of transportation was the competition among Southern seaports for the Western trade. The great period of railroad building in the South did not take place, however, until the decade of the 1850's, when it was pushed into being by the high price of Southern staples and the efforts of interior districts to obtain outlets for their crops. In the early stages of railroad development in the South, most of the capital for construction came from Southern sources, particularly from the subscription of stock by city corporations, state governments, and planters and merchants. In the 1850's some of the capital was obtained by selling bonds in Europe and the North, though European investors really preferred to put their surplus funds in Western developments.[22] South-

---

[21] See Lewis C. Hunter, *Steamboats on the Western Rivers* (Cambridge, Mass., 1949), pp. 367, 387; Gray, *History of Agriculture,* II, 761.

[22] See Leland H. Jenks, *The Migration of British Capital to 1875* (New York, 1927).

ern planters frequently subscribed to the stock of railroad companies by furnishing the labor of their slaves to build the roadbed. John Houston Bills of Bolivar, Tennessee, planter and versatile businessman, subscribed for stock in the Mississippi Central and Tennessee Railroad by paying for half of it in cash installments and the other half by the labor of his slaves on the railroad. He noted in his journal, December 19, 1854, that eighteen of his slaves had worked 299 days for the railroad during the past year. He also sold to the railroad company cordwood cut by his slaves on his Hickory Valley Plantation. In the fall of 1858 he noted with satisfaction that the railroad company had made upward of half a million dollars, and that his investment in its stock had paid handsome dividends.[23]

Notwithstanding the strong individualism of Southerners of the antebellum period, Georgia and North Carolina engaged in a sort of state socialism by building and operating railroads. In 1851 Georgia finished the building of the Western and Atlantic Railroad, connecting Atlanta and Chattanooga. After its completion the conservatives in the legislature tried to get the state to sell or lease the road and its equipment, but they failed. The state continued to operate the railroad efficiently, keeping it in good repair and receiving large profits until the Civil War. According to Ulrich B. Phillips, the Western and Atlantic Railroad was "scarcely at all involved in politics."[24] The North Carolina Railroad was also a successful example of state ownership and operation of a railroad. Completed in 1856, it ran through the center of the state from the seacoast to Raleigh, Greensboro, Charlotte, and Morganton, providing the Piedmont region with an outlet for its crops.

The letterbooks of John McRae, engineer of the South Carolina Railroad, give intimate glimpses into the problems of building Southern railroads. Slaves were hired from the adjoining planters to grade the roadbed, their masters being paid $10 to $12 a month. Malaria seriously hampered construction in the swampy lowlands during the spring and summer. Stockholders were slow in paying installments on their stock, and McRae had trouble in securing rights of way. In March, 1847, he wrote that the South Carolina Railroad was doing

[23] John Houston Bills Diary, December 19, 1854; April 10, 1857; August 9, 1858, typed copy of Vol. II, Southern Collection, University of North Carolina.
[24] U. B. Phillips, *A History of Transportation in the Eastern Cotton Belt to 1860* (New York, 1908), p. 331.

an immense business in freight, so that the Charleston depot had to be closed for seven days, and ten new locomotives had been ordered. In the summer of that year he wrote that "the people of the up country and Columbia are in a perfect fever on the Subject of Railroads." But local jealousies interfered with rational planning of railroads. For example, the South Carolina Railroad was not permitted to locate its depot at the Charleston wharves because of a variety of local interests, including "the fraternity of black barbers"; they feared that they would be deprived of the opportunity of shaving the passengers as they passed from the cars to the ocean ships.[25]

The railroads of the lower South operated under unusual handicaps. Their traffic was highly seasonal on account of the cotton crop. In the fall and winter they carried cotton and food to the seaports, but returning cars were often empty, and in the summer business dwindled greatly. The state of Georgia forbade railroads to operate on Sundays. The railroads also had to compete with steamboats, which often carried over three thousand bales of cotton on a trip. Although they had the advantage over steamboats of not being affected by low water in the river or by freezing weather, they faced serious handicaps. On the eve of the Civil War through traffic was prevented by there being three different gauges of track in use and by the unwillingness of many cities to permit the lines of different companies to connect; efforts to eliminate these bottlenecks were defeated by the teamster and hotel interests.

By 1861 the eleven Southern states which formed the Southern Confederacy possessed 8,783 out of the total 31,168 miles of railroads in the country. Although the white population of these states was less than one-fifth of the white population of the United States, during the last decade of the ante-bellum period the South Atlantic States more than tripled their railroad mileage and the Gulf States made an even greater gain. Virginia, possessing more than 1,800 miles of railway, led the Southern states in mileage, with Georgia ranking second; Louisiana, retarded by dependence on its rivers for transportation, had only 318 miles of tracks and Texas and Arkansas were virtually without railroads.[26] The railroads of the South were operated by 113 compa-

[25] Letter Books of John McRae. Entries of December 1, 1846; March 25, June 5, 1847, Wisconsin Historical Society Library; there are eighteen books, 1845–64; cited in Eaton, *A History of the Old South*, pp. 416–417, 422.
[26] Robert C. Black, III, *The Railroads of the Confederacy* (Chapel Hill,

nies that seldom owned more than 200 miles of track; the Manassas Gap Railroad, for example, destined to play a decisive role in the first battle of Bull Run, owned only sixty-two miles.

The Southern railroad system was designed primarily to transport the staple crops to seaports. To finance the growing and marketing of these crops as well as the purchase of slave labor, the planters and farmers were dependent on credit. Planters' factors in the first instance, and ultimately the banks, were the sources of this credit. According to Albert Gallatin's incomplete enumeration in 1830, the Southern states, containing at that time a third of the population of the United States, possessed 57 of the nation's 328 state banks.[27] The panic of 1819 hit the Southern states hard and produced political pressures to inflate the currency and establish banks with easy credit policies. Tennessee, for example, in 1820 created the Bank of Tennessee, promoted by the demagogue Felix Grundy, for the purpose of loaning sums as high as $500 to debtors on the security of their property. The bank notes of this institution were declared acceptable for state dues, and a law was passed that creditors who refused to receive them could not collect such debts for a period of two years. However, the supreme court of the state declared this law unconstitutional, and after the cashier defaulted, the so-called "Saddle Bags Bank" failed.[28]

Kentucky also in 1820 established an inflationary institution, the Bank of the Commonwealth of Kentucky, with officers paid by the state. This bank was authorized to issue a huge quantity of bank notes based only on the public credit, notes which were to be lent to needy debtors in amounts not exceeding $2,000. Furthermore, the legislature passed stay laws and abolished imprisonment for debt (December, 1821). In 1823 the court of appeals declared some of the laws for the relief of debtors unconstitutional, whereupon the legislature abolished the court and set up a new supreme court. The old court refused to abdicate, and the state was divided in bitter strife, so that John J. Crittenden described Kentucky politics at this time as based on feeling

---

1952), Chap. I; Robert S. Henry, "Railroads of the Confederacy," *Alabama Review,* VI (1953), 1–13; and R. S. Cotterill, *The Old South* (Glendale, Calif., 1939), pp. 215–227.

[27] Henry Adams (ed.), *The Writings of Albert Gallatin* (Philadelphia, 1879), III, pp. 352–356, 364.

[28] Joseph A. Parks, *Felix Grundy, Champion of Democracy* (Baton Rouge, 1940), Chap. VI.

and resembling a mighty quicksand.[29] The conservatives finally recovered control of the legislature in 1826 and restored the old court. The financial consequences of the struggle for the relief of debtors were seen in the depreciation of the bank notes of the Bank of the Commonwealth of Kentucky to 50 per cent of their face value.

South Carolina, Virginia, and Louisiana after 1842 developed the best banking systems of the Southern states. In 1812 the legislature of South Carolina chartered the Bank of the State of South Carolina, its capital being held exclusively by the government. The bank loaned money on real estate, but not more than $2,000 to any one person. So successful was its administration that it made a profit of 7 per cent; by 1848 it had paid $28 million to the state and had never suspended specie payments. Headed by a businessman-politician, Franklin Elmore, the bank exercised a conservative influence in state politics, stanchly supporting Calhoun. William Gilmore Simms wrote to his friend James H. Hammond on December 25, 1846, that South Carolina was ruled by an oligarchy and that the bank exercised a baneful influence on the political independence of the state through its power over the legislature. In the following year Simms declared that Calhoun was heavily in debt to the bank, to the amount of at least $20,000, and that the bank controlled the politics of the state.[30]

In contrast with the conservative practices of South Carolina and Virginia, the banks of the lower South, particularly of the Southwest, were probably the most reckless and speculative in the nation during the decades of the 1820's and 1830's. There was an orgy of buying of cotton lands, financed by easy loans from banks which issued notes that were not properly secured. Also the expansion of railroads during the period stimulated unsound banking and currency practices. The extent of speculation might be measured by the fact that the land offices of the federal government sold over twenty million acres during the peak of speculation in 1836; but after Jackson's Specie Circular, sales of land declined so precipitously that in 1842 only a million acres were sold. During the period of great speculation, individuals, with lordly disdain of realities, endorsed each other's notes to buy cotton

[29] John J. Crittenden to Henry Clay, November 25, 1826, Duke University Library.

[30] William Gilmore Simms to James H. Hammond, December 25, 1846, in Oliphant, *Letters of William Gilmore Simms,* II, 255, 294–295.

lands; a refusal to do so was regarded as an insult. Jackson's veto of the recharter of the Second Bank of the United States led to the closing of the branch banks in Southern cities and removed wholesome controls that had been exercised over the issue of notes by state banks. In order to avoid the necessity of redeeming their unsound bank notes, "wildcat banks" were established in remote spots in the Southwest, where wildcats presumably roamed.

Speculating planters as well as debt-ridden farmers desired the state to charter banks so that they might borrow bank notes easily. Bray Hammond has dispelled the myth of the poor debtor as the dominant type urging inflation.[31] Planters on the make, as well as established ones ever greedy to expand their landholdings and slaves, were seeking easy credit. Because of their demands, Louisiana in 1828 chartered a bank entitled the Consolidated Association of the Planters of Louisiana, supported by the assignment to it of a large amount of state bonds. The British house of Baring Brothers bought $1,666,667 face value of these bonds and four years later encouraged the state to charter the Union Bank of Louisiana with a capital of $7 million of state bonds assigned to the bank and marketed by Baring Brothers.[32]

Some of the Southern states chartered banks that were little more than state political arms, designed to aid the mass of the voters by making cheap money available. The Central Bank of Georgia, chartered in 1828, apportioned its loans to counties on the basis of population and limited loans to $2,500 per person.[33] The Bank of Alabama, established in 1823, became a political football, with the president and the board of directors elected annually by the legislature. When it was liquidated in 1841, after an investigation that revealed scandalous mismanagement, this venture in state banking cost the taxpayers over $35 million. Mississippi in 1830 chartered the Planters' Bank for the purpose of aiding agriculture, two-thirds of the capital of $3 million being provided by the sale of state bonds, and seven years later chartered the Union Bank with capital largely obtained through state bonds.[34]

[31] Bray Hammond, *Banks and Politics in America from the Revolution to the Civil War* (Princeton, 1957).

[32] R. W. Hidy, *The House of Baring in American Trade and Finance* (Cambridge, Mass., 1949), pp. 96, 110–112.

[33] T. P. Govan, "The Banking and Credit System in Georgia, 1810–1860," *Journal of Southern History*, IV (1938), 164–184.

[34] Sydnor, *Development of Southern Sectionalism*, Chap. V.

The panic of 1837 and the great decline in the prices of the Southern staples in the early 1840's resulted in a wave of repudiation of state bonds. Mississippi in 1842 repudiated the Union Bank bonds on the ground that their sale had been made in an illegal manner. The territory of Florida and the state of Arkansas also repudiated bonds of many millions of dollars that had been used to establish unnecessary banks.[35] Baring brothers, the Rothschilds, and Hope and Company of Amsterdam, who had bought large issues of American bonds, employed lobbyists such as Robert J. Walker of Mississippi and J. H. B. Latrobe of Maryland to influence state legislators to honor their obligations; they drew up petitions and spent considerable money subsidizing the press in order to prevent repudiation. They were finally successful in Maryland and Louisiana after a hard struggle. The Southern states were not alone in resorting to repudiation, for several of the Northern states also partially or completely repudiated their obligations to foreign bondholders.[36]

The disastrous experiences of the Southern states in the 1830's and 1840's led to reform in banking practices. Most of the states, after being stung, retired from the banking business and limited their activities in the field of banking to regulating banks. Georgia as early as 1833 required banks in the state to issue annual statements of their financial condition to the public. Texas reacted so violently to the unsound banking practices of the period as to prohibit in its constitution of 1845 the establishment of banks. Arkansas, also, after the failure of its real-estate banks in 1846, forbade the operation of banks within the state. Louisiana in 1842 adopted the admirable Louisiana Specie Reserve System. A state board of currency was set up to supervise the banks of the state. Banks were prohibited from loaning money on deposit for more than ninety days and had to keep a specie reserve of one-third of their deposit and bank note liabilities. The Louisiana system was so successful that in the financial crisis of 1857 the New Orleans banks suffered less than Northern banks, and the Louisiana system influenced the organization of the National Bank system during the Civil War.[37]

[35] Reginald McGrane, *Foreign Bondholders and American State Debts* (New York, 1935).

[36] John E. Semmes, *John H. B. Latrobe and his Times, 1803–1891* (Baltimore, 1917), pp. 457–458.

[37] Hammond, *Banks and Politics,* pp. 680–681.

In addition to state banks, the South had some powerful private bankers, such as James Robb and Alexander Brown & Sons of Baltimore. Robb was an uneducated poor boy from Pennsylvania who first gained his capital in the South by dealing in uncurrent money. Emigrating to New Orleans in 1837, in 1842 he acquired control of the New Orleans Gas Light and Banking Company, which became immensely profitable. He established a chain of banks under the name of the Bank of James Robb.[38] The Whigs elected him to the state senate, where he took a typical businessman's attitude in opposing a capital tax by the state and favoring a free system of banking without the interference of the government. He held that capital must be unencumbered by state regulations; otherwise New Orleans businesses would be placed at a disadvantage in competition with other firms. A great promoter of railroads in the South, he became the first president of the New Orleans, Jackson, and Great Northern Railroad, and was called the De Witt Clinton of the South. In 1858 he failed in business as a result of the panic of the preceding year. While he was affluent he built one of the most magnificent homes in the South in New Orleans and collected works of art, buying fifteen paintings from the sale of Jerome Bonaparte's collection. After his failure he sold his house and art treasures to John Burnside, another poor boy from Ireland who had become one of the wealthiest merchants of the South.

The emergence of Alexander Brown and Sons of Baltimore as the greatest merchant banking house of the Southern states was a remarkable example of the power of an individual in influencing economic development. In 1800 Alexander Brown emigrated from North Ireland, where he was engaged in the linen trade, to Baltimore. Here he founded a linen importing house, acquired ships, and expanded his business into buying tobacco and cotton and exporting them to Great Britain. In 1810 he sent his oldest son to Liverpool to found Brown, Shipley and Co.; later he established branches in Philadelphia, New York, and Boston that became known as Brown Brothers. In 1824 the Browns began to issue letters of credit to travelers going to Europe, and they developed an important business of dealing in sterling exchange. They were also influential in developing the Baltimore and Ohio Railroad. When Alexander died in 1834, he was worth approximately $2 million, one of the few millionaires in the United States. He

---

[38] *De Bow's Review*, XXV (1858), 559.

dominated the family business and the activities of his sons, basing the reputation of the firm on the highest probity. The Browns had agents in all the important ports of the South, and were the rivals of the English house of Baring as the leading cotton exporters of the South.[39]

The banking situation in the South at the close of the ante-bellum period presented a paradox. Though possessing a near colonial system, the Southern states held considerably larger specie deposits in their banks than did the Northern states.[40] In addition, the Southern banks were in the habit of keeping deposits in New York banks, drawing 4 per cent interest. The huge exports of the South provided the sterling bills to pay for a large proportion of the imports into the country (New Orleans exports alone providing sterling bills for 40 per cent of the imports into New York). One reason for the strong position of the Southern banks was that they had suffered so greatly from unsound banking practices of the 1830's that they were in general subjected to stricter regulation than were Northern and Western banks; Louisiana, in particular, required an unusually large specie reserve. Moreover, since the writing of checks was less developed below the Mason-Dixon Line than in the Northern states, banknotes, supported by specie, were more extensively used. Finally, Southern banks after 1837 employed their funds relatively more in short-term loans, in commercial transactions, than in long-term loans required in financing cotton and sugar planting.[41] The planters seemed to have borrowed principally from their factors instead of directly from the banks; for example, when Maunsel White, himself a former factor, proposed to make some improvements on his Deer Range sugar plantation, he asked his Richmond factors to advance him five or six thousand dollars for this purpose on the basis of consigning his next year's crop to them.[42]

In a speech before the Southern Commercial Convention in 1856,

---

[39] John Crosby Brown, *A Hundred Years of American Banking* (New York, 1909), and Frank R. Kent, *The Story of Alexander Brown and Sons* (Baltimore, 1925).

[40] Thomas Prentice Kettell, *Southern Wealth and Northern Profits* (New York, 1860), p. 96.

[41] Letters to the author from Arthur H. Cole, November 10, 1960, and Bray Hammond, November 13, 1960; J. Carlisle Sitterson, "Financing and Marketing the Sugar Crop of the Old South," *Journal of Southern History*, X (1944), 188–189. Sitterson points out the frequent practice of factors of selling the discounted drafts to money brokers, bankers, and individuals with money to loan.

[42] Maunsel White to Messrs. Dunlop, Moncure & Co., February 22, 1845, Maunsel White Papers.

James Robb analyzed the banking situation in the South. He declared, "We have more capital in the southern states for our wants, than any portion of the confederacy." He pointed out that New Orleans had $17 million of fixed capital and about $10 million of active capital. Although New York and Brooklyn had six times the population of New Orleans, their banking capital was less than three times that of the Southern port; Philadelphia, with a population triple that of New Orleans, had actually less capital; and Baltimore, with a population 50 per cent greater than the Crescent City, had $3 million less. Furthermore, he observed, the average price of money in New Orleans, i.e., "current price paid on undoubted security," was 33 per cent cheaper than in Boston; 25 per cent cheaper than in New York, Philadelphia, and Baltimore; and 50 per cent cheaper than in St. Louis or Cincinnati. Nevertheless, New Orleans was suffering from a lack of import trade and her prosperity was injured by her failure to build railroads. Other handicaps to the city's prosperity were a general lack of confidence in the financial reliability of all Southern states on account of the repudiations of Mississippi and Arkansas, an uneasy feeling produced by the agitation over slavery, and the strict laws of Louisiana, "unfavorable to the circulation of capital."[43]

The dependence of the Southern states on the North for credit, especially for manufactured goods, was the most salient aspect of its colonial status. It was a psychological as well as economic relation. James D. B. De Bow, editor of *De Bow's Review,* pointed out that country merchants in South Carolina who did not have the means to go to New York to buy goods and were forced to buy in Charleston carefully obliterated every mark on a box that indicated the goods were purchased there instead of in New York. "It was quite a plume in the cap of a trader," he reported, "to say he was just from New York, and had purchased his supplies there."[44] Many merchants made the trip to New York not only because of the delusion that they could get cheaper goods there but because of desire to see the life of a big city. Dependence on New York even went so far as to have the Charleston hotel keepers feeding their guests (so rumor said) on turkeys and chickens fattened in abolitionist Ohio and shipped via New York.

[43] J. D. B. De Bow, *The Southern States* . . . (New Orleans, 1856), II, 152–154.

[44] From *De Bow's Review,* in Louis M. Hacker, *The Shaping of the American Tradition* (New York, 1949), I, 528–530.

De Bow and other Southern patriots urged Southerners to patronize the importing merchants of the Southern ports, pointing out the economic advantages of this course. In New York the Southern country merchants did not purchase directly from the importers, who refused to break packages and sell in small lots, but from jobbers who sold at a great profit. If the local merchants bought in Southern ports they could save the profit they paid to the middleman as well as the expense of the trip to New York. The Southern Commercial Convention, meeting in Charleston in 1860, appointed a committee to report on the condition of Southern trade. The report observed that although the South provided three-fourths of the exports of the country, the importing merchants of the South, because of Northern monopoly of the import trade, had become "almost an extinct race." The high tariff was blamed to a large extent for such a situation; but actually the compromise tariff Act of 1833 had improved conditions, and the tariff of 1857 was one of the lowest in our history. The report declared that the merchants who obtained their supplies in Southern ports could save money on the exchange rate on bank notes and secure longer terms of credit than the six or eight months allowed by the New York jobbers.[45]

Southerners believed that the North, through its control of trade and manufactures, got forty cents out of every dollar that was received from the sale of Southern cotton. As Noah Cloud, editor of the *American Cotton Planter*, told the Scottish traveler Russell, after paying for goods and services in the North and visits to Northern resorts, not one-fourth of the money derived from the sale of cotton and sugar was left to be spent in the South.[46] A host of Northern middlemen, insurers, factors, transportation agents, importing merchants, jobbers, and bankers took their toll from the sale of Southern crops and the furnishing of supplies to Southern agriculturists. Thomas Prentice Kettell, editor of the *Democratic Review* of New York, in a work entitled *Southern Wealth and Northern Profits*, enumerated the various ways in which the South was exploited by the North, such as custom duties; federal bounties to New England fisheries; profits of Northern manufacturers on goods sold in the South; profits of importing merchants,

---

[45] Herbert Wender, *Southern Commercial Conventions 1837–1859* (Baltimore, 1930); John G. Van Deusen, *Ante-Bellum Southern Commercial Conventions* (Durham, 1926).

[46] Robert Russell, *North America*, pp. 290–291; an exaggeration that was inconsistent with the large bank reserves in Southern port cities.

factors, brokers, and commission men; interest on bank loans; profits on Southern travelers in the North; and money earned in the South by Northern tutors and teachers.[47]

The South was compared to Ireland, both exploited by a ruthless industrial power. It became a bitter jest below the Mason-Dixon Line that Southerners began life as babies rocked in Northern cradles and ended it buried in Northern coffins, and that throughout their existence they were dependent on the North for virtually all their manufactured articles. It is ironic that De Bow, the great crusader for Southern economic nationalism, had his industrial review published in the North (after trying several New Orleans printers) and that three-fourths of his income from advertisements came from Northern businesses.[48]

After the panic of 1857 New York City depended more on its Southern than its Western trade. When the Southern states seceded, the New York Chamber of Commerce estimated the Southern debt to Northern merchants to be $200 million, of which three-fourths was owed to New York businessmen.[49] It was natural, therefore, that the merchants of that city as a whole should oppose the abolitionists and on numerous occasions come to the political aid of the South. The merchants heartily supported such measures as the Compromise of 1850 and the Lecompton constitution. After the election of Lincoln, they held Union-saving meetings and exerted themselves to placate the South, which was threatening to throw off its economic vassalage to the great Northern port.

One of the principal objects of the Southern Commercial Conventions was to free their section from economic subjection to the North. The distress of the panic of 1837 seems to have inspired the first of these conventions, which met in that year. Thereafter, Southern Commercial Conventions were held in various Southern cities practically every year until the Civil War. These meetings, attended principally by businessmen, editors, and politicians, were likened by rhetorical Southerners to the meetings of the Greeks at the Olympic games in the way they developed a sense of unity among Southerners. The earlier

[47] Kettell, *Southern Wealth and Northern Profits*, Chaps. 6, 7.

[48] Otis C. Skipper, *J. D. B. De Bow, Magazinist of the Old South* (Athens, Ga., 1958), pp. 24–25, 129.

[49] Philip S. Foner, *Business and Slavery, the New York Merchants and the Irrepressible Conflict* (Chapel Hill, 1941), pp. 144–145, 218.

conventions emphasized the necessity of developing direct trade with Europe, while the later ones sought particularly to encourage the development of Southern manufactures and railroads. As the sectional controversy became more bitter they turned their attention to political subjects, to the reopening of the African slave trade, and to the exclusion of Northern teachers, textbooks, and magazines from the South. The members of the conventions listened to many eloquent speeches and passed many resolutions, but they succeeded in doing little in a practical way to remedy the ills of the South. Perhaps their chief effect was to engender and nourish sectional prejudice.

Not all Southerners, however, looked upon the North as exploiting the South. Some, such as Maunsel White, realized that the internal trade between the sections was mutually beneficial and constituted a strong reason for preserving the Union. In a letter to an Indiana editor in 1849 condemning the course of Northern fanaticism, he pointed out the powerful economic bonds between the sections by citing, as an example, the various items which he bought annually from Northern producers for his sugar plantation. These included Negro brogans, $680 (since he gave each slave two pairs a year); 6,000 yards of cottonade jeans and "Lowells," $750; hats, $50; pork, 175 to 180 barrels (besides hams for the family), $1,750; replacing mules and horses, $500 to $600; hickory hoop poles, $120 to $180; and coal, at least a thousand barrels, for his sugar mill—a total of $5,450. In this enumeration he did not list clothing for his family or the heavy outlays of capital in purchasing steam engines, boilers, vacuum pans, draining machines, saw mill and planing mill machinery, and agricultural implements—all purchased in the North. He estimated that the cotton planters expended about half the amount that the sugar planters did in buying Northern produce and manufactures.[50]

The Southern desire to escape economic dependence on the North led to various efforts at diversifying the economy of the region. Manufacturing was increasing, although unevenly, in the South during the last decades of the ante-bellum period. The upper South, too, made great progress in abandoning a one-crop type of agriculture. The prestige of the businessman also seems to have been rising. Changes were bound to be slow, however, in a region so predominantly agricultural

[50] Maunsel White to Charles Mason, September 14, 1849, Maunsel White Papers.

and so tied to slavery as was the ante-bellum South. The very prosperity of agriculture in the decade of the 1850's was a hindrance to the diversification of Southern economy. The main complaint of Southerners was not against the prevailing agrarian order of their society, but against the exactions of the Northern middleman. They were suffering from a feeling of injustice, a sense of being exploited, such as later affected the Western farmers during the Granger and Populist movements. Southern statesmen had largely removed one source of exploitation in 1857 by reducing the tariff to a reasonable level. Southern planters and farmers were powerless, however, to stop the exactions of the middleman because they were too individualistic to develop an effective union of producers. Their laissez-faire philosophy of government was opposed to seeking any of the modern devices of parity by subsidy and price supports.

CHAPTER 10

The Growth of the Business Class

BUSINESSMEN in the Old South lacked the prestige that they had held in the colonial period and were to acquire after the Civil War. Many of the prominent colonial families came from mercantile origins, and merchants like Henry Laurens and Christopher Gadsden of Charleston held honored positions in society. In the antebellum period, however, the businessmen as a group ranked below the planters, politicians, military officers, and professional class. This relatively low esteem was registered in the superfluous number of young men who went into the legal profession and the excessive admiration that Southern society accorded to the orator, the military man, and the politician. It was reflected in scorn for the Yankee, who was represented as engaged in an unseemly pursuit of the dollar. It was disclosed in the fact that the Southern states allowed New York to monopolize the cotton trade with Europe—by default of business enterprise. Except in a few urban centers, there did not develop a capitalist-labor relationship between the wage earners and the employers. The dominance of the agrarian ideal was exhibited by the aspiration of businessmen to become planters. Two striking examples were Maunsel White and John Burnside, both immigrants, who after making fortunes in commerce in New Orleans became large sugar planters.

William Gregg, the pioneer textile promoter in the South, lamented the tendency of the bright young men of his section to avoid business careers and seek the acclaim of society in other fields. In 1841 he wrote to James H. Hammond, soon to be elected governor of South Carolina, to ask him to encourage a young man to learn the textile business. "Paul Quattlebaum," he observed, "is by nature a mechanic, and but for his military & political propensity would make one of the most useful men in our state. This propensity has been sadly in his way, for notwithstanding his opportunity to make money I don't think from the time he entered the [army] for the Florida campaign to the present day he has made a living."[1] Quattlebaum, the son of a German miller and rifle maker in the upcountry, eventually found a way to thrive in business as a manufacturer of cotton gins and rifles and as a successful lumberman, and at the same time to win honors in the legislature and as brigadier general of the state militia.

Though trade did not rank in honor with planting or the professions, there is a tendency to underestimate the spirit of business enterprise in the Old South and to exaggerate the disdain among the upper class for the pursuit of business. Many planters did not regard it beneath their dignity to engage in money-making enterprises other than farming. Planters operated ferries, grist mills, lumber mills, stores, and contracted to dig canals and construct roadbeds of railroads with their slave gangs. The Guignard family of Columbia, South Carolina, was an example of such entrepreneurs. Descended from a French Huguenot immigrant, a cooper and merchant by trade, the Guignards expanded their fortunes by acquiring numerous scattered plantations, by operating a ferry across the Congaree River, by appropriating profits of many public offices, by speculating in land, administering estates, and constructing and repairing houses with a corps of skilled slaves whom they hired out. In the 1850's one of the Guignards had a commercial brickmaking business operated by the slaves on his plantation.[2]

The first businessmen of the South were merchants, shippers, and factors. Having accumulated capital from these sources or from plantations, some of the most enterprising became manufacturers, processing the natural resources of their region. Among the earliest factories in the Southern states were the textile mills, such as the Rocky Mount

[1] William Gregg to James H. Hammond, November 3, 1841, Hammond Papers, South Caroliniana Library.

[2] See Childs, *Planters and Businessmen, the Guignard Family,* pp. 17, 30, 41, 72.

Manufacturing Company, located at the falls of the Tar River in North Carolina, which Joel Battle, a wealthy planter, founded in 1817. He combined his capital and enterprise with the skill and knowledge of a New England cotton-mill man, Henry Donaldson, who had emigrated to the South for this purpose. Battle procured the machinery for his mill from New England and employed his own slaves as operatives. Modestly successful, the Rocky Mount Manufacturing Company continued in operation until the eve of the Civil War. Usually the capital for the founding of Southern cotton mills had to be obtained from Southern sources. A favorite method was to secure subscriptions to stock in the company from planters and merchants who paid for the stock in installments—often difficult to collect. Most of the Southern mills manufactured yarn and Osnaburg, a coarse cloth used to clothe slaves. The majority of the mill technicians came from New England and the cotton-mill machinery was obtained entirely in the Northern states, chiefly in Paterson, New Jersey, and Providence, Rhode Island, where companies gave liberal credit.[3]

The career of the most successful of the North Carolina pioneers in textile manufacturing, Edwin Michael Holt, illustrates the varied means by which capital was obtained for founding the early mills. Holt was a prototype of the successful businessman of the New South, who did not let the warm climate and false ideas of pride interfere with making money wherever the opportunity appeared. He started his rapid rise to wealth as a poorly educated farmer of the Piedmont section of the state. Remarkably enough for such a hustling man, he kept a diary (1844–1854), which reveals much concerning the characteristics of the emergent Southern capitalist.[4] He had a hand in various small enterprises, including farming, distilling whisky, running a country store, and operating a cotton mill. His liquor distilling business seems to have been as important as his store business or his early cotton mill. His diary shows that for many years his farming operations continued to engage a large part of his attention. He sent various products, whisky, brandy, butter, and flour, from the interior of the state by wagon to Fayetteville, the head of navigation of the Cape Fear River.

[3] Richard W. Griffin and D. W. Stanard, "The Cotton Textile Industry in Ante-Bellum North Carolina," *North Carolina Historical Review*, XXXIV (1957), 23–26.

[4] Diary of Edwin Michael Holt, 1844–54, Southern Collection, University of North Carolina Library.

He obtained his store goods, however, principally in the Northern cities.

In 1837 he erected a small cotton mill on Great Alamance Creek in the Piedmont, buying the machinery for it from Paterson, New Jersey. At first his mill manufactured only yarn, which was sold to the country stores of the state. The small scale of mill operations was indicated by the fact that in 1853 there were only nine hands employed. Almost all of his employees were white females who received extremely low wages. Work was often interrupted as a result of the water in the creek being either too high or too low for the water wheel, and occasionally operations were stopped in order that his employees could attend religious revivals. Difficulties in transporting his goods caused him to become a zealous promoter of railroads. He was distinctly different from the fox-hunting, cavalier type of Southerner—he arose early, worked hard, eschewed politics, was keen at a trade, and preached the doctrine of thrift and hard work.[5]

The center of textile manufacturing in North Carolina during the ante-bellum period was located at Fayetteville in the eastern part of the state. Here Henry Donaldson established a textile factory in 1825 and, like Battle at Rocky Mount, at first used slave labor. When Olmsted visited Fayetteville in 1853, he found Highland Scottish girls working in one of the cotton mills. They appeared to be modest, neat, and clean; however, the proprietor informed him that they seldom saved any of their earnings but spent them foolishly. Fayetteville possessed the largest factory in the state during the ante-bellum period, operating 4,500 spindles and 100 looms.

At Salem, the Moravian settlement in the Piedmont section of North Carolina, the Salem Cotton Manufacturing Company was founded in 1837. Church funds as well as private capital were invested in the mill, which sent some of its yarn to Philadelphia. When seven slaves were employed in 1847, there was a protest from the white workers, who maintained that the mill was intended only for whites. The factory failed in 1850, but one of the Moravian businessmen, Francis Fries, established a successful woolen mill in which he used his father's farm slaves.[6]

[5] Samuel A. Ashe, *Biographical History of North Carolina* (Greensboro, 1905—), VII.

[6] Adelaide L. Fries, "One Hundred Years of Textiles in Salem," *North Carolina Historical Review*, XXVII (1950), 1–19.

The most significant figure in the development of cotton mills in the South was William Gregg of South Carolina, a notable propagandist as well as a successful cotton-mill operator. Gregg obtained his early capital from a flourishing jewelry store which he conducted in Columbia. He became interested in cotton mills as a boy, when he was associated with his uncle in an unsuccessful cotton manufacturing venture in Georgia. In 1836 he bought a share of the Vaucluse cotton mill which had been founded by Senator George McDuffie, champion of nullification. In 1844–45 he toured New England to observe the textile manufacturing industry in that region, and upon his return wrote ten articles for the Charleston *Courier*, entitled "Essays on Domestic Industry," which were later published as a pamphlet. In these essays Gregg advocated the establishment of textile industries to diversify the economy of the South. The 1840's were a period of depression for the agricultural staples of the South, the lowest price for cotton in its history being reached in 1844, the year of Gregg's tour of New England. Gregg proposed the use in Southern mills of the labor of the poor whites, which hitherto had been largely unproductive. By bringing the poor whites into the factories, he maintained, not only would their labor be profitably employed, but their moral and social conduct would thereby be improved. He maintained also that the establishment of factories would check the emigration of the young people of the seaboard Southern states to the West. He advocated the manufacture of coarse cotton goods and advised the use of experienced Northern men to get the factories started.[7]

When Gregg began his agitation for industry in the South, the social atmosphere in the older communities was hostile to manufacturing. Charleston, for instance, had restrictions on the building of steam engines in the city. Legislatures controlled by planters were reluctant to grant charters of incorporation to manufacturing companies (which were associated in the public view with speculation). Fearing that his application for a charter for a company might not pass the legislature of South Carolina, Gregg applied at the same time to the Georgia legislature. The latter turned down his request, and the committee on manufactures of the South Carolina legislature recommended the passage of the act of incorporation by a majority of only one vote. To

[7] "William Gregg of South Carolina," *De Bow's Review*, X (1851), 348–352.

aid in the removal of prejudices against corporations, Gregg in 1845 published a pamphlet entitled *An Inquiry into the Expediency of Granting Charters of Incorporation for Manufacturing Purposes in South Carolina.* In this document he showed a remarkable spirit of modernity when he praised the example of the Merrimack Company of Lowell, Massachusetts, which had permitted its operatives to acquire $60,000 of its capital stock, and observed: "In this way, every industrious man, who is disposed to save his money, may become an owner and co-partner in the concern, which gives him employment, and thus become personally interested in its producing good results. By this means, the immense gulf, which would otherwise separate the owner and the operative, at once disappears, and although lines of distinction will always be seen, yet they will be so modified as scarcely to be felt."[8]

To test his ideas and set an example for other promoters to follow, in 1846 he built a model factory at Graniteville, South Carolina, near Aiken. The factory building was made of granite blocks and around it was established a village of one hundred cottages in Old Gothic style of architecture. Here families from the sand hills and pine barrens moved in; the father and mother frequently did not work, only the children. In the management of his factory Gregg pioneered in adopting a pattern of paternalism that was followed by many Southern textile-mill owners. He founded a school for children under twelve years of age and compelled them to attend; he established a company store, a company bank, and company churches. He strictly enforced prohibition of liquor in his village and prohibited dancing. On the other hand, he gave employees picnics and lectured them on politeness and the gospel of hard work and thrift.

The Graniteville mill became a notable success. By 1850 there were 325 persons employed in the mill, which supported a village of 900 people. The workers spent long hours in the factory, twelve at least, and the wages were four to five dollars a week for men, and three to four for women. Gregg imported the most up-to-date machinery from Massachusetts and employed Northern superintendents. The Southern mills had some advantages over their New England competitors: abundant water power, labor 20 per cent cheaper, brighter and cleaner cotton, and cheaper raw material. The Graniteville mill paid on an

[8] Broadus Mitchell, *William Gregg, Factory Master of the Old South* (Chapel Hill, 1928), p. 277, footnote 12.

average a 15 per cent dividend, and it was so successful that it became one of the mainstays of the Confederacy for textiles. Gregg's manufacturing interests converted him into a protectionist and so influenced his outlook in various other ways that he departed from the political philosophy of the planters in many respects.

Although Gregg was the outstanding personality in the development of cotton mills in the South, his state soon lost its primacy in textile manufacturing to other Southern states. Georgia's remarkable development of the textile industry caused the state to be called "the New England of the South" and Augusta the "Southern Lowell." Georgia led the Southern states in the number of hands engaged in textile factories, 2,813, as compared with the 1,441 hands of Virginia, the next largest employer below the Potomac, and with the 891 mill workers of South Carolina. Although the number of mills in the state declined between 1850 and 1860 from thirty-six to thirty-three, the value of the goods manufactured increased nearly 70 per cent. In the 1850's these mills had financial difficulties, and the largest one in Augusta failed.[9] The Augusta *Constitutionalist* attributed the failure of Southern mills to the lack of home patronage. Olmsted pointed out that Georgia merchants bought cotton goods made in Georgia mills from jobbers in New York.[10] Gregg wrote in *De Bow's Review,* "Graniteville goods are more popular in New York and Philadelphia than at home."[11] Southern manufacturers realized this prejudice against textiles of local manufacture, and at times took unethical means to combat it. Nathan Appleton of the Lowell Manufacturing Company, which sent large quantities of cotton cloth for slaves to New Orleans, complained to his agent there, "We are told that many small factories in the Southern states send their goods to N. O. calling them 'Lowell goods.' "[12]

Macon, Eatonton, and Columbus were thriving cotton-mill towns in Georgia. Athens, besides being the seat of the university, had several flourishing cotton mills. When Buckingham visited the town in 1839,

[9] Richard W. Griffin, "The Origins of the Industrial Revolution in Georgia Cotton Textiles, 1810–1865," *Georgia Historical Quarterly,* XLII (1958), 355–375.

[10] Olmsted, *Seaboard Slave States,* II, 184.

[11] *De Bow's Review,* XXIX (1860), 497.

[12] Nathan Appleton to Israel Whitney, Boston, November 5, 1842, Whitney-Burnham Papers, Box I, Library of Congress.

the three cotton mills there employed three hundred hands, half of them Negroes. One of the mills owned its slave labor force, while the others hired slaves from planters at $7 a month. The two races worked together in the mills without apparent repugnance. (Blacks and whites, he noted, shook hands with each other in the South but not in the North.) White labor, he observed, was cheaper than slave, for whites were paid the same wages as the Negroes and did not have to be fed and lodged.[13]

The great period in the founding of cotton factories in the South was in the 1840's, when cotton was selling at the lowest price in American history. In this decade thirty-two factories were established in North Carolina as compared with only eleven started in the decade of the 1850's.[14] In 1839, at the start of the cotton planting depression, the largest factory in Alabama was founded at Florence.[15] The cotton manufacturing business went into a relative decline during the last decade of the ante-bellum period.[16] The principal reasons for this state of affairs were, according to De Bow, the great increase in the price of raw cotton, the tariff on textiles, and the overstocking of coarse cotton goods by Southern mills. Another important point was that the mills paid larger dividends from their profits than were justified by good business practice, and thus failed to build up an adequate reserve— William Gregg was constantly fighting a rear-guard action against such a reckless practice. Moreover, the rise in the price of the Southern staples enhanced the prestige and profits of agriculture. The extensive newspaper campaign of propaganda for cotton-mill construction, characteristic of the 1830's and 1840's, had subsided, and editors were devoting their energies to the defense of slavery and Southern rights.

Although the number of cotton mills in eleven Southern states remained virtually stationary during the decade of 1850–60, the value of their product increased 43 per cent, twice the rate of the population growth. Georgia led the South in cotton manufacturing, followed in

[13] Buckingham, *Slave States of America*, II, 112.

[14] Griffin and Stanard, "The Cotton Textile Industry in Ante-Bellum North Carolina," 160–164.

[15] Richard W. Griffin, "Florence, Alabama: a Textile Manufacturing Center of the Old South, 1822–1871," *Bulletin of the North Alabama Historical Association*, II (1957), 21–24.

[16] Griffin, "The Origins of the Industrial Revolution in Georgia," 368–370.

order by Virginia, North Carolina, and Alabama. In 1860 the Southern mills produced one-third of the yarn, but only 6.7 per cent of the value of cotton goods manufactured in the United States. Lowell, Massachusetts, had more spindles than did the combined factories of eleven Southern states. (See note on page 246.)

The cotton-mill operatives in the Old South remained a people who kept to themselves, isolated from the other population. Gregg advised that cotton mills should not be located in large towns, for the employees would be corrupted by city life. He might also have added that in the cities they could not be controlled so well as in the remote mill villages. Here they bought their supplies from the company store, attended company schools and churches, and were protected from the evils of liquor by company prohibition measures. Some mills even had their own currency, such as the one-dollar bills of the Mount Hecla Steam Cotton Mills of Greensboro, N.C. (1837). Olmsted observed that the whites employed in the Columbus, Georgia, mills looked pale and unhealthy and were said to be short-lived. Gregg refused to exploit the labor of children under twelve years of age at Graniteville, but some other mill owners were not so scrupulous. When the mills were not running, the employees were reduced to asking for credit, or charity, to obtain food. Public entertainments were sometimes held to aid the unemployed mill people. The mill village represented in some degree the transfer of the plantation organization and paternalism into industry. Accordingly, independent yeomen were reluctant to give up their free life on the farm for the monotony and discipline of the mill, which also meant loss of status.[17]

One of the habits of Southerners which was responsible for the creation of a thriving industry was tobacco chewing and the dipping of snuff. In the later ante-bellum period, chewing tobacco displaced pipe smoking or taking snuff, Henry Clay's favorite form of using tobacco. This change of fashion was indicated by the small number of the Virginia factories at the end of the ante-bellum period that were engaged

[17] Richard W. Griffin, "Poor White Laborers in Southern Cotton Factories, 1789–1865," *South Carolina Historical Magazine,* LXI (1960), points out that although their wages seem very low, about half the amount received by New England workers, some poor whites were able to save money and raised their standard of living considerably over their pine-woods existence.

in manufacturing smoking tobacco, only 2 per cent, while 98 per cent manufactured plug chewing tobacco.[18]

The manufacture of chewing tobacco in the United States was concentrated in the Virginia cities. Richmond, with its fifty-two factories in 1860, was by far the largest center, making 36 per cent of the plug and smoking tobacco of the Virginia-North Carolina district, but other important tobacco towns were Petersburg, Lynchburg, and Danville. The typical tobacco factory of this period remained small, three-fourths of the factories employing less than fifty hands. In the last decade of the ante-bellum period the capital investment in the Virginia-North Carolina factories almost tripled, and both the number of hands and the value of the product more than doubled.

In contrast to the cotton industry, the tobacco factories employed slaves almost exclusively. The process of making plug tobacco required little skilled labor. It consisted of steaming the tobacco, steeping the leaves in pots of licorice flavoring and sugar, and prizing or pressing the lumps into flat cakes by means of screws and long levers. The perspiring Negro slaves were not sanitary in their handling of chewing tobacco. The English traveler Buckingham, who was prejudiced against the use of the filthy weed, narrated some practices of the Negroes in manufacturing plug tobacco calculated to turn squeamish stomachs.[19]

The most successful tobacco manufacturer of the Old South was James Thomas, Jr.[20] He had accumulated his capital while serving as a tobacco buyer for the French state monopoly. By 1860 his factory was employing 150 hands and making considerably over a million pounds of chewing tobacco annually. One of his special markets was California, where his brands, especially Wedding Cake, appealed to the miners. Thomas was a complex combination of businessman and devout religionist, who like many capitalists was able to keep his business practices separate from his religious zeal. He was so devoted to Baptist preachers and entertained them so hospitably that his home was jokingly dubbed "Baptist Hotel." He contributed liberally to the founding of a Baptist institution, Richmond College.

The panic of 1857 struck a severe blow at the tobacco manufactur-

[18] Robert, *Tobacco Kingdom,* p. 170.
[19] Buckingham, *Slave States of America,* II, 552–553.
[20] The Papers of James Thomas, Jr., are preserved in the Duke University Library.

ing industry. Seven-eighths of the Richmond factories stopped operations. Drafts on the New York commission merchants were returned unpaid to the Virginia banks. The panic accentuated the long-standing grievances of the tobacco manufacturers against the New York factors. The factor charged 7½ per cent commission as well as extra charges; especially galling was the practice of the New York merchants of settling accounts with the tobacco manufacturers only once a year, even when the factors had made cash sales. Accordingly, a Tobacco Manufacturers Convention met at Richmond on December 3, 1857, attended by a hundred Southern tobacco manufacturers, to devise measures against the villain of the industry, the Northern commission merchant. The convention resolved that credit for sales of tobacco should be restricted to four months instead of eight months, as at the time, and that the commission to factors should be reduced to 6½ per cent. When the Civil War came, the tobacco manufacturers were developing a defensive league against Northern businessmen. It was ironic that some of these Northern "exploiters" of the South, when captured in battle, were imprisoned in a Richmond tobacco warehouse converted into a jail for officers, the famous, or infamous, Libby Prison.

The Southern states had virtually no competition from the North in the manufacture of chewing tobacco, but it was a different story in regard to coal and iron. In 1820 Virginia was the leading coal producing state of the Union, but by the eve of the Civil War it had dropped behind Pennsylvania, Ohio, and Illinois. The smallness of the Southern coal industry at that time was indicated by the fact that Virginia, the largest producer, had twenty-two establishments employing only 1,847 hands, and Kentucky, the next largest, had thirty-three establishments employing 746 hands. Near Richmond were valuable bituminous pits, whose coal was used principally in manufacturing gas in Richmond and Northern cities. The miners were hired slaves, Englishmen, and Welshmen. Although the latter were paid higher wages than they could have earned in the North, they did not like living conditions in the South, particularly the lack of beer and the serving of cornbread instead of their accustomed wheat bread. The decline of salt making in the Kanawha Valley in the early 1850's injured the coal industry because a large proportion of Virginia coal was used by this industry. Furthermore, the use of charcoal by the Southern iron industry for smelting and of wood for fuel by the railroads and steamboats restricted the market for Southern coal.

In 1848 the discovery of cannel coal deposits at the present town of Cannelton, a short distance from Charleston, Virginia, gave a great impetus to coal mining in the Kanawha Valley. Besides being used for fuel, cannel coal produced coal oil and lubricating oils. After the discovery, the legislature of Virginia granted charters to forty-one coal companies in the Kanawha Valley and its tributaries. Most of these companies, having inadequate capital, failed or were combined into one of six larger companies before the outbreak of the Civil War. Capital for the Virginia mining companies was obtained partly from local sources and partly from Northern and English investors. The laborers in the Kanawha Valley mines were local white farmers and Irish and English immigrants. Good transportation facilities were vital to success, and accordingly some companies built their own railways and canals and put pressure on the Virginia legislature to improve the navigation of the Kanawha River and to speed the construction of the James River and Kanawha Canal.[21] The discovery of oil in western Pennsylvania in 1859 and the disruption of the Civil War ruined the market of the Virginia cannel coal producers.

Like the coal-mining business, the iron industry of the Southern states consisted of a group of small companies whose charcoal-burning furnaces and forges were located mainly in the Piedmont or mountainous country.[22] In 1860 Kentucky was the leading pig-iron producer among the Southern states. Its iron companies were concentrated in the hilly northeastern part of the state near the Ohio River and in the extreme western corner around Eddyville. Between 1840 and 1850, a decline occurred in pig-iron production in Kentucky, but the industry revived in the last decade of the ante-bellum period and increased production by 27 per cent. The Red River Iron Works of Estill County

[21] Jamison and Sewell's Report on "Mississippi Valley Coal Fields" cites an instance of a boatload of cannel coal from Elk River, Va., taking eighteen months to reach Louisville, Ky. *De Bow's Review*, XV (1853).

[22] For a description of the ante-bellum process of smelting pig iron, see Robert Scott, "Memoranda of My Visit to the East in 1829–30," September 17, 1829, pp. 82–84, University of Kentucky Library; see also J. Winston Coleman, Jr., "Old Kentucky Iron Furnaces," *Filson Club History Quarterly*, XXI (1959), 227–242.

was typical of Southern iron companies.[23] Established in 1844, this small company manufactured both pig iron and wrought iron, nails, horseshoes, castings, and bar iron. It sold its products through a commission merchant in Louisville, to whom it shipped its iron by boat down the Kentucky and Ohio rivers. The commission firm acted as selling agent for nine other furnaces in Kentucky, two in Tennessee, and six in Ohio. The Louisville firm was also a dealer in Western produce and furnished the iron companies with supplies.

The principal promoter of the iron industry in Kentucky was the Means family.[24] The founder of the fortunes of the family was Colonel John Means, a South Carolinian of Irish stock, who had emigrated to Ohio, bringing with him twenty-five slaves, whom he freed. In 1826 he entered into the iron business in the southern part of the state. The family expanded its iron business across the river into the northeastern corner of Kentucky, building Buena Vista Furnace in 1848 and acquiring Bellefonte Furnace four years later. About these furnaces developed little settlements with company stores and cottages for the wood cutters, iron workers, and teamsters. The labor was provided largely by the farmers of the vicinity rather than by slaves.[25] Although coal was available, the ante-bellum Kentucky furnaces mainly used charcoal to heat the furnaces, and therefore the companies had to own large areas of woodland. The Kentucky iron companies transported their product to market by boat down the Ohio River, selling their iron to rolling mills in southern Ohio, St. Louis, Wheeling, and Pittsburgh. Unfortunately the water in the rivers was often too low for transportation in the summer, when heavy iron could be hauled easily on dry roads to the river bank. The iron men of Greenup and Boyd counties, Kentucky, contributed capital to buy steamships and founded a packet line between the Big Sandy River and Cincinnati, and they also became active in promoting the building of railroads.

In 1854 a group of iron manufacturers, in which the Means family was prominent, organized the Kentucky Iron, Coal, and Manufactur-

[23] Much correspondence concerning this iron company is found in the Buckner Papers, University of Kentucky Library.

[24] The papers of the Means family are deposited in the University of Kentucky Library.

[25] In the other Southern states, hired Negro slaves were extensively used. S. S. Bradford, "The Negro Ironworker in Ante-Bellum Virginia," *Journal of Southern History*, XXV (1959), 194–206.

ing Company and purchased a large farm on the Ohio River near the mouth of the Big Sandy, where they founded the town of Ashland. To promote the growth of the town the company advertised in the Kentucky newspapers that it would donate iron manufacturing sites to new companies and that an excellent quality of coal for making coke was available.[26] A hotel was built, a bank established, and two newspapers founded in the new town, which soon had a thousand inhabitants. Ashland was destined to become a thriving iron manufacturing center of the New South, with important rolling mills.

Iron mining and manufacturing in the Old South were attended by many risks and vicissitudes. The firm of Jordans and Irvine, which in 1827 erected the Lucy Selina Furnace near Covington, Virginia, was an example of failure.[27] The company obtained its capital from a contract with the state to dig the Blue Ridge Canal, on which it realized a profit of 42 per cent. It expanded operations by establishing Clifton's Forge, where the pig iron from its furnace was converted into bar iron, kettles, pots, skillets, andirons, and Dutch ovens. Its products were shipped by the James River to commission agents in Richmond and Lynchburg. On account of the burden of debts and the decline in the price of iron resulting from a glut of this commodity in the Virginia market, after fifteen years of struggle the firm went into bankruptcy.

On the other hand, William Weaver, a Philadelphia merchant who had settled in Virginia, started an iron smelting business in the western part of the state with modest capital and made a considerable success. In 1828 he was operating three furnaces in Rockbridge County and making iron of high quality, which he sold in Richmond and Lynchburg for a lucrative profit. Since none of the iron works in western Virginia operated continuously through the year, he employed his unneeded slaves in cultivating his farms, which not only supplied food for his mine hands but also provided a surplus to sell. In the 1850's he operated Etna Furnace and Buffalo Forge with the assistance of some of his Philadelphia relatives. When he died in 1863, he had accumulated considerable wealth, including seventy slaves.

[26] Frankfort *Commonwealth*, December 31, 1856.
[27] Francis R. Holland, Jr., "Three Virginia Iron Companies, 1825–1865," M.A. Thesis, University of Texas, 1958, based on MS. records in the McCormick Historical Collection, Madison, Wis.

The pig-iron industry as a whole did not flourish in the late ante-bellum South. Indeed, Virginia, Georgia, and South Carolina made less pig iron in 1860 than they had ten years earlier. The principal reason for this decline was the competition of the Pennsylvania furnaces, which had abandoned charcoal for anthracite coal as fuel.[28] Particularly had the South Carolina industry, located in the western part of the state, languished. The ambitious Nesbitt Company, which had included some of the most prominent men of the state, failed as a result of the panic of 1837, and its assets were acquired by a group of Swedes and Germans who organized the Swedish Iron Manufacturing Company of South Carolina. The only company in the state that had a moderate success was the King's Mountain Company, which during the decade of the 1850's paid dividends of 6 or 7 per cent.[29]

The Tennessee pig-iron industry, consisting of seventeen establishments employing approximately a thousand slaves, was somewhat more prosperous. John Bell, the Whig leader, had acquired large iron interests in Stewart County on the Cumberland River in 1835, when he married a wealthy widow. During the 1850's his company, the Cumberland Iron Works, owned a rolling mill, four furnaces, 51,000 acres of land, and 365 slaves. Managed by his partners, it seems to have been successful until its destruction by the Union army.[30] A progressive step in the Tennessee iron industry took place in 1860, when a New Jersey man who had settled in the Chattanooga area began the revolutionary process of using coke instead of charcoal to fire the furnaces.[31]

Prior to the founding in 1871 of Birmingham, Alabama, the iron center of the New South, the most important iron manufacturing city below the Mason-Dixon Line was Richmond. Here was located the Old Dominion Nail Works, which in the 1850's was producing over a thousand tons of nails a year, and the Tredegar Iron Works, by far

[28] See Lester J. Cappon, "Trend of the Southern Iron Industry under Plantation Management," *Journal of Economic and Business History*, II (1929), 353–381; J. P. Leslie, *The Iron Manufacturer's Guide to the Furnaces, Forges, and Rolling Mills of the United States* (New York, 1859), pp. 182, 747.

[29] Ernest M. Lander, Jr., "The Iron Industry in Ante-Bellum South Carolina," *Journal of Southern History*, XX (1954), 337–355.

[30] Joseph H. Parks, *John Bell of Tennessee* (Baton Rouge, 1950), pp. 114–116.

[31] Gilbert Govan and James Livingood, *The Chattanooga Country, 1540–1951* (New York, 1951), pp. 163–168.

the largest iron manufacturing company in the South. Founded in 1837, the company went through a struggle to survive, but in 1848, after ownership was acquired by a masterful Virginian of Scottish ancestry, Joseph Reid Anderson, a graduate of West Point, the company expanded greatly. When the Civil War came the Tredegar Works was employing nine hundred men, and, aided by a protective tariff, doing an annual business of approximately a million dollars.[32] The labor force consisted of about equal numbers of slaves and white mechanics, many of the latter imported from the North. The chief market of the company was in the North, for in the Southern states a prejudice existed against homemade iron products. The most important contributions of the company to Southern economic development were the building of over forty railroad locomotives, the making of iron rails, and the supplying of boiler plate for sugar mills. The United States government was a large customer of the company, buying over 1,300 cannon as well as large quantities of cannonballs before 1860. During the War for Southern Independence the Tredegar Works became the mainstay of the Confederate government in providing artillery, and its location at Richmond was one of the reasons for not abandoning the city earlier in the war.

A now forgotten industry of the Old South was gold mining. Until the discovery of the precious metal in California, the states of North Carolina and Georgia were the chief gold-producing region of the United States. Indeed, the federal mint depended entirely upon the mines of North Carolina for its supply of gold between the years 1804–27.[33] Mrs. Anne Royall, a sharp-tongued Northern journalist, in 1830 visited the North Carolina gold region; she had no good word to say for the slow-moving, cotton-coated Tar Heels whom she saw poking about like snails in the gold diggings and using absurd machinery.[34] Gold was discovered in the Cherokee country of northeastern Georgia in 1828 and a mining rush brought at least 6,000 gold-diggers into the region. Even before the Cherokees were removed, the state divided some of their lands into 160-acre farms and 40-acre gold sites,

[32] See Kathleen Bruce, *Virginia Iron Manufacture in the Slave Era* (New York, 1931).

[33] Fletcher Green, "Gold Mining; A Forgotten Industry of Ante-Bellum North Carolina," *North Carolina Historical Review*, XIV (1937), 1–19, 135–155.

[34] Anne Royall, *Mrs. Royall's Southern Tour* (Washington, 1830).

which were distributed to the citizens by a lottery. At first individual miners engaged in placer mining with spades, pans, and crude cradles, but soon companies were organized that sank shafts and used stamping mills and mercury to extract the gold. Two gold-mining towns, Auraria and Dahlonega, sprang up in 1831–32, and the federal government established branch mints at Dahlonega and Charlotte, North Carolina. Charles Lanman, a Northern traveler, visited Dahlonega in 1848 and reported that few fortunes had been made in the Georgia gold fields and that the expense of digging the ore exceeded the gain by about 100 per cent.[35] Nevertheless, between 1828 and 1861 Georgia sent nearly $8 million worth of gold to the mints at Dahlonega and Philadelphia. The California gold rush drew miners from the declining region and Auraria after the Civil War became one of the dead towns of Georgia.[36]

In a remote corner of southeastern Tennessee was located one of the richest deposits of copper known in the United States before the Civil War, the Ducktown mines. Ducktown was a former Indian village so remote from civilization that the first task of the miners was to build roads. Mining began in 1850, twelve years after the removal of the Cherokees. By 1855 twenty-eight companies had been chartered by the Tennessee legislature to exploit the copper deposits of the region. The capital for operating the mines was provided largely by English companies, New York capitalists, and businessmen of Charleston, Savannah, and New Orleans. Labor in the mines was procured by importing Cornish and Northern miners and hiring local white men. Toward the close of the decade most of the small mine owners had sold their properties to the larger companies. The dominant figure in the development of the mines and management of the companies was Julius E. Raht, a well-educated German immigrant. In 1860 there were seven smelting works around Ducktown employing five hundred miners as well as an equal number engaged in cutting wood, making charcoal, and hauling ore. The Confederate government early in the war confiscated the mining properties of Northern men and sold them at auction to Southern citizens. Under their control the Ducktown mines continued to operate, furnishing copper ingots to the Confederate munitions industry. At the close of 1863, Union cavalry captured

[35] Lanman, *Letters from the Alleghany Mountains*, pp. 2–19.
[36] See E. M. Coulter, *Auraria, the Story of a Georgia Gold-Mining Town* (Athens, 1956).

Ducktown and closed this vital source of copper to the Confederate armies.[37]

The mining interests of the South were not comparable in value or extent of employment to those industries that arose from processing agricultural products. In 1860 the milling of flour and cornmeal still ranked at the top of Southern manufactures. Thousands of small grist-mills all over the South, operated by water wheels, served local needs, but commercial milling was concentrated in a few urban centers. At Richmond were located the largest grain mills in the world, the Gallego Mills, and Baltimore was also a great flour-mill city. From these two centers vast quantities of flour and meal were exported to Brazil and the lower South. The value of flour and meal produced in the eleven Southern states in 1860, approximately $38 million, was nearly twice as great as that of the next important industry of that region, the sawmill or lumber business.[38]

The processing of the forest resources of the South was highly dispersed. Numerous small sawmills, operated by water or by steam engines, produced over $19.5 million worth of lumber a year. Georgia was the leading lumber state in the lower South, Kentucky in the upper South. The Dismal Swamp of North Carolina and Virginia was an important source for cypress shingles. Yellow-pine lumber, live-oak timber, and staves for barrels were cut in great quantities from the coastal plain forests. The lumber industry in the South employed approximately 16,000 persons, the largest labor force engaged in any Southern manufacturing enterprise. In the last decade of the ante-bellum period the Southern states increased the value of their lumber production by 102 per cent.

Though a large exporter of lumber, the Southern states had to supplement many of their industries, such as the production of salt, by importations. The blockade during the Civil War revealed how dependent the South was on outside sources for this vital commodity.[39] Much salt needed to preserve meat was imported from Turks Islands in the Caribbean and from England. Next to New York, Virginia was the largest producer of salt in the country in 1860, for it had valuable

[37] See R. E. Barclay, *Ducktown Back in Raht's Time* (Chapel Hill, 1946).

[38] Secretary of the Interior, *Manufactures of the United States in 1860: the Eighth Census* (Washington, 1865), p. 716.

[39] Ella Lonn, *Salt as a Factor in the Confederacy* (Baltimore, 1933).

deposits in the Great Kanawha Valley and at Saltville in the south-western corner of the state. Another Southern source of salt was at Petit Anse, the salt lake in Louisiana. And in this state, also, near New Iberia, Judge Avery sank a shaft in 1862 on Avery Island and discov-ered a rich deposit of rock salt. The salt industry in the Kanawha Valley used crude methods to produce salt by boiling in furnaces the briny water that was pumped from wells. Beginning in 1817, coal was used to heat the furnaces; indeed the salt makers provided the chief customers of the western Virginia coal companies until the decline of the Kanawha industry after 1850.

The letters of Dr. John J. Cabell of Lynchburg and the diary of Luke Willcox of Marmet in West Virginia, two salt producers of the Kanawha Valley, reveal some of the problems of this fiercely competi-tive industry. In 1832, when Dr. Cabell began feverishly to build salt furnaces in the Kanawha Valley, he was hindered by an epidemic of cholera among his hired slaves, which caused their owners to recall them. Finally he was able to construct a railroad from the coal banks to his furnaces and to import a steam engine from Pittsburgh. His furnaces began to produce four hundred bushels of salt a day. When prices fell he tried to arrange a cartel among the saltworks proprietors of the Kanawha Valley, assigning each owner a quota of salt produc-tion. The attempt at a cartel failed, for some producers were too indi-vidualistic to join and the others were unable to reach an agreement on individual quotas. Luke Willcox's diary, 1844–54, shows that, like Dr. Cabell, he had many other business interests, such as storekeeping, lending money, hiring out slaves, operating a farm.[40] Both proprietors marketed their salt by sending it on flatboats or steamers down the Ohio River and its tributaries to Southern towns.

Another minor but distinctive industry of the South was the manu-facture of cordage and hemp bagging, used as wrappers for cotton bales. Cordage was made in long narrow buildings called ropewalks, where slaves, walking backward and manipulating the dressed hemp carried around their waists, twisted the strands into rope. As late as 1860, few of the hemp factories were operated by steam power. The industry in the South was confined to Kentucky and Missouri, where hemp were staple crops; the factories were concentrated in Lexington and Louisville.

[40] The Willcox Diary is in the Library of Western Virginia University.

The height of the Kentucky industry was reached in 1850, when more than two thousand persons, mostly slaves, were employed, and the state contained over a third of the bagging, bale, rope, and cordage factories in the United States. The industry declined in the last decade of the ante-bellum period, from 159 to 42 factories.[41] Foreign competition was the principal cause, although the dishonesty of some of the Kentucky manufacturers in disposing of their goods had an adverse effect on the market in the lower South. The industry could not have existed without a protective tariff, usually 25 per cent ad valorem, reduced to 15 per cent in 1857. This was not adequate to save the industry from the competition of Indian hemp and Scottish bagging. Moreover, iron bands were being used to some extent as substitutes for rope on cotton bales. During the decade 1850–60 numerous small factories were driven out of business and hemp manufacturing was gradually taken over by five companies. By 1860 Kentucky had declined to fourth rank in the nation in the production of cordage, being surpassed by Massachusetts, New York, and Missouri. Nevertheless, the state manufactured 60 per cent of the bagging of the United States and also led in the making of bale rope.

The manufacture of agricultural implements and machines, which were of such importance to the South, was left largely to Northern firms, though many of the simple tools used on the plantation were made by slave artisans or local blacksmiths. The most influential invention designed by an ante-bellum Southerner was the reaper which Cyrus H. McCormick, a Shenandoah Valley farmer, patented in 1834. His machine was not as well suited to the hilly country of the Virginia Piedmont and Valley as to the level fields of the West. Accordingly, being a good businessman, he moved to Chicago to be near the developing Western wheat belt. Here in 1848 he began to manufacture his machine in large numbers.[42] Obed Hussey also received a patent in 1833 on a successful reaper shortly before McCormick did, but he unwisely moved from Cincinnati to Baltimore, where he located his factory. In competition with the McCormick reaper his business declined so greatly that in 1858 he retired from the contest. At the close of the ante-bellum period Louisville and Richmond were developing

[41] Hopkins, *History of the Hemp Industry in Kentucky*, Chaps. IV, VI.
[42] See William T. Hutchinson, *Cyrus Hall McCormick* (New York, 1930–35), 2 vols.

as important centers for making farm implements and machinery. Nevertheless, between 1850 and 1860, with the exception of the making of cotton gins, there was a decline in the already slight manufacture of agricultural implements in the South.

The Southern states had a monopoly of the manufacture of cotton gins. The great manufacturer of these machines was Daniel Pratt, a New England carpenter, who had emigrated to Georgia, where he learned to construct gins. In 1833 he moved to Alabama and developed a thriving industrial village named Prattville, thirteen miles from Montgomery. He was a versatile manufacturer who, besides his cotton gin factory, established a cotton mill, a foundry, machine and blacksmith shops, a gristmill, a wagon manufactory, a tin manufactory, a printing business, a mercantile business, and a sash, door, and blind factory. These various industries supported a village of over eight hundred people and manufactured goods valued in 1860 at nearly $750,-000.[43]

Indeed, the typical industrial pattern of the Old South was a diversity of small industries concentrated in a town, usually located on the fall line. Except for its situation, Charleston, South Carolina, was a good example of the diversified manufacturing towns of the South. In 1850 the city ranked as the third manufacturing center of the South, with Richmond holding first place and New Orleans second. Its foundries and machine shops were particularly important, making railroad locomotives, steam engines, and steamship machinery. Textile mills, however, did not succeed in this seaport city. In 1848 a cotton mill was established, to whose capital stock the merchant Jacob Schirmer subscribed. When it failed three years later he recorded in his diary: "a regular burst up—my patriotism is to the tune of $750, all to be lost."[44] Charleston reached its peak as a manufacturing center in 1856 and then declined. A series of fires that destroyed some of its largest factories contributed to its decline.[45] The insurance of cotton and sugar in transit to markets was standard practice, but the insurance business in respect to factories, houses, and lives was largely undeveloped in the South.

[43] De Bow, *Commercial Review of the South and West,* IV (1847), 136–137.
[44] Jacob Schirmer Diary, October 11, 1851, South Carolina Historical Society, Charleston.
[45] Ernest M. Lander, Jr., "Charleston: Manufacturing Center of the Old South," *Journal of Southern History,* XXVI (1960), 330–351.

Although the states that formed the Southern Confederacy produced less than 10 per cent of the manufactured goods of the United States in 1860, their output was greater proportionally than in 1900. But the development of manufacturing in the Old South had a history of ups and downs instead of a steady progress. In the later ante-bellum period some manufactures, such as the tobacco industry, the making of finished products of iron, the sawing of lumber, and the milling of cereals, were prospering. Other important industries, notably hemp, salt, pig iron, gold mining, agricultural implements and machines (except cotton gins), and cotton manufacturing in some states, had gone into a decline. The primary reason for this decline was the revival of high prices for the Southern agricultural staples. Thus the movement of capital went into agricultural exploitation, which seemed to offer more assured profits and less competition than manufacturing. Moreover, during the last decade of the ante-bellum period, there was a general movement toward the elimination of small factories and the consolidation of manufacturing into larger units. This drift was undoubtedly accelerated by the expansion of transportation facilities. A prophet in 1860 might well have predicted the coming of a depression in agriculture as a result of overproduction, to be followed by a renaissance of Southern manufacturing.

Southern businessmen were not very different from those of the North. Indeed, a considerable proportion of them were Northern men, such as Daniel Pratt, James Guthrie of Louisville, and J. Edgar Thomson, the chief engineer of the Georgia Railroad before he became president in 1852 of the Pennsylvania Railroad. One of the most remarkable of these men was Judah Touro, son of a rabbi of Newport, Rhode Island, who emigrated in 1802 to New Orleans, where, starting as a peddler of soap, candles, and fish, he acquired great wealth. Somewhat eccentric, he never left the city except in 1815 to fight against the British. His modesty and his philanthropies won the affection of his fellow citizens. Especially notable was his donation of a church, free of rent, to the Unitarian minister.

Southern businessmen were less specialized than their Northern counterparts, many of them combining the occupations of planter and lawyer with those of manufacturer, merchant, or banker. They had a paternalistic attitude toward their workers, to whom they paid low wages, and they would not tolerate strikes. Some of them felt twinges of conscience because of their absorption in money making. Such a man was the salt manufacturer and planter Dr. John J. Cabell of Lynchburg. Plagued by a world of troubles in his business affairs, he believed that God was scourging him for his sins. He tried to justify his hectic pursuit of gain by his good intentions. "My ardent desire," he wrote, "is to do justice and to love and fear the Lord and do his commandments as far as my weak nature will allow. I now know I have been too anxious to accumulate fortunes for my children, which have been one of my errors of my natural life because I have made myself a Slave to it, to the neglect of higher and more important duties."[46]

The glorification of the Southern businessman was a salient theme of *De Bow's Review,* the Southern counterpart to Hunt's *Merchant's Magazine* of New York. In the issues from December, 1850, to April, 1853, De Bow published thirty short biographies of notable Southern businessmen and agriculturists under the title "Gallery of Industry and Enterprise." Surprisingly, the first sketch was not of a Southern man but of Charles T. James of Providence, Rhode Island, who had published a pamphlet, *The Culture and Manufacture of Cotton at the South,* in which he had urged Southerners to establish cotton mills. He himself was owner of one of the largest of the New England mills, yet in reply to New England cotton-mill men like Abbott Lawrence who condemned his pamphlet, he declared that, though a New Englander, he was also an American and wished to see each section develop its resources. De Bow selected Vardry McBee of South Carolina as a "Model Man of Enterprise for the South and the Country." Born in Spartanburg District, McBee quit school on account of poverty when he was twelve years old, worked as a farm laborer, learned the saddler's trade, and became a country merchant. As he acquired capital he expanded his enterprises to include a paper mill, a cotton factory, and gristmills. He purchased a large plantation near Greenville from a planter emigrating to the West, restored the fertility of its soil with manure, stopped erosion, and won numerous prizes for his skill as an agriculturist. De Bow praised him for his encouragement of home industry, his public spirit, and his leadership in railroad development.[47]

Certain characteristics of Southern businessmen stand out in the

[46] John J. Cabell to Richard K. Crallé, July 7, 1833, John J. Cabell Papers.
[47] *De Bow's Review,* XIII (1852), 314–318.

"Gallery" of business leaders of the Old South. In general, they were men of unusual public spirit, like Gregg in promoting cotton mills; or Glendy Burke, the great New Orleans merchant, who founded the public-school system of New Orleans; or C. S. Tarpley of Mississippi, who led a delegation from his state to stir the businessmen of New Orleans from their lethargy in regard to building a railroad northward to the Ohio River. Most of the men in the "Gallery" had been poor boys who had worked hard, saved their money, and established reputations for integrity and good judgment. Several of the business leaders, such as Franklin Elmore, had gone to college, but the majority had been trained in shops and stores and had little schooling. Many had gotten their start as merchants. Few confined their activities to one form of industry, such as Gregg to manufacturing, but developed wide-ranging economic interests. Henry W. Conner of Charleston, for example, beginning his career as a factor and commission merchant, introduced light-draft steamers on the Southern rivers for trade and transportation of cotton, then became president of the Bank of Charleston, organizer of the Charleston Gas Light Company, builder of a resort hotel on Sullivan's Island, and president of the South Carolina Railroad.

The agrarian ideal that permeated all classes of Southern society undoubtedly hampered the growth of the business class. When young Jason Niles, educated at the University of Vermont, came South in 1839 to seek a teaching position, he heard an argument in the barroom of a Nashville hotel on the tendencies of the commercial spirit. One of the disputants expressed a typical Southern point of view when he declared that the independent farmer was ten times more an aristocrat than was the merchant, "because the merchant lived by being complaisant and civil to all; and when he ceased to be so he starved; while the farmer who was not dependent on others for his living, could be as aristocratic and haughty as he pleased with perfect impunity."[48] Also the agrarian interests of the South caused many Southerners to be dubious about developing manufactures in their region for fear that it would weaken the opposition to a protective tariff. Actually the growth of manufacturing enterprises did result in causing many Southern businessmen to advocate a protective tariff on textiles, hemp products, salt, sugar, and iron.

[48] Diary of Jason Niles, November 23, 1839, typed copy, II, 229, Southern Collection, University of North Carolina.

The business class, the editors, and to a lesser extent the politicians produced most of the champions of the industrial gospel.[49] The work of William Gregg in propagandizing for the development of Southern cotton mills has been noted. Daniel Pratt used the press to urge Southerners to go in for manufactures. He pointed out that the amount of capital that was invested in a plantation would bring more wealth to the state if put into manufacturing, for the planter often wore out his land and moved out of the state. He urged the Southern states to encourage manufacturing by granting liberal charters, particularly to banks.[50] One of the most widely used arguments of the promoters of industry in the 1840's and 1850's was that factories provided jobs for the unproductive poor whites and elevated them in every respect. Many editors, particularly Noah Cloud of the *American Cotton Planter* and James D. B. De Bow of *De Bow's Review,* preached the industrial gospel. Mark Cockrill of Tennessee, one of the greatest sheep raisers of the South, urged that associations of planters should be formed to establish cotton mills.

Among the most persuasive methods used to spread industrial propaganda were the holding of industrial fairs and the Southern Commercial Conventions. The Kentucky Mechanics Institute in 1853 held an industrial exhibition in a large tobacco warehouse of Louisville, attended by a huge crowd, including many Negroes. Here was exhibited a large assortment of manufactures made in Louisville, pianos, buggies and carriages, iron mantels, stoves, gas fixtures, plows, carpets, furniture, and cooperage articles.[51] Although the Southern Commercial Conventions passed resolutions encouraging the development of Southern manufactures, their chief interest was in promoting direct trade with Europe. Many Southern businessmen attended these meetings in the hope of advancing Southern economic independence, but found the assemblies dominated by orators and politicians, and accomplishing little.

The businessmen as a whole were a conservative element in Southern society, opposed to the agitation of sectional issues. Some of the notable business leaders of the South, such as Senator John King, cot-

---

[49] See Herbert Collins, "The Southern Industrial Gospel before 1860," *Journal of Southern History,* XII (1946), 386–402.

[50] *De Bow's Review,* X (1851), 225–228.

[51] Louisville *Daily Courier,* August 27, October 14, 15, 1853.

ton manufacturer and president of the Georgia Railroad, and James Guthrie of Louisville, Kentucky, president of the L. & N. Railroad, were Democrats. The great majority, however, seem to have belonged to the Whig, Know-Nothing, and Union parties. Although they were loyal to their region and opposed to abolition, they distrusted the inflammatory politicians and sought to put a brake on the secession movement. Not all the industrialists, however, were antisecessionists. Ross Winans of Baltimore, whose railroad machine shops were the greatest in the South, was an example of a Southern businessman who supported the secession cause; he was arrested for making munitions in 1861 for Southern states. Richard Lathers, a native Southerner who became a New York merchant, made a tour of the Atlantic seaboard states early in 1861 to ascertain the attitude of the business community toward secession. He found that many of the businessmen, such as ex-Governor William Aiken, "the Astor of Charleston," and Donald McKay, president of the principal Charleston bank, were strongly opposed to it.[52] Yet when their influence proved unavailing to stop the movement, they became loyal Confederates.

Re note on page 229: The census statistics of 1860 on the textile industry of the South are highly unreliable. Professor Richard W. Griffin, who has studied this subject more thoroughly than any other scholar, has collated various types of evidence and concluded that in 1860 there were far more textile mills than are recorded by the census takers, and that the slave states produced between 20 and 25 per cent of the national manufacture of cotton textiles.

[52] Alvan F. Sanborn, *Reminiscences of Richard Lathers* (New York, 1909).

CHAPTER 11

Town Life

IN THE romantic legend of the South, Charleston and New Orleans had a great place, but the ordinary towns and cities were ignored almost as though they did not exist. Moreover, the older historians of the region, U. B. Phillips, William E. Dodd, and Walter L. Fleming, were too obsessed with the plantation and politics to give more than a fleeting glance to city life. Yet the cities and towns of the Old South deserve close scrutiny, for they were the centers of change in that slowly changing society. In the cities could be discerned the signs of the breaking down of slavery, particularly as the result of the hiring system and the greater sophistication of town slaves. The introduction of factories and railroads was subtly modifying typical agrarian attitudes, even to the point of relaxing opposition to a protective tariff.

A Southern town had a different appearance and atmosphere from the urban communities of the Northern states. The architecture was adapted to a warmer climate, in which the veranda or porch was a prominent feature. The streets were often shaded by pride of China (chinaberry) trees, palmettoes, magnolias, crepe myrtles, and mimosas, filling the air with fragrance. The Southern towns, with few exceptions, reflected the untidy, slipshod, and individualistic characteristics of an agrarian society dependent on slave labor. There was a conspicuous absence of paint on the frame buildings and a lack also of the neat green commons of New England villages. The Southern towns were full of activity during the early fall, when crops were being moved to markets, but ordinarily, except on Saturday afternoon, an air of somnolence and listlessness lay on them. The whistle of a steamboat, the arrival of a train, the movement of a sulky down the street, a street fight, a political speech—any such thing was welcomed.

Most of the towns had grown up haphazardly and therefore had no plan of arrangement or regularity. There were important exceptions, however: Columbia, South Carolina, and Augusta and Macon, Georgia, were built on a rectangular plan and the streets were spacious. Raleigh was regularly laid out in squares, dominated by the beautiful Greek Revival capitol. Savannah's City blocks, bordered by shade trees, gave the impression of *rus in urbe*. Among the unattractive features of the Southern towns were the alleys back of the imposing residences, where the slave domestics and the free Negroes lived in miserable shanties.

In the decade of the 1830's the towns of the south Atlantic seaboard exhibited signs of decline and decay. During a tour of them in 1831, William Gilmore Simms found many, such as Cahawba, the abandoned capital of Alabama, to be "stagnated depots." Of Savannah, he wrote: "Like most of our Southern townships and depots it remains stationary and has an air of utter languishment."[1] He attributed this condition to the relative decline of cotton culture in the seaboard slave states. Simms's native city of Charleston impressed the actress Fanny Kemble as having an air of genteel decay and eccentricity which rendered its citizens indifferent to what Mrs. Grundy would say and freed them from "devotion to conformity in small things and great, which pervades the American body-social from the matter of church-going to the trimming of women's petticoats."[2] The decline of this proud city was dramatized by the fact that although in 1820 its population was nearly equal to that of New Orleans, during the last twenty years of the ante-bellum period, the number of its inhabitants declined from 42,985 to 40,578, while its rival grew rapidly. Norfolk was another Southern town which failed to breathe the air of progress: it stood absolutely stationary during the decade 1850–60 at a population of approximately 14,500 blacks and whites.

On the other hand, many Southern cities grew by leaps and bounds

[1] Oliphant, *Letters of William Gilmore Simms,* I, "Notes of a Small Tourist."
[2] Frances Anne Kemble, *Journal* [1823–33] (Philadelphia, 1835).

during the decade preceding the Civil War. The river towns, profiting from the steamboat trade, showed the most progress. Louisville gained in population by 55 per cent, St. Louis by 93 per cent, and New Orleans by nearly 45 per cent. Mobile, the outlet of the booming cotton country of Alabama, increased from 1,500 people in 1820 to 30,000 in 1850, and Savannah, reviving in the last decade of the ante-bellum period, expanded at the rate of 45 per cent. The growth of Memphis to become the largest city of Tennessee was astonishing. Founded in 1819 by General Marcus Winchester and John Overton, promoter of Andrew Jackson's political career, it remained little more than a flatboat town until 1850, when its population skyrocketed during the next ten years by 155 per cent, from 8,839 to 22,263. During that decade the cotton economy of the hinterland was prospering and the city was linked by railroad (1857) with Charleston on the Atlantic coast.[3] Columbus, Georgia, was another town of remarkable growth, rising from an Indian trading post in 1828 to a thriving textile center in the 1850's as a result of being located at the falls of the Chattahoochee River and having the benefit of real-estate speculators. Solon Robinson described Atlanta in 1851 as "a sort of Jonah's gourd city," which had arisen as a result of railroads.

The constitution and functions of the town governments were determined by the charter of incorporation granted by the legislature. Many Southern towns were incorporated when their populations hardly justified it. Mobile, for example, was incorporated in 1819, when it contained only 809 people; Memphis in 1826, with a population of less than 500 people; and Lexington in 1831, with a population of 6,167. Lexington's charter provided for annual elections of a mayor and a council of twelve members, the electorate to consist of male citizens twenty-one years of age who had resided in the town six months and paid a tax. When a town had grown into a city, it was divided into wards (Nashville and Louisville in 1860 each had eight wards), which elected representatives to the city council.

City and town elections were usually listless occasions. In the election for mayor of Lexington, Kentucky, in 1852, only 642 of the 1,218

[3] Gerald M. Capers, Jr., *The Biography of a River Town, Memphis: Its Heroic Age* (Chapel Hill, 1939); Williams, "Early Ante-Bellum Montgomery," *Journal of Southern History,* VII (1941), 495–525.

white male residents voted.[4] Emotional issues, such as nullification and nativism, however, led to spirited contests. The Charleston merchant Jacob Schirmer recorded in his diary that the city elections during the nullification controversy were disgraced by bribery, corruption, and "persecution in every shape and form."[5] Thomas Hicks Wynne, a city employee of Richmond, wrote in May, 1856, "We have so much canvassing and electing that one-fourth of our time is devoted to these duties." Wynne thought that the frequent elections in cities resulted in the choice of ridiculous men for local office and weak city councils that were inefficient and wasted the people's money.[6]

In the 1850's city elections frequently became turbulent affairs as a result of the rise of the Know-Nothing movement. The Know-Nothings in the South seemed to have been less anti-Catholic in sentiment than in the North. They were mostly old Whigs who were concerned over the fraudulent voting of unnaturalized foreigners encouraged by the Democrats, and they sought to find an issue that would distract attention from the dangerous sectional controversy over slavery. The clash between Know-Nothings and Democrats in the Southern towns and cities was often violent because the towns had a surprising number of foreign-born immigrants in their population. Such residents in New Orleans in 1860 amounted to 40 per cent of the population, greater than that of Boston, approximately 36 per cent. The foreign-born of St. Louis at that time constituted nearly 60 per cent of the population, while New York, Chicago, and Milwaukee had a foreign-born population of only 50 per cent. Other Southern cities that had large foreign-born groups were Louisville with 34 per cent of the total population, Memphis with 36 per cent of white population, Charleston with 30 per cent of white population (15.5 per cent of total population), Baltimore and Mobile with 24 per cent, and Natchez with 25 per cent of total population.[7]

The foreign-born element in the Southern states was heavily concen-

---

[4] Trustee Minutes of Lexington, 1830–54, microfilm in University of Kentucky Library, January 5, 1852, p. 217.

[5] Jacob S. Schirmer, Diary, September 4, 1832 (see also August 31, 1852), South Carolina Historical Society, Charleston.

[6] Thomas Hicks Wynne Diary, May 18, 1856, Brock Collection, Huntington Library.

[7] Ella Lonn, *Foreigners in the Confederacy* (Baton Rouge, 1940), p. 4.

trated in the towns and cities along the coast because relatively few immigrants were farmers; most were employed mainly as merchants, peddlers, skilled craftsmen, and laborers. In Memphis, the Irish far outnumbered any other foreign group, living in the slum sections of "Pinch" and "Happy Hollow." German immigrants dominated the foreign-born population in St. Louis, Louisville, Baltimore, and in some Texas towns, notably New Braunfels. These foreign-born groups founded national fraternal societies, such as the German Friendly Society, the Turn Verein, St. Andrew's Society, and the Hibernian Society, which gave aid to their members in sickness and distress and celebrated national festivals. The Germans were the only foreign group in the South to establish a foreign-language press, although French-language newspapers continued to be published in New Orleans throughout the ante-bellum period.[8]

Hatred of the foreign-born was displayed in city elections during the Know-Nothing movement. Violent mobs, led by the Vigilantes in New Orleans and the "Plug Uglies," "Rip Raps," and "Blood Tubs" in Baltimore attacked the foreign-born groups on election days. In August, 1855, on election day there occurred a riot in Louisville, called "Bloody Monday," in which twenty-two persons, three-fourths of whom were foreign immigrants, were killed. The bitter antiforeign feeling revived interest in city elections, so that more people voted in local contests in some of the large cities in 1855 and 1856 than in the presidential election. The result was that the Know-Nothing party won control in most of the large cities of the South.[9]

Except in New Orleans, there does not seem to have been much corruption in the conduct of city government, but great inefficiency and extravagance prevailed. Local governments often plunged their communities into heavy debt by subscribing to the stock of railroad companies. The city of Richmond in 1839, with a population of approximately 20,000 people, of whom a large part were slaves and free Negroes, had a debt of $700,000, incurred partly in building a water-works. The budget of Richmond at this time was revealing of the main functions of municipal government in the Old South. The city

[8] See Carl Wittke, *The German-Language Press in America* (Lexington, 1957).

[9] W. D. Overdyke, *The Know Nothing Party in the South* (Baton Rouge, 1950).

spent $40,000 annually for interest, $20,000 for salaries, $5,000 for support of the poor, $2,000 for free schools and the orphanage asylum, $4,000 for repairing the streets, $9,000 for the night watch, and $5,000 for fire protection, upkeep of the market, and contingent expenses.[10] The revenue of the town of Lexington in 1832 was $9,407, which was derived from a tax of 25 cents on each $100 worth of property, a poll tax, a dog tax, rent of markets, tax on stores, licenses, and fines from the Mayor's Court.[11]

City government in the Old South was a surprising blend of laissez faire and strict regulation of economic affairs. Louisville, for example, had an array of inspectors: of flour, weights and measures, salt, liquor, coal, markets, taverns, and the city pump, but not of meat. The boards of aldermen or councils attended to a wide variety of civic interests— the free schools; the pesthouse, in which smallpox victims were isolated; city health through a health officer; care of the poor; supervision of the streets; and regulation of the police. The night watch was usually more numerous than the daytime police. Equipped with rattles and lamps, the watch patrolled the streets; in New Orleans its members, colloquially called "Charlies," were accompanied by trained dogs.[12] The council passed such typical ordinances as those requiring free Negroes to wear badges, prohibiting slaves from hiring their time from masters, enforcing the curfew laws, prohibiting cockfights or the playing of bandy (a boys' game) on the streets, requiring the use of lime in privies, and prohibiting hogs and cattle from running at large.

One of the responsibilities of the city government was the paving of the streets, which was generally neglected. In 1805 the streets of New Orleans were so muddy in the winter that when ladies attended the grand balls they waded through the mud with their silken dresses tucked up, carrying their shoes and stockings in their hands; upon their arrival, they washed their feet and legs, put on their shoes and stockings, and were ready for the dance.[13] By the 1830's travelers reported that the sidewalks of the main streets in most of the Southern towns were paved with brick and the streets had stone cobbles. Nevertheless, James

[10] Buckingham, *Slave States,* II, 416.

[11] Trustee Minutes of Lexington, Report of Mayor, May 30, 1832, p. 137.

[12] E. M. Coulter, *The Other Half of Old New Orleans: Incidents from the Recorder's Court* (Baton Rouge, 1939), p. 12.

[13] Saxon, *Old Louisiana,* p. 108. Memoir of Judge Thomas Nicholls (1840).

Silk Buckingham wrote of Richmond in 1839 that its streets were "wretchedly paved, imperfectly drained and never lighted, as I believe there is not a single street light in the city—the most dirty, rough, and disagreeable streets to walk on that are to be found perhaps in the Union—filled with dirt and dust all through the dry weather and dirt and mud all through the wet. Of all the reforms needed for Richmond I would say that 'Street Reform' was the most urgent and pressing."[14] Henry Benjamin Whipple in 1844 found a similar condition in the streets of Mobile, which he reported were "worse than any I have ever seen"—the pedestrian either waded in mud or was suffocated with the dust.[15]

The sanitation of Southern towns remained bad throughout the antebellum period. Ignorance of the germ theory of disease was universal. Open sewers were the rule in the Southern towns. Whipple described the streets of New Orleans as extremely dirty, the gutters covered with a green scum that gave forth an offensive odor. When a cholera epidemic occurred in Richmond in 1854, the city fathers, recorded Thomas Hicks Wynne in his diary, had "a vast deal of filth removed, but owing to the imperfect sewerage system of the city it is impossible to keep many parts of it clean."[16] The health of the citizens of Southern towns was continually threatened by the presence of livery stables and barns, swarms of flies, open privies, and polluted wells. A large number of vultures, which were protected by law, acted as scavengers in Charleston. New Orleans, Memphis, and other cities used slave convicts, both men and women, wearing chains, to clean and repair the streets.

A major problem of the cities was to obtain an adequate supply of pure water. In 1818 Benjamin H. Latrobe, the great architect and engineer, went to New Orleans to complete the waterworks for the city started by his son who had died of yellow fever. He secured a pump from New York which pumped water from the river through wooden pipes bored from logs. He planned to sell water to individuals, but he too fell a victim of yellow fever and the city took over his private venture.[17] Augusta, William Gilmore Simms noted in his journal of

1831, possessed a waterworks that brought water to the town from springs. Nashville, Tennessee, had a city-owned waterworks as early as 1833. Water was pumped from the Cumberland River by a steam engine to an elevated reservoir from which it flowed to homes through cast-iron pipes. The first American water filtering plant, and the only one in the ante-bellum South, was built in Richmond in 1832 by Albert Stein, but it was not successful. An immigrant from Düsseldorf, Germany, Stein inaugurated a new era in building municipal waterworks in the South. During the 1830's and 1840's he constructed waterworks for five of the principal Southern cities.

Some of the Southern cities provided pure drinking water for their citizens by boring artesian wells. Edmund Ruffin in his diary describes some artesian borings that he saw on his visit to Charleston in 1857. One well owned by the city was over 1,200 feet deep; water gushed from it through a pipe three inches in diameter. Before the introduction of these artesian wells the supply of drinking water was obtained from shallow wells ten or twelve feet in depth and from barrels of rain water drained from the roofs. Ruffin observed that such sources of water were polluted either by privies and dead bodies or by the filth from a multitude of buzzards that roosted on the housetops. Before the era of city-owned artesian wells and deep private wells, Ruffin, during visits to Charleston in the summer, had found when washing his face that the water available was "offensive to the smell."[18]

Another threat to the health of Southern towns was the recurrence of epidemics, particularly of cholera and yellow fever. The first great scourge of Asiatic cholera came to the Southern cities in the summer of 1833.[19] Apparently this deadly disease had been introduced into the United States from Canada, and then advanced along the river highways into the lower South. It was propagated by polluted drinking water or by contaminated food. Whenever cholera struck a town there was a mass exodus to the country, thus spreading the disease. According to the English traveler E. S. Abdy, Maysville, Kentucky, was estimated to have a population of 4,000 people before the cholera pestilence of 1833; when he arrived the next year, only 500 remained.[20]

[18] Edmund Ruffin Diary, May 15, 1857, p. 103, Library of Congress.
[19] See J. S. Chambers, *The Conquest of Cholera* (New York, 1938), Chaps. V, VI, VIII.
[20] Abdy, *Journal*, pp. 339, 349.

Victims of the plague died with dramatic suddenness. The Negroes seemed to be more susceptible to its ravages than the whites. A resident of northern Kentucky at this time wrote to a relative that the inhabitants were so terrified that they would not reap and all business was prostrated. "The Cholera appears to spare no age nor sex," he observed, "but sweeps whole families off in a day or so. We here believe that it is most contagious from the dead bodies," which frequently lay unburied for days. The doctors had slight defense against the dread disease; their main prescription was the taking of huge doses of calomel; thousands drank whisky excessively as a preventive.[21]

In a letter to Peter B. Porter of New York in 1833, Henry Clay described its effect on Lexington: "All the stores and shops are closed, and no one moving in the streets except those concerned with the dead or the sick."[22] At its height in June approximately five hundred of the citizens of Lexington died, and it was difficult to find grave diggers to bury their bodies. James Lane Allen, in his story "King Solomon," tells of the heroism displayed by the town drunk and loafer who risked his life in burying the infected bodies, but who, after the crisis was over, however, relapsed into his old way of living. In the epidemic of 1849 New Orleans was the worst sufferer from its ravages, which killed approximately one-seventh of the population. Some of these victims were reported to have died from fright. When the fearsome disease appeared in Richmond, Virginia, in the summer of 1854, the newspapers suppressed any reference to it in order not to hurt business by alarming the country people.[23]

Yellow fever was a more frequent and devastating scourge of Southern communities than cholera. It attacked the health of lowland towns during warm weather, the season of mosquitoes, which carried the germs of the disease. The cause of the disease remained a mystery throughout the ante-bellum period. It was generally believed to originate from the accumulation of filth in a city or from the miasma of low places. Doctor Josiah C. Nott of Mobile seems to have been the only one who suspected that yellow fever was spread by the bite of a

[21] A. P. Thompson, Mason County, Kentucky, to Thornton K. Thompson, June 24, 1833, University of Kentucky Library.
[22] Henry Clay to Peter B. Porter, June 16, 1833, Henry Clay Collection, University of Kentucky Library.
[23] Wynne Diary, August 13, 1854.

mosquito. The doctors frantically tried all kind of remedies, but the favorite prescriptions were huge doses of calomel and quinine, while tar was burned at street intersections to purify the air.[24]

New Orleans had the greatest death rate of any city and Louisiana of any state in the Union. The Southern metropolis had a large floating population and many visitors; these were the persons who succumbed most readily to yellow fever rather than the natives or those who were acclimated. Theodore Clapp, pastor of an independent church in the city, lived through twenty yellow-fever epidemics in his thirty-five years of residence in New Orleans. During epidemics, when others fled the city, he and the Catholic priests heroically remained to care for the sick and dying.[25] During the great epidemic of 1853 it was estimated that 40,000 people in New Orleans contracted the disease, of whom 8,000 died. When a Southern community suffered a disaster from plague or fire, Northern as well as other Southern cities contributed generous sums for relief, and doctors from neighboring towns would go to the aid of the stricken city.

In addition to suffering from recurrent epidemics, the Southern towns were peculiarly vulnerable to fires. They had a special reason for fearing the outbreak of fires, because arson was a favorite weapon of disgruntled slaves. Every householder was required by town regulations to keep a fire bucket, usually made of leather; when a fire occurred the citizens formed a line to pass buckets of water from wells, rivers, or cisterns to the scene of the conflagration. By 1820 most of the Southern towns had the protection of volunteer fire companies.[26] The members were exempted from militia duty, an inducement so attractive that eventually laws were passed limiting the number who could belong to a fire company. In some cities, such as Norfolk, members of the fire companies were also exempted from jury duty. The volunteer firemen, often dressed in colorful costumes, developed great *esprit de corps* as companies of rival cities competed with each other in contests of skill, particularly in the height to which their engines could

[24] Jo Ann Carrigan, "Yellow Fever in New Orleans, 1853: Abstractions and Realities," *Journal of Southern History*, XXV (1959), 337–355.

[25] Theodore Clapp, *Autobiographical Sketches and Recollections during a Thirty-Five Years' Residence in New Orleans* (Boston, 1859), Chaps. VI, VII.

[26] See John B. Clark, Jr., "Fire Protection in the Old South," Ph.D. Dissertation, University of Kentucky, 1957.

throw a stream of water. The visiting firemen held parades, ate barbecues, listened to orations, and got drunk.

In fighting fires the principal implements used were ladders, buckets,
hooks to pull down walls, gunpowder to clear spaces for stopping the
advance of an extensive fire, and fire engines. The latter were hand-
operated pumps, which were pulled on wheels to the scene of the fires.
They were purchased almost entirely from Northern manufacturers.
At the close of the ante-bellum period pumps operated by steam engines and horse-drawn vehicles were introduced in the larger Southern
cities. These innovations greatly reduced the need for man power and
led to the hiring of full-time paid firemen. In Louisville the city government furnished the engines and exercised control over them, but
in many cities and towns the volunteer firemen raised funds to buy
their uniforms and engines. Charleston in 1857 had ten engines manned
by volunteer white companies and ten operated by Negro slaves under
white direction. The Richmond Fire Association, which controlled
seven volunteer companies in 1850, sold fire insurance, each member
of the companies being a stockholder. The New Orleans Firemen's
Charitable Association, an organization of volunteer companies, contracted with the city in 1855 to provide fire protection for an annual
sum of $70,000.

A great increase in the safety of the larger towns came with the introduction of gas lighting for the streets. Baltimore in 1816 was the
first American city to light its streets with gas lamps. Until 1835 the
streets of New Orleans were lighted by whale-oil lamps suspended over
the middle of the street by chains, but in that year the enterprising
actor-manager James H. Caldwell, who had illuminated his theater
with gas lighting, organized the New Orleans Gas Lighting and Banking Company and received a franchise to light the city streets. After
his retirement from theatrical management in 1843, he made a fortune
from establishing gas lighting in Mobile and Cincinnati. In Richmond
the diarist Thomas H. Wynne joined the Know-Nothing party in 1855
in order to obtain the office of superintendent of the city-owned gas-
works. The Know-Nothings won the city election, with the result that
the incumbent superintendent, a foreigner, was turned out and Wynne
obtained his position.[27] The great majority of Southern towns during

[27] Wynne Diary, April 9, May 6, 1855.

the ante-bellum period did not have the advantage of gas lighting but had to depend on whale-oil lamps.

A considerable number of Southern towns and cities established good free public schools. The story of the Lexington schools seems to have been typical of the development of public schools in Southern towns. In 1833 there was a school in Lexington which charged tuition at moderate rates but gave free tuition to those who could not pay. Twenty years later the town, with a population of 8,367, of whom 5,526 were white, was supporting four public schools, in three of which Latin and Greek were taught. The school term lasted for eleven months. The number of children of school age in the town was 1,484, of whom 1,378 were enrolled in the public schools. Despite a large percentage of absentees, the schoolrooms were crowded, averaging sixty-six pupils to a room. In addition to the regular schools, there was a municipal night school of 103 students, in which arithmetic, penmanship, and bookkeeping were taught. A committee of the city council adopted a uniform set of textbooks for all the city schools, among which were the famous "Peter Parley" readers prepared by Samuel Goodrich, a Northern man, and Rand's *System of Penmanship*. In order to stimulate the teachers to their highest exertions, the committee adopted a rule declaring the positions of all teachers vacant at the end of the school year. The principals received salaries of $700 and the teachers ranged from $250 to $300 a year. The town spent approximately a fourth of its revenue, or $8,000, in operating the four public schools.[28]

Good schools were only one of the many cultural advantages which city life offered. The development of urban communities made possible the establishment of lyceums, public libraries, and theaters, providing cultural advantages for the citizens. In the decade of the 1830's, the lyceum movement, which had originated in Massachusetts in 1826 though the efforts of Josiah Holbrook, spread below the Mason-Dixon Line. Carl Bode describes the course of this movement in the South as a flurry of interest followed by apathy.[29] The lyceum did not take root as strongly in the South as it did in the North partly because in the North there existed a close connection between this institution and

[28] Trustee Minutes of Lexington, January 6, 1853, p. 361; August 4, 1853, pp. 403–404.

[29] See Carl Bode, *The American Lyceum, Town Meeting of the Mind* (New York, 1956).

the various reform movements, especially the abolition movement. The scattered population of the South, the existence of slavery, and the fact that the mass of Southerners were not as literate or well educated as the majority of the people in the North were also serious handicaps to the founding of lyceums. Furthermore Southerners, with their love of rhetoric and interest in politics, preferred debating societies and orations to the didactic lectures which formed the staple of Northern lyceums.

Nevertheless, many Southern towns gave a hospitable reception to lecturers from Great Britain and, before the 1850's, from the Northern states. In 1839 James Silk Buckingham, a British traveler, lectured in the Southern states on Palestine and Egypt. He noted that in Charleston his lectures were attended by larger audiences in proportion to its population than in any other city where he had spoken, and also that they were better reported by the Charleston newspapers than in any other city. In Mobile, with a population of 12,000 people including slaves, 500 persons listened to one of his lectures.[30] Professor Benjamin Silliman of Yale College gave twelve lectures in New Orleans in 1845 on geology and fossils, and Louis Agassiz of Harvard College a few years later lectured in Charleston on geology. Thackeray was greeted by large and enthusiastic audiences when he lectured in Southern cities in 1853 on the literary men of Great Britain. William Gilmore Simms, the novelist, added to his income by lecturing in Southern towns, and P. T. Barnum, the Yankee showman, edified Southern audiences with his lecture "The Advantages of Temperance."

A significant movement in the larger Southern cities, particularly in the decade of the 1850's, arose with the establishment of Athenaeums and Mechanics' Institutes. The Maryland Institute in Baltimore, founded in 1826 by John H. B. Latrobe, was an early example of the Mechanics' Institute. It supported an extensive library, a cabinet of minerals, chemical and philosophical apparatus, and promoted lectures on useful subjects.[31] The Mechanics' Institutes in most Southern cities seemed to have been designed to broaden the culture of the citizens as a whole rather than specifically devoted to the interests of the mechanic class. The Kentucky Mechanic's Institute, of Louisville, organ-

---

[30] Buckingham, *Slave States*, I, 83.
[31] John E. Semmes, *John H. B. Latrobe and his Times, 1803–1891* (Baltimore, 1917), Chap. XV.

ized in 1853, had at the close of the decade about a thousand readers, of whom many were "ladies." The Institute was managed by various committees on Exhibition of Paintings, Lectures, Finance, Instruction, Library, Arts and Sciences.[32]

The Richmond Athenaeum encouraged the development of the fine arts in the city and provided a library and a series of lectures. Among the paintings placed in the lecture room was a copy of Murillo's *Ascension of the Virgin.* Alexander Galt, the Norfolk sculptor, who had studied in Italy, had a studio in the Athenaeum Hall where in 1853 he exhibited his works with the object of securing a commission from the Virginia Legislature for a statue of Jefferson. His *Psyche,* his *Bacchante,* and his *Virginia* aroused high praise from the patriotic Virginians.[33] The directors of the Athenaeum in 1853 purchased 1,500 books in London to add to the library. Among the lectures delivered during the year was one by the British consul and novelist G. P. R. James, entitled "The Connection between Literature, Science, and Art," and another by O. P. Baldwin on the woman's rights movement, "treating his subject in such a ludicrous style as to elicit roars of laughter."

The growth of towns and cities in the South was accompanied by a remarkable expansion of public libraries. Between 1850 and 1860 the federal census recorded that the number of volumes in the Southern libraries, other than private, had increased fivefold. The three public libraries in Georgia at the beginning of the decade, for example, had increased to 288; the sixteen libraries of Alabama had multiplied to 361; the twenty-one in Virginia to 1,350. Virginia and South Carolina (the latter possessing the famous Charleston Library Society) had by far the largest number of volumes in public libraries in the Southern states.[34]

The phenomenal expansion of public libraries in the South during the last decade of the ante-bellum period, however, should not be interpreted too sanguinely, for the number of volumes available to the public in these libraries did not average more than a single volume for every two or three white persons. South Carolina was an outstanding exception, possessing one and one-half volumes per white person, which

---

[32] Louisville *Daily Courier,* February 1, 1855.
[33] Wynne Diary, December 17, 1853.
[34] *Census of 1860,* "Mortality and Miscellaneous Statistics," p. 505.

was equivalent to the ratio in Massachusetts. Besides municipal libraries there were Sunday School libraries; of the latter, Georgia had fifty-
two and Kentucky ninety-one. Some of the municipal libraries charged
a fee for books taken out. The Transylvania law student, William Little
Brown, paid 87½ cents when he joined the Lexington Library in 1810,
but he was thereby enabled to borrow such volumes as Lady Mon-
tagu's *Letters, The Devil on Two Sticks,* Volney's *View of America,*
Locke's *Essay on Human Understanding,* Goldsmith's *History of England,* Hume's *Essays,* two volumes of *The Guardian,* Johnson's *The
Rambler,* Malthus, and Mitford's *History of Greece.*[35]

Entertainment in the cities and the towns was provided by the theater, the circus, concerts, and lectures. Some of the Southern towns had
Thespian societies, or amateur theatrical groups, which built theaters
and produced comedies and farces, such as *She Stoops to Conquer,
Secrets Worth Knowing,* and *The Bee Hive.* Brown noted in his diary
on February 29, 1812, that he saw *Othello* performed in Lexington
but that some hatters had conspired to spoil the performance by hisses
and clamor, in which they succeeded. The development of the theater
in the South was impeded by strong Puritan feeling in many communities. When Sol Smith's company came to Huntsville, Alabama, in 1829,
the players had to compete with "preaching every night." The preachers condemned those who attended the theater, warning them that
they would be roasted in hell. Smith commented upon their effect on
attendance at the theater and box-office receipts, "the preachers carried
the day." When the company played in Tuscaloosa, the bigoted portion
of the citizens discouraged the performance of "prophane stage plays
in a Christian community," and consequently the actors played to
houses which barely paid expenses.[36]

Indeed, the crowds seemed to prefer such forms of entertainment as
balloon ascensions, revivals, and camp meetings to the more sophisticated entertainment of the theater. Thomas Hicks Wynne noted in his
diary of 1854 that Ole Bull, the violinist, and Patti, the singer, had
given concerts in Richmond, but that "a wonderful preacher" and lady's
man named Cummings (an ante-bellum Billy Graham) had thrown

[35] Brown, "His Book," May 16, 1801–June 13, 1807, pp. 29–35.
[36] Sol Smith, *Theatrical Management in the South and West for Thirty Years*
(New York, 1868), p. 60.

the performances of these artists in the shade, drawing the crowds though he had only a small amount of merit.[37]

James H. Caldwell, a British actor, is regarded as the founder of the English stage in New Orleans. In 1822 he built the American Theater, later called the Camp Street Theater, and in 1835 he erected the elaborate St. Charles Theater. Five years later he expanded his theatrical business by building a theater in Mobile, driving Sol Smith's company there out of business. The history of the stage in the South is filled with accounts of the burning of theater buildings. The most dramatic case was the destruction of the Richmond Theater in 1811 by a fire that took the lives of many of the audience; the godly must have rejoiced when a church was built on its site. The St. Charles was burned to the ground in 1842. Caldwell attempted to start another theater, but because of competition retired instead the following year.

Next to Caldwell, the most important theatrical manager in the South was Sol Smith, who has left a valuable account of the growth of the theater in the South and West. This versatile man, the son of a New York goldsmith, drifted to the Ohio Valley, working as a printer's apprentice and as a newspaper editor until 1823, when he began his career as a theatrical manager. Although he himself was a comedy actor of great skill, he devoted his energies primarily to managing traveling stock companies. In 1835, in partnership with Noah M. Ludlow, he founded a pioneer theater at Mobile. Earlier his stock company had traveled through Kentucky, Tennessee, Alabama, and Georgia in a wagon pulled by six horses. They encountered many rough conditions, such as almost impassable roads and a scarcity of candles to light the performance. The rural audiences at times took the play as a real happening, with ludicrous results. Their most popular play on the road was *Don Juan or the Libertine Destroyed*, because of the melodramatic scene depicting the infernal region with flaming fires and brimstone. In 1840, Smith moved from Mobile to New Orleans, where he started the New American Theater and several years later the New St. Charles Theater. He also founded and managed a theater at St. Louis until his retirement in 1853.

The theatrical business was not remunerative in the Southern states. Strolling companies often lived from hand to mouth, for rural audi-

[37] Wynne Diary, February 6, 1854.

ences had little money and the companies usually had to be content with charging 25 or 50 cents for admission. Sol Smith estimated that Caldwell, over a period of twenty-five years as a theatrical manager, did not average a profit of $1,000 a year, and that he himself had about the same profit from his labors. One of the financial troubles which stock companies encountered was the unsound currency which the box office had to accept.[38]

Except in several large cities, the theaters were makeshift buildings. In Mobile, Smith began his performances in a room above a billiard hall; in St. Louis the stage was in an old salthouse; in Natchez in a renovated warehouse; and in some towns the wandering stock players used the courthouse or the building of the local Thespian Society. However, Tyrone Power, the Irish actor, described the American Theater in New Orleans in 1835 as "a large well-proportioned house with rows of boxes, a pit, or parquette, as it is termed, subdivided as in the French Theater." The Opera, or the New French Theater, opened in 1818, had a company of actors superior to the American Theater company, he observed, and its handsome, well-appointed building contained, besides the auditorium, a large ballroom, supper rooms, and "gambling hells."[39]

The different types of actors in a Southern stock company are indicated by the composition of Sol Smith's company in New Orleans. The troupe of eleven members included a leading actor, "heavy man," leading actress, first old man, light and eccentric comedian, and female singer. It became a custom to employ a visiting "star" to act with the regular company. The most prominent of the stars were English and Irish actors, such as the elder Joseph Jefferson, who died from yellow fever in Mobile in 1842, and Junius Brutus Booth, who settled on a farm near Belle Aire, Maryland. Ellen Tree and Fanny Kemble were the favorites among English actresses. William Charles Macready, during his last American tour in 1849, played four weeks in the roles of Julius Caesar and Othello before "great houses" in New Orleans before returning to New York, where he was mobbed in the Astor Place Opera House by partisans of the American actor, Edwin Forrest.

Tyrone Power, whom Sol Smith described as the "greatest Irish comedian that ever graced the American stage," was immensely pop-

[38] Smith, *Theatrical Management*, p. 172.
[39] Power, *Impressions of America*, II, 171, 172, 175.

ular in the South as well as in the North. In November, 1833, he played in one theater in Baltimore nearly as large as Covent Garden in London, while Charles Kemble and his daughter Fanny played in another. The Kembles attracted the aristocratic audience, Power the sturdy democracy; as he noted in his travel account, "the people are with me against the Kembles." In Savannah he played four nights a week in a well-designed theater before a "merry and intelligent audience." In New Orleans he reported that at his performances the parquet and dress boxes were almost exclusively filled with ladies, coiffeured with the taste of French women and dressed in the latest Parisian fashions. "When the New Orleans Theatre is attended by the belles of the city," he wrote, "it presents decidedly the most elegant-looking auditory of this country."[40] In Natchez the theater was located in a graveyard, and his first performance in the play *Born to Good Luck* was postponed because the oil for the lamps, on account of exposure to frost, refused to burn. The planters, whom he described as fine-looking men, leisurely assembled at the theater, where they occupied the pit exclusively.

The taste of Southern audiences was far from highbrow. Shakespeare's plays were performed more frequently than they are today, but were not nearly as popular as farces and comedies. Sol Smith noted that in Mobile in the 1830's *The Hunchback* was twice as popular as *Romeo and Juliet*. Such farces as *The Lying Valet, Of Age Tomorrow,* and *Three Weeks after Marriage,* or light comedies such as *Cherry and Fair Star, Town and Country, Soldier's Daughter, A Roland for an Oliver,* and *Hypocrite* provided the heaviest box-office receipts. *The School for Scandal* and *She Stoops to Conquer* were also perennial favorites. The Richmond Theater advertised in the newspapers in the fall of 1859 *Dreams of Delusion,* "the sparkling comedy" *Wild Oats, Simon Seigel,* and the pantomime, *Kim-ka, or the Aeronaut.*[41] Sex does not seem to have been emphasized nearly as much on the ante-bellum stage as in the middle of the twentieth century.

More popular than the plays were the Negro Minstrels, the dancing of Fanny Elssler, and the singing of Jenny Lind. The founder of minstrel shows in the United States was "Daddy" Thomas D. Rice. Born in New York City of poor parents, he wandered to Louisville, Ken-

[40] *Ibid.,* II, 172.
[41] Richmond *Whig,* December 23, 1859.

tucky, where he was employed in Ludlow and Smith's Southern Theater as property man, lamp lighter, and stage carpenter. According to Sol Smith, Rice composed in Louisville in 1830 the popular Negro song "Jim Crow," singing it first in "a little piece entitled the Rifle" by Solon Robinson. Rice had heard an old Negro named Jim Crow, who worked in a livery stable near the theater, singing a song accompanied by a shuffling dance and step. He mimicked the Negro's dance and memorized his stanza, to which he later added hundreds of verses. The words of the original stanza were:

> First on de heel, den on de toe,
> Ebery time I wheel about I jump Jim Crow.
> Wheel about and turn about and do jis so,
> And ebery time I wheel about I jump Jim Crow.

From 1840 to 1880 the Negro minstrels, with faces blackened by burnt cork, were the most popular form of entertainment in the country.[42]

In the 1840's another immensely popular entertainer, the Austrian ballet dancer, Fanny Elssler, toured the cities of the South. In New Orleans "the divine Fanny" was the rage as she danced "the Smolenski" at the rate of $1,000 a night. Her dancing was described as "sinuous, human and fired by a great energy." In the early 1850's Jenny Lind, hailed as "the Swedish Nightingale," sang to rapt audiences in the South. She was so popular that in New Orleans seats to her concert sold for $50. Her manager, P. T. Barnum the circus man, with a shrewd insight into the sentimentality and Victorian decorum of the age, advertised her "angelic" qualities as much as her modest musical talent.

A mirror, though often a distorted one, of life in the towns was furnished by the newspapers. It was easy to found a newspaper in the Old South. The expenses for physical equipment were not great—principally the cost of a hand-operated press, type, and a quantity of rag paper. The presses and most of the paper were bought in the Northern states. This dependence on the North was typical of Southern newspapers, for as late as 1860 only 5 per cent of the paper produced in the United States was manufactured in the Southern states. A few editors

[42] Carl Wittke, *Tambo and Bones, a History of the American Minstrel Stage* (Durham, 1930), Chap. I.

like Joseph Gales in Raleigh, North Carolina, and Amos Kendall, proprietor of the *Western World* at Frankfort, built and operated paper mills to supply their newspapers with newsprint. The great economic prize for editors was to be elected state printer. Joseph Gales, editor of the Raleigh *Register,* which supported the Republican party, was annually elected state printer by the legislature from 1800 to the election of Jackson as President.[43]

The patronage of a political party seems to have been a prerequisite for newspaper success. The *Jeffersonian,* of Lynchburg, Virginia, edited by Richard K. Crallé and financed by Dr. John J. Cabell, for example, became unprofitable after it departed from the support of Jackson in 1832, and was offered for sale at a price of $3,000. Dr. Cabell advised Crallé, who had become an ardent supporter of Calhoun, to secure 1,500 subscribers before starting a new journal in Richmond.[44] Among the great handicaps to operating a newspaper business in the South were the difficulties of securing reliable journeyman printers and of collecting cash from subscribers.

The Southern newspapers, aside from the heat and passion of political partisanship, were dull publications. The front page was frequently devoted to advertisements. The editors published little local news. Murders and sex crimes were relegated to a small space, except for a few sensational trials, such as the Ward trial of 1854 in Kentucky, involving the murder of a schoolmaster who had flogged the son of a wealthy family. James Silk Buckingham observed in 1839 that there was not much original matter in the Southern newspapers aside from the editorial column, the main contents being extracts from other papers. The debates in Congress and the state legislature were frequently published as well as political letters, almost always anonymous. Also many Southern newspapers published poems and anecdotes. Flashes of humor enlivened the reports of police courts in some newspapers; George W. Kendall in the New Orleans *Picayune,* and George D. Prentice, editor of the Louisville *Journal,* were famous for their witty squibs.

A considerable proportion of the Southern editors were born in the

[43] Winifred Gales, "Reminiscences," pp. 141, 160, Southern Collection, University of North Carolina; see also Clement Eaton, "Winifred and Joseph Gales, Liberals in the Old South," *Journal of Southern History,* X (1944), 461–474.

[44] John J. Cabell to Richard K. Crallé; March 16, November 13, December 17, 1831; Crallé to Cabell, September 11, 1831, July 4, 1832, Cabell Papers.

North. One of these, George D. Prentice, a native of Connecticut, came to Kentucky in 1830 to write a campaign biography of Henry Clay and remained to edit the Louisville *Journal,* which became one of the great Whig newspapers devoted to the preservation of the Union. Amos Kendall, a New England Yankee who was employed as a tutor for Henry Clay's children, edited the Frankfort *Argus of Western America* until he went to Washington to become a member of Jackson's "Kitchen Cabinet." In Charleston, western Virginia, a former Vermont schoolteacher, Enos W. Newton, edited the *Kanawha Republican* for many years; A. W. Campbell, a native of Ohio, championed the interests of the western part of Virginia and opposed slavery in his Wheeling *Intelligencer* (1856–61). The editor of the Mobile *Register* for twenty-six years from its founding in 1828 was the Connecticut Yankee Thaddeus Sanford, and the Nashville *Union* was edited in the latter part of the ante-bellum period by Jeremiah George Harris, who had left his New Bedford, Massachusetts, paper to settle in Tennessee and redeem the Whig state for the Democratic party. The Charleston *Courier* for many years prior to the Civil War was edited by the moderate Aaron Willington of Massachusetts. In 1851 six of the editors of the leading newspapers of North Carolina were Northern men, and some of the prominent editors of Georgia came from beyond the Mason-Dixon Line. One of the greatest Southern newspapers, the New Orleans *Picayune,* was founded by George S. Kendall, a Yankee who had worked on the New York *Tribune* under the tutelage of Horace Greeley.

Almost invariably these men used their influence to preserve the Union, and many of them advocated democratic reforms in government and the establishment of free schools. Also, with few exceptions, they denounced the abolitionists and accepted the point of view of their communities with regard to slavery. George D. Prentice, "originally educated to think slavery wrong," declared in an editorial of 1858: "We think, that, where the climate and soil are favorable the blacks are better off in slavery than out of it—we wish to see it left everywhere to the will of the whites and the operation of natural causes." He denounced the abolitionists, demanded that the fugitive-slave law be enforced, and advocated that the territories be open to slavery, "for it will not go there to any considerable extent unless invited by natural causes."[45] Nevertheless, in the latter part of the ante-bellum period, the position of Northern-born editors was always insecure, and they were liable to be denounced as "squinting toward abolitionism."[46]

The life blood of the Southern newspapers of the ante-bellum period was political warfare. Certain of the Southern editors became bell-wethers of their parties, determining policies and providing political arguments and slogans for the country newspapers. Such an editor was "Father" (Thomas) Ritchie, who founded the Richmond *Enquirer* in 1804 and for forty-one years edited it. Ritchie became a dominant figure in the Republican and Democratic parties. He strongly opposed centralization and sought to preserve the principles of the Virginia and Kentucky Resolutions of 1798–99.[47] Thomas Jefferson in his old age said that the *Enquirer* was the best paper in America, and, because of the general scurrility of the press, it was the only newspaper that he read. The rival newspaper in Richmond was the *Whig*, founded by John Hampden Pleasants in 1824 and ably edited by him until he was killed in a duel in 1846 by Thomas Ritchie, Jr., who had succeeded his father as editor of the *Enquirer*. Pleasants was a strong supporter of the American System of Henry Clay. He and other Whig editors in the South tended to take their cue from the *National Intelligencer* at Washington, edited by Gales and Seaton, the son and son-in-law of Joseph Gales. The *National Intelligencer* was noted for its reports of the debates in Congress, taken down in shorthand, and for its modera-tion and conservatism. It was "the Bible of the Whigs."

The personal journalism of this era gave an outlet to strong and colorful editors. Many of the journalists were uninhibited in their use of sarcasm and defamation in attacking rival editors. Yet libel suits were rare. Editors and their patrons settled their differences by fisti-cuffs, canings, and duels. One of the most pugnacious and colorful of the Southern editors was "Parson" (William G.) Brownlow, who in slashing editorials and picturesque language in the Knoxville *Whig* supported the Whig cause in eastern Tennessee. A former carpenter

[45] Louisville *Journal*, August 31, 1858; see also November 19, 1855.

[46] See Clement Eaton, *Freedom of Thought in the Old South* (Durham, 1940), Chap. VII.

[47] C. H. Ambler, *Thomas Ritchie; a Study in Virginia Politics* (Richmond, 1937).

and Methodist preacher, he represented the views of the common man, including a violent sectarian spirit. Although he hated the abolitionists, he upheld the cause of the Union until he was forced to suspend his paper in October, 1861, and flee to the North.[48] William W. Holden, editor of the *North Carolina Standard* of Raleigh, was another poor boy who became a strong power in politics as the champion of the Democratic party. He changed his views and allegiance so often that he was called "the Talleyrand of North Carolina politics." From a different social stratum, Francis Preston Blair, plantation owner and banker, wrote articles for Kendall's Frankfort *Argus* and in December, 1830, was appointed editor of the Washington *Globe,* powerful organ of President Jackson. The Rhett family dominated the editorial policy of the Charleston *Mercury,* which had been founded in 1823 by Henry L. Pinckney, introducer of the famous Gag Resolution in Congress. In the 1850's Robert Barnwell Rhett's son, Barnwell Rhett, Jr., edited the paper, championing the ideas of the fire-eaters. Another advocate of the extreme Southern position was John M. Daniel of the Richmond *Examiner,* noted for his biting sarcasm.[49]

During the last decade of the ante-bellum period the circulation of Southern newspapers more than doubled (117.6 per cent); only in South Carolina did they show no appreciable increase. This notable growth of circulation was owing not only to the expansion of population and transportation but also to the greater literacy of the people and the conversion of weekly papers into dailies. The difference between the Southern states and comparable rural states of the North in respect to the per capita circulation of newspapers was surprisingly small. Indeed, the white per capita circulation in Alabama, fourteen copies annually, was ahead of the circulation in the free state of Indiana, with eleven copies. Virginia and New Hampshire had approximately equal white populations in 1860; the white per capita circulation of newspapers in Virginia was twenty-six, in New Hampshire twenty-nine. Louisiana, with a large urban population, had a circulation among whites considerably larger than the circulation in Con-

[48] E. M. Coulter, *William G. Brownlow, Fighting Parson of the Southern Highlands* (Chapel Hill, 1937).

[49] George W. Bagby, *John M. Daniel's Latch-Key: a Memoir of the Late Editor of the Richmond Examiner* (Lynchburg, 1868); F. L. Mott, *American Journalism* (New York, 1950).

necticut.[50] The majority of the Southern newspapers were weeklies such as the Greenville *Mountaineer,* with only 400 subscribers; even the daily New Orleans *Picayune* had a circulation of less than 6,000.

The newspapers, particularly in their humorous stories, revealed the existence of a certain antagonism between town and country. The country folk were suspicious of town people, who they believed took advantage of them and cheated them. Hamilton C. Jones's story of "Mc Alpin's trip to Charleston" illustrates the naïveté of the Southern farmers and their sense of uncomfortableness upon entering a city. The cities were regarded by the countrymen as places of sin, as the homes of dandies and extreme fashions which they detested. Thomas Wynne, the Richmond diarist, commented in 1855 that extravagance and luxury were making great inroads in Richmond society. Both sexes dressed in a manner that "throws all ideas of our fathers in the shade." The ladies, for instance, wore large straw bonnets, called "Bloomers," twenty-four to thirty-six inches wide, which they protected from the wind by a string attached to the hand.[51] Hostility to towns led to a discrimination against them in the legislature, so that they were usually underrepresented.

The values of the city residents were different from those of the planter and the yeoman. The spirit of feverish moneymaking and of business enterprise that was emerging in the Southern cities brought their inhabitants closer to the sense of values of the Yankees than to the ideals of the agrarian gentry. In the cities were settled most of the foreign immigrants to the region as well as Northern businessmen— both threats to Southern orthodoxy. City religion became less emotional and more decorous than the shouting religions of the rural areas. Chivalric ideals, also, were less honored by the mercantile and commercial community than by the planters. Moreover, the city electorates were less disposed than their brethren in the country to follow the fire-eaters.[52]

[50] *Census of 1860,* "Mortality and Miscellaneous Statistics," compiled from tables, pp. 320–322.

[51] Wynne Diary, May 6, 1855.

[52] Ollinger Crenshaw, *The Slave States in the Presidential Election of 1860* (Baltimore, 1945).

CHAPTER 12

Social Justice

SOCIAL reform movements developed very slowly in the Old South, almost at a glacial pace. At a time when the Northern states were experiencing a fermentation of social experiments, when Dorothea Dix and "Chevalier" Howe and John Humphrey Noyes were rampant, the Southern states were resisting the introduction of the "isms." Yet both sections upheld, at least in theory, the same ideals of social justice—ideals derived from the precepts of Christianity, the natural rights philosophy, and the common law of England. In the semifrontier condition of much of the South, reform movements were difficult to organize. Moreover, the state of Southern society did not encourage the rise of bold reformers like William Lloyd Garrison in the North, who were largely the products of middle-class enthusiasms. Many Southern leaders shared the point of view of Robert E. Lee, who relied on God's providence and the slow melting influence of time to remove social injustices. Perhaps strongest of all influences in delaying reform was the conservative influence of slavery. Nevertheless, the best of the Southern people, animated by a feeling of *noblesse oblige,* sought to carry out Christian justice by their individual conduct if not through reform organizations.

The Southern states did accomplish some notable reforms, too, particularly in a progressive humanization of their criminal codes. This movement did not arise from the concept, so prevalent today, that the individual criminal is a product of his environment and that society, therefore, rather than the individual, is responsible for crime. On the contrary, there was a strong feeling in the Old South that every individual was morally accountable for his acts. The change from the draconic punishments of colonial days to a more humanitarian code arose from a variety of influences: the ideas of the Italian writer Beccaria; the recognition of the dignity of the human individual in the American political system; the teachings of Christianity, which inculcated the virtue of mercy rather than vengeance; and the growth of population, which made it more convenient to punish the criminal in other ways than the crude methods of branding, cropping of ears, flogging, and confinement in the stocks.

Every Southern state except Louisiana preserved the death penalty for grave crimes. In Georgia there were seven capital crimes, arson (i.e., burning a house in a town), killing a person in a duel, castration, murder, treason, inciting a slave insurrection, and perjury resulting in a conviction and death. In Tennessee in 1835 the death penalty was reserved for first-degree murder and murder committed in attempted arson, rape, burglary, or larceny. In Missouri death was decreed for murder, treason, rescuing a person convicted of a capital crime, and killing a person in a duel. The penalty for rape of a white woman varied in different states, ranging from imprisonment for periods of one to twenty-one years in Virginia and castration in Missouri to death in Maryland. Louisiana seems to have had the mildest criminal punishments, consisting of one to five years' imprisonment for larceny, twenty years for manslaughter, and life for murder. Pierre Soulé, who had emigrated from France, led the successful fight in 1846 to abolish compulsory capital punishment.[1]

Kentucky also had an admirable record in the early humanization of its criminal code. Until 1798 Kentucky followed the Virginia code, which decreed the death penalty for treason, murder, burglary, manslaughter, rape, sodomy, perjury, forgery, arson, and grand larceny. But in that year it reformed its criminal code, retaining the death penalty for only one crime, first-degree murder, which was defined as premeditated murder, and murder committed in an attempt to per-

[1] Roger W. Shugg, *Origins of Class Struggle in Louisiana; A Social History of White Farmers and Laborers during Slavery and After, 1840–1875* (Baton Rouge, 1939), pp. 58–61.

petrate arson, rape, or burglary. The preamble to this revision of the criminal code stated that cruel and sanguinary punishments defeated their purpose, because men would not prosecute or convict, and also that a meritorious object of the laws should be the reformation of the criminal and his restoration to society as a useful citizen.[2]

The treatment of the criminal in North Carolina, on the other hand, is a remarkable story of legal conservatism. The Hillsborough *Recorder* declared on March 21, 1844, that "North Carolina has the bloodiest code of laws of any state in the Union."[3] During the following year Hardy Carroll, after escaping hanging three times for stealing horses, was hanged in Louisburg for stealing a pair of suspenders. In the Revised Code of 1855, the number of capital crimes was reduced from the twenty-eight in effect in 1817 to seventeen, including arson, bestiality or sodomy, burglary, castration, dueling, highway robbery, infanticide, insurrection, murder, obstructing railroads, rape, selling free Negroes into slavery, stealing slaves or aiding them to escape, and any second-time offense of circulating seditious publications, exciting insurrection, malicious maiming, and manslaughter. The severity of the criminal code, however, had been ameliorated by the ancient English custom of benefit of clergy, by which persons convicted of a felony who could read received lesser sentences than hanging, such as branding the hand or receiving a public whipping of thirty-nine lashes. In North Carolina the legislature at various times removed by statute certain crimes from being subject to benefit of clergy, and in 1855 this hoary privilege was completely abolished.

The criminal code of South Carolina was as drastic as that of its neighbor. The death penalty was prescribed for 165 crimes in 1813 and 22 in 1850. Of 10,000 indictments prior to 1860 which Williams examined, 60 per cent were for assault and battery, 4 per cent for murder, 2 per cent for bastardy (a much higher ratio than exists in South Carolina today), and 1½ per cent for rape, approximately the same ratio as today.[4] These statistics indicate that the people of South Carolina resorted to fistfights and assaults to a much greater degree than they do today; furthermore, most homicides in the ante-bellum

[2] F. Garvin Davenport, *Ante-Bellum Kentucky: a Social History, 1800–1860* (Oxford, Ohio, 1943), Chap. VIII.

[3] Johnson, *Ante-Bellum North Carolina,* Chap. XXII.

[4] Jack K. Williams, *Vogues in Villainy: Crime and Retribution in Ante-Bellum South Carolina* (Columbia, 1959), p. 6; see Chap. I.

period were committed with knives or clubs instead of with firearms.

Nevertheless, the carrying of pistols, bowie knives, and sword canes was a strong encouragement to crime. In New Orleans the sheriff told the English traveler Russell in 1861 that the city was a "perfect hell upon earth, and that nothing would ever put an end to the murders, manslaughters, and deadly assaults, till it was made penal to carry arms."[5] The citizens of Alabama, on the other hand, were restrained from carrying deadly weapons by a law making the carrying of concealed weapons in the streets of a town a penal offense incurring a prison sentence and a $500 fine for violation. Whipple observed that this law had an excellent effect on the peace and order of Mobile, although it was daily broken.[6]

The legal codes did not make special provision for the punishment of juvenile crime, but juries and judges exercised great leniency in such cases. In South Carolina no child under seven years of age could be indicted for a capital crime or a youth under fourteen years of age tried for rape. Juvenile crime was not much publicized, though in South Carolina half of the relatively few indictments of children were for murder or attempted murder. Juvenile delinquency did not seem to pose the massive problem that it does today.

Although a decided movement took place after 1815 toward substituting fine and imprisonment for cropping ears, branding, the pillory, and the stocks, these barbarous punishments were not entirely eliminated before the Civil War. Cropping of both ears was the punishment in North Carolina for the first offense of counterfeiting and for perjury. In 1816 branding was abolished in North Carolina and a fine was substituted. All through the ante-bellum period, criminals were hanged before large crowds of people, as in Scotland and England. Women comprised a large proportion of these crowds. Public hangings had the character of a holiday or circus, engendering much drunkenness and many street fights. The reformers were not able to abolish this practice, but in most parts of the South by 1830 they were able to remove the pillory, public stocks, and whipping post from the courthouse square to the jailyard.

Another important humanitarian victory was won by the abolition of imprisonment for debt. The panic of 1819, which caused many

[5] Russell, *My Diary North and South*, p. 244.
[6] Whipple, *Southern Diary*, pp. 85–86.

worthy citizens to become bankrupt, helped to change the laws in regard to debt. The constitutions of Mississippi in 1817 and of Alabama in 1819 prohibited imprisonment if the debtor surrendered his estate. Richard Mentor Johnson, the Old War Hawk and reputed slayer of Tecumseh, was one of the numerous Kentuckians who could not pay his debts in the period following the panic. He was prominent in securing a state law in Kentucky that abolished imprisonment for debt and, as a member of Congress, in the passage in 1832 of a federal law abolishing imprisonment in federal cases.[7] In 1820 North Carolina enacted a law abolishing imprisonment for debt, but during the next year repealed it. The eminent reformer Judge Archibald De Bow Murphey spent twenty days in prison in 1820 because of his inability to pay his debts. Tennessee abolished imprisonment for debt in 1842 and North Carolina two years later.

The Southerner had a cavalier attitude in regard to the laws regulating personal conduct, shown especially in his attitude toward dueling. A large segment of life below the Mason-Dixon Line, a scholar has pointed out, was regulated by an unwritten code—a code derived from the customs of the English gentry, the military punctilio of French and British officers, chivalric ballads, and Scott's novels.[8] Insult must never be tolerated. An illustration of this compulsion to avenge insult was the duel between Benjamin F. Perry, editor of the Greenville, South Carolina, *Mountaineer,* and Turner Bynum, editor of the rival nullification newspaper, *The Southern Sentinel,* in the summer of 1832. The cause was a sarcastic editorial by Bynum on Perry's championship of moderation in resisting the protective tariff, an editorial far less invidious than many book reviews today. The two editors fought their duel on a romantic island in the Tugaloo River between South Carolina and Georgia. Observing all the punctilious etiquette of duels, Perry killed his opponent, having before the tragic event implored God in prayer to protect him. In his autobiography he commented that after this duel the nullifiers treated him with the greatest courtesy: "When a man knows that he is to be held accountable for his want

[7] See Leland W. Meyer, *Life and Times of Colonel Richard M. Johnson of Kentucky* (New York, 1932).

[8] Charles S. Sydnor, "The Southerner and the Laws," *Journal of Southern History,* VI (1940), 1–23; for extralegal action, see also Clement Eaton, "Mob Violence in the Old South," *Mississippi Valley Historical Review,* XXIX (1942), 351–370.

of courtesy," he observed, "he is not so apt to indulge in abuse. In this way duelling produces a greater courtesy in society & a higher refinement."[9]

Another editor, O. Jennings Wise, of the Richmond *Enquirer,* fought eight duels in less than two years. Educated at Indiana University and William and Mary College, Wise spent three years as attaché of the American Legation in Berlin and Paris before becoming editor of the Richmond paper. He was both sophisticated and religious, praying every night before retiring. In the age of the weekly bath, he took a cold plunge in the bathtub every morning.[10] On July 15, 1859, he fought a duel with Patrick Henry Aylett of the Richmond *Examiner* as a result of a controversy over the westward extension of slavery. Wise applied the name of "Augustus Tomlinson," a pickpocket in Bulwer's novel *Paul Clifford,* to his rival. Aylett demanded that the *Enquirer* editor withdraw the epithet and upon his refusal challenged him to a duel. They evaded the Virginia law against dueling by crossing over the line into North Carolina. Thomas Hicks Wynne, the Richmond diarist, described this encounter as follows: "They stood at 30 ft— Old [editor of the Richmond *Whig,* with Aylett as second] & Lot Davis with Wise. The word 'Fire, one-two-three,' was given. Aylett standing with his pistol pointed at Wise and Wise with his pointing upward and neither fired—some explanation was asked & Aylett's second explained, the word was again given & Aylett fired at Wise (missing him) and Wise fired in the air."[11] Wise (according to his young brother John) was an execrable shot, but his opponents must have been worse, for in numerous duels he was never hit. He regarded it as a quixotic duty to defend the reputation of his father, Governor Henry A. Wise; according to Wynne, "if you do not bow down to and worship [Governor] Wise the son will challenge you instanter."

The enforcement, or lack of it, of the laws dealing with dueling reveal a curious conflict between legal enactments and social practice. The Southern states tried to stamp out this custom by legislation prescribing imprisonment, fine, and temporary or permanent loss of the right to hold either civil or military office. Sending or carrying a chal-

[9] Lillian A. Kibler, *Benjamin F. Perry, South Carolina Unionist* (Durham, 1946), p. 135.
[10] John S. Wise, *The End of an Era* (Boston, 1902), Chap. VII.
[11] Wynne Diary, July 18, 1859.

lenge was also made a criminal offense. These laws were so out of accord with public sentiment, however, that they were hardly ever enforced. A common way of evading them was for the duelists to cross over into a neighboring state to fight. A number of antidueling associations arose in the South to combat the evil; editors, churchmen, and statesmen deplored it. Many prominent statesmen, including Henry Clay, had an ambivalent attitude toward dueling; theoretically they condemned it, but, afraid of being called cowards or of seeming to lack a strict sense of honor, they continued to send challenges and accept them.[12]

Despite the severity of criminal codes in the Old South, it is doubtful that criminals were punished more harshly than they are today. Indeed, in ante-bellum South Carolina, grand juries returned true bills in only 63 per cent of the indictments presented to them, as contrasted with 97 per cent in 1950. Of cases tried by the juries only 39 per cent resulted in convictions as compared with more than 90 per cent in 1950. The major reason for the leniency of the ante-bellum juries was the severity of the laws. Another important reason for acquittals was the oratory of ante-bellum lawyers before Southern juries. The power of the spoken (not written) word in the South can hardly be exaggerated. The system of court challenges was also used frequently to exclude men of character, intelligence, and impartiality from the juries. Moreover, men of the upper class were reluctant to serve on juries and used various expedients to escape doing so.

The jury system in many parts of the South was a crude and uncertain method of arriving at justice. Whipple, after observing a motley jury in action in Florida, commented: "Murder here costs about 2 yrs. imprisonment or a $1,000 fine."[13] Micajah Clark crossed over the South Carolina line in 1857 to attend a magistrate's court in northeastern Georgia as a spectator. He wrote in his diary that he was much amused at the ignorance and self-importance of the magistrate and the people. Two village lawyers addressed the jury in behalf of their clients, but "they had a hard time to make the fool officers, witnesses, and people understand what was law."[14]

[12] Eaton, *Henry Clay and the Art of American Politics,* pp. 17, 60–61, 144, 177.

[13] Whipple, *Southern Diary,* p. 24.

[14] Micajah Clark Travel Journal, p. 53.

The rich man and the member of an influential family probably had a greater advantage over the poor man in court in the South than in the more democratic and literate society of the North. An example of such favoritism was the trial of Lafayette Shelby, the grandson of Governor Isaac Shelby, accused of killing a young man in front of the Phoenix Hotel in Lexington, Kentucky, in May, 1846. Shelby shot the young man merely because the latter stared at him. Henry Clay, in the last great criminal case of his life, was employed to defend Shelby. The jury was divided, and the defendant was released on heavy bail. The Reverend William Pratt, who attended the trial, wrote in his diary, "the community has been outrageously treated and the laws trampled under foot. Old men say for 30 years a white man has not been hung in Fayette County, although a number of murders have been committed."[15] The judge and the eight jurors who voted for acquittal were hung in effigy before a large and angry crowd gathered in front of the courthouse. After the trial Shelby left the community for Texas; he was never punished for his cold-blooded crime. The English correspondent Russell noted a similar miscarriage of justice in New Orleans, where he was introduced to a man who had murdered a rival at a dance and was acquitted partly because of "able and ingenious counsel," but mainly because of "a judicious distribution of money."[16]

The Ward case in Louisville, Kentucky, in 1854 posed the question whether wealth and influence or justice should rule in Kentucky courts. Matt Ward, scion of a wealthy and prominent family of the city, shot and killed a Yankee schoolteacher who had whipped his young brother to discipline him.[17] The family hired eighteen lawyers, headed by John J. Crittenden, and brought forward 120 witnesses. When the young man was acquitted, resolutions from meetings all over the state condemned the decision, the judge and jurors were burned in effigy, and the newspapers in general attributed the acquittal to the influence of money and family prestige.[18]

The humanizing of the criminal codes in the Southern states was closely connected with the building of state penitentiaries. As early as

[15] William M. Pratt Diary, I, p. 223, May 24, July 4, 1846.
[16] Russell, *My Diary North and South*, p. 241.
[17] A. D. Richardson, *A Full and Authentic Report of the Testimony on the Trial of Matt F. Ward* (New York, 1854).
[18] Louisville *Daily Courier*, April 21, 24, May 4, 5, 6, 1854.

1799 Kentucky established a state prison at Frankfort, and by 1820 Virginia, Maryland, and Georgia were confining criminals in penitentiaries. Reformers in North Carolina, beginning in 1791, introduced bill after bill in the legislature to erect a penitentiary, but their efforts were defeated, primarily because the people were unwilling to pay taxes for this purpose. In 1810 a bill for establishing a penitentiary was defeated by the vote of the presiding officer of the Senate. The most cogent argument of the reformers was that juries, because of the severity of the law, would not convict in many cases and governors for the same reason would pardon many of those sentenced. In 1816 they pointed out that only 29 per cent of those indicted for murder and 26 per cent of those indicted for petty larceny were convicted. The construction of a penitentiary and the substitution of imprisonment for hanging, cropping the ears, branding, and flogging, they argued, would lead to stricter justice and to protection of the community from released criminals. Nevertheless, the people were not impressed, and voted overwhelmingly in a popular election in 1846 against the proposal to erect a penitentiary and thus increase taxes.[19] Accordingly, North Carolina shared the unenviable position, along with South Carolina, Florida, and Arkansas, of having no penitentiaries when the Civil War began. In these states prisoners were confined in inadequate county jails with no program for rehabilitation.

In the reform of prisons the Southern states as a whole were not greatly behind the North. The two leading examples of prison reform in the North were in Pennsylvania, which inaugurated solitary confinement at hard labor in its prison at Philadelphia, and in New York, whose Auburn prison provided separate cells for prisoners to sleep in, though they worked together in the daytime under the rule of silence.[20] The Auburn system was generally adopted in the more advanced Southern prisons. James Silk Buckingham, when he visited the Richmond prison in 1839, observed that it attempted to follow the Auburn system, but that the rule of silence was often broken by the convicts as they worked together and that the association of first offenders with older criminals brought bad results.[21] The greatest progress in prison reform,

[19] Johnson, *Ante-Bellum North Carolina*, pp. 661–673.
[20] See Blake McKelvey, *American Prisons, a Study in American Social History Prior to 1915* (Chicago, 1936).
[21] Buckingham, *Slave States*, II, 421.

wrote Dorothea Dix in 1845, after visiting many prisons both in the North and the South, was the rising standard in the type of men who administered prisons.[22]

Entries in the diary of Robert Scott, a young law student of Frankfort, Kentucky, during a trip that he made to the East in 1829–30, give detailed descriptions of the Maryland and Virginia penitentiaries. The Maryland Prison, located outside of Baltimore, consisted of three apartments, one for men, one for women, and one for youths. The whole number of prisoners at that time was 360, of whom 230 were blacks, and 45 females (only two of them white). The prisoners slept in hammocks and their heads were shaven every other week. They occupied separate cells but ate in a common dining hall and worked in a common shop under the rule of silence. They were employed principally in weaving striped cotton cloth and in making horn combs, and were allowed to keep their earnings after paying their board. Scott noted that the whole prison showed order, decency, and good management, the prisoners working industriously, and that corporal punishment, though in use, was rarely resorted to. The inmates were supplied with Bibles; they had a Sunday School and were required to listen to preaching on Sundays. The Virginia Penitentiary at Richmond was an imposing semicircular building designed in 1796 by Benjamin Latrobe. The cells, Scott reported, were clean and comfortable, but the convicts themselves were squalid. Although its inmates worked at various crafts, the penitentiary was operated at a loss to the state of several thousand dollars annually.[23]

Alexis de Tocqueville and Gustave Beaumont, two young Frenchmen who visited the United States in 1830–31 to study American penal systems, found great variations among Southern prisons—from the good condition of the Baltimore Prison to the wretched state of the New Orleans Prison. They praised particularly the practice of the Maryland Prison of paying convicts for all work done above a daily task, a practice unique among prisons in the United States. De Tocqueville wrote of New Orleans: "We saw there men thrown in pell-mell with swine, in the midst of excrement and filth. In locking up criminals, no thought is given to making them better but simply to taming

[22] Dorothea L. Dix, *Remarks on Prisons and Prison Discipline in the United States* (Philadelphia, 1845), p. 18.
[23] Robert Scott Diary, October 26, December 22, 1829.

their wickedness; they are chained like wild beasts; they are not refined but brutalized."[24] They talked to Governor A. B. Roman about the terrible conditions in the prison, and as a result his message to the legislature of January 2, 1831, was largely devoted to urging prison reform. The legislature responded by authorizing the construction of a modern penitentiary at Baton Rouge, which was opened in 1835 and contained one hundred cells and a cotton mill and shoe factory.

In 1835 William Crawford made an extensive report to the British government on American prisons. The Maryland Prison, opened in 1812, he found self-supporting, but the discipline was lax and the punishments, such as flogging and gagging, degrading. Most of the white prisoners could read and write. The Virginia Penitentiary contained well-lighted and ventilated cells, but they were often cold and damp. In Virginia one-twelfth and in Kentucky at least one-twentieth of a prisoner's sentence had to be served in solitary confinement. The Richmond Prison had a system of grading prisoners, giving honor badges and special privileges as a reward for good behavior; this was the first prison to do so in the United States. When Crawford visited it, all the white prisoners could read but none of the Negroes could. Fifteen of the prisoners were between sixteen and twenty years of age, sixteen being the minimum age of imprisonment. In the Kentucky and Tennessee prisons there were no female inmates. The Tennessee law prohibited corporal punishment and refractory prisoners were punished by solitary confinement. In the Southern prisons the Negroes were usually far more numerous than the whites, and usually there for stealing.[25]

One thing prison management in the South had to try to do was to make the prisons self-supporting, so that the citizens would not have to be taxed for them; opposition to taxes was unusually strong in the Old South partly because the rural population had little cash. Out of this effort at self-support arose a pernicious practice of the state's of leasing convicts' labor to private contractors. Joel Scott, superintendent of the Kentucky Penitentiary (1825–34), paid the state $1,000 a year for the right to hire the labor of the convicts, thus starting a practice that became one of the greatest evils of the New South. Scott made a

[24] Pierson, *Tocqueville and Beaumont in America,* pp. 493, 629.
[25] William Crawford, *Report on the Penitentiaries of the United States* (London, 1835).

fortune estimated at $40,000 from prison labor, which he obtained without competitive bidding. A successful textile factory was established in the penitentiary at Jackson, Mississippi, which furnished supplies to the Confederate army. From 1845 to 1862 Alabama leased the labor of criminals in the penitentiary to private contractors.

Toward the end of the ante-bellum period two European visitors, Fredrika Bremer of Sweden and William Russell, correspondent of *The Times* of London, examined some of the Southern prisons. Fredrika visited the "House of Correction" in Richmond in 1850 and found not a single white prisoner among the two hundred inmates, which included some Negro women. In New Orleans she observed that the outward management of the prison was excellent; order and cleanliness prevailed, and the prisoners were wearing good clothes. Yet a group of slave women were confined with the criminals because their master had put them up as security for a bankrupt. They had been in jail for two years waiting until he could obtain the money to recover them.[26]

Russell gave an unfavorable report on the New Orleans Prison in 1861. He saw in its courtyard "hardened and desperate criminals" associating with teen-age boys who had been convicted of larceny; seventy murderers, burglars, and pirates were mingling with men awaiting trial; one desperate criminal with irons on his legs was playing cards with another inmate and "smoking in supreme content." Debtors were crowded three and four to a cell; they were freed after ninety days if their board was paid. The women's ward was a disgrace; maniacal women with disheveled hair, shrieking and gesticulating indecently, were being held in jail until there was room for them in the lunatic asylum. The women's quarter had "a horrible stench," and they were confined five to a cell, without beds or blankets. Women who had committed small offenses were huddled with "vile criminals."[27]

Besides the state prisons there were city jails and workhouses to which those convicted in the recorders' courts for slight offenses were sent. James Silk Buckingham found that of the two hundred prisoners in the Richmond jail half were Negroes, and that a large proportion of the whites were foreigners. No females were in jail, as contrasted

[26] Bremer, *Homes of the New World,* II, 210.
[27] Russell, *My Diary North and South,* p. 247.

with conditions in Northern prisons.[28] In Charleston, South Carolina, Harriet Martineau in 1835 observed drunkards and vagrants in the workhouse who had been sentenced to one month at hard labor engaged in making coffins and breaking stone.[29] Until 1847 vagrants convicted in the magistrates' courts of South Carolina were sold as indentured servants for a period of time. In New Orleans petty crimes, such as loafing on the levee, fighting, or stealing fish from the tanks of the fishermen, were tried in the recorder's court, with a usual punishment of thirty days in the calaboose. The majority of the defendants were drunks, arrested by the night watchmen.[30] Thomas Watson, a foreigner in the city jail at Richmond, who had been sentenced for drunkenness, wrote to Governor Wise for a pardon, stating that he was often compelled to work for eight and a half hours on the public streets with a ball and chain around his leg; when he returned to jail, his food was "the coarsest poorest kind and not enough of that," and his wife and children were in the poorhouse.[31]

One of the notable steps of progress in the humanitarian movement in the Old South was the improvement in treatment of the insane. In the early part of the nineteenth century the mentally sick were treated shamefully. The Bible had portrayed crazy people as possessed of devils, and a stigma was attached to any family with a mentally sick person. Consequently, many families tried to hide the fact and to take care of their mentally sick members by confining them at home. Indigent psychotics were usually imprisoned in jails and workhouses, where they mingled with criminals. Often they were put in strait jackets, iron collars, and leg chains, imprisoned in unheated rooms in winter, and subjected to various medieval instruments of restraint. These horrible conditions so shocked Dorothea Dix, when in 1841 she visited a jail in her native state, that she began a crusade to secure humane treatment for the insane. Her method was to agitate for reform by presenting memorials to state legislatures and speaking before them in behalf

[28] Buckingham, *Slave States*, II, 421.

[29] Harriet Martineau, *Retrospect of Western Travel* (New York, 1838), I, 334.

[30] Coulter, *The Other Half of Old New Orleans*, pp. 3–4, 39–43, 53–55.

[31] Thomas Watson to James Lyons, October, 19, 1856; James Lyons to Henry Wise, October 21, 1856, James Lyons Papers, Brock Collection, Huntington Library.

of the mentally sick. Her crusade carried her ultimately into every Southern state.

Before Miss Dix began her efforts to arouse public opinion, some of the Southern states had already built insane asylums and had separated the mentally sick from the criminal element. Virginia was a pioneer in the United States in this field, establishing in 1773 an insane asylum at Williamsburg and in 1828 a second institution, Western Lunatic Asylum, at Staunton. Maryland opened a hospital for the insane at Baltimore as early as 1816. Eight years later Kentucky founded Eastern Kentucky Insane Asylum at Lexington. Here Henry Clay's son Theodore was for many years a patient. South Carolina established a state lunatic asylum at Columbia in 1828 and Tennessee built the Tennessee Hospital for the Insane at Nashville in 1840. When Miss Dix investigated the treatment of the insane in the United States in 1845–46, she found little difference between the Northern and Southern states. Helen E. Marshall, her biographer, has written, "Taken as a section, the south showed no great contrast to other sections which Miss Dix had visited."[32]

The improvement that occurred in the 1840's and 1850's was apparent not only in respect to physical facilities, but in a more enlightened attitude toward the mentally diseased. When E. S. Abdy visited the Southern states in 1834, he reported that at the lunatic asylum in Staunton a quarter of a dollar was charged as the price of admission to see the lunatics—a practice that also existed in England. He was told that only a small proportion of the patients were ever cured. At the asylum in Lexington he observed no signs of coercion in the rooms, but in the yards some of the patients had irons on their legs, and shower baths were used as a means of discipline.[33] Conditions had greatly improved when Fredrika Bremer visited the Staunton institution in 1850. Cure there, she wrote, was the rule when the patient was brought to the asylum at the onset of his malady.[34]

The theory of the causes of insanity also had changed. Formerly it was believed that insanity was a disease of inflammation, which required a liberal employment of cupping and bloodletting, of blisters

[32] Helen E. Marshall, *Dorothea Dix: Forgotten Samaritan* (Chapel Hill, 1937), p. 113.
[33] Abdy, *Journal*, II, 284, 345–346.
[34] Bremer, *Homes of the New World*, II, 521.

and purgatives. By the decade of the 1850's the theory had arisen that mental disease was one of debility and should be treated by a mild discipline, by tranquilizing and occupying the mind of the patient through recreation, drama, concerts, dances, reading, religious services, lectures, and manual labor. Following the reforms of the great French physician Philippe Pinel, the Southern as well as the Northern asylums had abolished physical restraints and coercion of mental patients to a large degree.

American physicians believed the principal causes of insanity to be (1) the intemperate use of liquor, described as "the most fertile exciting cause of insanity," (2) domestic unhappiness, (3) masturbation, and (4) religious excitement. The fact that religious excitement was one of the most frequent causes of insanity during the ante-bellum period throws a rather lurid light on the nature of religion as frequently practiced then. An article on the development of insane asylums in the United States, to be found in the population volume of the Census of 1860, attributed religion's role in insanity to "the intemperate style of preaching wherein the terrors and consequences of Divine wrath are portrayed with all the vigor and force of a vivid imagination." Also, the article observed, patients had been brought to mental asylums as a result of attending exciting revivals and protracted religious meetings, and engaging in solitary reading and meditation on the Bible "until personal demerit and its consequent punishment became the sole occupants of the thoughts."[35] Some deluded persons were tormented continually by the belief that they had committed the unpardonable sin against the Holy Ghost.

Dorothea Dix had a great effect on the South. During her trips she found antiquated laws governing the commitment of afflicted persons to hospitals for the insane, and in some of the states she uncovered the practice of farming out the care of the pauper insane at public auction. One of her greatest victories was won when she persuaded the North Carolina legislature to appropriate money to build an insane asylum. The legislature had rejected the appeal of Governor John M. Morehead in 1844 for an asylum, and two years later the people had voted against a penitentiary—they were unwilling to pay the necessary taxes for such institutions. But in 1848 the legislature responded to Miss Dix's ability as a lobbyist by levying a tax to establish an insane

[35] *Eighth Census of the United States, 1860,* "Population," Introduction, pp. xc–xci.

asylum, which opened its doors to patients in 1856 and was named Dix Hill. Her appeal to the legislature of Alabama in 1849 seemed on the point of success when the burning of the state capitol at Montgomery necessitated financial retrenchment, and an asylum was not opened in that state until October, 1860. In Mississippi her eloquence led the legislature in 1856 to make a large appropriation for an insane asylum; she described this achievement as "a conquest over prejudice and determination not to give a dime."[36] The institution, located at Jackson, was opened in 1855. By the time the Civil War came, all the states of the nation had asylums for the care of the mentally sick except Florida, Arkansas, and Delaware.

Yet in all sections of the United States the asylums and hospitals for the care of the mentally sick were totally inadequate. In Kentucky, with a population of 919,484 whites, the Eastern Lunatic Asylum at Lexington, from its founding in 1824 to 1860, admitted a total of only 2,439 persons, of whom over one-third were discharged as cured. The superintendent reported in 1859 that because of crowded accommodations he had been forced to turn away half of those who had applied during the past year.[37] Kentucky started a second asylum at Hopkinsville in 1854, but it was burned six years later.

Another unfortunate class for which the state provided care was the deaf. They constituted a much more numerous group in America than did the blind, and consequently most states established schools for them before they made provision for the blind. The states of the upper South, according to the inaccurate Census of 1860, had a larger proportion of deaf mutes in their populations than any other section of the country. In the nation as a whole there was one deaf mute to every 2,275 persons, but in Virginia the ratio was one to 1,550 and in Kentucky one to 1,602 persons. This striking disproportion, the Superintendent of the Census speculated, may have been owing to the fact that those states had large mountainous areas containing an isolated homogeneous population where marriage of cousins frequently occurred.[38]

[36] Marshall, *Dorothea Dix*, p. 121.
[37] *Report of the Board of Managers and Superintendent of the Kentucky Lunatic Asylum (at Lexington, Kentucky) for the Year 1858–9* (Frankfort, 1859), p. 7.
[38] Joseph C. Kennedy, *Population of the United States in 1860 . . .* (Washington, 1864), Introduction, p. lxviii.

The earliest institution for the deaf in this country was the American Asylum at Hartford, Connecticut, founded in 1817 by Thomas Gallaudet. It served as a training school for teachers of the deaf in Southern as well as Northern institutions. One of the earliest of the state schools for the deaf was founded in 1823 at Danville, Kentucky. Here for forty years the superintendent was John A. Jacobs, an honor student at Centre College, who had prepared himself for his duties by studying at the American Asylum. He taught his pupils to read and write through a sign language and trained them for useful tasks. The state paid the expenses of the poor students, as it did those of the indigent insane. At the time of the Civil War the deaf-and-dumb school at Danville had nearly one hundred pupils and a staff of six trained instructors.

The participation of the South in the care of its handicapped members of society was hindered by its theory of the state and by the small amount of taxes levied on the people. North Carolina did not establish an institution for the deaf and dumb until action was stimulated in 1845 by a visit of the principal of the Virginia Institute for the Deaf and Dumb at Staunton. Some Southern states, such as Georgia, appropriated money to send their indigent deaf children to the American Asylum at Hartford. In Georgia a remarkable propagandist, John Jacobus Flournoy, himself afflicted by deafness, had aroused interest in the plight of the deaf. In 1833 an investigation was ordered by the legislature, which revealed the existence of only 145 deaf mutes of all ages in the state. The legislature, regarding this number as too few to justify the establishment of a school, appropriated $3,000 for the education of Georgia's deaf children at the American Asylum at Hartford. Sixteen were selected to attend, but only three could be induced to leave home for this distant Northern city. It was not until 1846 that Georgia established a state school for deaf mutes.[39] But by the time of the Civil War all of the Southern states except Florida and Arkansas had established schools for this handicapped class.

The education of the blind in the United States started in Boston in 1833 with the foundation of the Perkins School for the Blind by the crusading Samuel Gridley Howe. To arouse interest in the blind he toured the South as well as the North, giving exhibitions of the

[39] E. M. Coulter, *John Jacobus Flournoy; Champion of the Common Man in the Ante-Bellum South* (Savannah, 1942), pp. 40–42.

achievements of his blind students, who sang, played on the piano, recited, read Braille, and displayed handicrafts that they had made. Virginia was the first of the Southern states to establish a school for the blind; in 1838, after an exhibition of some blind students from Massachusetts before the legislature, the state created a department for the blind in the deaf-and-dumb school at Staunton. Howe traveled to Columbia, South Carolina, in the autumn of 1841 and exhibited some of his pupils before the legislature. Professor Francis Lieber of South Carolina College and Christopher Memminger of Charleston were active in that state in agitating for an institution for the blind. Howe crossed the mountains to appeal to legislatures in Kentucky and Tennessee, and then traveled to New Orleans. Upon his return to Boston he wrote Lieber, May 2, 1843, "succeeded beyond my expectation in establishing a school for the blind in Kentucky—the School was endowed with $10,000 by the legislature and went into operation yesterday under the charge of one of my former pupils, a young man of very fine talents but nearly blind."[40] By 1860 all of the Southern states had established schools for the blind, and the Virginia institution had published in Braille Peter Parley's histories, a history of Virginia, a book of fables, and several elementary textbooks.

One of the sad institutions in America was the county poorhouse. The indigents, consisting principally of cripples, aged people, and afflicted children unable to earn a living, were under the care of overseers and wardens of the poor, elected by the voters of the county and usually unpaid. The officials often farmed out paupers to be cared for; they would be given to the lowest bidders, in one county in North Carolina for eight cents a day. Sometimes the officials furnished provisions to poor people outside the poorhouse; at other times they placed paupers in the house of correction or workhouse together with petty offenders against the law, such as drunkards, gamblers, and prostitutes. The county courts apprenticed orphans and illegitimate children to farmers or artisans until they had reached the age of eighteen (if girls) or twenty-one (if boys). The terms of their indenture prescribed that they should be taught a trade and to read and write.[41] Some orphans were cared for in orphanages founded by churches, such as Bethesda in Georgia, which George Whitefield had established in the

[40] Samuel Gridley Howe to Francis Lieber, May 2, 1843, Lieber Papers.
[41] Johnson, *Ante-Bellum North Carolina*, Chap. XXIII.

eighteenth century; or by benevolent individuals, such as those in New Orleans created by bequests of two Scottish merchants.

Only in the large towns of the South were there hospitals; most people who became sick were attended in their homes by physicians and nursed by relatives. In New Orleans was the famous Charity Hospital, founded in 1815 and operated by the city. Its new quarters erected in 1839 had beds for five hundred patients. Many of its patients were homeless sailors and destitute immigrants. A Catholic organization, the Sisters of Charity, cared for the sick gratuitously; indeed, during epidemics the Catholic Church was outstanding in its unselfish service to the afflicted. In the decade of the 1850's the city of Louisville supported the Louisville Marine Hospital. Also, in the larger towns, numerous benevolent societies aided their members in times of illness and death.

Inebriates constituted another class that required the help of Southern society. Unfortunately, their treatment and cure were regarded as primarily a moral problem. According to the Superintendent of the 1860 Census, there was only one institution in the United States for the cure of inebriates, located at Binghamton, New York. Nevertheless, drunkenness was recognized as one of the greatest evils of Southern society. Henry Benjamin Whipple wrote in his diary in New Orleans in 1844, "Drinking is an awful vice here."[42] The Louisville *Daily Courier* of November 10, 1853, reported that of the 240 convicts in the Tennessee Penitentiary, 127 were drunk when they committed crime and 202 were addicted to intemperate drinking.[43]

The chief methods used to combat drunkenness in the Old South, apart from fine and imprisonment, were the appeals of the churches and the formation of temperance societies. When Robert Scott, the Kentucky law student, passed through Lexington in the autumn of 1829, he noted that the town had a temperance society and that "similar societies existed in almost all the churches of the neighborhood." In Lewisburg, western Virginia, he found that the temperance society of eighty members was composed principally of persons who were not "professors of Religion," and that the preachers of the town did not patronize this organization.[44] The North Carolina Temperance Society

[42] Shippee, *Bishop Whipple's Southern Diary*, p. 110.
[43] Louisville *Daily Courier*, November 10, 1853.
[44] Robert Scott, "Memoranda Itineris," October 4, 1839, pp. 85–86.

sent out the Reverend Thomas P. Hunt, a Presbyterian preacher, to organize societies throughout the state and obtain total abstinence pledges, but he reported that his efforts had met with indifference, opposition, and ridicule.[45] Nevertheless, in 1834 there were more than fifty auxiliary societies in the state, with 4,700 members.

More dramatic methods than those adopted by such quiet organizers were needed to make any great impression on Southern society. In 1840 a group of hard drinkers in Baltimore was persuaded by an evangelist to renounce drinking, and organized a crusade movement, called the Washingtonian Movement. These reformed drunkards campaigned against drunkenness by reciting stories of their former degradation to intensely moved audiences. In 1842, at Teetotaler's Hall in New York City, the most effective of all the ante-bellum temperance organizations was founded, the Sons of Temperance. This organization spread widely into the Southern states, partly because it was a secret society with a ritual, grips, and signs and symbols. It held colorful processions in full regalia, picnics, and temperance lectures, thus affording to a simple people amusement that competed with barbecues and stump speakings. A temperance parade of the Negroes of Savannah on July 4, 1845, was described by a Mobile mechanic as follows: "a procession of darkies who has formed a temperance Society and paraded thro the streets with music and marshalls mounted with their regalia streaming in the wind and each of those on foot with ribbons around their waist and a tin cup to drink with."[46]

The diary of the Reverend William Pratt, pastor of the First Baptist Church of Lexington, Kentucky, reveals that many men in his community ruined promising careers by drunkenness. One of the political leaders of the city in the decade of the 1840's was Thomas Marshall, a lawyer and Democratic congressman who had taken an active role in suppressing the antislavery newspaper, the *True American,* edited by Cassius M. Clay. On December 28, 1845, he became very drunk at a hotel in the city, and a few days later sold his library at auction. On December 30 he came to the Temperance Society meeting as "an humble penitent, confessed his sin, and renewed the pledge and made a powerful speech." In May of the following year he broke his pledge

---

[45] Johnson, *Ante-Bellum North Carolina,* pp. 170–171.
[46] John W. Evans to William H. Garland, July 4, 1845, Garland Papers.

again; he subsequently joined the volunteers to fight in the Mexican War, where he continued to drink heavily.

If the Reverend Mr. Pratt was disappointed in the weak conduct of Marshall, he was cheered by the victory of the temperance cause in the municipal election of January 1, 1858. The main issue in the election was whether coffeehouses that sold liquor should be denied licenses. There were many handbills and much public speaking on both sides. Pratt exerted his influence to suppress the liquor houses, and the no-license party won the election. On February 22, 1858, he noted in his journal the effect: "On Washington's birthday not one in the work-house, jail, or watchhouse, such an event not known for years—this is owing to the suppression of the liquor traffic."[47] But the following year the liquor party defeated the idealists and reformers by electing pro-liquor councilmen.

In 1851 Maine, after a vigorous campaign led by Neal Dow, passed a state prohibition law. Other Northern states enacted similar laws, which, however, were declared unconstitutional by their courts. Southerners believed too much in personal liberty to adopt such restrictive legislation, which they regarded as one of the Northern "isms." One method of control, however, that some Southern communities adopted was a high license on stores that sold liquor. Wilmington, North Carolina, for example, placed a tax of $50 on these establishments. Robert Russell noted in 1859 that this tax reduced the number of stores to nine in number, but that nearly fifty others sold liquor "on the wink."[48] The opponents of liquor in Georgia entered into politics and in 1855 cast over six thousand votes for B. H. Overby, a Methodist preacher, the candidate of the Temperance party for governor. Moreover, prominent political leaders, notably Robert Barnwell Rhett in South Carolina, Governor Henry A. Wise in Virginia, and Governor Joseph E. Brown in Georgia, championed the temperance cause. Many Southern newspapers and churches also supported the movement. *The Kentucky New Era* of Louisville in 1852 listed 265 temperance societies in the state as well as eighty post offices where ten or more copies of this temperance newspaper were taken.[49]

The most notable figure in the temperance movement in the Old

[47] William M. Pratt Diary, I, December 28, 1845; II, February 22, 1858.
[48] Russell, *America*, pp. 158–159.
[49] *The Kentucky New Era*, September 4, 1852.

South and the outstanding social reformer in that region was the Virginia planter John Hartwell Cocke. Despite his avoidance of politics and his preference for the quiet life of a country gentleman, he had great prestige in his state, first as an officer in the War of 1812, and then as a civic leader and progressive planter. His personality had been formed in the liberal period of Virginia's history. He was the aristocratic type of planter like Jefferson, with the latter's humanitarian spirit but without his wide-ranging intellectual interests. Next to Jefferson and Joseph C. Cabell, he was the most influential person in the founding of the University of Virginia and was a member of its Board of Visitors for thirty-three years. A man of wealth, yet of simple tastes, he owned a cotton plantation in Alabama as well as his Virginia estate of Bremo, forty miles from Charlottesville. Its beautiful mansion, designed by Jefferson, still stands.

Back of General Cocke's reforming zeal lay a deep religious faith; he was in truth a puritan cavalier. Mrs. Cocke's diary reveals that she regularly read a portion of the Bible to her husband in the early morning by candlelight. Both she and her husband were deeply concerned that their slaves should have religious instruction. She herself conducted a school for the children of the Negro quarter.[50] While Cocke was at his Alabama cotton plantation in 1847, he wrote to his son that he was glad the latter had secured a preacher for the chapel on Bremo Plantation. "This is but part of the duty of religious instruction we owe our slaves," he observed; "if we were faithful in this respect, we might with more propriety use for defence the Scriptural arguments which so distinctly recognize the Institution."[51]

Cocke regarded the slaves as human beings, capable of noble sentiments and actions. Though he believed that the Bible sanctioned slavery, he emancipated a number of his slaves and sent them to Liberia. Their letters to him from Africa are touching in their gratitude and deep affection.[52] To his son, Dr. Cary Charles Cocke, he wrote in 1857 concerning his former slave James, whose wife and children were owned by Cary: "he has shown himself man enough to work out his own salvation in seven years [by earning his emancipation]—and I

[50] Louise C. Cocke Diary, October 3, 11, December 1, 1834, University of Virginia Library.
[51] John H. Cocke to Dr. Cary Charles Cocke, January 5, 1857, Cocke Papers.
[52] See Bremo Slave Letters, University of Virginia Library.

believe he will under God in seven years more be able to claim his wife & children for their value—I do not expect to live to that period but I trust that you and Nannie Oliver [Cary's wife] will find it in your hearts to reward such distinguished Nobility in human Nature."[53] Cocke became so active in the colonization movement that he was elected president of the society.

Cocke is especially famous for his activity in the temperance movement and in his opposition to the cultivation of tobacco and to the smoking and chewing of it. He sent out temperance tracts, attended temperance conventions, and erected a beautiful Greek Revival structure over a temperance spring on his estate near the James River and the Kanawha Canal. The tradition has been handed down that the boatmen stopped often to drink its refreshing water, but only in small quantities well mixed with their corn liquor. A young tutor in the Selden family at Westover on the James wrote to the old general a pessimistic letter about the progress of the temperance cause. "This part of Va.," he observed, "preserves too decidedly still her old grog-drinking habits to make such a movement as the temperance reformation a very pleasing one, even among the young. Mr. Selden himself makes no regular business of drinking every day, but I don't think he speaks of the temperance cause in a way to make his children think it very deserving of their attention." The tutor remarked that he himself was regarded as a prodigy because he was a temperance fellow, and that when he attended a Christmas party he found himself the center of observation as "a live specimen of a *cold water* man."[54]

The neglect of social reform in the South was partly owing to the politicians' obsession with federal politics. Benjamin F. Perry, the South Carolina Unionist, was sagacious in his comment in 1853: "What might not South Carolina now be if her Calhouns, Haynes, McDuffies, Hamiltons, and Prestons had devoted their great talents and energies to the commercial and internal improvement of the state, instead of frittering them away in political squabbles, which ended in nothing?"[55] The reforms which South Carolina desperately needed were an enlightened system of public schools, good roads, manufactures, a

[53] John H. Cocke to Dr. Cary Charles Cocke, November 4, 1857, Cocke Papers.
[54] William G. Strange to John H. Cocke, April 18, 1847, Cocke Papers.
[55] Kibler, *Benjamin F. Perry*, p. 304.

penitentiary for criminals, railroads, and democratic changes in government, such as the abolition of the overrepresentation of the lowland parishes in the legislature and of the aristocratic method of choosing the governor and presidential electors by the legislature. But Calhoun was dictator of the state from 1830 to his death in 1850, and he thwarted all efforts toward progressive reforms, for he did not wish South Carolina to be distracted by bitter internal fights. Rather, he was determined to preserve the unity of the state and devote its harmonious energies to fighting the battles for slavery in Congress and in presidential elections. In Kentucky, Clay occupied a somewhat similar position, and he too was concerned with federal politics rather than state reforms. The editors, as well as the politicians, throughout the South had their eyes primarily on the federal capital, on the slavery and territorial issues, on the victory of a national political party—to the detriment of state issues and of social reforms.

CHAPTER 13

The Southern Mind in 1860

"ROONY" (W. H. F.) LEE, whom Henry Adams met at Harvard College in the class of 1858, seemed to the critical New Englander to embody the mind and the spirit of the South. This tall, handsome, extroverted son of Robert E. Lee had the manners and bearing of a gentleman and the habit of command. To Adams he appeared to be "a Virginian of the eighteenth century, little changed from the model of his grandfather, 'Light Horse Harry' Lee." During Roony's first year in Harvard he was the most popular and prominent man in his class; then he "seemed slowly to drop into the background." He was a splendid creature, but his mind was completely unanalytical and simple. A total failure as a student, he left college when he was offered a commission by General Winfield Scott to join the expedition against the Mormons. He asked his New England classmate to write his letter of acceptance, which in this period of sectional acrimony showed the good temper of the Virginian and "flattered Adams's vanity more than any Northern compliment could do." Despite the fact that he was a poor student, Roony Lee served his section well, first as a gentleman planter, and then as a major general of cavalry in the Confederate army.

The New England historian generalized concerning the Southerner as a type. "Strictly, the Southerner," Adams wrote, "had no mind; he had temperament. He was not a scholar; he had no intellectual training; he could not analyze an idea and he could not conceive of admitting two; but in life one could get along very well without ideas if one had only the social instinct."[1] Adams's view of the Southerner was more favorable than that of such Northerners as Emerson, Thoreau, Longfellow, Holmes, and Whittier, who saw the South through an abolitionist lens. If the Northern intellectuals as a whole (there were some exceptions, such as Bryant and Whitman) so viewed the South, what must have been the warped and unreal image of the land of Dixie held by the great majority of Northerners on the eve of the Civil War?

Had Adams visited the South, he might have discerned that the Southern mind displayed many facets. These were produced partly by the subregions into which the land was divided, for there was not one *South,* but many souths. Far from being an abstraction, the Southern mind represented an accumulation of experiences that were different from those of contemporary New Englanders or Westerners or Middle States people. Perhaps the best definition of "the Southern mind" is the dominant thought of the section, which changed greatly between 1800 and 1860. Until about 1835 Virginia held the leadership in formulating the thought of the South. After that date the intellectual leader was South Carolina, whose writers and statesmen, Calhoun, Harper, Hammond, Grayson, Simms, and De Bow, expressed the dominant thought of the Cotton Kingdom.

It is surprising that New Orleans, the South's second largest city, did not assume a more commanding position in Southern thought than it did. Perhaps its transitory population, its unhealthy and enervating climate, and its powerful commercial interests tended to inhibit creative thought. Although the city had the best opera in America, its citizens showed little taste for intellectual interests. Not until 1847 did the city acquire a university, the University of Louisiana, but it was a feeble institution. The chief intellectual expression of the city, *De Bow's Review,* had been founded (in Charleston) by a South Carolinian, who carried the extreme South Carolina doctrines into the lower South.

No single theme explains the complex society below the Mason-Dixon Line. Ulrich B. Phillips sought to interpret Southern behavior

[1] Henry Adams, *The Education of Henry Adams, an Autobiography* (Boston, 1918), pp. 56–59. In contrast to the Roony Lee type of Southerner was H. H. Richardson, the architect, who entered Harvard from Louisiana. Of him, Adams wrote that he had met no one in his student days whom he valued as much in later life (p. 64).

first in terms of climate and later in terms of race—the central theme
of Southern history, he argued persuasively, was the determination of
the ruling whites to keep the South "a white man's country."[2] But
shortly after he announced his thesis in 1928, conditions began to
change so that, whatever validity it may have had in explaining the
past, it became increasingly outmoded in its application to the modern
South. In 1860 the South was differentiated from the North more by
the character of its upper class than by the distinguishing qualities of
its great middle class, the yeoman farmers. The plantation gentry still
preserved some of the traditions of the English country gentlemen—
noblesse oblige, particularly the obligation of public service in local
affairs, the practice of hospitality, and the adherence to the code of
the gentleman. Especially did they cherish the idea of personal dignity,
of honor. William Gilmore Simms trained his son, as did many a Southern father, in this tradition, so that he wrote proudly: "He will resent
the smallest indignity of another boy, but a single sharp word from his
mother, or myself, will flood his eyes with tears."

The masses of the Southern people, however, were too strongly
molded by rural isolation to exhibit much of the country-gentleman
ideal. James H. Hammond noted in his diary, July 3, 1841, that he
had passed seven years living at Silver Bluff "among the most ignorant, vulgar & I may add most narrow minded set of people in the
world. There is not a soul to whom I can converse of anything save
neighborhood news & crops."[3] Simms wrote five years later to a Northern friend that there was strong opposition to his election to the legislature because of his frequent visits to the North: "The cry is that I
am a Northern man, that my affinities are with the North, etc. . . .
Among a people so ignorant as many of our poor farmers are it is not
difficult for cunning men who are unprincipled to effect a great deal."[4]
He was defeated.

Professor Lucian Minor of William and Mary College pointed out
the danger of such provincialism, which existed in the North also, in a
letter to John Hartwell Cocke, May 13, 1857:

[2] U. B. Phillips, "The Central Theme of Southern History," *American Historical Review,* XXXIV (1928), pp. 30–43.

[3] James H. Hammond Diary, July 3, 1841, Library of Congress.

[4] William Gilmore Simms to James Lawson, October 9, 1846, in Oliphant,
Letters of William Gilmore Simms, II, 191.

We are, I fear, within a few years of disunion & perhaps of civil war; and all because neither side knows the other. Each has a hundred excellencies, entirely unknown to the other, and a knowledge of which would substitute mutual esteem if not mutual affections for the hate that is now waxing bitterer and bitterer on both sides. What a pity that a hundred men & women of known character & of some skill in writing would [not] go from the South to explore the North—mingling intimately with the people & studying their ways & traits at home and would then publish here the results of their espionage, while a Northern hundred should do the like by the South. It wd. dispel hosts of prejudices.[5]

More Southerners journeyed North, not for friendly espionage, but for pleasure and profit, than Northerners visited the South. Thousands of merchants made the annual buying trip to the North; many of the upper class, impelled by hot weather, went to Newport and Saratoga; and thousands of Southern youths attended Northern colleges, particularly the medical college of the University of Pennsylvania. Yet Southern youths educated in Northern colleges do not seem to have become more national-minded or more liberal on the slavery question as a result of their Northern experience.

On no other subject did the Southern mind reveal itself more distinctly than on the institution of slavery. Here was an interest which tended to unify the heterogeneous elements of Southern society and to differentiate, particularly after the 1830's, Southern from Northern thought. The defense of slavery involved two powerful and constant human interests, the retention of profitable property, for which men will always fight furiously and tenaciously as long as they can see the slightest semblance of legal right, and the preservation of public safety. Southerners differed on many political measures, but when the institution of slavery was threatened they closed their ranks. In 1820 the members of Congress from the slave states voted as a solid phalanx against the Tallmadge amendment to the Missouri bill. The circumstance that one congressman, Willard Hall of Delaware, who was reared in Massachusetts, voted in favor of the antislavery measure only served to dramatize the uniformity of Southern thought.[6]

Between 1800 and 1830, Southern opinion on slavery seems to have

[5] Lucian Minor to John Hartwell Cocke, May 13, 1857, Cocke Papers.
[6] Glover Moore, *The Missouri Controversy, 1819–1821* (Lexington, Ky., 1953), p. 52.

been, over all, rather liberal, but attitudes varied in different parts of the South. One of the main sources of evidence, the reports of travelers, is open to suspicion of its objectivity, for planters talking to travelers usually tried to be polite and agreeable and also to present the best side of Southern life. Nevertheless, it is striking how much the travelers in the upper South prior to 1830 were in agreement about the willingness of planters to concede that slavery was an evil which should be removed. Although in conversation Southerners admitted the abstract evils of slavery, they maintained that it would require many years for the institution to die out and that any movement toward the manumission of slaves should be extremely gradual—and come from them. Henry Knight, a New England visitor to Virginia in 1824, observed: "There are many planters who wish there never had been a slave brought into the country, and who would make great sacrifices to emancipate them, if it could be safely done. But this must be done gradually and provision made for them when free."[7]

Liberal sentiments in regard to slavery were strongest in Virginia, Maryland, and North Carolina, where exhausted soil and depression in the tobacco market greatly reduced the profitableness of that system of labor. Indeed, slavery was in a moribund condition in the tobacco country at this time; later it was resuscitated by the rise of the internal slave trade as cotton culture expanded into the Gulf region. Nevertheless, there were nobler motives than economic pressures behind Virginia liberalism at the end of the eighteenth century and during the first quarter of the nineteenth. George Washington, for example, in discussing Southern slavery with the actor John Bernard shortly before his death in 1799, remarked that there was need to emancipate the slaves, not only "on the score of human dignity" but also "to perpetuate the existence of our Union by consolidating it in a bond of common principle."[8] He spoke in the afterglow of the Revolution, suffused by a generous feeling for the rights of man. But the liberal Revolutionary generation was passing away: Jefferson died in 1826; Charles Carroll, the last of the signers of the Declaration, in 1832; and James Madison in 1836.

[7] "Arthur Singleton Esq." [Henry C. Knight], *Letters from the South and West* (Boston, 1824), p. 80.
[8] John Bernard, *Retrospections of America, 1797–1811* (New York, 1887), p. 91.

Representative of the idealistic group in Virginia society was a young aristocrat of the Piedmont, Edward Coles. After the latter had listened to Bishop James Madison, president of William and Mary College, lecture on the rights of man, he asked him whether it was right to hold slaves. In an embarrassed manner, the venerable church-man replied that "it could not rightfully be done & that slavery was a state of things that could not be justified on principle & could only be tolerated in our Country, by our finding it in existence, & the difficulty of getting rid of it." The young student could not convince the amiable college president, however, that the latter should carry out his theory by freeing his own slaves.

When Coles's father died in 1807, a few weeks after Edward's twenty-first birthday, the young Virginian resolved to emancipate his share of inherited slaves. This decision meant giving up the appealing life of a Virginia planter. In 1809, after becoming President Madison's secretary, he talked freely with the old statesman about the great wrong of holding slaves, but he could not persuade him to emancipate his own bondsmen. Coles commented, "no man had a more instinctive repugnance to doing wrong to another than he had; yet from the force of early impressions, the influence of habit & association & a certain train of reasoning, which lulled in some degree his conscience without convincing his judgment (for he never justified or approved of it) he continued to hold slaves."[9] Coles, on the other hand, followed the dictates of his conscience and in 1819 took his slaves to Ohio, freed them, and gave to each head of a family a farm of 160 acres.

There are not many men like Edward Coles in any society. Most Southerners who disapproved of slavery in this period, even Jefferson in his old age, to whom Coles also appealed, were not willing to lead a crusade or act as individuals to free their slaves. In North Carolina, Thomas Oliver Larkin, a Massachusetts Yankee who kept a store at Wilmington, 1821–25, and later served as consul at Monterey, California, believed that many slaveowners in the state favored the emancipation of the bondsmen. But they were neither articulate nor crusaders.[10]

[9] Ralph L. Ketcham, "The Dictates of Conscience: Edward Coles and Slavery," *Virginia Quarterly Review*, XXXVI (1960), 46–62.

[10] Robert J. Parker, "A Yankee in North Carolina: Observations of Thomas Oliver Larkin, 1821–1826," *North Carolina Historical Review*, XIV (1937), 340.

The holding of slaves was strongly opposed by two religious sects in the South. The journal of Francis Asbury shows that the Methodist Church, in the period when most of its members were humble men, held antislavery opinions. Asbury attended a conference of Southern itinerant preachers near Petersburg, Virginia, on November 25, 1794, in which "the preachers almost unanimously entered into an agreement and resolution not to hold slaves in any State where the law will allow them to manumit them on pain of forfeiture of their honour and their place in the itinerant connexion, and in any State where the law will not admit of manumission they agreed to pay them the worth of their labour, and when they die to leave them to some person or persons or society, in trust, to bring about their liberty."[11] The Quakers were even more zealous in their opposition to slavery, not only emancipating their own slaves, but seeking to secure the repeal of laws prohibiting the instruction of slaves. The Quaker editor William Swaim of Greensboro, North Carolina, advocated the manumission of the slaves until his death in 1834.

Captain Basil Hall of the Royal Navy and Timothy Flint, a New England schoolmaster and preacher, noted that there were various opinions held in the lower South in regard to slavery. Some defended the institution as a positive benefit to society, since every civilized society must have a class of hewers of wood and drawers of water, and the Negro slaves were well suited to that function. Others recognized that slavery was an evil, but one that had been "attentuated by long habits of thinking both of the slaves and of the master." The British traveler was convinced that the South Carolinians would maintain slavery inviolate "in spite of their own admission that it is a grievous evil and certainly in spite of all attempts to compel them to change it."[12] Flint observed, in the lower Mississippi Valley in 1826, "if you introduce the subject [of slavery] with any delicacy, I have never yet heard one, who does not admit that slavery is an evil and injustice, and who does not at least affect to deplore the evil."[13] Nevertheless, he remarked that these inhabitants of the lower South condoned and rationalized the preservation of the institution, arguing that the Bible clearly recognized the right of the master to own slaves.

[11] Elmer T. Clark (ed.), *The Journal and Letters of Francis Asbury* (Nashville, 1958), II, 33.
[12] Hall, *Travels*, III, 154, 162.
[13] Timothy Flint, *Recollections of the Last Ten Years*, p. 342.

The turning point in the attitude of the upper South to slavery came in 1831–32 after the shock of the Nat Turner insurrection of August, 1831. This event caused a momentous debate in the Virginia legislature on the adoption of a plan of gradual emancipation. The two leading newspapers of the state, the Richmond *Enquirer* and the Richmond *Whig*, which had previously been silent on the slavery question, published editorials and letters from contributors urging the legislature to adopt a plan of gradual emancipation. In the legislature the reformers—largely young representatives from the western part of the state—criticized the institution of slavery as retarding the progress of the state and as being injurious to the welfare of the whites. They attributed Virginia's backward condition in comparison with the Northern states solely to the existence of slavery, failing to realize that many other factors besides slavery, such as the westward movement, the exhaustion of the soil, the ruralness of the state, the African heritage of a retarded Negro population, were also responsible for Virginia's condition. Furthermore, they spoke eloquently against slavery as a violation of the rights of man. They proposed the adoption by the legislature of a plan for the gradual emancipation of the slaves in the state by a postnati method and the deportation to Africa or Haiti of the emancipated Negroes.

The conservatives of the tidewater opposed the adoption of such a plan as violating the rights of property and as being impractical. A consideration of great importance in the conservatives' reluctance to give up slavery was the rich profits being made from the sale of Virginia slaves to the lower South, for this was the period when the domestic slave trade was approaching its height. Furthermore, they were appalled by the difficulties of determining what to do with the freedmen should a plan of manumission be adopted.

The decision in the legislature seems to have been made mainly on the basis of economic interests. The legislature of 1831–32 consisted of 134 members, three-fourths of whom were slaveholders, but only eighteen of whom could be classed as planters (owning as many as twenty taxable slaves, i.e., slaves over twelve years of age). In this body there were thirty-four nonslaveholders, of whom twenty-six were residents of the trans-Alleghany section of the state. On January 25, 1832, when the legislature voted on the crucial resolution introduced by William B. Preston of the West, declaring it expedient for the legislature to enact laws abolishing slavery within the state, there was a close correlation between the way the delegates voted on this measure and the percentage of slaves held in the districts from which they came. Representatives from the trans-Alleghany part of the state, where slaves constituted only 10 per cent of the population, voted solidly, thirty-one to zero, in favor of the antislavery resolution. The delegates from the tidewater and Piedmont, where the slaves composed 56 and 54 per cent of the population respectively, voted overwhelmingly against the resolution. Only nine representatives from these areas, including Thomas Jefferson Randolph, Jefferson's grandson, who owned thirty-six slaves, rose above their economic interests to vote in favor of a great liberal reform.[14] The revolutionary proposal was defeated by an overwhelming majority.

The Virginia debate was especially significant, for other Southern states were watching its outcome and the decision would influence their course. Moreover, the debate gave an impetus to the developing proslavery argument, one of the great rationalizations of American history. Even before this dramatic debate and before the rise of the Northern abolitionists, the proslavery argument had begun in South Carolina in the 1820's after the spread of slavery into Missouri had been challenged. Such leaders as Senator William Smith, Whitemarsh Seabrook, and Robert J. Turnbull maintained that slavery was not an evil but a positive good.[15] This elaborate apology for slavery may well have been designed to convert Southerners themselves to the belief it was morally justifiable and to quiet any guilty feelings that they might have. Certainly the first important publication by a Southerner justifying slavery, *Review of the Debates in the Virginia Legislature of 1831 and 1832,* by Thomas Roderick Dew, was designed primarily not as a reply to Northern abolitionists but to convince Virginians that slavery was a necessary institution. In a review of Paulding's *Slavery in the United States* in the *Southern Literary Messenger* in 1836, Beverley Tucker declared that Southern writers must defend the institution of slavery "to convince our own people" of its rightness.[16] His father, St. George Tucker, professor of law at William and Mary College, had

[14] Joseph C. Robert, *The Road from Monticello: a Study of the Virginia Slavery Debate of 1832* (Durham, 1941).

[15] W. S. Jenkins, *Pro-Slavery Thought in the Old South* (Chapel Hill, 1935).

[16] *Southern Literary Messenger,* II (1836), 339.

published a pamphlet in 1796 advocating the gradual emancipation of the slaves.

The attack of the abolitionists on slavery, led by such extremists as Garrison and Weld, broadened into an assault on Southern society and the moral character of the slaveholders. This aroused the greatest resentment below the Mason-Dixon Line. Francis Lieber reported to Charles Sumner on October 27, 1835, shortly after he had arrived in Columbia, South Carolina, that the moderate Senator William C. Preston had told him, "if the Abolitionists go on at this rate a man like myself will not be at liberty any more to speak his mind."[17] At the same time the Virginia planter, John Hartwell Cocke of Bremo, in a letter to William C. Rives deplored the agitation of the slavery question by ambitious Southern politicians "who had rather be first in Hell than second in Heaven (that is as far as relates to human affairs) and such men will not fail to stir any source of agitation which will suit their purposes. They know that slavery is our sorest sin, and to touch it, excites feelings allied to madness."[18]

The proslavery argument can best be studied in a volume of essays published in Charleston in 1852 entitled *The Pro-Slavery Argument*. Here are articles by Thomas R. Dew and the South Carolinians, Chancellor William Harper, Senator James H. Hammond, and William Gilmore Simms. South Carolina was the leader in forging the proslavery argument, for it had the largest proportion of slaves in the South, 57.6 per cent in 1850; Virginia had a slave population of only 32.2 per cent. Moreover, the swampy rice plantations needed Negro laborers more urgently than the other staple-crop areas; for the Negroes, though not immune, were less susceptible to malaria than the white man, and the ignorant and primitive Gullah Negroes seemed to require the control of the masters. The Carolinians also had developed an exaggerated sense of pride and a tradition of standing up for their rights.

The proslavery argument was a many-sided and ingenious defense of an institution that earlier had been condemned by the South's finest minds. It had the respectability of being based in part on the philosophy of Aristotle, who had justified Greek slavery on the ground that

[17] Francis Lieber to Charles Sumner, October 27, 1835, Francis Lieber Papers.
[18] John Hartwell Cocke to William C. Rives, August 10, 1835, William C. Rives Papers, Library of Congress.

it recognized the natural inequality of man in an organic society. The apologists for slavery also maintained that the Africans alone could endure working in the scorching heat of the Southern climate. (Actually thousands of white farmers worked in the fields with no bad effects.) The proslavery justification appealed to experience, maintaining that the free Negro had proved to be shiftless and criminally disposed, and citing the ruin of staple agriculture in Jamaica after the emancipation of the slaves in 1833. The argument that the Southerners leaned upon most heavily, however, was the sanction of the Bible, derived from a literal interpretation. The considerations which seem strongest today, the great property loss involved (for the abolitionists were opposed to compensation of the masters) and the need of slavery as a temporary police system until the slaves could be educated in the responsibilities of freedom, were not stressed in the proslavery literature.

In the decade of the 1850's the proslavery argument took a relatively new and militant turn. It was stimulated by the publication of *Uncle Tom's Cabin* in 1852 and the controversy over the extension of slavery into the territories. The origin of the races was explored to justify Southern slavery. On February 10, 1850, Francis Lieber wrote from Columbia, South Carolina, to a Northern friend, "There is a contest brewing here about the unity or diversity of our race. I confess to you that I do not see how a negro, with his anatomical and physiological difference, ever can have grown out of a white man, or vice versa, and so with the Mongolian race."[19] In 1854, Dr. Josiah C. Nott, a Mobile physician, and George R. Gliddon, an archaeologist, published *Types of Mankind,* in which they presented the theory that the different races were separately created species, the Negro being at the lowest scale of human creation and permanently inferior to the white man. This doctrine of the diversity of the races aroused a storm of protest in the South because it conflicted with the Biblical account of the origin of man.[20]

Following the axiom that the best defense is offense, the Southern defenders of slavery in the 1850's made an attack on the ethics of Northern industrial society. The most prominent protagonists were

[19] Francis Lieber to George Hillard, February 10, 1850, Francis Lieber Papers.
[20] See William Stanton, *The Leopard's Spots, Scientific Attitudes toward Race in America 1850–1859* (Chicago, 1960).

William J. Grayson, a former collector for the port of Charleston, and George Fitzhugh, a Virginia lawyer. Grayson in 1856 published a long rhymed poem entitled *The Hireling and the Slave,* in which he contrasted the security which the Southern slave enjoyed with the brutal exploitation of the Northern and British workingman. Fitzhugh published a powerful indictment of the treatment of factory workers, or "wage slaves," in the North and in England in his *Sociology for the South, or the Failure of Free Society* (1854) and *Cannibals All! or Slaves without Masters* (1857). Neither Fitzhugh nor Grayson actually investigated conditions in Northern or British factories (or, for that matter, in Southern textile mills, where working conditions were similar), but engaged in generalizations. The Virginia polemicist derived most of his material from reading British reviews, newspapers, and the works of Carlyle.

Fitzhugh had so many contradictory sides to his nature that he has been called by a modern scholar a writer *sui generis.*[21] Unlike most of the other proslavery propagandists, he was not a racist, although he did accept the current view that the Negro was inherently inferior to the white man; nor was he an agrarian, for he was a strong advocate of manufactures, opposed free trade, and praised Governor Wise, to whom he dedicated *Cannibals All,* for endeavoring "to Virginianise Virginia" in opposing centralization from without and promoting it from within through encouraging railroads, education, and manufactures. His major effort was directed toward showing the failure of free society to protect the working class from being ruthlessly exploited as to wages; moreover, during unemployment, sickness, and old age, the workers were completely neglected. Because of these evils of capitalism, he predicted that Northern society was headed toward socialism; the only remedy against this threat was the adoption of slavery in the North as well as in the South—for the white workingman as well as for the Southern Negro. He anticipated and perhaps influenced Lincoln's "House Divided" speech of 1858 by declaring in the Richmond *Enquirer* that slavery would prevail everywhere in the United States or everywhere be abolished.[22]

[21] C. Vann Woodward (ed.), *Cannibals All! or Slaves without Masters by George Fitzhugh* (Cambridge, 1960).

[22] Harvey Wish, *George Fitzhugh, Propagandist of the Old South* (Baton Rouge, 1943), pp. 150–151.

Fitzhugh's importance in Southern thought is difficult to evaluate. Although his volumes were praised by the proslavery intellectuals, notably by De Bow and Professor Holmes of the University of Virginia, it seems probable that the majority of Southerners did not accept his extreme views. His larger significance was his realization of the evils of unregulated capitalism, in which he was a forerunner of the Populists and Progressives. Despite overstatement, the proslavery writers of the 1850's such as Fitzhugh rendered service in criticizing the evils of Northern industrialism, which the abolitionists ignored. As Jay Hubbell has observed, "The defeat of the South in the Civil War left Northern industrialism almost without critics among American writers."[23] Fitzhugh was remarkable also in that he was one of the relatively few philosophical conservatives in America who have boldly dissented from the general drift of liberal conformity that has characterized American political thought.

The supreme feat of harmonizing slavery with democracy as a just institution was accomplished by John C. Calhoun and other statesmen of the lower South. In condemning some antislavery resolutions of the Vermont legislature introduced into Congress at the close of 1837, Calhoun said in the Senate: "Many in the South once believed that it [slavery] was a moral and political evil. That folly and delusion are gone. We see it now in its true light and regard it as the most safe and stable basis for free institutions in the world."[24] Governor James H. Hammond in a letter to Thomas Clarkson, president of the British Anti-Slavery Society, March 24, 1845, declared that the attacks of the abolitionists had driven the Southerners to examine the moral basis for holding slaves, which some of them had doubted; this close examination had convinced them of the rightness of slavery, so that slaveholders were indebted to the abolitionists for a "perfect ease of conscience."[25]

Speaking in the House of Representatives in 1836 and again in the Senate twenty-two years later, Hammond proclaimed that every civilized society was based on a "mud sill" of a laboring class that did the

[23] Hubbell, *The South in American Literature*, p. 412.

[24] Richard K. Crallé (ed.), *The Works of John C. Calhoun* (New York, 1853), III, 180.

[25] E. N. Elliott (ed.), *Cotton Is King and Pro-Slavery Arguments* (Augusta, 1860), pp. 684–685.

hard, sweaty work of society. The slaves were fitted by nature, he argued, to form this "mud sill" in the South. By their labor they freed the planter class from the necessary drudgery connected with civilized life and gave it leisure for the cultivation of the mind and for political affairs.[26] The society of the Old South, extravagantly admiring the Greek culture of the fifth century, thought that it was necessary to suppress the lower class in order to refine a relatively small part of its upper class. Only in the twentieth century did a different concept of culture emerge in America—namely, that the goal of society should be mass culture, irrespective of race.

The inevitable result of the growth of a doctrine justifying the permanent suppression of black men as slaves was the rejection of the principles of the Declaration of Independence. Hammond in his first letter to Clarkson, January 28, 1845, wrote: "I indorse without reserve the much abused sentiment of Governor M'Duffie, that slavery is the true corner-stone of our republican edifice; while I repudiate, as ridiculously absurd, that much lauded but nowhere accredited dogma of Mr. Jefferson, that 'all men are born equal.' "[27] Calhoun, also, in his *A Disquisition on Government,* written at the end of his career, repudiated the Jeffersonian doctrine of the equality of man. Instead, he affirmed that men are created unequal, and that they are not entitled to liberty as a natural right but must achieve it by struggle and by superior ability and virtue.[28]

Such ideas represented mainly a theory of the black belts. They were not the views of the millions of inarticulate farmers, the villagers and townsmen, the great middle class of the South. Undoubtedly a majority of these citizens believed that slavery was a necessary institution which was sanctioned by the Bible, but that was as far as they went. The conditions in South Carolina or the black belts should not be taken as typical of the whole South. William E. Dodd may be right when he asserts that in the Cotton Kingdom "there was the most perfect agreement ever known in Anglo-Saxon history," if that statement is confined to the question of the preservation of slavery. On the other hand, his sweeping generalization that "Before 1850 the older Jeffersonian ideal was totally abandoned, and the contrary ideal of the inequality

[26] John C. Rives (ed.), *Congressional Globe,* 35th Cong., 1st Sess., p. 962.
[27] Eliott, *Cotton Is King and Pro-Slavery Arguments,* pp. 637–638.
[28] Crallé, *Works of John C. Calhoun,* I, 55–58.

of men had been adopted," did not represent the sentiment of the common people.[29] As the Civil War approached, the South was becoming more democratic. The growth of popular education, the wide distribution of land ownership in the last decade of the ante-bellum period, the democratization of government by constitutional changes, and the strong Jeffersonian tradition that survived among the plain folk were all against a caste system.

Indeed, the most notable trait that distinguished Southern farmers from European peasants was a conviction of the equality of all white men. This frontier virtue never disappeared from the lives of the great middle class, as John Basil Lamar's humorous story "Polly Peablossom's Wedding" illustrated. When the preacher failed to appear at the wedding and a squire was asked to perform the ceremony, Mrs. Peablossom objected that "the quality" in her day in Duplin County, North Carolina, had a prejudice against being married by a magistrate. But old Mr. Peablossom remonstrated, "None of your Duplin County aristocracy about here, now . . . North Ca'lina ain't the best state in the Union nohow. . . . Quality, eh! Who the devil's better than we are? An't we honest? An't we raised our children decent, and learned them how to read, write, and cipher? An't I *fout* under Newnan and Floyd for the country? Why, darn it! We are the *very best* sort of people."[30] This boast was the voice of Jacksonian democracy that prevailed until the South went down in defeat at Appomattox.

The upcountry yeomanry produced Calhoun, but he became the spokesman of the aristocratic lowlanders. He was pre-eminently the philosopher of the *status quo*. His profound conservatism was expressed during a conversation in Washington with Marcellus, the brother of Governor Hammond, on September 18, 1844. Calhoun said, so Marcellus reported, that if Carolina adopted the proposed plan of electing a governor by the people, her influence would be destroyed; that if she changed her constitution, "she will become a pygmy."[31] The witty Charleston lawyer James L. Petigru, on the other hand, opposed an aristocratic government, remarking to his friend Hugh S. Legaré that

[29] William E. Dodd, *The Cotton Kingdom* (New Haven, 1921), pp. 62, 70.

[30] T. P. Burke (ed.), *Polly Peablossom's Wedding: and Other Tales* (Philadelphia, 1851), pp. 20–21.

[31] Marcellus Hammond to J. H. Hammond, September 22, 1844, Hammond Papers, South Caroliniana Library.

life tenure of judges was an anomaly in a democracy, for the judges take on the hue of their party.[32]

Calhoun was wise and prophetic in many things and blind in others. He looked far into the future and predicted that if the slave should be liberated from the care of the master, the Negro would become the bondsman of society. He envisaged also a conflict between capital and labor when conditions in the United States should approximate those in the old countries of Europe. The Southern slave system, he maintained, was "the balancer" of the Union, "the great conservative power, which prevented other portions, less fortunately constituted, from rushing into conflict." In the Southern states, capital and labor were united; the laborer was cared for by a lifelong system of social security. It would be wisdom, he suggested, for Northern businessmen to collaborate with Southern conservatives. He thus adumbrated the formation of an alliance between Northern and Southern conservatives that was consummated in the twentieth century in the Senate of the United States.[33]

The valid contribution that Calhoun made to political science was his penetrating analysis of the danger of unchecked majority rule. The Carolina leader had a more realistic view of human nature than Jefferson; he approached close to the point of view of Madison, who realized how powerful economic groups are in formulating governmental policy. The great Carolinian, with his Calvinistic heritage, perceived the evil and greed in human nature. He wrote to his daughter two years before his death that he regarded life as very much of "a struggle against evil."[34] Calhoun held that the federal Constitution did not provide sufficient checks against the tyranny of the numerical majority. In order to preserve liberty and a fair distribution of the benefits and burdens of the Union, it was necessary to protect the minority from the selfish action of the majority. This could be done, he held, by the application of the doctrine of the concurrent majority, by which major issues between sections should be decided only through agreement of a ma-

[32] James Louis Petigru to Hugh S. Legaré, June 3, 1843, Petigru Papers, South Caroliniana Library.

[33] See Richard N. Current, "John C. Calhoun, Philosopher of Reaction," *Antioch Review* (Summer, 1943), pp. 223–234, and Eaton, *Freedom of Thought in the Old South*, Chap. VI.

[34] Hubbell, *The South in American Literature*, p. 418.

jority in both sections.[35] This doctrine was presented in the impractical form of "state interposition" (he did not use the word "nullification"), or a suspensive veto by the state of a federal act deemed unconstitutional until three-fourths of the sovereign states in convention had overruled the state veto. In the last years of his life he sought unsuccessfully to organize a Southern bloc in Congress that would transcend party lines. It is strange that he overlooked the potentialities of the filibuster in the Senate, in recent days so formidable an obstacle to the majority will.

Even as enlightened a mind as Calhoun's lent itself to a movement to suppress all criticism of slavery both north and south of the Mason-Dixon Line. Using the analogy of comity between sovereign nations, he demanded that the Northern states suppress the abolition societies, that the federal government allow the Southern states to censor the mails, and that freedom of petition in regard to slavery be denied.[36] The policy of suppressing the circulation of abolition publications among the slaves, many of whom could read, could be justified on the ground that the preservation of public safety is the supreme law. But the "gag rule" in Congress and the suppression of all criticism of slavery or of the advocacy of emancipation, which was supported by the united will of the Southern states after 1836, went far beyond any reasonable requirement of public safety.

After the middle 1830's it became increasingly dangerous below the Mason-Dixon Line for even native-born Southerners to attack slavery publicly. The experience of Cassius Marcellus Clay, a Bluegrass aristocrat and a graduate of Yale College, demonstrated this fact when he attempted to estabish a newspaper devoted to the gradual emancipation of the slaves in Lexington, Kentucky. His *True American* was suppressed in 1845 by an orderly mob (paradoxical as that phrase may seem) that boxed his press and sent it out of the state to Cincinnati.[37] University professors, such as Benjamin S. Hedrick of the University of North Carolina, who held free-soil opinions were forced to go into exile or conceal their heterodox views. In the decade of the 1850's the

[35] See J. T. Carpenter, *The South as a Conscious Minority 1789–1861* (New York, 1930), Chap. IV.

[36] See Clement Eaton, "Censorship of the Southern Mails," *American Historical Review*, XLVIII (1943), 266–280.

[37] *Appeal of Cassius M. Clay to Kentucky and the World* (Boston, 1845); Brutus J. Clay Papers.

South lost two of its finest scholars, Francis Lieber and F. A. P. Barnard, president of the University of Mississippi, because of their liberal views. Barnard resigned his position after he was severely criticized for violating Southern mores by accepting Negro testimony in the faculty trial of a student accused of raping a colored girl.[38] The acme of suppression of criticism of slavery was reached when the supreme court of North Carolina in 1860 upheld the sentence by a lower court of Daniel Worth, a Wesleyan preacher, to a year in jail for circulating Hinton Rowan Helper's *The Impending Crisis of the South*.[39]

As the rancor between the sections increased over the slavery controversy, a movement arose below the Mason-Dixon Line to exclude Northern textbooks and magazines that were hostile to slavery, and to keep Southern youth from attending Northern schools and colleges.[40] Even the liberal Thomas Jefferson as early as 1821 had protested against sending Southern boys to Northern colleges, where they would imbibe "opinions and principles in discord with those of their own country."[41] Nevertheless, in 1850 nearly half of the students at Princeton and also at the University of Pennsylvania Medical School were from the Southern states. The number from the South at Harvard was smaller, yet even in this citadel of antislavery a third of the law students came from below the Mason-Dixon Line; at Yale 57 of the 432 students enrolled were Southerners.[42] The campaign against Southerners attending Northern colleges seems to have had little effect until after the John Brown Raid. Then in December, 1859, more than two hundred Southern students withdrew from the University of Pennsyl-

[38] John Fulton (ed.), *Memoirs of Frederick A. P. Barnard* (New York, 1896), pp. 246–253.

[39] One prominent Virginian, John Hartwell Cocke, tried to interest his friends in reading it, but was rebuffed. Professor Lucian Minor wrote: "Do not send me the Helper book. I should not have time for more than a brief glance into it. What you say of its Strange oscillations between sublimity and absurdity excites my curiosity to peep over some of its pages." Minor to Cocke, October 14, 1857, Cocke Papers.

[40] See "Southern School Books," *De Bow's Review*, XIII (1852), 259, 261–65; "Home Education at the South," *ibid.*, X (1851), 362; "Southern Education for Southern Youth," *ibid.*, XIX (1855), 462–464.

[41] Thomas Jefferson to General James Breckinridge, February 15, 1821, in A. A. Lipscomb and A. L. Bergh (eds.), *The Writings of Thomas Jefferson* (Washington, 1903), XV, 315.

[42] See John S. Ezell, "A Southern Education for Southrons," *Journal of Southern History*, XVII (1951), 390–391.

vania Medical School and returned South, many of them to enter
Richmond Medical College. In 1860 Bishop Leonidas Polk founded
the University of the South at Sewanee, Tennessee, to teach sound doctrines on slavery as well as to strengthen the Episcopal Church in the
South.

William M. Pratt, the Baptist minister at Lexington, Kentucky,
wrote in his diary, January 11, 1856, "James Brady, principal of Morton School no 1, was mobbed, taken out of his house, head shaved and
varnished on the face with varnish—he had written a letter to Ohio
reflecting severely on the institution of slavery and on Mr. Berkeley,
Episcopal preacher. The committee discharged him and he was advised to leave immediately."[43] Pratt condemned the mob spirit, but he
commented that the principal had acted foolishly in writing such a
severe letter on the Kentuckians and their institutions, thus depriving
himself of a good position that paid him a salary of $900.

What the Southern states desperately needed in 1860 was the free
exercise of the critical spirit. Although they possessed some realistic
thinkers, the social atmosphere was so hostile to outspoken criticism of
the social order that most persons who disagreed with the prevailing
ideas must have concealed their opinions.[44] One prominent individual
who did not, however, was the Charleston lawyer James L. Petigru,
the finest mind in South Carolina. He spoke out against fanaticism of
all kinds, yet he had such wit and bonhomie that the Charlestonians
respected him and tolerated his nonconformity. Far more typical of
Southern thought was the attitude of the historian Hugh Blair Grigsby,
"the Virginia Froissart," who sought to glorify the past of his state and
to justify the present. While he was writing his history of the Virginia
Constitutional Convention of 1788, he felt at times as though he was
working in vain, but he was encouraged to continue by "the thought
of saving so many noble fellows from oblivion, gratifying the honest
pride of so many of their descendants, rearing a monument to Virginia
genius," and perpetuating his own name.[45]

The conservatism of the Southern mind of this period was furthermore exhibited in the field of religion. As a result of the Great Revival

[43] William M. Pratt Diary, II, January 11, 1856.
[44] See Eaton, *Freedom of Thought in the Old South,* Chaps. VII–X, for non-
conformists.
[45] Hugh Blair Grigsby Diary, August 19, 1859, Virginia Historical Society
Archives, Richmond.

of 1800 and subsequent outpourings of religious enthusiasm, a striking change had occurred in the religious life of the section.[46] By 1830 the Southern people had become thoroughly converted to orthodoxy in religion; the skepticism that had existed among the gentry of the eighteenth century, the age of reason, had virtually disappeared. The last great outspoken skeptic was Dr. Thomas Cooper. In 1829, when he was seventy years old, he wrote to a friend in Birmingham, England, describing his strenuous life as president of South Carolina College, where he lectured five times a week on chemistry "with very full experiments." "I should live here more comfortably," he wrote, "if this land & the people were not so theologically ignorant and bigotted, but altho' very unpleasant it gives me stimulus to constant exertion in opposition."[47] Two years later he had much to stimulate him when a legislative committee brought charges against him of corrupting the young, "inculcating the folly of keeping the Sabbath, of public prayer, of preaching, and of all outward observances in Religion; denying the divine authority of the Old Testament and of the greater part of the New—by sneers and insinuations attempting to bring into contempt Christianity as taught by the sects most prevalent in this state."[48] His bold defense before the Board of Trustees secured his acquittal at this time, but in 1834 he was forced to resign.

Despite the doctrine of the separation of church and state in the early Republic, religious qualifications for officeholding continued in some of the Southern states throughout the ante-bellum period. The Mississippi constitution of 1830 declared, "No person who denies the being of God or a future state of rewards and punishments shall hold any office in the civil departments of the state." Arkansas in its constitution of 1836 went further and disqualified an atheist from taking an

---

[46] See Clement Eaton, "The Ebb of the Great Revival," *North Carolina Historical Review*, XXIII (1946), 1–12; Walter B. Posey, *The Presbyterian Church in the Old Southwest 1778–1838* (Richmond, 1952), *The Baptist Church in the Lower Mississippi Valley* (Lexington, 1957), and "The Protestant Episcopal Church: an American Adaptation," *Journal of Southern History*, XXV (1959), 3–30.

[47] Thomas Cooper to Joseph Parker, February 21, 1829, Thomas Cooper Papers, South Caroliniana Library.

[48] Report of the Committee of the Legislature to the Board of Trustees, December 14, 1821; Cooper, "Letter to the Board of Trustees December 14, 1831," and "Observations on the Prest. State of the South Carolina College, Nov. 26, 1834," Thomas Cooper Papers.

oath in court.[49] It was not until 1835 that North Carolina revised its constitution to permit Catholics to be elected to the legislature, and not until 1868 could Jews serve as officeholders.

A salient characteristic of Southern religion was its puritanism, which affected not only the great middle class but also many of the aristocracy. In 1846 a prominent Presbyterian minister of Richmond, the Reverend Joseph Stiles, sent a questionnaire to preachers of various sects in the South asking whether they believed that promiscuous dancing in public was "a Scriptural recreation." Without exception the replies were an emphatic "No." One minister wrote that "The spirit of dancing is the spirit of the *world*. . . . All public amusements such as pantomimes, shows, tragedies, comedies, theatre, circus, etc., were regarded by the primitive Christians as the pomps of idolatry."[50] Until 1850 the rural churches held frequent trials of their white and slave members for such transgressions as dancing, swearing, fighting, gambling with cards, Sabbath breaking, and neglecting church services. According to a record of 501 cases of church discipline of a Baptist church in North Carolina between 1791 and 1860, drunkenness was by far the most frequent offense, 117 cases, while sex immorality constituted only 33 cases.[51]

The religious belief of an overwhelming majority of Southerners in 1860 was of a type that would today be called fundamentalism, resting on a literal interpretation of the Bible. It was the type of religion that prevails in the Appalachian highlands today. A recent study of the religious thought of this region shows that the folk religion of the Old South survives there with little change. The questionnaire used in this study was answered by 1,500 persons and indicated that 99 per cent believed in the existence of a God (only five persons in the entire sample answered "No"), 98 per cent had faith that God answers prayers, 68 per cent believed in the literal interpretation of the Bible, and 91 per cent believed in immortality.[52]

Religious conservatism had its counterpart in political conservatism,

[49] Francis N. Thorpe (ed.), *The Federal and State Constitutions . . . of the United States of America* (Washington, 1909), II, 2044; I, 284.

[50] Leo Rosser to the Reverend Joseph C. Stiles, January 28, 1846, Joseph C. Stiles Papers, Huntington Library.

[51] Johnson, *Ante-Bellum North Carolina*, pp. 450–451.

[52] Sample survey conducted by Southern Appalachian Studies, 1958, under the direction of Dr. Thomas R. Ford, University of Kentucky.

expressed in almost an idolatry of the federal Constitution as interpreted by the Virginia and Kentucky resolutions of 1798. A striking
example of such conservatism was Jefferson Davis' speech in the Senate in 1859 against the Morrill Land Grant Act for establishing agricultural colleges, in which he argued that the act would violate state
rights, although such federal aid would have been an immense boon
to education in the South.[53]

The Southern states formed a minority section within the Union,
and increasingly the fate of the Southern way of life depended upon
preserving the old interpretation of the Constitution. It also depended
upon skill in politics, and therefore politics was an absorbing interest
among Southerners. Edwin Hall, the Virginia tutor, wrote in 1837 that
in order to get along with the ladies in Virginia one must talk non-
sense and resort to flattery, but to get along with men one must know
how to talk politics: "a knowledge of the politics of the day turns to
a very good account [in society] as almost every gentleman here is
more or less a politician."[54] Francis Grund, the perceptive Austrian
visitor, noted two years later: "The Southerners are the only people
in the Union who study politics as a science, having both the leisure
and education for that purpose. The Southern papers, therefore, are
on an average much better edited than those of the North."[55]

Nevertheless, many of the large planters did not participate actively
in politics. Samuel Hairston of Pittsylvania County, Virginia, the largest slaveholder of the South, owning personally nearly two thousand
Negroes and controlling another thousand owned by his mother-in-
law, was not unusual in his class in eschewing politics. Francis W.
Pickens, governor of South Carolina in 1861, wrote that it was a profound error to think that the Civil War had been brought on by the
large planters:

I know the fact that the largest slaveholders were generally the conservative
men in the commencement and were for moving with caution and prudence,
while the small-property-holders were for the most part fiery and uncalculat-
ing. It was a great ground swell of the masses that forced the country forward, having no guide but devotion to the country and the indignant feelings

[53] Knight, *Documentary History of Education in the South before 1860*, III,
446–452.
[54] Gara, "A New Englander's View of Plantation Life," p. 349.
[55] Grund, *Aristocracy in America*, p. 193.

of a wronged people. As a general rule the large slaveholders and cotton planters had but little to do with politics, and it was the great masses of the other class who have ever held a large control over the public opinion of the Southern states.[56]

Fully as conservative as the political thought of the Old South was the literary taste of the people. No longer did Southerners read skeptical works, Thomas Paine's *Age of Reason,* Voltaire, Gibbon, Hume, and Volney; nor the older British writers, Pope, Addison, and Godwin, whose works were popular at the beginning of the nineteenth century. Their taste had turned to romantic works—but so had the taste of Northern readers. In 1854 two of the most popular novels in the South were *Alone* by "Marion Harland" (Mary Virginia Terhune, daughter of a Virginia merchant), which was selling in Richmond, according to the Wynne diary, "like hot cakes," and *Tempest and Sunshine, or Life in Kentucky* by Mary Jane Holmes, a Massachusetts woman who had moved to Kentucky.[57] Walton R. Patrick's careful studies of the reading tastes of the people of Louisiana in the period 1830–60 indicate that the public bought recent literary works rather than the Greek and Latin classics or the older British authors. The advertisements in the newspapers show that the books which were most salable were the novels of Scott, Bulwer-Lytton, Dickens, Thackeray, Disraeli, G. P. R. James, Dumas, George Sand, Eugène Sue, James Fenimore Cooper, Joseph Holt Ingraham, Caroline Lee Hentz, and Mrs. E. D. E. N. Southworth. The popular poets of the period were Byron, Tom Moore, and Feliciana Dorothea Hemans, a sentimental Northern poetess.[58]

After 1830 a new element entered the Southern book market, namely, a prejudice against Northern books because of the antislavery movement. J. W. Randolph's bookstore in Richmond, for example, advertised in the Williamsburg *Weekly Gazette,* April 24, 1856:

The ice having prevented the usual avalanche of Yankee Books, which,

[56] *Letter of Hon. Francis W. Pickens, The Crops and Condition of the Country* (Baltimore, 1866), pp. 5–6, a pamphlet in the University of Kentucky Library.

[57] Wynne Diary, October 29, 1854.

[58] Walton R. Patrick, "Literature in the Louisiana Plantation Home Prior to 1861," Ph.D. Dissertation, Louisiana State University, 1937, and "A Circulating Library of Antebellum Louisiana," *Louisiana Historical Quarterly,* XXIII (1940), 3–12.

for the most part, teach bad government and worse morals, the reading public can fall back upon the safer and purer literature of home production:

Edith Allen, or Life in Virginia, by Laurence Neville, $1. It is the best work from a Southern pen.

Grigsby, *Virginia Convention of 1776.*

Uncle Robin in His Cabin in Virginia and Tom Without One in Boston. Too much cannot be said of its true and correct picture of the Southern slaveholder.

Dew's Essay on Slavery. Timid statesmen should read these books and be satisfied of the blessings of slavery.

Beverley's *History of Virginia.*

Jefferson's *Notes on Virginia.*

Virginia Debates of 1798-9. Politicians who never read it swear by this book.

Campbell's *Colonial History of Virginia.*

Ruffin's *Agricultural Essays.* Buy it and the earth will return the compliment with a smile.[59]

Uncle Tom's Cabin, despite violent condemnation, seems to have had a widespread sale in the South. A young Northern tutor on the Galloway plantation in western North Carolina wrote in his diary in the fall of 1852 that a copy of Mrs. Stowe's novel had been brought from New York by the planter. "Mr G. likes Uncle Toms Cabin," he recorded, "but Mrs. G. is bitter against it." A few days later Mr. Galloway changed his mind and decided to burn the book. His wife had prevailed. "Mrs. G. thinks Mrs. Stowe is worse than Legree!"[60]

The greatest literary vogue in the Old South was for the novels of Sir Walter Scott. Thomas Jefferson attempted to read *Ivanhoe* (1820), but found it too artificial and boring to complete.[61] He and his generation belonged to the age of reason and of enlightenment. The new generation, on the other hand, was so entranced with the novels of the Scottish lord that Mark Twain accused it of having the "Sir Walter disease." The tremendous popularity of Scott's historical romances, *Waverley, Rob Roy,* and *Guy Mannering,* had been preceded by the publication of Jane Porter's *Scottish Chiefs* (1810), which may have prepared the way for the reception of Scott's novels. It became a

[59] Williamsburg *Weekly Gazette,* April 24, 1856, William and Mary College Library.

[60] D. D. Hall (ed.), "A Yankee Tutor in the Old South," *New England Quarterly,* XXXII (1960), 82-91.

[61] Hubbell, *The South in American Literature,* 127-128, 188-193.

perennial favorite of Southern youth; Andrew Jackson, who himself scarcely read a book, recommended its hero, William Wallace, to his nephew as a model upon which to form his character.[62]

Scott's influence on the social life of the Old South is impossible to evaluate, but it seems to have been significant.[63] The influence of books upon a society, such as *Uncle Tom's Cabin* on the North, the Scott novels on the South, and the works of the English democratic thinkers of the seventeenth and eighteenth centuries on the American revolutionists, depends on whether the seed falls upon good or stony ground. Scott's novels were read widely in the North as well as the South, but the more democratic nature of Northern society and economic conditions there were not favorable to the reception of Scott's ideas. The romantic spirit of the period affected the North somewhat differently from the South. In the Northern states, where industrialism was emerging, the spirit expressed itself in the transcendentalist movement and in social reform. In the Southern states, on the other hand, the conditions of rural life gave the romantic spirit a different direction. Plantation life, with its lonely homesteads, its monotony, its brooding quietness and closeness to nature, stimulated the social-minded individuals to frequent traveling and visiting and the introverts to escape into reverie, romantic dreams, promoting ring tournaments, and reading such novels as Scott's.[64]

Scott's novels were read principally by the upper classes, which constituted only a small part of the population. Some middle-class farm families doubtless perused his romances about lords and ladies and serfs, but it is difficult to believe that they saw any connection between medieval chivalry and their own daily lives.[65] They must have laughed at the make-believe tournaments which the aristocracy around them at times staged, just as the Kentucky farmers today laugh at the bless-

[62] Andrew Jackson to Andrew Jackson Donelson, April 16, 1820, in Bassett, *Correspondence,* III.

[63] See Rollin G. Osterweis, *Romanticism and Nationalism in the Old South* (New Haven, 1949), Chap. IV; Grace W. Landrum, "Sir Walter Scott and His Literary Rivals in the Old South," *American Literature,* II (1930), 256–276; Harrison Orians, "The Romance Ferment after Waverley," *American Literature,* III (1932), 408–431.

[64] Eaton, *Freedom of Thought in the Old South,* Chap. II.

[65] Wynne Diary, November 4, 1855. Wynne commented, concerning a tournament held in the Richmond fairgrounds, that some people had ridiculed the tournaments, "comparing them to gander pullings."

ing of the hounds before a foxhunt. Their contact with the romantic
spirit came chiefly through the florid rhetoric of Southern orators, their
unworldly religion, their folk songs, and their absorption at second hand
of the idea of "Southern honor." The love of military titles in the
South was only slightly inspired by Scott's novels. Mark Twain vastly
exaggerated the influence of these novels when he wrote, "It was Sir
Walter Scott that made every gentleman in the South a major or a
colonel, or a general or a judge, before the war; and it was he, also,
that created rank and caste down there, and also reverence for rank
and caste, and pride and pleasure in them."[66] The militia system of
the South—a great source of pleasure and companionableness in this
isolated rural society—was the real origin of the custom of conferring
military titles upon prominent citizens.

The best-seller list in the United States during the ante-bellum period contains only five authors associated with the South, and all of
them, except Poe, belonged to what Hawthorne called "the damned
mob of scribbling women."[67] The popularity of the novels of "Marion
Harland," Mary Jane Holmes, and Augusta Jane Evans of Mobile was
based on their appeal to the sentimental taste of the age and to their
moral and didactic content. Emerson, whose essays were a best seller
in 1841, as was Thoreau's *Walden* in 1854, had few readers in the
Southern states. Fredrika Bremer wrote, "It is remarkable how very
little, or not at all, the authors of the Northern states, even the best of
them, are known in the South. They are afraid of admitting their
liberal opinions in the Slave States." She found that Joel Poinsett, one
of the most cultivated of Southerners, was unacquainted with Emerson's philosophy, which, upon Miss Bremer telling him of it, he condemned as "unpractical."[68]

Indeed, the Southern mind at this period was a curious combination
of romanticism and practicality. Southerners as a whole looked with
suspicion upon the artist and the literary man. John Esten Cooke, a
young Virginia lawyer, like many other Southerners with literary aspirations, felt constrained to conceal his authorship of literary works
in order not to injure his career as a lawyer and practical man. He

[66] Samuel L. Clemens, *Life on the Mississippi,* Chap. XLVI, "Enchantments
and Enchanters."

[67] Frank L. Mott, *Golden Multitudes, the Story of the Best Sellers in the
United States* (New York, 1947), pp. 319–320.

[68] Bremer, *The Homes of the New World,* I, 298.

wrote Evert Duyckinck, editor of the New York *Literary World*, to suppress his name as author of the novel *Leatherstocking and Silk:* "Being identified as the writer of such a book would materially injure me I fear in my profession."[69] And Maunsel White, the New Orleans merchant and sugar planter, undoubtedly reflected the Southern sense of values when he peremptorily denied the request of his son, off at school, to take piano lessons. It was a waste of precious time, he declared, to "drum" on the piano, and his son should turn his attention, instead, to acquiring "manly" and useful training. He concluded his reprimand as a good Victorian father would do, saying, "Let me hear no more of pianos!"[70]

Romantic feeling in the South was displayed most clearly in the exaltation of women. Yet, as Francis Grund, the Austrian immigrant noticed, homage was often paid to women in general rather than to the particular woman.[71] Olmsted, in the upland districts of the South, observed women in sunbonnets hoeing in the fields. The Southern attitude toward women did not differ greatly from that held by Northerners. In both sections the great majority of the people scorned the woman's rights movement. Sarah and Angelina Grimké were exceptional Southern women in their adoption of feminism, but this did not occur until after they had exiled themselves from their native Charleston and joined the Quaker society in Philadelphia. In the North they encountered strong prejudice when they progressed from being abolitionists to advocates of woman's rights. When Angelina stepped out of her conventional sphere and lectured to an audience in Groton, Massachusetts, the local minister declared that "he would as soon be caught robbing a hen roost as encouraging a woman to lecture."[72] Sarah in 1838 published a feminist tract entitled *Letters on the Equality of the Sexes and the Condition of Women,* in which she pointed out that the man mingled in the world and improved himself by "the collision of intellects with cultivated minds," while the woman attended

[69] John Esten Cooke to Evert A. Duycinck, November 24, 1853, May 6, 1854, Evert A. Duycinck Papers, New York Public Library.

[70] Maunsel White to Maunsel White, Jr., April 25, 1847, Maunsel White Papers.

[71] Grund, *Aristocracy in America,* p. 40.

[72] G. H. Barnes and D. L. Dumond (eds.), *Letters of Theodore Dwight Weld, Angelina Grimké Weld and Sarah Grimké, 1822–1844* (New York, 1934), I, 430.

to domestic duties and was so dependent on her husband that she had to ask him for pin money.

Even such a prominent Southern reformer as John Hartwell Cocke strongly condemned the feminist movement. After attending the World Temperance Convention, he wrote from Saratoga on September 23, 1853, to his friend William H. McGuffey, the famous author of the *McGuffey Eclectic Readers:*

> You have doubtless seen the struggle we had with the "strong-minded women" as they call themselves in the World Temperance Convention. If you have seen the true account of the matter, you will see that we gained a perfect triumph and I believe have given a rebuke to this most impudent clique of unsexed females and rampart abolitionists which must put down the petty-coats—a least as far as their claim to take the platforms of public debate and enter into all the rough and tumble of the war of words.[73]

The professor of moral philosophy at the University of Virginia replied: "I most heartily rejoice with you in the defeat of those shameless Amazons who gave so much trouble at the World Convention—I trust and believe that it will be *final*."[74] While Northern society was being agitated by such movements as antislavery, transcendentalism, feminism, the Southern people remained virtually unmoved.[75]

Nevertheless, the Southern mind in some respects had undergone significant changes between 1790 and 1860. Travelers in this later period were impressed by the new materialistic spirit of the Southern people. In the Cotton Kingdom men were continually talking about the price of cotton and of Negroes. Cotton and slaves seemed to be an obsession that monopolized conversation and occupied all minds. There was also a restless migration farther and farther westward to exploit more fertile lands, and in the last decade before the Civil War, Texas and Arkansas had become the new El Dorado. But despite improvements in transportation and communications, the Southern people remained provincial and isolated. The new transportation system did not result in a free trade in ideas. Although businessmen were emerging

[73] John Hartwell Cocke to William H. McGuffey, September 23, 1854, Cocke Papers.

[74] William H. McGuffey to John Hartwell Cocke, October 10, 1854, Cocke Papers.

[75] See Clement Eaton, "The Resistance of the South to Northern Radicalism," *New England Quarterly*, VIII (1935), 215–231.

as a new class, they had not as yet acquired the status of the planter, the lawyer, or the politician. Indeed, the revival of prosperity in agriculture in the 1850's delayed their progress in Southern society.

The rule of the country gentleman in many parts of the South had been upset by the victory of a realistic democracy, which Beverly Tucker said had no sense of honor. No longer did moderate Virginia gentlemen lead the South, as in the days of the Virginia dynasty. The Old Dominion had sent twenty congressmen to the House of Representatives in 1800, but in 1860 it could send only fourteen. But more important than the decline of the South to a minority position within the nation was the lowering of the quality of its statesmanship. The fine qualities of the Southerner, his generous hospitality, his naturalness, his high sense of honor, could not compensate for limited vision in politics. The South had lost its poise largely as a result of the abolitionist attack.

The "sovereign people" showed little regard for minority opinion within the section. The Charleston merchant, Jacob Schirmer, recorded in his diary in 1848 an instance of it: "a man selling Birds in Broad St. made use of some expression in regard to our domestic institution —was knocked down by Mr. Geo. Walter & was then taken to the Police Office and he left here this afternoon in the Wilmington Boat."[76] Nor did the sovereign people or their leaders have that decent respect for the opinion of mankind to which Jefferson had appealed in the Declaration of Independence. Like South Africa today, the aroused South of 1860 was prepared to defy world opinion and go it alone. When Johnston J. Pettigrew made the minority report to the South Carolina legislature in 1858 against reopening the African slave trade, he said: "The opinion, then, of the outside world on slavery is entitled to less weight than upon almost any other subject, being destitute of every foundation which renders opinion respectable."[77] Though Pettigrew had had an outstanding scholastic record at the University of North Carolina and was a man of great personality, he shared the ruinous provincialism and overweening pride of South Carolina.

"Bull Run" Russell's account of an interview with Governor J. J. Pettus of Mississippi on the eve of the Civil War reveals much concerning the limitations of the Southern mind. He found the governor

[76] Jacob S. Schirmer Diary, January 1846.
[77] *Charleston Mercury,* January 11, 1858.

sitting in an office with mildewed walls and broken panes in the windows; while they were talking, various citizens walked casually through the room. The governor was a grim, blunt man who had for years hunted and trapped in the forests like Natty Bumpo or David Crockett. As he conversed with the Englishman, he dropped "a portentous plug of tobacco just outside of the spittoon, with the air of a man who wished to show he could have hit the centre if he liked." He displayed a wonderful confidence in the Southern people and announced that although England was powerful in "Eu—*rope*," "the sovereign State of Mississippi can do a great deal better without England than England can do without her."[78] He was convinced that Southern society represented the highest development of civilization. Such parochial self-esteem was not confined to Southerners, however; it was characteristic of most Americans of the period, who believed that the United States had created a democratic government and a civilization immensely superior to the decadent institutions of Europe.

The Mississippi governor typified only the dominant political mind of the South; he did not reflect the Whig outlook, the point of view of the Southern moderates. The Whigs of the 1850's prided themselves on their conservatism, a conservatism of the Burke school that believed in orderly progress. They had almost as much scorn for the extreme proslavery men as for the abolitionists. A mixed party, as all of our national parties have been, its leadership was especially responsive to men of property. The Southern Whigs opposed territorial expansion, but favored business or material progress—making the nation strong industrially by protective tariffs, federal aid to internal improvements, and a stable currency controlled by the national government. They wished to conserve the nation, though many of them believed in state rights. It is a pity that the leaders of this group in 1860 were in general old men, such as John J. Crittenden and John Bell; Southern youth belonged to the other side. After being overwhelmed during the emotional crisis that preceded the Civil War, the Whig tradition survived to become the core of the New South movement.

[78] Russell, *My Diary North and South,* p. 89.

Bibliography

MANUSCRIPTS

Library of Congress and National Archives
  American Colonization Papers
  Breckinridge Family Papers
  Jabez L. M. Curry Papers
  George Denison Papers
  Franklin Elmore Papers
  Lewis R. Gibbes Papers
  James H. Hammond Papers
  Andrew Johnson Papers I (1839–59)
  Daniel W. Lord Travel Journal
  Nathaniel Macon Papers
  Matthew Fontaine Maury Papers
  James Monette Plantation Diary
  Joel R. Poinsett Papers
  Carter G. Woodson Papers (Hiram Revels Autobiography)
  William C. Rives Papers
  Edmund Ruffin Diary
  U.S. Manuscript Censuses, 1850 and 1860
  Moses Waddel Diary
  Whitney-Burnham Papers

Alderman Library, University of Virginia
  Bremo Slave Letters
  John Hartwell Cocke Papers
  Robert L. Dabney Papers
  Richard Eppes Plantation Journal

William and Mary College Library
  Thomas R. Dew Papers

Virginia Historical Society Archives
  Hugh Blair Grigsby Papers
  Henry A. Wise Papers

West Virginia University Library
  Luke Willcox Diary

University of Kentucky Library
  James H. Atherton Diary
  Bedford Family Papers
  Buckner Family Papers
  Henry Clay Collection
  Freedman Letters from Liberia
  David Gist Papers
  Mary Austin Holley Transcripts
  Lulbegrud Baptist Church Minutes
  Means Family Papers
  Morton and Griswold (textbook publishers) Papers
  William Moody Pratt Diary
  Providence Baptist Church Minutes
  William Reynolds Journal
  Robert C. Scott, Memoranda Itineris, "Memoranda of My Visit to the
    East in 1829–30"
  Shelby Family Papers
  William Smith of Smithville, S.C., Store Ledger
  Trustee Minutes of Lexington, Kentucky
  Augustus Woodward Diary

Transylvania College Library
  Horace Holley Letters

University of North Carolina Library, Southern Collection
  John Houston Bills Diary
  Winifred Gales Reminiscences
  William Harris Garland Papers
  John Berkeley Grimball Diary
  James C. Harper Diary
  Charles A. Hentz, "My Autobiography"
  Edwin Michael Holt Papers

Daniel R. Hundley Diary
George W. Mordecai Papers
Jason Niles Diary
Benjamin F. Perry Diary
Ebenezer Pettigrew Papers
James Roach Diary
Private Diary of Ed. Ruffin
David L. Swain Diary
Maunsel White Papers (microfilm at the University of Kentucky Library)

North Carolina State Department of Archives and History
Catherine Ann Edmondston Diary
Dr. Francis J. Kron Diary in Littleton Papers
Nathaniel Macon Papers

Duke University Library (has a valuable collection of the papers of Southern
literary men)
James Thomas Jr. Papers
Henry Watson Papers
U.S. Manuscript Censuses 1850 and 1860, Schedule II (Agriculture)

University of South Carolina, South Caroliniana Library
Ball Family Papers
Micajah Clark Travel Journal
Thomas Cooper Papers
Franklin Elmore Papers
James H. Hammond Papers
James L. Petigru Papers
W. Thacher Diary

South Carolina Historical Society
Abiel Abbott Journal of a Voyage to South Carolina
Thomas B. Chaplin Plantation Journal
Stephen Ravenel Travel Journal
Jacob S. Schirmer Diary

Charleston Library Society
Mitchell King Diary

Alabama State Library
John Witherspoon DuBose Papers

Louisiana State Department of Archives
Mrs. Isaac Hilliard Diary
T. J. Knight, "Account of Newton Knight"
Thomas Affleck Papers

Tulane University Library
Bishop Kemper, "Diary of a Trip Down the Mississippi"
John McDonogh Papers
Samuel Walker, "Diary of a Louisiana Planter"

Northwestern College of Louisiana
Placide Bossier Diary (microfilm)
P. Lestant Prudhomme Diary (manuscript owned by Mrs. Irma Sompaynac, microfilm lent by Eugene P. Watson, Librarian)

Privately Owned Manuscripts
Dr. Daniel G. Brinton Diary, owned by Dr. Brinton Thompson, Trinity College, Hartford, Connecticut
W. S. Hyland Plantation Journal, Mississippi, owned by Dr. Thomas D. Clark, University of Kentucky, Lexington, Kentucky
R. A. Moen (ax salesman) Letters, owned by Dr. Thomas D. Clark
Brutus J. Clay Papers, owned by Rudolf Berle Clay of Paris, Kentucky

New York Public Library
William Little Brown Diary (typed copy)
E. A. Duyckinck Papers (containing correspondence of John Esten Cooke and John R. Thompson)

State Historical Society of Wisconsin
John McRae Letter Books

Huntington Library
John J. Cabell Papers
Lewis and Robert Hill Papers
Francis Lieber Papers
James and W. H. Lyons Papers
Joseph C. Stiles Papers

PUBLISHED CORRESPONDENCE, DIARIES, AND MEMOIRS

See also under such categories below as agriculture, slavery, and commerce and industry.

Thomas Hart Benton, *Thirty Years' View* . . . (New York, 1875), 2 vols.; Louis B. Wright and Marion Tinling (eds.), *The Secret Diary of William Byrd of Westover, 1709–1712* (Richmond, 1941); M. H. Woodfin and Marion Tinling, *Another Secret Diary of William Byrd of Westover, 1739–1741* (Richmond, 1942); John Fulton (ed.), *The Memoirs of Frederick A. P. Barnard* (New York, 1896); Elmer T. Clark (ed.), *The Journal and Letters of Francis Asbury* (Nashville, 1958), 3 vols.; R. K. Crallé (ed.), *The Works of John C. Calhoun* (New York, 1853–55), 6 vols.; J. F. Jameson (ed.), "Correspondence of John C. Calhoun," *American Historical Association Report*, II (1899); Robert L. Meriwether (ed.), *The Calhoun Papers* (Columbia, 1959—), I; Mary Boykin Chesnut, *A Diary from Dixie* (New York, 1905); Dunbar Rowland (ed.), *Official Letter Books of W. C. C. Claiborne, 1801–1816* (Madison, 1917), 6 vols.; Cassius M. Clay, *The Life of Cassius Marcellus Clay, Memoirs, Writings, and Speeches* (Cincinnati, 1886); Calvin Colton (ed.), *The Works of Henry Clay* (New York, 1857), 6 vols.; James F. Hopkins (ed.), *The Clay Papers* (Lexington, 1959–61), I and II; Victoria C. Clayton, *White and Black under the Old Regime* (Milwaukee, 1899); Theodore Clapp, *Autobiographical Sketches and Recollections during a Thirty-Five Years' Residence in New Orleans* (Boston, 1859); Dunbar Rowland (ed.), *Jefferson Davis, Constitutionalist, His Letters, Papers, and Speeches* (Jackson, Miss., 1923), 10 vols.; H. D. Farish (ed.), *Journal and Letters of Philip Vickers Fithian, 1773–1774* (Williamsburg, 1942); Philip Henry Gosse, *Letters from Alabama* (London, 1859); Larry Gara (ed.), "A New Englander's View of Plantation Life; Letters of Edwin Hall to Cyrus Woodmason," *Journal of Southern History*, XVII (1952); Henry S. Foote, *Casket of Reminiscences* (Washington, 1874); Charles E. Cauthen (ed.), *Family Letters of the Three Wade Hamptons, 1782–1901* (Columbia, 1953); A. R. Newsome (ed.), "A Miscellany from Thomas Henderson's Letter Book, 1810–1811," *North Carolina Historical Review*, VI (1929); D. H. Hall (ed.), "A Yankee Tutor in the Old South" [Charles W. Holbrook], *New England Quarterly*, XXXII (1960), 82–91; [Catherine C. Hopley], *Life in the South; from the Commencement of the War, By a Blockaded British Subject* (London, 1863), 2 vols.; Julian Boyd (ed.), *The Papers of Thomas Jefferson* (Princeton, 1950—), 15 vols. to date covering years to 1789; A. A. Lipscomb and A. L. Bergh (eds.), *The Writings of Thomas Jefferson* (Washington, 1903), 20 vols.; Robert J. Parker (ed.), "A Yankee in North Carolina, Observations of Thomas Oliver Larkin, 1821–1826," *North Carolina Historical Review*, XIV (1937); John S. Bassett (ed.), *The Correspondence of Andrew Jackson* (Washington, 1926–35), 7 vols.; Frances Anne Kemble, *Journal of a Residence on a Georgian Plantation in 1838–1839* (New York, 1863); Alvan F. Sanborn (ed.), *Reminiscences of Richard Lathers* (New York, 1909);

Everett S. Brown (ed.), "Letters from Louisiana, 1813–1814," *Mississippi Valley Historical Review*, XI (1925), 570–579; Gideon Lincecum "Autobiography," *Mississippi Historical Society Publications*, VIII (1904); W. H. Hoyt (ed.), *The Papers of Archibald De Bow Murphey* (Raleigh, 1914), 2 vols.; Vincent Nolte, *The Memoirs of Vincent Nolte or Fifty Years in Both Hemispheres* (New York, 1934); Samuel G. Stoney (ed.), "Memoirs of Frederick Adolphus Porcher," *South Carolina Historical and Genealogical Magazine*, XLVII (1946); J. G. Hamilton (ed.), *The Papers of Thomas Ruffin* (Raleigh, 1918–20), 2 vols.; John R. Shaw, *The Life and Travels of John Robert Shaw, the Well Digger* (Lexington, Ky., 1807); Mary C. Simms Oliphant *et al* (eds.), *The Letters of William Gilmore Simms* (Columbia, 1954–56), 5 vols.; Sol Smith, *Theatrical Management in the South and West for Thirty Years* (New York, 1868); Gaillard Hunt (ed.), *The First Forty Years of Washington Society Portrayed by the Family Letters of Mrs. Samuel Harrison Smith* (New York, 1906); William H. Sparks, *The Memories of Fifty Years* (Macon, 1872); Dorothy Stanley (ed.), *The Autobiography of Sir Henry Morton Stanley* (Boston, 1909); Frances Dugan and Jacqueline Bull (eds.), *Bluegrass Craftsman, Being the Reminiscences of Ebenezer Stedman, Papermaker, 1803–1885* (Lexington, 1959); Jared Sparks (ed.), *Letters and Recollections of George Washington* (New York, 1906); G. H. Barnes and D. L. Dumond (eds.), *Letters of Theodore Dwight Weld, Angelina Grimké Weld, and Sarah Grimké, 1822–1844* (New York, 1934), 2 vols.; John S. Wise, *The End of an Era* (Boston, 1902); Richard J. Hooker (ed.), *The Carolina Back Country on the Eve of the Revolution; the Journal and Other Writings of Charles Woodmason, Anglican Itinerant* (New York, 1934), 2 vols.

PUBLISHED TRAVEL ACCOUNTS

Of the following accounts, the most useful are those by the Englishmen Sir Charles Lyell, Basil Hall, James S. Buckingham, and William H. Russell; and the Northerners Solon Robinson, De Puy Van Buren, Bishop Whipple, and Frederick Law Olmsted. Despite an antislavery bias, Olmsted's books are by far the most valuable travel accounts of the Old South.

Thomas D. Clark (ed.), *Travels in the Old South, A Bibliography* (Norman, Okla., 1956–59), 3 vols., is indispensable. E. S. Abdy, *Journal of a Residence and Tour in the United States, 1833–1834* (London 1835), 3 vols.; Robert Barclay Allardice, *Agricultural Tour in the United States and Upper Canada* (Edinburgh, 1842); C. D. Arfwedson, *The United States and Canada* (London, 1834), 2 vols.; Henry Barnard, "The South Atlantic States in 1833 as Seen by a New Englander," edited by Bernard C. Steiner, *Maryland Historical Mazagine*, XIII (1918); John Bernard, *Retrospections of*

America, 1797–1811 (New York, 1887); Bernhard, Duke of Saxe-Weimar Eisenach, *Travels through North America during the Years 1825 and 1826* (Philadelphia, 1828); Fredrika Bremer, *The Homes of the New World, Impressions of America* (New York, 1853), 2 vols.; W. N. Blane, *Excursion through the United States and Canada during the Years 1822–23* (London, 1824); H. M. Brackenridge, *Views of Louisiana* (Baltimore, 1817); William Cullen Bryant, "A Tour of the South," Parke Godwin (ed.); *Prose Writings of William Cullen Bryant* (New York, 1884), 2 vols.; A. Candler, *A Summary View of America . . . by an Englishman* (London, 1824); Herbert A. Kellar (ed.), "A Journey through the South in 1836: Diary of James D. Davidson," *Journal of Southern History,* I (1935); John Davis, *Travels in the United States* (New York, 1803); T. F. McDermott (ed.), "Diary of Charles De Hault De Lassus from New Orleans to St. Louis, 1836," *Louisiana Historical Quarterly,* XXX (1944), 359–438; Gottfried Duden, *A Report of a Journey in the Western States of North America,* translated by William G. Bek (St. Louis, 1919); William Faux, *Memorable Days in America* [1818–20] (London, 1823), also vols. XI–XII in R. S. Thwaites, *Early Western Travels 1748–1846* (Cleveland, 1904–7), 32 vols.; G. W. Featherstonhaugh, *Excursion through the Slave States* (London, 1844), 2 vols.; Timothy Flint, *Recollections of the Last Ten Years Passed in Occasional Residence and Journey in the Valley of the Missisippi* (Boston, 1826); Elias P. Fordham, *Personal Narrative of Travels in Virginia, Maryland, Pennsylvania, Ohio, Indiana, Kentucky* (Cleveland, 1906); George J. Joyaux (ed.), "Forest's Voyage aux États Unis de Amérique en 1831," *Louisiana Historical Quarterly,* XXXIX (1956); T. C. Grattan, *Civilized America* (London, 1859), 2 vols.; *The Journals of Welcome Arnold Greene; Journey in the South,* edited by Alice E. Smith (Madison, 1957); Francis J. Grund, *Aristocracy in America* (New York, 1959); Captain Basil Hall, *Travels in North America in the Years 1827–28* (Edinburgh, 1829), 3 vols.; Mrs. Margaret [Basil] Hall, *The Aristocratic Journey,* edited by Una Pope-Hennessey (New York, 1931); Thomas Hamilton, *Men and Manners in America* (Philadelphia, 1833), 2 vols.; Adam Hodgson, *Letters from North America . . .* (London, 1824), 2 vols.; Isaac Holmes, *An Account of the United States of America during a Residence of Four Years* (London, 1823); Mathilda C. F. Houston, *Texas and the Gulf of Mexico or Yachting in the New World* (Philadelphia, 1845); [William Kingsford] *Impressions of the West and South during a Six Weeks' Holiday* (Toronto, 1858); Charles Lanman, *Letters from the Alleghany Mountains* (New York, 1849); Benjamin H. Latrobe, *The Journal of Latrobe* (New York, 1905); Augustus Levasseur, *Lafayette in America, 1824 and 1825, or Journal of Travels* (New York, 1829), 2 vols.; *Letters on the Condition of Kentucky in 1825,* edited by Earl G. Swem (New York, 1916); Fletcher Green (ed.), *The Lides Go South and West* (Columbia, 1952); Charles

Lyell, *Travels in North America* (New York, 1845), 2 vols.; Charles Lyell, *A Second Visit to the United States* (New York, 1849), 2 vols.; Alexander MacKay, *The Western World* (Philadelphia, 1849), 2 vols.; Charles MacKay, *Sketches of a Tour in the United States and Canada* (London, 1859); J. M. Mackie, *From Cape Cod To Dixie and the Tropics* (New York, 1864); Harriet Martineau, *Society in America* (London, 1837), 3 vols., and *Retrospect of Western Travel* (London, 1838), 3 vols.; Frederick Marryat, *A Diary in America* (London, 1839), 3 vols.; John Melish, *Travels in the United States* (Philadelphia, 1812); F. A. Michaux, "Journal," in Thwaites, *Early Western Travels,* III; Hon. Mathilda Amelia Murray, *Letters from the United States, Cuba, and Canada* (New York, 1856); Charles Augustus Murray, *Travels in North America during the Years 1834, 1835, and 1836* (London, 1839), 2 vols.; Henry A. Murray, *Lands of the Slave and the Free* (London, 1855), 2 vols.; Frederick Law Olmsted, *A Journey in the Seaboard Slave States* (New York, 1856), also a later edition, 2 vols. (New York, 1904), *A Journey in the Back Country* (New York, 1860), *A Journey through Texas, or a Saddle Trip on the Southwestern Frontier* (New York, 1857); and *The Cotton Kingdom by Frederick Law Olmsted,* edited by Arthur M. Schlesinger (New York, 1953); James K. Paulding, *Letters from the South* (New York, 1816), 2 vols.; Richard Parkinson, *Tour in America* (London, 1805); John Palmer, *Journal of Travels in the United States and Canada* (London, 1818); F. M. Perrin du Lac, *Voyage dans les deux Louisianes, Collections of Modern Voyages* (London, 1807), VI; Tyrone Power, *Impressions of America* (Philadelphia, 1836), 2 vols.; Herbert A. Kellar (ed.), *Solon Robinson, Pioneer and Agriculturalist* (Indianapolis, 1936), 2 vols.; Oswald Mueller (ed.), *Roemer's Texas 1845–1847* (San Antonio, 1935); Francis, duc de la Rochefoucald-Liancourt, *Travels through the United States of America* (London, 1799), 2 vols.; Anne Royall, *Mrs. Royall's Southern Tour* (Washington 1830), 2 vols.; William H. Russell, *My Diary North and South* (Boston, 1863); Robert Russell, *North America, its Agriculture and Climate* (Edinburgh, 1857); Charles Sealsfield, *The Americans as They are Described in a Tour through the Valley of the Mississippi* (London, 1828); William Gilmore Simms, "Notes of a Small Tourist," in Oliphant (ed.), *Letters of William Gilmore Simms,* I; "Arthur Singleton Esq." [pseudonym of Henry C. Knight], *Letters from the South and West* (Boston, 1824); Christian Schultz Jr., *Travels on an Inland Voyage* (New York, 1810); James Stirling, *Letters from the Slave States* (London, 1857); James Stuart, *Three Years in North America* (Edinburgh, 1833), 2 vols.; Lady Emmeline Stuart-Wortley, *Travels in the United States . . . during 1849–1850* (New York, 1851); Louis F. Tasistro, *Random Shots and Southern Breezes* (New York, 1842); George W. Pierson (ed.), *Tocqueville and Beaumont in America* (New York, 1938); Henry Reeve (ed.), *Democracy in America, by De Tocqueville* (New

York, 1946); "A Tourist's Description of Louisiana in 1860," edited by Walter Pritchard, *Louisiana Historical Quarterly*, XXI (1938); Frances Trollope, *Domestic Manners of the Americans* (London, 1832), 2 vols.; Isabella Trotter, *First Impressions of the New World* (London, 1859); Mark Twain [Samuel L. Clemens], *Life on the Mississippi* (Boston, 1883); A. De Puy Van Buren, *Jottings of a Year's Sojourn in the South* (Battle Creek, Mich., 1859); Archibald Henderson (ed.), *Washington's Southern Tour* (Boston, 1923); Isaac Weld, Jr., *Travels through the States of North America* (London, 1799), 2 vols.; L. B. Shippee (ed.), *Bishop Whipple's Southern Diary, 1843-1844* (Minneapolis, 1937).

NEWSPAPERS AND PERIODICALS

The most influential newspapers of the Old South were the Baltimore *Sun;* Washington *National Intelligencer;* Richmond *Enquirer, Whig,* and *Examiner;* Norfolk *Southern Argus;* Alexandria *Gazette;* Williamsburg *Virginia Gazette;* Wheeling *Intelligencer;* Charleston, Va., *Kanawha Republican;* Raleigh *North Carolina Register,* and *North Carolina Standard;* Salisbury *Western Carolinian;* Memphis *Daily Avalanche;* Nashville *Union* and *Republican Banner;* Knoxville *Whig;* Louisville *Journal* and *Courier;* Frankfort *Argus of Western America* and *Commonwealth;* Lexington, Ky., *Gazette* and *Observer and Reporter;* Charleston, S.C., *Courier* and *Mercury;* Savannah *Republican;* Augusta *State Rights Sentinel;* Montgomery *Advertiser* and *Mail;* Mobile *Register;* New Orleans *Picayune, Bee, Crescent* and *True Delta;* Baton Rouge *Daily Comet;* Natchez *Free Trader;* Woodville, Miss., *Republican;* Jackson *Mississippian;* Austin, Tex., *State Gazette;* St. Louis *Missouri Republican* and *Missouri Democrat.*

The leading agricultural papers were the Petersburg *Farmers' Register;* Baltimore *American Farmer;* Montgomery *American Cotton Planter;* Columbus *Soil of the South;* Augusta *Southern Cultivator;* Charleston *Southern Agriculturist.* The most successful magazines of the Old South were the literary *Southern Review,* Charleston; *Southern Literary Messenger,* Richmond; *Southern Quarterly Review,* Charleston; *The Magnolia,* Charleston; *Russell's Magazine,* Charleston; *Southern Rose,* Charleston; *Southern Rosebud,* Charleston; and the industrial and agricultural *De Bow's Review,* New Orleans; *Niles' Weekly Register,* Baltimore.

GENERAL WORKS

A perceptive analysis of interpretations of Southern history is found in Wendell H. Stephenson, *The South Lives in History* (Baton Rouge, 1955). The most comprehensive history of the South is Wendell H. Stephenson and

E. M. Coulter (eds.), *History of the South* (Baton Rouge, 1949—), 10 vols., which include Charles S. Sydnor, *The Development of Southern Sectionalism 1819–1848,* and Avery O. Craven, *The Growth of Southern Nationalism, 1848–1861.* Avery Craven, *The Coming of the Civil War* (New York, 1942), and Allan Nevins, *The Ordeal of the Union* (New York, 1947), 2 vols., have valuable chapters on the South and slavery. One-volume accounts that combine political and social history are R. S. Cotterill, *The Old South* (Glendale, 1939); W. B. Hesseltine and D. L. Smiley, *The South in American History* (rev. ed., Indianapolis, 1960); Francis B. Simkins, *A History of the South* (rev. ed., New York, 1953); and Clement Eaton, *A History of the Old South* (New York, 1949). U. B. Phillips, *Life and Labor in the Old South* (Boston, 1929), concentrates on the large plantation and the institution of slavery. C. Vann Woodward, *The Burden of Southern History* (Baton Rouge, 1960), is a thoughtful interpretation of the unique qualities of the South.

AGRICULTURE

Lewis C. Gray, *History of Agriculture in the Southern United States to 1860* (New York, 1941), is a classic in its field. U. B. Phillips, *Life and Labor in the Old South* (Boston, 1929), and Paul W. Gates, *The Farmer's Age: Agriculture 1815–1860* (New York, 1960), Chaps. 5–7, are especially good for the study of the staple crops of the South. More specialized studies are Avery O. Craven, *Soil Exhaustion as a Factor in the Agricultural History of Virginia and Maryland, 1606–1860* (Urbana, 1925); see also U. B. Phillips (ed.), *Plantation and Frontier Documents, 1649–1863* (Cleveland, 1909), 2 vols.; J. C. Robert, *The Tobacco Kingdom, Plantation, Market and Factory in Virginia and North Carolina, 1800–1860* (Durham, 1938); Nannie M. Tilley, *The Bright Tobacco Industry, 1860–1929* (Chapel Hill, 1948); John Taylor, *Arator* (Petersburg, Va., 1818); Avery O. Craven, *Edmund Ruffin, Southerner . . .* (New York, 1932); Kathleen Bruce, "Virginia Agricultural Decline to 1860: A Fallacy," *Agricultural History,* VI (1932), 3–13; Cornelius O. Cathey, *Agricultural Developments in North Carolina, 1783–1860* (Chapel Hill, 1956); Bennett H. Wall, "Ebenezer Pettigrew; an Economic Study of an Ante-Bellum Planter," Ph.D. Dissertation, University of North Carolina, 1947; Emmett B. Fields, "The Agricultural Population of Virginia, 1850–1860, Ph.D. Dissertation, Vanderbilt University, 1954; Richard Troutman, "The Social and Economic Structure of Kentucky Agriculture, 1850–1860," Ph.D. Dissertation, University of Kentucky, 1958; James F. Hopkins, *A History of the Hemp Industry in Kentucky* (Lexington, 1951); Paul C. Henlein, *Cattle Kingdom in the Ohio Valley, 1783–1860* (Lexington, 1959); J. S. Bassett (ed.), *The Westover Journal of John A. Selden* (Northhampton, 1931), and *The Plantation Overseer as Revealed in His Letters*

(Northampton, 1925); J. C. Bonner, "The Plantation Overseer and Southern Nationalism," *Agricultural History,* XIX (1945), 1–11; J. C. Bonner, "Genesis of Agricultural Reform in the Cotton Belt," *Journal of Southern History,* IX (1943), 473–500; Jeannette Mirsky and Allan Nevins, *The World of Eli Whitney* (New York, 1952); Herbert Weaver, *Mississippi Farmers, 1850–1860* (Nashville, 1945); John H. Moore, *Agriculture in Ante-Bellum Mississippi* (New York, 1958); Alfred G. Smith, Jr., *Economic Readjustment of an Old Cotton State, South Carolina, 1820–1860* (Columbia, 1958); Charles S. Davis, *The Cotton Kingdom in Alabama* (Montgomery, 1939); Weymouth T. Jordan, *Hugh Davis and His Alabama Plantation* (University, Ala., 1948), and *Ante-Bellum Alabama, Town and Country* (Tallahassee, 1957); Duncan C. Heyward, *Seed From Madagascar* (Chapel Hill, 1937); Arney R. Childs (ed.), *Rice Planter and Sportsman, The Recollections of J. Motte Alston, 1821–1909* (Columbia, 1953); E. Merton Coulter, *Thomas Spalding of Sapelo* (University, La., 1940); Arney R. Childs (ed.), *Planters and Businessmen: the Guignard Family of South Carolina 1795–1930* (Columbia, 1957); Albert V. House, *Planter Management and Capitalism in Ante-Bellum Georgia: The Journal of Hugh Frazer Grant, Rice Grower* (New York, 1954); James H. Easterby, *The South Carolina Rice Plantation as Revealed in the Papers of Robert F. W. Allston* (Chicago, 1945); J. Carlyle Sitterson, *Sugar Country, the Cane Sugar Industry in the South, 1753–1950* (Lexington, 1953); Charles H. Moffatt, "Charles Tait, Planter, Politician, and Scientist of the Old South," *Journal of Southern History,* XIV (1948); U. B. Phillips, "The Origin and Growth of the Southern Black Belts," *American Historical Review,* XI (July, 1906), 798–816; Barnes Lathrop, "The Pugh Plantations, 1860–1865; a Study of Life in Lower Louisiana," Ph.D. Dissertation, University of Texas, 1946; J. Carlyle Sitterson, "The McCollams; a Planter Family of the Old and New South," *Journal of Southern History,* VI (1940), 347–367, "The William J. Minor Plantations: A Study in Ante-Bellum Absentee Ownership," *ibid.,* IX (1943), 59–74, "Magnolia Plantation, 1852–1862; a Decade of a Louisiana Sugar Estate," *Mississippi Valley Historical Review,* XXV (1939), 197–211; "Lewis Thompson and his Louisiana Plantation, 1848–1888: A Study in Absentee Ownership," in Fletcher M. Green (ed.), *Essays in Southern History* (Chapel Hill, 1949); Wendell H. Stephenson, "A Quarter-Century of a Mississippi Plantation: Eli J. Capell of Pleasant Hill," *Mississippi Valley Historical Review,* XXIII (1936); Frank L. Owsley, *Plain Folk of the Old South* (Baton Rouge, 1949); Blanche Henry Clark, *The Tennessee Yeoman, 1840–1860* (New York, 1941); W. T. Jordan, "The Elisha F. King Family, Planters of Alabama Black Belt," *Agricultural History,* XIX (July, 1945), 152–162; H. L. Coles, "Some Notes on Slave Ownership and Land Ownership in Louisiana, 1850–1860," *Journal of Southern History,* IX

(1943), 380–394; P. S. Postell, "John Hampden Randolph, a Louisiana Planter," *Louisiana Historical Quarterly*, XXV (1942), 140–223; Fabian Linden, "Economic Democracy in the Slave South; an Appraisal of Some Recent Views," *Journal of Negro History*, XXXI (1946), 140–189; Fletcher Green, *The Lides Go South and West* (Columbia, 1952); Susan D. Smedes, *Memorials of a Southern Planter* (Baltimore, 1887), delightful, but romantically colored; E. M. Coulter, "A Century of a Georgia Plantation," *Mississippi Valley Historical Review*, XVI (1929), 334–336; W. T. Jordan, "The Peruvian Guano Gospel in the Old South," *Agricultural History*, XXIV (1950), 211–221; Donald L. Kemmerer, "The Pre-Civil War South's Leading Crop: Corn," *Agricultural History*, XXIII (1949), 236–239. Valuable material on agriculture can be found in the manuscript censuses of 1850 and 1860, Schedule II; in the travel accounts, particularly those of Solon Robinson and Olmsted; *De Bow's Review;* and in the various studies of slavery.

SLAVERY AND THE NEGRO

Among the more significant studies of Southern slavery are U. B. Phillips, *American Negro Slavery* (New York, 1929), which presents the more favorable aspects, and Kenneth Stampp, *The Peculiar Institution: Slavery in the Ante-Bellum South* (New York, 1956), which is highly critical. A useful general survey is provided by John Hope Franklin, *From Slavery to Freedom, A History of American Negroes* (New York, 1947), and valuable accounts are to be found in Gray, *History of Agriculture in the Southern United States,* and Phillips, *Life and Labor in the Old South;* B. A. Botkin, *Lay My Burden Down, A Folk History of Slavery* (Chicago, 1945), presents testimony of old slaves collected in the 1930's; Frederick Douglass, *Narrative of the Life of . . . an American Slave* (Boston, 1845), is an account by the most distinguished Negro of his period of his personal experience with slavery. The history of the African slave trade is told in W. E. B. DuBois, *Suppression of the African Slave Trade to the United States of America, 1638–1870* (Cambridge, Mass., 1896), and Elizabeth Donnan, *Documents Illustrative of the History of the Slave Trade to America* (Washington, 1930–35); and of the domestic slave trade in Frederic Bancroft, *Slave-Trading in the Old South* (Baltimore, 1931), and Wendell H. Stephenson, *Isaac Franklin, Slave Trader and Planter of the Old South* (University, La., 1938). Slavery in the several states is treated in James C. Ballagh, *A History of Slavery in Virginia* (Baltimore, 1902); Charles S. Sydnor, *Slavery in Mississippi* (New York, 1933); Harrison A. Trexler, *Slavery in Missouri, 1804–1865* (Baltimore, 1914); R. B. Flanders, *Plantation Slavery in Georgia* (Chapel Hill, 1933); Rosser H. Taylor, *Slave-holding in North Carolina; an Economic View* (Chapel Hill, 1926); John S. Bassett, *Slavery in the State of North Carolina* (Baltimore, 1899); V. Alton

Moody, "Slavery on Louisiana Sugar Plantations," *Louisiana Historical Quarterly,* VII (1927); James B. Sellers, *Slavery in Alabama* (University, Ala., 1950); J. Winston Coleman, Jr., *Slavery Times in Kentucky* (Chapel Hill, 1940); Orville Taylor, *Negro Slavery in Arkansas* (Durham, 1958); and Chase C. Mooney, *Slavery in Tennessee* (Bloomington, 1957). The slave code is analyzed by a Northern student, J. C. Hurd, in *The Law of Freedom and Bondage in the United States* (Boston, 1858–62), 2 vols., and a southern judge, Thomas R. R. Cobb, *Inquiry into the Law of Negro Slavery* (Savannah, 1848); see also Helen T. Catterall (ed.), *Judicial Cases Concerning American Slavery and the Negro* (Washington, 1926–36), 4 vols. Some of the best sources for the study of Southern slavery are the travel accounts, notably those by F. L. Olmsted, Sir Charles Lyell, and Solon Robinson. Also plantation journals give realistic pictures of slavery, notably U. B. Phillips and J. D. Glunt (eds.), *Florida Plantation Records* (St. Louis, 1927), and Edwin Davis, *Plantation Life in the Florida Parishes of Louisiana.* Particular aspects of slavery are presented in Herbert Aptheker, *Negro Slave Revolts, 1526–1860* (New York, 1939), extremely exaggerated; W. S. Drewry, *The Southampton Insurrection* (Washington, 1900); Joseph C. Carroll, *Slave Insurrections in the United States, 1800–1865* (Boston, 1938); Harvey Wish, "American Slave Insurrections before 1861," *Journal of Negro History,* XXII (1937), 299–320; Carter G. Woodson, *The Education of the Negro Prior to 1861* (New York, 1915), and *The Mind of the Negro as Reflected in Letters* (Washington, 1926); Bennett H. Wall, "Medical Care of Ebenezer Pettigrew's Slaves," *Mississippi Valley Historical Review,* XXXVII (1950), 451–470; William D. Postell, *The Health of Slaves on Southern Plantations* (Baton Rouge, 1951); Clement Eaton, "Slave-Hiring in the Upper South; a Step toward Freedom," *Mississippi Valley Historical Review,* XLVI (1960), 663–678; H. M. Henry, *The Police Control of the Slave in South Carolina* (Emory, Va., 1914); C. G. Woodson "Negro Owners of Slaves," *Journal of Negro History,* XXIX (1944), 109–125; Luther P. Jackson, *Free Negro Labor and Property Holding in Virginia, 1830–1860* (New York, 1921); E. L. Fox, *The American Colonization Society 1817–1840* (Baltimore, 1919); Bell I. Wiley, *Southern Negroes 1861–1865* (New Haven, 1938); Larry Gara, "The Liberty Line; the Legend of the Underground Railroad" (Lexington, Ky., 1961); Wilbur Siebert, *The Underground Railroad from Slavery to Freedom* (New York, 1898); John Hope Franklin, *The Free Negro in North Carolina, 1790–1860* (Chapel Hill, 1943); John H. Russell, *The Free Negro in Virginia 1619–1865* (Baltimore, 1913); Merton England, "The Free Negro in Ante-Bellum Tennessee," *Journal of Southern History,* IX (1943); Clement Eaton, "A Dangerous Pamphlet in the Old South," *Journal of Southern History,* II (1936), 1–12, and "Mob-Violence in the Old South," *Mississippi Valley Historical Review,* XXIX (1942); W. R. Hogan and E. W. Davis, *William John-*

son's *Natchez, the Ante-Bellum Diary of a Free Negro* (Baton Rouge, 1951);
E. M. Lander, "Slave Labor in South Carolina Cotton Mills," *Journal of Negro History,* XXXIII (1953), 161–173; Richard B. Morris, "The Measure of Bondage in the Slave States," *Mississippi Valley Historical Review,* XLI (1954), 230–240; R. R. Russel, "The General Effects of Slavery Upon Southern Economic Progress," *Journal of Southern History,* IV (1938), 34–54, and *Ante Bellum Studies in Slavery, Politics, and the Railroads* (Kalamazoo, Mich., 1960); Lorenzo D. Turner, *Africanisms in the Gullah Dialect* (Chicago, 1949); Gunnar Myrdal, *The American Dilemma* (New York, 1944), 2 vols.; Melville Herskovits, *The Myth of the Negro Past* (New York, 1941); M. Crum, *Gullah: Negro Life on the Carolina Sea Islands* (Durham, 1940). The argument whether Southern slavery was profitable or not is debated by T. P. Govan, "Was Plantation Slavery Profitable?" *Journal of Southern History,* VIII (1942), 513–535; R. W. Smith, "Was Slavery Unprofitable in the Ante-Bellum South?" *Agricultural History,* XX (1946), 62–64; and Alfred Conrad and John R. Meyer, "The Economics of Slavery in the Ante-Bellum South," *Journal of Political Economy,* LXVI (1958), 95–130. The psychological effects of slavery on the Negro are considered by Stanley Elkins, *Slavery, A Problem in American Institutional and Intellectual Life* (Chicago, 1959); Frank Tannenbaum, *Slave and Citizen, the Negro in the Americas* (New York, 1947); William Stanton, *The Leopard's Spots; Scientific Attitudes toward Race in America* (Chicago, 1959); and W. F. Allen *et al., Slave Songs of the United States* (New York, 1867). Important sources of the proslavery argument are *Pro-Slavery Arguments as Maintained by the Most Distinguished Writers of the Southern States* (Charleston, 1852); E. N. Elliott (ed.), *Cotton Is King and Pro-Slavery Arguments* (Augusta, 1860); and *De Bow's Review.* W. S. Jenkins, *Pro-Slavery Thought in the Old South* (Chapel Hill, 1935), is a good survey of the defense of slavery. George Fitzhugh, *Sociology for the South, or the Failure of Free Society* (Richmond, 1854), and *Cannibals All; or Slaves Without Masters* (Richmond, 1857), represents the extreme in proslavery defense. William J. Grayson, *The Hireling and the Slave, Chicora, and Other Poems* (Charleston, 1856), attacks Northern wage slavery and defends patriarchal character of slavery. Henry Hughes, *A Treatise on Sociology* (Philadelphia, 1859), and James D. B. De Bow, *The Interest in Slavery of the Southern Non-Slaveholder* (Charleston, 1860), are important works defending slavery. Two good biographies of outstanding protagonists for slavery are Harvey Wish, *George Fitzhugh, Propagandist of the Old South* (Baton Rouge, 1943), and Otis C. Skipper, *J. D. B. De Bow, Magazinist of the Old South* (Athens, 1958). Richard N. Current, "John C. Calhoun, Philosopher of Reaction," *Antioch Review* (Summer, 1943), 223–234, and Calhoun's works, edited by Crallé, deal with the political

defense of slavery. Censorship of antislavery publications is discussed by Clement Eaton in "Censorship of the Southern Mails," *American Historical Review,* XLVIII (1943), 266–280, and John S. Ezell, "A Southern Education for Southrons," *Journal of Southern History,* XVII (1951), 303–327. Antislavery sentiments are studied in Louis Filler, *The Crusade against Slavery, 1830–1860* (New York, 1960), and Dwight L. Dumond, *The Anti-Slavery Movement in the United States* (Ann Arbor, 1961). Clement Eaton, *Freedom of Thought in the Old South* (Durham, 1940); Joseph C. Robert, *The Road from Monticello, a Study of the Virginia Slavery Debate of 1832* (Durham, 1941); Glover Moore, *The Missouri Controversy 1819–1821* (Lexington, 1953); Asa E. Martin, *The Anti-Slavery Movement in Kentucky Prior to 1850* (Louisville, 1918); L. Minor Blackford, *Mine Eyes Have Seen the Glory, The Story of Mary Berkeley Minor Blackford* (Cambridge, 1954); Frank Freidel, *Francis Lieber, Nineteenth Century Liberal* (Baton Rouge, 1947); and Ralph L. Ketcham, "The Dictates of Conscience: Edward Coles and Slavery," *Virginia Quarterly Review,* XXXVI (Winter, 1960), 46–62, all discuss aspects of antislavery sentiment in the South. The most notable published attacks on slavery made by Southerners in the nineteenth century were Henry Ruffner, *An Address to the People of West Virginia, Shewing that Slavery is Injurious to the Public Welfare* (Lexington, 1847); Daniel R. Goodloe, *An Inquiry into the Causes which have Retarded the Accumulation of Wealth and Increase of Population in the Southern States* (Washington, 1846); Hinton Rowan Helper, *The Impending Crisis of the South, and How to Meet It* (New York, 1857); and Cassius Marcellus Clay, *The Life of Cassius Marcellus Clay, Memoirs, Writings, Speeches* (Cincinnati, 1886).

COMMERCE AND INDUSTRY

Transportation in the Southern states is discussed in Louis C. Hunter, *Steamboats on the Western Waters* (Cambridge, 1949), an excellent study; W. F. Dunaway, *History of the James River and Kanawha Company* (New York, 1922); Ulrich B. Phillips, *A History of Transportation in the Eastern Cotton Belt to 1860* (New York, 1908); and Robert C. Black, III, *The Railroads of the Confederacy* (Chapel Hill, 1952). The merchants of the South are presented in *De Bow's Review,* January, 1850–April, 1853, "Gallery of Industry and Enterprise"; William T. Childs, *John McDonogh, His Life and Work* (Baltimore, 1939); Lewis E. Atherton, *The Pioneer Merchant in Mid-America* (Columbia, Mo., 1939) and *The Southern Country Store* (New York, 1949); and Thomas D. Clark, *Pills, Petticoats, and Plows: The Southern Country Store* (Indianapolis, 1944), which is largely devoted to the mercantile business after 1865. The cotton trade is ably described in Robert G. Albion, *The Rise of New York Port, 1815–1860* (New York, 1939), and

Charles G. Summersell, *Mobile, History of a Seaport Town* (University, Ala., 1949); see also Matthew B. Hammond, *The Cotton Industry* (New York, 1897); Ralph H. Haskins, "The Cotton Factor, 1800–1860, a Study in Southern Economic and Social History," Ph.D. Dissertation, University of California, 1956), and "Planter and Cotton Factor in the Old South: Some Areas of Friction," *Agricultural History,* XXIX (1955), 1–14; A. H. Stone, "The Cotton Factorage System of the Southern States," *American Historical Review,* XX (1915), 557–665; J. H. Easterby, "The South Carolina Rice Factor as Revealed in the Papers of Robert F. W. Allston," *Journal of Southern History,* VII (1941), 160–172, and *The South Carolina Rice Plantation as Revealed in the Papers of Robert F. W. Allston* (Chicago, 1945). The most important studies on banking in the Southern states are Bray Hammond, *Banks and Politics in America from the Revolution to the Civil War* (Princeton, 1957); R. W. Hidy, *The House of Baring in American Trade and Finance* (Cambridge, Mass., 1949); Charles S. Sydnor, *The Development of Southern Sectionalism, 1819–1848* (Baton Rouge, 1948); T. P. Govan, "The Banking and Credit System in Georgia, 1810–1860," *Journal of Southern History,* IV (1938), 164–184; John C. Brown, *A Hundred Years of American Banking* (New York, 1909); J. D. B. De Bow, *The Industrial Resources of the Southern and Western States* (New Orleans, 1852–56), 2 vols.; R. C. McGrane, *Foreign Bondholders and American State Debts* (New York, 1935); Joseph H. Parks, *Felix Grundy, Champion of Democracy* (Baton Rouge, 1940); Leland H. Jenks, *The Migration of British Capital to 1875* (New York, 1927); Frank R. Kent, *The Story of Alexander Brown and Sons* (Baltimore, 1925). Mining in the South is described in Fletcher Green, "Gold Mining; a Forgotten Industry of Ante-Bellum North Carolina," *North Carolina Historical Review,* XIV (1937), 1–19, 135–155; E. M. Coulter, *Auraria, the Story of a Georgia Gold-Mining Town* (Athens, 1956); R. E. Barclay, *Ducktown Back in Raht's Time* (Chapel Hill, 1946); Lester J. Cappon, "Trend of the Southern Iron Industry under Plantation Management," *Journal of Economics and Business History,* II, 353–381; J. W. Coleman, Jr., "Old Kentucky Iron Furnaces," *Filson Club History Quarterly,* XXXI (1959), 227–247; Francis R. Holland, "Three Virginia Iron Companies, 1825–1865," M.A. Thesis, University of Texas, 1958; Kathleen Bruce, *Virginia Iron Manufacture in the Slave Era* (New York, 1930). The history of Southern manufactures is described by Adelaide Fries, "One Hundred Years of Textiles in Salem," *North Carolina Historical Review,* XXVII (1950), 1–19; Broadus Mitchell, *William Gregg, Factory Master of the Old South* (Chapel Hill, 1941); Richard W. Griffin and D. W. Standard, "The Cotton Textile Industry in Ante-Bellum North Carolina," *North Carolina Historical Review,* XXXIV (1957), and Griffin, "The Origins of the Industrial Revolution in Georgia; Cotton Textiles, 1810–1865," *Georgia Historical Quarterly,* XLII

(1958); James F. Hopkins, *A History of the Hemp Industry in Kentucky* (Lexington, 1951); Joseph C. Robert, *The Tobacco Kingdom, Plantation, Market, and Factory in Virginia and North Carolina, 1800–1860* (Durham, 1938); William T. Hutchinson, *Cyrus Hall McCormick* (New York, 1930–35), 2 vols.; Philip G. Davidson, "Industrialism in the South," *South Atlantic Quarterly*, XXVII (1928), 405; Herbert Collins, "The Southern Industrial Gospel before 1860," *Journal of Southern History*, XII (1946), 386–402; A. R. Childs, *Planters and Businessmen, the Guignard Family of South Carolina, 1795–1930* (Columbia, 1957). For the influence of sectionalism on trade, see R. R. Russel, *Economic Aspects of Southern Sectionalism, 1840–1861* (Urbana, Ill., 1924); P. S. Foner, *Business and Slavery, the New York Merchants and the Irrepressible Conflict* (Chapel Hill, 1941); Herbert Wender, *Southern Commercial Conventions 1837–1859* (Baltimore, 1930); Thomas P. Kettell, *Southern Wealth and Northern Profits* (New York, 1860); Weymouth T. Jordan, *Rebels in the Making: Planters' Conventions and Southern Propaganda* (Tuscaloosa, 1958); and E. Q. Hawk, *Economic History of the South* (New York, 1934).

SOUTHERN SOCIETY AND CULTURE

Daniel R. Hundley, *Social Relations in Our Southern States* (New York, 1860), was a pioneer attempt to analyze the social structure of the South. Other primary works are George Fitzhugh, *Sociology for the South* (Richmond, 1854), and *Cannibals All, or Slaves without Masters* (Richmond, 1857); Hinton Rowan Helper, *The Impending Crisis of the South* (New York, 1857); and Josiah C. Nott, *Types of Mankind* (Philadelphia, 1854). Modern studies include R. B. Vance, *Human Geography of the South* (Chapel Hill, 1932); F. P. Gaines, *The Southern Plantation: a Study in the Development and Accuracy of a Tradition* (New York, 1925); Everett Dick, *The Dixie Frontier* (New York, 1948); Frank L. Owsley, *Plain Folk of the Old South* (Baton Rouge, 1949); Blanche Henry Clark, *The Tennessee Yeomen, 1840–1860* (Nashville, 1942); William E. Dodd, *The Cotton Kingdom* (New Haven, 1921); Guion G. Johnson, *Ante-Bellum North Carolina, A Social History* (Chapel Hill, 1937); F. Garvin Davenport, *Ante-Bellum Kentucky, a Social History, 1800–1860* (Oxford, Ohio, 1943); M. C. Boyd, *Alabama in the Fifties* (New York, 1937); Wilbur I. Cash, *The Mind of the South* (New York, 1941); Clement Eaton, "Class Differences in the Old South," *Virginia Quarterly Review* (Summer, 1957); J. C. Bonner, "Profile of a Late Ante-Bellum Community," *American Historical Review*, XLIX (1944); U. B. Phillips, "The Central Theme of Southern History," *American Historical Review*, XXXIV (1928), 30–43; Roger W. Shugg, *Origins of Class Struggle in Louisiana* (University, La., 1939); C. S. Sydnor, *A Gentleman of Old*

Natchez: Benjamin L. C. Wailes (Durham, 1938); G. G. Johnson, *A Social History of the Sea Islands* (Chapel Hill, 1930); Katherine Jones (ed.), *The Plantation South* (Indianapolis, 1957); Ina Van Noppen (ed.), *The South, A Documentary History* (Princeton, 1957); Paul H. Buck, "The Poor Whites of the Ante-Bellum South," *American Historical Review,* XXXI (1925), 44–46; A. N. J. Van Hollander, "The Tradition of the 'Poor Whites,'" in W. T. Couch (ed.), *Culture in the South* (Chapel Hill, 1935); Horace Kephart, *Our Southern Highlanders* (New York, 1913). Various aspects of Southern society are considered in Charles H. Ambler, *Sectionalism in Virginia from 1776 to 1861* (Chicago, 1910); W. R. Hogan, *The Texas Republic, a Social and Economic History* (Norman, 1946); J. F. H. Claiborne, *Mississippi as a Province, Territory, and State* (Jackson, 1880); John Hope Franklin, *The Militant South 1800–1861* (Cambridge, 1956); J. Winston Coleman, Jr., *Famous Kentucky Duels* (Frankfort, 1953); Sarah N. Randolph, *The Domestic Life of Thomas Jefferson* (Cambridge, Mass., 1939); Percival Reniers, *The Springs of Virginia* (Chapel Hill, 1941); A. C. Cole, *The Irrepressible Conflict, 1850–1865* (New York, 1934). Social problems are considered in Dorothea Dix, *Remarks on Prisons and Prison Discipline in the United States* (Philadelphia, 1845); Helen E. Marshall, *Dorothea Dix: Forgotten Samaritan* (Chapel Hill, 1937); E. M. Coulter, *John Jacob Flournoy, Champion of the Common Man in the Ante-Bellum South* (Savannah, 1942); Blake McKelvey, *American Prisons, a Study in American Social History Prior to 1915* (Chicago, 1936); Charles S. Sydnor, "The Southerner and the Laws," *Journal of Southern History,* VI (1940), 1–23; Clement Eaton, "Mob Violence in the Old South," *Mississippi Valley Historical Review,* XXIX (1942), 351–370; J. K. Williams, *Vogues in Villainy; Crime and Retribution in Ante-Bellum South Carolina* (Columbia, 1959); Paton Yoder, "Private Hospitality in the South, 1775–1850," *Mississippi Valley Historical Review,* XLVII (1960), 419–433; A. B. Longstreet, *Georgia Scenes* (Augusta, 1840); Grace E. King, *Creole Families of New Orleans* (New York, 1921); J. G. Baldwin, *The Flush Times of Alabama and Mississippi* (New York, 1853); G. P. Jackson, *White Spirituals in the Southern Uplands* (Chapel Hill, 1933). City and town life is realistically portrayed in travel accounts by Buckingham, Bremer, Russell, Abdy, Arfwedson, Hall, and Olmsted. Histories of individual cities are Gerald Capers, *The Biography of a River Town, Memphis: Its Heroic Age* (Chapel Hill, 1939); John C. Gobright, *The Monumental City, or Baltimore Guide Book* (Baltimore, 1858); Raphael Semmes, *Baltimore as Seen by Visitors, 1783–1860* (Baltimore, 1953); Thomas J. Wertenbaker, *Norfolk, Historic Southern Port* (Durham, 1931); Harold Sinclair, *The Port of New Orleans* (Garden City, 1942); Lyle Saxon, *Fabulous New Orleans* (New York, 1928); Clanton W. Williams, "Early Ante-Bellum Montgomery," *Journal of Southern History,* VII (1941), 495–525; F. Garvin Davenport, *Cultural Life in*

Nashville on the Eve of the Civil War (Chapel Hill, 1941). Richard C. Wade, *The Urban Frontier, the Rise of Western Cities, 1790–1830,* presents a fresh interpretation. Architecture is discussed in Talbot F. Hamlin, *Greek Revival Architecture in America* (New York, 1944); Oliver Larkin, *Art and Life in America* (New York, 1949); Rexford Newcomb, *Architecture in Old Kentucky* (Urbana, 1953); J. Frazer Smith, *White Pillars, Early Life and Architecture of the Lower Mississippi Valley* (New York, 1941); Clay Lancaster, *Back Streets and Pine Trees . . .* (Lexington, 1956); J. C. Bonner, "Plantation Architecture of the Lower South," *Journal of Southern History,* XI (1945), 370–388. Education is treated in Charles W. Dabney, *Universal Education in the South* (Chapel Hill, 1936), I; Eaton, *Freedom of Thought in the Old South,* Chap. 3; Frank L. McVey, *The Gates Open Slowly, a History of Education in Kentucky* (Lexington, 1949); Charles L. Coon (ed.), *A Documentary History of Education in the South before 1860* (Chapel Hill, 1908), 3 vols.; Edgar Knight, *Public Education in the South* (Boston, 1922); E. Merton Coulter, *College Life in the Old South* (New York, 1928); Dumas Malone, *The Public Life of Thomas Cooper, 1783–1839* (New Haven, 1926); Philip A. Bruce, *History of the University of Virginia, 1819–1919* (New York, 1920–22), 5 vols.; Albea Godbold, *The Church College of the Old South* (Durham, 1944); W. D. Armes (ed.), *The Autobiography of Joseph Le Conte* (New York, 1903); Kemp Battle, *History of the University of North Carolina* (Raleigh, 1907–12), 2 vols.; T. C. Johnson, Jr., *Scientific Interests in the Old South* (New York, 1936); Daniel W. Hollis, *University of South Carolina* (Columbia, 1951). The most valuable works on Southern religion are C. C. Cleveland, *The Great Revival in the West* (Chicago, 1916); W. W. Sweet, *The Story of Religion in America* (New York, 1939), and *Revivalism in America* (New York, 1944); Clement Eaton, "The Ebb of the Great Revival," *North Carolina Historical Review,* XXIII (1946), 1–12; Niels H. Sonne, *Liberal Kentucky, 1780–1829* (New York, 1939); Clarence Gohdes, "Some Notes on the Unitarian Church in the Ante-Bellum South," in David K. Jackson (ed.), *American Studies in Honor of William Kenneth Boyd* (Durham, 1940); Benjamin M. Palmer, *The Life and Letters of James H. Thornwell* (Richmond, 1875); William M. Polk, *Leonidas Polk* (New York, 1844), 2 vols.; Thomas C. Johnson, *The Life and Letters of Benjamin M. Palmer* (Richmond, 1906), and *The Life and Letters of Robert L. Dabney* (Richmond, 1903); Walter B. Posey, *The Presbyterian Church in the Old Southwest, 1778–1838* (Richmond, 1952), *The Baptist Church in the Lower Mississippi Valley* (Lexington, 1957), *The Development of Methodism in the Old Southwest, 1783–1824* (Tuscaloosa, 1933), and "The Protestant Episcopal Church, an American Adaptation," *Journal of Southern History,* XXV (1959), 3–30. The most useful volumes on the intellectual life of the Old South, particularly in respect to literature, are Vernon Parrington, *The Ro-*

mantic Revolution in America 1800–1860 (New York, 1927); Jay B. Hubbell, *The South in American Literature, 1607–1900* (Durham, 1954); Gregory Paine, *Southern Prose Writers* (New York, 1947); William P. Trent, *William Gilmore Simms* (Boston, 1892); W. T. Couch (ed.), *Culture in the South* (Chapel Hill, 1935); John D. Wade, *Augustus Baldwin Longstreet: a Study of the Development of Culture in the South* (New York, 1924); Richard B. Davis, *Francis Walker Gilmer: Life and Learning in Jefferson's Virginia* (Richmond, 1939); *Southern Literary Messenger,* 1834–60, and B. B. Minor, *The Southern Literary Messenger, 1834–1864* (New York, 1905); Mary C. Simms Oliphant *et al.* (eds.), *The Letters of William Gilmore Simms* (Columbia, 1954–1956), 5 vols.; Frank L. Mott, *A History of American Magazines* (New York, 1930–57), 4 vols.; *American Journalism* (New York, 1950), and *Golden Multitudes, the Story of the Best Sellers in the United States* (New York, 1947); Franklin J. Meine (ed.), *Tall Tales of the Southwest, an Anthology of Southern and Southwestern Humor, 1830–1860* (New York, 1937); Charles H. Watts, *Thomas Holley Chivers; His Literary Career and His Poetry* (Athens, 1956); Linda Rhea, *Hugh S. Legaré* (Chapel Hill, 1934); Arthur H. Quinn, *Edgar Allan Poe, a Critical Biography* (New York, 1942); F. G. Davenport, *Cultural Life in Nashville on the Eve of the Civil War* (Chapel Hill, 1941); W. S. Hoole, *The Ante-Bellum Charleston Theatre* (Tuscaloosa, 1946); Rollin G. Osterweis, *Romanticism and Nationalism in the Old South* (New Haven, 1949); and Arthur P. Hudson, *Humor of the Old Deep South* (New York, 1936). Professor T. Harry Williams, in *Romance and Realism in Southern Politics* (Athens, 1961), has presented the most recent interpretation of the distinctive element in Southern culture—its romanticism, which has led to disastrous results in politics.

Index